90 0788434 2

KW-467-123

Charles Seale-Hayne Library
## University of Plymouth
**(01752) 588 588**
LibraryandITenquiries@plymouth.ac.uk

.

*Also in the Variorum Collected Studies Series:*

**ANNA ZARNOWSKA**
Workers, Women, and Social Change in Poland, 1870–1939

**JANUSZ ZARNOWSKI**
State, Society and Intelligentsia
Modern Poland and its Regional Context

**SIMON FRANKLIN**
Byzantium – Rus – Russia
Studies in the Translation of Christian Culture

**IVAN T. BEREND AND GYÖRGY RÁNKI**
Studies on Central and Eastern Europe in the Twentieth Century
Regional Crises and the Case of Hungary

**PETER F. SUGAR**
East European Nationalism, Politics and Religion

**NIKOLAI TODOROV**
Society, the City and Industry in the Balkans, 15th–19th Centuries

**THOMAS S. NOONAN**
The Islamic World, Russia and the Vikings, 750–900
The Numismatic Evidence

**BARISA KREKIC**
Dubrovnik: A Mediterranean Urban Society, 1300–1600

**ANTONI MACZAK**
Money, Prices and Power in Poland, 16th–17th Centuries
A Comparative Approach

**PASCHALIS M. KITROMILIDES**
Enlightenment, Nationalism, Orthodoxy
Studies in the Culture and Political Thought of Southeastern Europe

**JERZY TOPOLSKI**
The Manorial Economy in Early-Modern East-Central Europe
Origins, Development and Consequences

**ERIK FÜGEDI**
Kings, Bishops, Nobles and Burghers in Medieval Hungary

VARIORUM COLLECTED STUDIES SERIES
*Studies in East-Central Europe*
*General Editor: Ivan T. Berend*

# Comparative Studies in Modern European History

Miroslav Hroch

Miroslav Hroch

Comparative Studies in
Modern European History

Nation, Nationalism, Social Change

ASHGATE
VARIORUM

This edition © 2007 by Miroslav Hroch

Miroslav Hroch has asserted his moral right under the Copyright, Designs and Patents Act, 1988, to be identified as the author of this work.

**Published in the Variorum Collected Studies Series by**

Ashgate Publishing Limited
Gower House, Croft Road,
Aldershot, Hampshire
GU11 3HR
Great Britain

Ashgate Publishing Company
Suite 420
101 Cherry Street
Burlington, VT 05401–4405
USA

Ashgate website: http://www.ashgate.com

ISBN 978–0–7546–5935–8

**British Library Cataloguing in Publication Data**
Hroch, Miroslav
    Comparative studies in modern European history: nation, nationalism, social change. – (Variorum collected studies series: 886)
    1. Nationalism – Europe – History 2. Europe – History – 1492–3. Europe – History – Autonomy and independence movements
    I. Title
    940.2

UNIVERSITY OF PLYMOUTH

**9007884342**

    ISBN 978–0–7546–5935–8

**Library of Congress Cataloging-in-Publication Data**
Hroch, Miroslav.
    Comparative studies in modern European history : nation, nationalism, social change / by Miroslav Hroch.
        p. cm. – (Variorum collected studies series ; 886)
    Chiefly in English with essays in French and German.
    Includes bibliographical references and index.
    ISBN 978–0–7546–5935–8 (alk. paper)
    1. Europe – History – 1492–2. Europe – History – Autonomy and independence movements. 3. Nationalism – Europe – History.
    I. Title.

    D208.H76 2007
    940.2–dc22                                                        2007001428

The paper used in this publication meets the minimum requirements of the American National Standard for Information Sciences – Permanence of Paper for Printed Library Materials, ANSI Z39.48–1984. ∞ ™

Printed by by TJ International Ltd, Padstow, Cornwall

VARIORUM COLLECTED STUDIES SERIES CS886

# CONTENTS

Preface                                                                    ix–xii

Acknowledgements                                                              xiii

PART 1: NATIONAL MOVEMENTS

I     The social composition of the Czech patriots in
      Bohemia, 1827–1848                                                    33–52
      *The Czech Renaissance of the Nineteenth Century, eds P. Brock*
      *and G. Skilling, Toronto: University of Toronto Press, 1970*

II    From ethnic group toward the modern nation: the
      Czech case                                                           95–107
      *Nations and Nationalism 10. London, 2004*

III   Zionism as European national movement                                73–81
      *Jewish Studies 38. Jerusalem, 1998*

IV    De l'ethnicité à la nation: un chemin oublié vers la
      modernité                                                            71–85
      *Anthropologie et Sociétés 19. Quebec, 1995*

V     The social interpretation of linguistic demands in
      European national movements                                          67–96
      *Regional and National Identities in Europe in the XIXth and*
      *XXth Centuries, eds H-G. Haupt, M.G. Müller and S. Woolf.*
      *Alphen aan den Rijn: Kluwer Law International, 1998*

VI    Social and territorial characteristics in the composition
      of the leading groups of national movements                        257–275
      *Comparative Studies on Governments and Non-Dominant*
      *Ethnic Groups in Europe, 1850–1940, Vol. VI, ed. A Kappeler.*
      *Dartmouth, MA: New York University Press, 1992*

VII    Real and constructed: the nature of the nation            91–106
       *The State of the Nation, ed. J.A. Hall, Cambridge: Cambridge*
       *University Press, 1998*

VIII   National minority movements and their aims                189–207
       *In the National Interest. Demands and Goals of European*
       *National Movements of the Nineteenth Century: A Comparative*
       *Perspective, M. Hroch. Prague: Charles University Press, 2000*

PART 2: NATIONALISM

IX     How much does nation formation depend on nationalism?     101–115
       *East European Politics and Societies 41. Berkeley, CA, 1990*

X      Nationalism and national movements: comparing the
       past and present of Central and Eastern Europe              35–44
       *Nations and Nationalism 2. London, 1996*

XI     An unwelcome national identity, or what to do about
       'nationalism' in the post-communist countries?            265–276
       *European Review 4. Cambridge, 1996*

XII    Eugen Lembergs "Nationalismustheorie"                       1–11
       *Bohemia 45.1. Munich, 2004*

PART 3: HISTORICAL HERITAGE

XIII   Historical belles-lettres as a vehicle of the image of
       national history                                           97–108
       *National History and Idenity, ed. M. Branch. Helsinki: The*
       *Finnish Literature Society, 1999*

XIV    Historical heritage: continuity and discontinuity in the
       construction of national histories (with J. Malečková)      15–36
       *Studia Historica 53. Prague, 2000*

XV     The Czech discourse on Europe, 1848–1948                   243–261
       *The Meaning of Europe. Variety and Contention Within and*
       *Among Nations, eds. M. af Malmborg and B. Stråth. Oxford:*
       *BERG, 2002*

PART 4: SOCIAL CHANGE

XVI    Die Rolle des Zentraleuropäischen Handels im Ausgleich
       der Handelsbilanz zwischen Ost- und Westeuropa
       1550–1650                                                              1–27
       *Der Aussenhandel Ostmitteleuropas, ed. I. Bog. Cologne:*
       *Böhlau Verlag GmbH & Cie, 1971*

XVII   Die Rezeption der Französischen Revolution als
       Indikator des Fortschritts?                                          185–195
       *Westmitteleuropa Ostmitteleuropa: Vergleiche und*
       *Beziehungen. Festschrift für Ferdinand Seibt zum 65.*
       *Geburtstag, eds W. Eberhard, H. Lemberg, H-D. Heimann and*
       *R. Luft. Munich: R. Oldenbourg Verlag, 1992*

XVIII  Zur Typologie der europäischen Revolutionen. Einige
       Überlegungen zur nicht bestehenden Diskussion                         20–30
       *Revolutionen in Ostmitteleuropa 1789–1989, ed. K. Mack.*
       *Munich: R. Oldenbourg Verlag, 1995*

XIX    Criteria and indicators of uneven development                         11–26
       *Criteria and Indicators of Backwardness: Essays on Uneven*
       *Development in European History, eds M. Hroch and*
       *L. Klusáková. Prague: Charles Univerity Press, 1996*

Index                                                                         1–4

This volume contains xiv +320 pages

# PUBLISHER'S NOTE

The articles in this volume, as in all others in the Variorum Collected Studies Series, have not been given a new, continuous pagination. In order to avoid confusion, and to facilitate their use where these same studies have been referred to elsewhere, the original pagination has been maintained wherever possible.

Each article has been given a Roman number in order of appearance, as listed in the Contents. This number is repeated on each page and is quoted in the index entries.

# PREFACE

The proposal to publish a collection of my scholarlyc essays as a volume in the Variorum Collected Studies Series generously offered by Ivan Berend, encouraged me to think in more general terms about the results of the historical research that I have conducted over a period of half a century. Most of my books and essays concern two basic problems of European history: firstly, the social and political aspect of the transition from pre-modern, feudal, traditional societies to modern, capitalist ones and the uneven pace of this transition across Europe. The second aspect of my research focuses on the creation of national identity during the nineteenth century, particularly among the "smaller" European nations, i.e. those without statehood.

If these two topics are not represented equally in this volume, the explanation is more technical and political than scientific. I did most of my research on different aspects of social change in the sixteenth-seventeenth centuries during the decades of Communist rule in Czechoslovakia, making it rather difficult to publish in English (everything that I published was in Czech or German). The situation partially changed in the mid-1980s, and allowed two books of mine to be published in English: *Ecclesia Militans: The Inquisition*[1] and *Social Preconditions of National Revival in Europe*[2] (as an enlarged and heavily revised translation from my German book published already in 1968[3]). Although the first attracted little interest, the second one was successful and became a text much quoted by historians and social scientists in various European countries, except my own.

At the same time, important changes in the former Soviet block countries (but also in Spain, Belgium and Great Britain) demonstrated the significance of studies on "nationalism" and my book – although the result of research done

---

[1] Miroslav Hroch, Anna Skybova, *Eccesia Militans: The Inquisition*, Dorset Press, Edition Leipzig 1988.

[2] Miroslav Hroch, *Social Preconditions of National Revival in Europe. A Comparative Analysis of the Social Composition of Patriotic Groups among the Smaller European Nations*, Cambridge UP 1985.

[3] *Die Vorkämpfer der nationalen Bewegung bei den kleinen Völkern Europas. Eine vergleichende Analyse zur gesellschaftlichen Schichtung der patriotischen Gruppen* (Acta Universitatis Carolinae, Monographia XXIV), Prague 1968.

during the 1960s – became stimulating and inspiring. By the 1990s, my research and publications focused on the study of nations and nationalisms. The end of Communist rule across Eastern Europe led to a greater exchange of academic thought; I was invited to participate in several international projects and conferences and as a result of this, the core of this volume is formed from this new wave of studies on "nationalism", even though my basic concept of the nation and the methodological approach to studying the process of nation-formation originated during an earlier period. Some of my essays that were published in English during the 1990s, were partially based on earlier work first published in Czech. A book of mine focusing on comparative studies of national demands was published in English[4] and a generalizing conclusion of all my recent research was published in German in 2005.[5]

The most important argument of my academic work, and where I disagree with the majority of contemporary research, is the belief that we cannot study the process of nation-formation as a mere by-product of nebulous "nationalism". We have to understand it as a part of a social and cultural transformation and a component of the modernization of European societies, even though this modernization did not occur synchronically and had important regional specificities. Because of this, I have included my critical discussion on the (non)sense of using the term "nationalism" as the central tool of analysis in the second part of volume.

As a historian, I was strongly interested in the role of history, and of "collective memory" in the process of nation-formation and undertook some research on this issue. Even though I am well aware that systematic comparative studies will have to be undertaken in the future, I have included some of my preliminary results in part three as a way of trying to provoke and inspire this research.

The last part – on "Social change" – is, for the aforementioned reasons, only a very limited selection and may be regarded as a small and not very representative example of this sometimes forgotten component of my historical research. What is, unfortunately, totally absent, are my studies on the Thirty Years War and its economic aspects,[6] and on the "crisis" of the seventeenth century,[7] since I have not published any of my work on these subjects in English.

---

[4] *In the National Interest. Demands and Goals of European National Movements of the Nineteenth Century: A Comparative Perspective*, Prague 2000.

[5] *Das Europa der Nationen. Die moderne Nationsbildung im europäischen Vergleich*, Göttingen, Vandenhoeck-Ruprecht 2005.

[6] *Handel und Politik im Ostseeraum während des Dreissigjährigen Krieges. Zur Rolle des Kaufmannskapitals in der aufkommenden allgemeinen Krise der Feudalgesellschaft* (Acta Universiatis Carolinae, Monographia), Prague 1976.

[7] *Das 17. Jahrhundert – Krise der Feudalgesellschaft?* (co-author Josef Petran), Hamburg, Hoffmann & Campe 1981.

Aside from case-studies, the first section includes the essays that I regard as essential to understanding my concept of nation-formation. Sometimes, this concept is called "theory", but it was never my intention to create an analytical framework. My aim is far more modest: to determine which social circumstances were favorable to the emergence of the idea of nationhood among a "non-dominant ethnic group" and what were the reasons for the success of most national movements. If I had any ambitions beyond the realm of empirical research, these lay in the field of methodology. I have tried to check and to demonstrate the utility of the comparative approaches that became the crux of my research during the 1960s, when its use was not yet commonplace in European (and even less in Czech) historiography. Since today the comparative approach belongs ostensibly to the self-evident part of methodology in social sciences, it seems to me to be useful to present, at the end of my introduction, a short overview of my concept of the comparative method. Although an important part of my work is comparative, this method as such is not explicitly presented in the essays published in this volume.

Perhaps it would be interesting for new researchers to read a shortened version of my now forty-year old attempt to characterize the comparative method, published in my book *Die Vorkampfer der nationalen Bewegung* (1968). In this work I distinguished the comparative method, as a complex of various procedures and techniques, from simple comparison and stressed that its application has to follow four basic requirements.

Firstly, the object being compared must be defined as precisely as possible: it must be known in advance that the comparison is between objects belonging to the same category, without regard to the level of abstraction used. It also has to be decided if the comparison is to be made between processes or singular structures of events.

Secondly, the aim of the comparative procedure must be stated. Several kinds of results may be pursued. An elementary procedure is the simple search for similarities and differences between two or more objects of comparison. A more complex procedure uses the similarities and differences between the objects of comparison as the starting point or instrument of typology. An even more challenging objective is the interpretation of causal relations, of social or cultural determinants and the search for general models of causality. The search for similarities and differences can also be used in an "asymmetrical" way, when comparing a larger number of objects with a single one regarded as central, by ascertaining which characteristic of that central object are of general application, and which ones are specific to it. This procedure plays an important role as a corrective to the study of the history of one individual nation, city or region.

Thirdly, the relation of comparative procedure to the chronological axis has to be clarified. Generally, the comparative method can be applied both diachronically, i.e. along the chronological axis, and synchronically, i.e. across the chronological axis. The comparison of events and data along the historical axis is one of commonest procedures of historical research: we confront prior with consequent occurrences. A synchronic comparison in the narrower sense of the word involves the comparison of historical processes or events occurring in different countries at the same time. These processes might be mutually related and interdependent, or they might occur relatively independently. Nevertheless, another type of synchronic comparison may be more productive: comparison according to analogous historical situations. If we can establish that the objects of comparison passed through the same stages of development, we can compare these analogous stages, even if from the standpoint of absolute chronology they occurred at different times.

Fourth, the criteria of analysis used for all the objects of comparison must be established. The criterion of comparison means the feature (distinction) with reference to which the comparison is made: the qualities being compared must always be applicable to each of the objects of comparison: The criterion of comparison between a carriage and a motor car could be the length of the chassis, the carrying capacity, the weight, but definitely not the power of the motor or the petrol consumption. It is, however, not enough to make sure that we are in a position to apply the chosen criterion to all the objects of comparison; it is also necessary that this criterion is relevant to the problem to be solved and adequate to the aim in view. The more complex the problem and the process, the greater the number of criteria of comparison required. The greater the number of objects of comparison, the more advantageous it is to restrict the number of criteria of comparison to a minimum. In the first case, there is the risk of parallel narratives with minimum comparative results, in the second case, using one or two aspects isolated from the complexity of life means that the results must be interpreted as partial, although they can serve as inspiration for further research.

In some of my essays I have used the comparative perspective only as an implicit methodological approach in the context of transnational history. Sometimes, I used asymmetric comparison in order to characterize a crucial point in national history. With the exception of the three case-studies in the first section, I have always preferred to use the European dimension of my comparative or generalizing reflections. Naturally, the dimensions of Europe usually corresponde to the place of origin of the observer. European history looks different if observed from Prague than if observed from Paris or from Helsinki. Differences in perspective are inevitable, but it is preferable if they do not disturb traditional consensual opinions.

MIROSLAV HROCH

*Prague*
*October 2006*

# ACKNOWLEDGEMENTS

Grateful acknowledgement is made to the following persons, journals, institutions and publishers for their kind permission to reproduce the essays included in this volume: University of Toronto Press, Toronto (for essay I); *Nations and Nationalism* and The Association for the Study of Ethnicity and Nationalism, London (II, X); World Union of Jewish Studies, Jerusalem (III); l'Université Laval, Quebec (IV); Kluwer Law International, Alphen aan den Rijn (V); New York University Press, New York, NY (VI); Cambridge University Press, Cambridge (VII, XI); Charles University Press, Prague (VIII, XIV, XIX); The University of California Press, Berkeley, CA (IX); R. Oldenbourg Verlag, Munich (XII, XVII, XVIII); Michael Branch and The Finnish Literature Society, Helsinki (XIII); BERG, Oxford (XV); Böhlau Verlag, Cologne (XVI).

# I

# The Social Composition of the Czech Patriots in Bohemia, 1827–1848

MUCH RESEARCH has been done on the Czech national renascence which tells us in great detail about the development of the national programme, about how Czech patriots (*vlastenci*) thought, what books they printed, and how they organized their activity. However, we know less about the structural changes undergone by Czech society during the first half of the nineteenth century. So far, the question of who these patriots were, what social groups they came from, and in what social environment they moved, has been almost entirely neglected. Yet, it is necessary to obtain the most concrete knowledge possible regarding the social composition of the widest circle of activist patriots in order to gather more reliable data on the causes and social presuppositions of the birth of the modern national movement – not only in Bohemia but in all small European nations.

This essay is an attempt to characterize the community of Czech patriots from several points of view: (a) social composition, (b) territorial distribution, (c) occupation of parents (i.e. social origin), and (d) environment in which they spent their youth. For the execution of such a task, it is first necessary to obtain the largest possible number of individuals with national consciousness and then to gather biographical data for them. The criterion used here for inclusion of an individual in the group is whether he engaged in public patriotic activity or gave active and

Translated from the Czech.

conscious support to such activity – be it in the form of financial subventions for patriotic purposes, collaboration with patriotic journals, or membership in patriotic organizations. The period chosen for concentrated study is a key one in the Czech national movement. It is a period of successful national agitation displaying great tenacity of purpose. It followed a time of predominantly scholarly interest and preceded the beginning of the mass national movement, which first manifested itself in the revolutionary year of 1848. It is in our limited period that the activity of the small patriotic group was of special significance.

A number of sources can be used to determine the social composition of patriots between the 1820s and 1840s. During this period some periodicals were already being published in the Czech language and a relatively large number of publications were put out at irregular intervals. Needless to say, not every periodical in the Czech language can be regarded as a patriotic one, and not every reader as a patriot. Only some of the Czech periodicals had a wider impact on the Czech renascence. One of these was the *Časopis Českého musea* (Journal of the Czech Museum; 1827 ff.), which had as its aim to gather around itself the Czech patriotic public and thus distinguished itself from the very beginning from contemporary periodicals of other nations. Even the act of subscribing to this periodical was of significance. For other periodicals, however, only the contributors should be considered significant.

For our purposes, the most valuable sources of identification of Czech patriots are, however, the lists of members and collaborators of the Czech Literary Foundation, the Matice česká. This institution, from the beginning of the 1830s, served as a centre for those who favoured and supported Czech patriotic literature and, before 1848, it became the central organ of Czech patriotic activity (especially for southern Bohemia, although the Matice was weak there).[1] Because of its solely patriotic preoccupation, the Matice differed from an analogous organization publishing religious literature in the Czech language, the Dědictví svatojanské (The Heritage of St. Jan Nepomuk), in which the Catholic aspect took precedence over the patriotic. The Matice was generally recognized as the main institution for the publication of Czech books, as can be verified from its lists as well as from private correspondence of Czech patriots, and the funds required to finance their publication came solely from the voluntary contributions of those who shared the Matice's aims. Fortunately for our present study, the names of the contributors to the Matice were regularly published as an appendix to the "Journal of the Czech Museum," along with the occupation and domicile of the donor. This appendix, which at the time of its origin aimed especially at propaganda goals, has preserved source

---

1 On the activity of the Matice cf. K. Tieftrunk, *Dějiny Matice české* (Prague, 1881); *Stolet Matice české, 1831–1931* (Prague, 1931); W. Nebeský, *Geschichte des Museums des Konig-reichs Böhmen* (Prague, 1868), esp. chap. III. Stanley B. Kimball presents more detailed data on the publishing and organizational activity of the Matice in the following study in the present volume.

material of singular value, since the contributors were necessarily backers of the Matice's stand. Of course, the publication of the names also served a practical purpose: it was a check on book-keeping (and on the basis of random checks we can say that the lists are reliable). The fact that the contributions were perhaps partly motivated by personal vanity, by the attempt to keep up with the neighbours, and so on, is not of too great consequence to our study, since we start with the assumption that national consciousness is not in itself a proof of the personal noble-mindedness and unblemished character of the individual. Vanity, too, must undoubtedly be considered as an expression of national consciousness – rejoicing in the publication of one's own name in the pages of a patriotic journal, side by side with well-known patriots – especially if popularization in such manner carried with it some risk of social or even political discrimination.

The publication of lists of contributors to the Matice in the "Journal of the Czech Museum" was not entirely accidental, for the Matice was closely linked to the Museum from its beginning. The lists of contributors followed directly the lists of subscribers to the Journal. During the twenty years from 1827 (the year in which publication of the Journal was started) to 1847, both institutions underwent a number of changes. The programme of their activities turned increasingly from scholarly patriotic efforts to patriotic work for the benefit of the popular reader, as expressed by a new conception of the Matice's editorial policy from the beginning of the 1840s. We can assume, therefore, that the representation of the educated public during the earlier period is exaggerated and that only in the 1840s does the composition of contributors begin to encompass the whole patriotic community. The composition of patriots obtained from these lists is distorted, however, because the contributions to the Matice were relatively high (the smallest recorded contribution of an individual was five florins) and poorer patriots would not have appeared often since they would have had to save for a long time to be able to send this amount to the Matice. The results of this analysis have therefore to be verified by comparison with another patriotic enterprise, where property was not an obstacle to such an extent. We refer to collections on behalf of the Czech industrial high-school, taken on the eve of 1848 and later up into the early 1850s. Again, in individual cases, there could be distortion because of personal reasons or reasons of principle. For scholarly and artistic circles, this difficulty can be overcome by supplementing the lists with data in the *Riegrův naučný slovník* (Rieger Dictionary).

During the pre-March period, renascence passed through Moravia considerably later than, and on the whole independently of, the development in Bohemia. Therefore, the lists of the Matice cannot be considered as reliable in identifying Moravian patriots as in identifying Czechs of Bohemia. Since, in addition, we do not have other sources of similar character for this period, we have disregarded the Czech renascence in Moravia before 1848 and have concentrated on the renascence in Bohemia.

I

Having made the above remarks by way of introduction, we may now turn to consider the results of our analysis of the social composition of patriots in Bohemia. A picture of the variable part played by individual social groups, which is the easiest problem to survey, emerges from a review of the social composition of contributors to the Matice (and until 1833 also of subscribers to the Journal) on the basis of individual years in which they sent in their contributions (cf. Table 1). In analysing the figures of Table 1 it should, of course, be remembered that individual contributors could appear on the lists several times, either in one year or over several years, although they could appear at most five times if they wished to become founding members.[2] It is difficult to say whether such distortion has a greater effect on the figures for the more propertied or for the poorer strata of the patriots. Some of the more propertied ones contributed a lump sum of fifty florins and as a result appeared only once on the lists, but others paid ten florins on five occasions and appeared five times. In spite of numerous considerations of this sort, Table 1 does demonstrate a number of explicit changes in the representation of individual groups. In the period in which the main body of patriots consisted of the subscribers to the "Journal of the Czech Museum" (i.e. to 1833) men of education of the old type predominate among the subscribers; the proof is to be found in the relatively high proportion of the gentry and the relatively low proportion of students in comparison with the later period. However, the interest expressed by bourgeois circles is surprising. The beginnings of the Matice (i.e., the 1830s) are characterized by an increase in the proportion of students and a sharp decrease in that of the gentry and also – a fact which is as yet difficult to explain – of the burghers. The change in the orientation of the Matice in the early 1840s manifested itself above all in a growth of interest among the ranks of officials and professional people, and a temporary drop in that of students and a permanent one in that of the clergy.

A more thorough analysis on a more reliable basis can, of course, only be made through the compilation of a broader list of patriots. This we drew up after adjusting the lists of contributors to the Matice on the basis of the criteria mentioned above. An analysis of the social composition of almost 2800 patriots, as indicated in Table 2, confirms the basic trends of development apparent in Table 1, i.e. a strong participation of students, clergy, and officials (especially seigniorial officials).[3] Not all groups shared equally in the sharp numerical increase of contributors.

As shown in Table 3, typical features are the relatively insignificant increase in the number of gentry, clergy, and to some extent also those in professional occupations, and the considerable dynamism of the students, officials, and the popular strata (whose numbers were, of course, insignificant in the earlier stages). The

2 M. Hroch and A. Veverka, "K otázce sociální skladby české obrozenecké společnosti," *Dějepis ve škole* (Prague, 1957), 155ff.
3 The classification of social groups is arranged on the twofold basis of division into basic social classes and division according to professional groups and is done in more detail for the members of the intelligentsia.

TABLE 1

Social composition of contributors to the Matice česká, 1827–48 (per cent)

| YEAR | Gentry | Professional occupations | Officials | Teachers | Students | Merchants, burghers, artisans | Peasants | Workers | Clergy | TOTAL NUMBER OF CONTRIBUTORS |
|------|--------|--------------------------|-----------|----------|----------|-------------------------------|----------|---------|--------|------------------------------|
| 1827 | 8.5 | 7.5 | 11.5 | 5.5 | 10.0 | 6.0 | | | 45.0 | 375 |
| 1828 | 9.0 | 8.0 | 13.0 | 8.5 | 6.0 | 11.0 | | | 45.0 | 173 |
| 1829 | 10.0 | 7.0 | 14.0 | 8.0 | 7.5 | 8.5 | | | 45.5 | 140 |
| 1830 | 8.5 | 8.5 | 14.0 | 8.5 | 5.0 | 9.5 | | | 44.5 | 157 |
| 1831 | 13.5 | 12.0 | 9.0 | 9.0 | 5.5 | 5.5 | | | 44.5 | 134 |
| 1832 | 9.5 | 7.0 | 17.0 | 8.0 | 9.5 | 8.5 | | | 40.0 | 279 |
| 1833 | 2.0 | 6.5 | 12.0 | 7.0 | 23.0 | 5.5 | | | 44.0 | 223 |
| 1834 | 1.0 | 6.0 | 11.5 | 9.5 | 25.5 | 5.5 | | | 41.5 | 222 |
| 1835 | 1.0 | 8.0 | 12.0 | 6.0 | 23.0 | 6.0 | | | 44.0 | 227 |
| 1836 | 4.0 | 5.0 | 14.5 | 7.0 | 23.5 | 4.0 | | | 42.0 | 183 |
| 1837 | 7.5 | 8.5 | 13.0 | 5.0 | 10.5 | 6.5 | 1.5 | | 41.0 | 219 |
| 1838 | 3.0 | 11.0 | 12.5 | 3.0 | 18.5 | 5.0 | | 0.5 | 47.0 | 125 |
| 1839 | 2.5 | 8.5 | 13.0 | 7.0 | 22.0 | 6.5 | 1 | | 39.0 | 74 |
| 1840 | 4.0 | 10.0 | 8.0 | 4.0 | 20.0 | 6.0 | | | 48.0 | 49 |
| 1841 | 2.5 | 12.0 | 22.0 | 4.0 | 14.0 | 4.0 | 1.5 | | 40.0 | 76 |
| 1842 | 4.0 | 16.5 | 20.0 | 8.5 | 13.0 | 10.0 | | | 28.0 | 231 |
| 1843 | 2.5 | 15.5 | 16.5 | 7.0 | 17.0 | 12.5 | 0.6 | 0.5 | 28.0 | 381 |
| 1844 | 1.5 | 15.0 | 18.0 | 4.0 | 22.0 | 11.0 | | 0.5 | 28.0 | 517 |
| 1845 | 0.5 | 11.0 | 18.0 | 6.0 | 22.0 | 8.5 | | 0.5 | 33.5 | 917 |
| 1846 | 1.5 | 6.0 | 20.0 | 6.0 | 24.0 | 12.5 | 1.5 | 2.0 | 30.5 | 1157 |
| 1847 | 1.5 | 3.5 | 20.0 | 7.0 | 23.5 | 11.5 | 1.0 | 2.0 | 29.0 | 1443 |
| 1848 | 0.1 | 1.0 | 16.5 | 7.5 | 30.0 | 11.0 | 1.5 | 2.5 | 29.0 | 1135 |

TABLE 2

Social composition of Czech patriots, 1827–48

| | Prague | | Towns, pop. over 5000 | | Towns, pop. 2000–5000 | | Towns, pop. 1000–2000 | | Villages and small towns | | TOTAL | |
|---|---|---|---|---|---|---|---|---|---|---|---|---|
| | 1827–41 | 1842–48 | 1827–41 | 1842–48 | 1827–41 | 1842–48 | 1827–41 | 1842–48 | 1827–41 | 1842–48 | 1827–41 | 1842–48 |
| Gentry, land-owners, high officials | 54 | 28 | 6 | 4 | 3 | | | | 6 | 12 | 69 | 44 |
| Merchants | 5 | 19 | 3 | 17 | 10 | 12 | | 7 | | 4 | 18 | 59 |
| Entrepreneurs | 1 | 8 | 1 | 3 | 4 | 3 | | 2 | | | 6 | 16 |
| Artisans | 14 | 34 | 9 | 13 | 15 | 42 | 2 | 16 | 7 | 31 | 47 | 136 |
| BURGHERS, TOTAL | 20 | 61 | 13 | 33 | 29 | 57 | 2 | 25 | 7 | 35 | 71 | 211 |
| Doctors | 19 | 26 | 1 | 7 | 7 | 17 | | 3 | | 3 | 27 | 56 |
| Lawyers | 17 | 8 | 1 | 1 | | | | | | | 18 | 9 |
| Artists, etc. | 33 | 21 | 5 | 2 | | 1 | | | | | 38 | 24 |
| PROFESSIONALS, TOTAL | 69 | 55 | 7 | 10 | 7 | 18 | | 3 | | 3 | 83 | 89 |
| Seigniorial officials | 4 | 4 | 2 | 4 | 15 | 38 | 14 | 20 | 40 | 79 | 75 | 145 |
| Other officials | 21 | 59 | 5 | 23 | 19 | 26 | 1 | 19 | 3 | 24 | 49 | 151 |
| OFFICIALS, TOTAL | 25 | 63 | 7 | 27 | 34 | 64 | 15 | 39 | 43 | 103 | 124 | 296 |
| Clergy | 20 | 21 | 13 | 29 | 72 | 85 | 44 | 70 | 164 | 248 | 313 | 453 |
| High-school teachers | 6 | 16 | 6 | 9 | 8 | 12 | 1 | | | | 21 | 37 |
| Other teachers | 13 | 25 | 3 | 11 | 9 | 11 | 1 | 8 | 8 | 25 | 34 | 80 |
| TEACHERS, TOTAL | 19 | 41 | 9 | 20 | 17 | 23 | 2 | 8 | 8 | 25 | 55 | 117 |
| Officers, soldiers | 4 | 8 | | 4 | 1 | 5 | | 1 | | | 5 | 18 |
| Students | 113 | 257 | 14 | 77 | 28 | 107 | 1 | 9 | 4 | 40 | 160 | 490 |
| Millers | 1 | 7 | | 2 | | 2 | | 2 | 2 | 15 | 3 | 28 |
| Peasants | | | | | | | | 1 | 2 | 28 | 2 | 29 |
| Wage labourers | 1 | 5 | | 2 | 2 | 2 | | 4 | 2 | 10 | 5 | 23 |
| Women, etc. | 3 | 10 | 3 | 6 | 2 | 14 | | 1 | 2 | 15 | 10 | 46 |
| TOTAL | 329 | 556 | 72 | 214 | 195 | 376 | 64 | 163 | 240 | 534 | 900 | 1843 |

TABLE 3

Social composition of Czech patriots according to period when contributions were begun
(percentage of total in category in parentheses)

| | 1827–34 | 1835–41 | 1842–48 | TOTAL |
|---|---|---|---|---|
| Landowners and gentry | 27 (41) | 9 (13) | 30 (46) | 66 (100) |
| Merchants and artisans | 63 (23) | 8 (3) | 213 (74) | 283 (100) |
| Professional occupations | 54 (30) | 31 (17) | 91 (53) | 176 (100) |
| Officials | 112 (25) | 35 (8) | 307 (67) | 456 (100) |
| Clergy | 268 (34) | 64 (8) | 461 (58) | 793 (100) |
| Teachers and high-school teachers | 46 (27) | 10 (6) | 120 (67) | 176 (100) |
| Officers and non-com. officers | 5 (21) | | 18 (79) | 23 (100) |
| Students | 122 (17) | 41 (7) | 483 (76) | 646 (100) |
| Peasants and millers | 5 (9) | | 57 (91) | 62 (100) |
| Servants and workers | 4 (14) | 2 (3) | 23 (83) | 28 (100) |
| Other and undetermined | 8 (13) | 2 (4) | 48 (83) | 58 (100) |
| TOTAL | 714 (26) | 202 (7) | 1851 (67) | 2767 (100) |

speed of growth in the participation of the burghers was somewhat above average. An over-all survey can be obtained by gathering all social groups into larger entities according to the degree to which a particular group was linked to the old society and partly also according to its living standard.[4] The average ratio of the number of patriots up to 1841 to those after is 33:67. Considering the groups linked with the old society, the ratio of "notables" (291 patriots) was 53:47, and that of the other groups, especially the clergy (i.e., altogether 1081 patriots), was 39:61. For groups linked with production (artisans, burghers) the ratio was 24:76, and for petty intelligentsia and students (1000 patriots) it was 23:77. The national movement was, then, clearly losing ground among the "notables," whose position was, as can be seen elsewhere, close to the provincial patriotism (*Landespatriotismus*) of the eighteenth century, and, by contrast, it was gaining ground among the young intelligentsia and among the burghers.[5] If medical doctors are not counted among the "notables," the increase in their number would be even less, the ratio becoming 63:37.

As can be seen from Table 2, the great majority of the patriots lived in the towns, and in Prague and medium-sized towns they were especially strong. That merely one-quarter of the patriots were active in the villages is certainly surprising in

4 Among the patriots whom we equate with the "old pre-industrial society" we include as "notables" the gentry, high officials, and the elite of the educated of the old type; clergy, seignorial and other officials, and officers belong to the other group. By "phase B" we understand the period of conscious national agitation directed towards the broad masses in an attempt to win them for the programme of national, cultural (and eventually even political) emancipation, i.e. the period which superseded that of scholarly concern for the nation ("phase A"). The period of mass nationalist activity is designated as "phase C." In Bohemia "phase B" may be dated from the 1820s to 1840s, and 1848 marks the beginning of "phase C."

5 This fact reflects the change in attitude of the broader patriotic strata towards the Matice during the 1830s.

view of the agrarian character of Czech society. We would at least expect this proportion to grow during phase B, but this was not the case. Although the ratio of growth for Prague was indeed actually below average (it was 38:62, clearly because of the decrease in the representation of the "notables"), in other cities it was slightly above average (ratio 30:70), and in the villages it remained average (31:69).

Now we can finally consider the distribution of the relevant social groups among the various types of settlement (cf. Table 4). The majority of those belonging to the professional occupations and the majority of students lived in Prague. By contrast, more than half of the patriotic clergy were active in the countryside; they formed the majority of village patriots. Seigniorial officials formed the second largest group of village patriots. The rest of the officials, as well as artisans and burghers, were distributed on the whole among the various types of settlements in roughly the same proportion as the over-all distribution of patriots, which was: Prague, 31.5 per cent; larger towns, 10.5 per cent; medium-sized towns, 21 per cent; small towns, 8 per cent; and villages, 28 per cent.

The data obtained regarding the social composition of our community of patriots will now be compared with the corresponding figures for the social composition of the reading public of two popular reading enterprises of the pre-March period, and with the composition of contributors to the Czech industrial school before 1848. The lists of the supporters of the Dědictví svatojanské could be analysed as has been done for the Matice lists, but we shall be satisfied with a basic classification according to social groups, and with the trends of development.[6] The percentages for the various groups (considerably rounded off) are given in Table 5. The proportion of artisans and burghers was roughly the same as in our previous analysis, but the proportion of secular intelligentsia decreased sharply and was on the whole insignificant. The predominance of clergy is not surprising; however, the sharp decrease, caused by the mass influx of the peasantry into the Dědictví, is surprising. It is an incontestable expression of the penetration, if not of the national awakening, then of education to the peasant masses. This development is the basis for our periodization of the beginning of phase C in Bohemia (cf. footnote 4).

The social composition of subscribers to the popular journal Večerní vyražení for the year 1831 gives us the picture shown in Table 6. It is surprising how close the social composition of the readers of Večerní vyražení is to that of our community of patriots at the time of the founding of the Matice; we find here a similarly low proportion of students and peasants and a roughly similar distribution for the various types of settlements. Only the proportion of artisans and burghers is considerably higher, and the proportion of the clergy is considerably lower.

From the end of phase B lists of contributors to the Czech industrial school have been preserved. The complicated problem of analysing these lists would require

6 Cf. lists in K. Borový, *Dějiny Dědictví svatojanského* (Prague, 1885).

TABLE 4

Social composition of patriots according to the size of their place of activity

| | Prague | Towns, pop. over 5000 | Towns, pop. over 2000 | Small towns, pop. over 1000 | Villages and small towns, pop. up to 1000 | TOTAL | Per cent |
|---|---|---|---|---|---|---|---|
| Landowners and gentry | 46 | | 1 | 27 | 18 | 66 | 2.3 |
| Merchants and artisans | 81 | 46 | 86 | 3 | 42 | 283 | 10.2 |
| Professional occupations | 124 | 17 | 25 | 54 | 3 | 176 | 6.3 |
| Officials | 110 | 44 | 99 | 124 | 146 | 456 | 16.8 |
| Clergy | 55 | 42 | 158 | 10 | 412 | 793 | 28.7 |
| Teachers and high-school teachers | 60 | 29 | 40 | 10 | 33 | 176 | 6.3 |
| Students | 360 | 91 | 135 | 1 | 44 | 646 | 23.3 |
| Officers | 12 | 4 | 6 | 3 | | 23 | 0.8 |
| Peasants and millers | 8 | 2 | 2 | 4 | 47 | 62 | 2.2 |
| Servants and workers | 6 | 2 | 4 | 1 | 12 | 28 | 1.0 |
| Other and undetermined | 13 | 9 | 16 | | 17 | 58 | 2.1 |
| TOTAL | 875 | 286 | 572 | 237 | 774 | 2767 | 100.0 |

I

TABLE 5

|  | 1834–40 | 1841–45 | 1847–48 |
|---|---|---|---|
| Artisans and burghers | 9 | 15 | 12 |
| Officials, professionals, teachers | 16 | 8 | 6 |
| Clergy | 65 | 60 | 21 |
| Peasantry | 3 | 11 | 54 |
| Other | 7 | 6 | 7 |
| TOTAL | 100 | 100 | 100 |

an independent study.[7] For our purposes, a rough break-down of the social composition of the first contributors in 1847 will suffice.[8] The burgher and artisan subscriptions make up 32 per cent, the secular intelligentsia, 24 per cent; students, only 3.5 per cent; clergy, 8 per cent; and peasants, 14 per cent. In the course of the following years workers especially were added to the subscription lists; otherwise the relative proportions were substantially maintained. Here we encounter, then, a social structure which is characteristic of phase c of the national movement in Bohemia. It should be noted, however, that this structure differs from the composition of readership of the *Večerní vyražení* only by having a lower proportion of the clergy and a higher proportion of peasants.

On the basis of the above data we consider the decisive proportion of urban patriots in the Czech national renascence to be incontestable. This determines the basic ratio in the analysis of "patriotic topography," the geographic distribution of patriots on the territory of Bohemia. Did all towns participate more or less equally in national activity? In which regions do we find the largest number of patriots? To find the answers to these questions we have gathered the data on contributors to the Matice and projected them on the "map" of Bohemia. At the same time we have taken into consideration patriotic groups – even those found in the countryside. A

TABLE 6

Social composition of subscribers to the journal *Večerní vyražení* in 1831 by place of activity (per cent)

|  | Prague | Towns | Countryside | Undetermined | TOTAL |
|---|---|---|---|---|---|
| Artisans and burghers | 13.0 | 10.0 | 0.5 | 6.0 | 29.5 |
| Officials, professional occupations, teachers | 9.0 | 9.0 | 8.0 | 6.0 | 32.0 |
| Clergy | 2.0 | 6.0 | 10.0 | 0.5 | 18.5 |
| Students | 3.0 | 0.5 |  | 4.0 | 7.5 |
| Peasants and millers | 0.5 |  | 2.0 |  | 2.5 |
| Undetermined | 1.5 | 0.5 | 6.0 |  | 8.0 |
| TOTAL | 29.0 | 26.0 | 26.5 | 16.5 | 98.0 |

7 See E. Mandler, "Počátky Jednoty pro povzbuzení průmyslu v Čechách," unpublished dissertation, University of Prague, 1956.
8 Cf. also lists published regularly in the issues of *Časopis Českého musea* for the year 1847.

town or a community is considered to be a seat of a patriotic group when we have proof that it has had at least three contributors to the Matice in the same period, or two contributors of different occupations in the same period and another in the period immediately preceding or following. We wish to ascertain which environment was more favourable for national awakening, if we can ascertain any regularities at all in this direction. The designation "patriotic community" for a three-member group of contributors is in no way exaggerated. We assume logically, and we know from some partial regional studies, that patriots gathered around themselves others who were interested, and that journals and books were lent and borrowed, or collectively read.[9] However, we must not overestimate the significance of the geographic distribution of those patriotic groups which were composed predominantly of persons unable to decide for themselves where they would be active and about whom we have no proof that they grew up in the place of their activity. The clergy, in particular, and partly also high-school teachers and to a lesser degree officials, belong to this category. Accordingly, we need only to summarize some basic facts.

The size of the patriotic groups was not directly proportionate to the population in the localities where the patriots were active. The patriotic communities were not distributed evenly over the territory of Bohemia. On the basis of the density of distribution of patriots in towns (and in larger village patriotic groups), we can distinguish three regions in Bohemia: (a) areas where patriotic groups were active in all towns and small towns with population over 1000 (central Polabí, Pojizeří, eastern Bohemia), (b) areas where we find patriotic groups only in larger towns and in some administrative or governmental centres (above all in southwest and west Bohemia), (c) areas with single patriotic groups fairly remote from one another (southeast Bohemia, south Bohemia). Interpretation of these facts will be possible only on the basis of a comparative study. In the meantime we can only express some negative judgments. The density of the patriotic communities did not depend on their location relative to language frontiers; sometimes at such a frontier we find a dense network of communities, while at other times we find only single contributors. The density did not even depend on the location in Bohemia; e.g., the southern part of central Bohemia was almost inactive. Finally, it did not even depend on the degree of language purity; sometimes we find patriotic communities in linguistically mixed areas, and in contrast a number of solidly Czech regions remained aloof.

Patriotic groups differed from one another not only in size but also in social composition. We shall attempt, therefore, to characterize briefly the types of patriotic communities with regard to both social composition and location. Without

---

9 Patriotic activity of local groups is described with reference to Nové Město nad Metují in Z. Nejedlý, *Bedřich Smetana*, III (Prague, 1929), 447ff. Activity in Polička is described in J. Růžička, *O Drašarovi a poličských buditelích. Román a skutečnost* (Polička, 1966), esp. chap. I.

a detailed enumeration of the names of localities, we can draw the following conclusions on the basis of detailed research:

1  Groups in the nationally more active regions of Bohemia were composed, more often than elsewhere, of members of all basic social elements (i.e., officials, burghers, and clergy).

2  Burghers were represented most strongly in patriotic groups in east Bohemia and in the eastern parts of central Bohemia (Polabí), but are scarcely represented at all in patriotic groups in the nationally less active territories of Bohemia.

3  Officials were strongest in patriotic groups in nationally active territories, which stretched from west Bohemia to the basin of the river Jizera in northern Bohemia.

4  Small patriotic groups in nationally passive regions were most often composed mainly of clergy, with sometimes some officials.

The question of the social origin of the patriots, or to put it more accurately the patriotic intelligentsia, is not one which has gone unnoticed in Czech literature. Most authors see in Czech patriots the sons of peasants who went to Germanizing or Germanized towns for education and there began their national awakening,[10] but E. Chalupný has pointed out that a number of patriots came from the towns.[11] Although such statements have been made, no reasonably accurate or concrete analysis has yet been carried out. However, from the catalogues of students at the University of Prague and at theological seminaries outside Prague very valuable material on the social origin of the patriotic intelligentsia can be obtained.[12] These catalogues make it possible to ascertain the occupation of parents and the birthplace of almost all students after 1815. With the exception of some catalogues in which the birth-place is indicated only by the name of region, we have at our disposal reliable and carefully kept source materials.[13]

A somewhat more serious distortion may arise as a result of our inability to identify all members of the intelligentsia. Out of a total number of 1800 members of the intelligentsia and students we succeeded in ascertaining complete data for 800

10  E. Denis, *Čechy po Bílé Hoře*, II/1 (Prague, 1931), 14: K. Krofta, *Dějiny selského stavu* (Prague, 1949), 349; A. Klíma, *Rok 1848 v Čechách* (Prague, 1949), 16.

11  E. Chalupný, *Havlíček* (Prague, 1929), 133.

12  The sources for the identification of the origin of the patriotic intelligentsia are the lists of students of individual university faculties and of diocesan theological seminaries, which, from the second decade of the nineteenth century, carefully noted such data as father's employment (and changes of employment where these occurred), the place and date of birth, and high-school education. The lists are in the Archives of Charles University in Prague.

13  Since the majority of entries were made on the basis of data given by the students, the possibility that there is some distortion "upwards" of the social composition cannot be excluded. A random check of the data on the social origin of a student given in different catalogues of the same faculty or in catalogues of different faculties (e.g. philosophy and law), however, showed that the data are very reliable. Substantial fluctuations are evident only in two areas: between the general designation "burgher" and the concrete designation of craft, or father's trade, and between the term *Bauer* and *Landmann* and occasionally also *Gutsbesitzer*.

patriots, while for 140 patriots the data are incomplete. The success, however, varied considerably from one individual group of the intelligentsia to another. The social origin of almost all university students was ascertained, as well as of a majority of doctors and lawyers and a large part of the clergy. In contrast to this, we did not succeed in identifying the majority of officials, probably because by no means all of them had a university education or were educated at the University of Prague. The older generation of patriots, born roughly before 1795, though small, is also poorly represented in our sample, since complete catalogue lists had not been established at the time they pursued their studies. With these exceptions, however, we can consider the sample of identified patriotic intelligentsia as sufficiently representative.

Again, as in the case of the social composition of the patriots, we shall be interested first in social origin (i.e., occupation of parents) and in place of birth. Table 7 is constructed on the basis of these indicators.[14] The largest part of the patriotic intelligentsia came from artisan or burgher families, while not quite one-fifth came from peasant families. Similarly, a majority of the patriots were born in towns and only one-quarter in villages. The relatively low percentage of sons from doctors' and lawyers' families is not surprising, and the very low percentage of patriots from teachers' families only confirms the insignificant representation of this stratum in the national renascence. The figure for sons of seigniorial officials in the countryside is also surprisingly low, but this may not reflect the true state of affairs since we succeeded in identifying the social origin of only a small part of patriotic officials. Only an insignificant proportion of Czech patriots came from families which we could classify as among the "notables," while the highest proportion came from urban and rural families of small manufacturers. The insignificant proportion from the ranks of the poor in the towns and in the countryside can be explained by the relatively low influx from these strata into institutions of higher learning. The nature of the data obtained above forces us to re-examine critically the traditional view, which is still held, that thatched-roofed cottages were the cradle of Czech patriots. They also lead us to adopt a position of scepticism in regard to traditional conceptions about the social origins of patriots in other nations as well.

We can establish, to some extent, the degree of validity of our findings so fas as the social origin of single generations of the patriotic intelligentsia is concerned. To do this, we must take into consideration the distortion in the figures due to gaps in the data given in the catalogues, and eliminate as much as possible the oldest patriotic generation. For this reason we take as our first dividing line the year 1810, and as our second the year 1820; the older generation will then be composed of patriots who studied during the beginning period of phase B; the middle

---

14 Social groups are determined on the basis of the same criterion as social origin. Sons of non-gentry landowners and sons of officers are listed under "other." The size of places is determined on the basis of the year 1844; according to F. Palacký, *Popis království Českého* (Prague, 1848).

TABLE 7

Social origin of patriotic intelligentsia according to size of birth-place
(figures in parentheses are the percentage share, of the total, of each occupation in each category)

| OCCUPATION OF PARENTS | Prague | Towns, pop. above 4000 | Towns, pop. 1500–4000 | Small towns, pop. under 1500 | Villages | Undetermined birth-place | TOTAL |
|---|---|---|---|---|---|---|---|
| Merchants | 17 (1.8) | 8 (0.8) | 16 (1.7) | 6 (0.6) | 9 (1.0) | 7 (0.7) | 63 (6.7) |
| Artisans and burghers | 37 (3.9) | 76 (8.1) | 118 (12.5) | 57 (6.1) | 36 (6.8) | 26 (2.8) | 350 (37.1) |
| Professional occupations | 12 (1.2) | 4 (0.4) | 10 (1.1) | | 1 (0.1) | | 27 (2.8) |
| Officials | 32 (3.4) | 17 (1.8) | 25 (2.7) | 9 (1.0) | 17 (1.8) | 3 (0.3) | 103 (10.9) |
| Teachers | 5 (0.5) | 1 (0.1) | 5 (0.5) | 8 (0.9) | 13 (1.3) | 9 (1.0) | 41 (4.3) |
| Millers | 3 (0.3) | 8 (0.9) | 6 (0.6) | 5 (0.5) | 18 (1.9) | 13 (1.3) | 53 (5.6) |
| Peasants | | 1 (0.1) | 2 (0.2) | 9 (1.0) | 119 (12.6) | 30 (3.3) | 161 (17.1) |
| Employees and workers | 9 (1.0) | 4 (0.4) | 2 (0.2) | 7 (0.8) | 7 (0.8) | 6 (0.6) | 35 (3.7) |
| Other and undetermined | 19 (2.0) | 19 (2.0) | 30 (3.2) | 15 (1.5) | 24 (2.1) | | 107 (10.2) |
| TOTAL | 134(14.2) | 138(14.6) | 214(22.7) | 116(12.3) | 244(25.8) | 94(10.4) | 940(100) |

TABLE 8

Social origin of patriotic intelligentsia according to date of birth

| OCCUPATION OF PARENTS | Born up to 1810 | | | Born 1811–20 | | | Born 1821–30 | | | TOTAL (per cent) |
|---|---|---|---|---|---|---|---|---|---|---|
| | number | A* | B† | number | A | B | number | A | B | |
| Merchants | 20 | 6.2 | 2.5 | 21 | 7.9 | 2.6 | 14 | 6.3 | 1.7 | 6.8 |
| Artisans | 141 | 44.3 | 17.6 | 92 | 35.5 | 11.5 | 75 | 33.3 | 9.4 | 38.5 |
| Professional occupations | 4 | 1.2 | 0.5 | 14 | 5.5 | 0.7 | 8 | 3.6 | 1.0 | 3.2 |
| Officials | 22 | 6.4 | 2.6 | 38 | 14.6 | 4.7 | 34 | 15.1 | 4.2 | 11.5 |
| Teachers | 12 | 3.8 | 1.5 | 12 | 4.6 | 1.5 | 6 | 2.2 | 0.7 | 3.7 |
| Millers | 13 | 4.0 | 1.6 | 15 | 5.8 | 1.9 | 12 | 5.1 | 1.5 | 5.0 |
| Peasants | 36 | 11.4 | 4.5 | 34 | 13.1 | 4.2 | 49 | 21.8 | 6.1 | 14.8 |
| Employees and workers | 6 | 1.8 | 0.7 | 12 | 4.8 | 1.5 | 11 | 4.6 | 1.4 | 3.6 |
| Other and undetermined | 66 | 20.1 | 8.3 | 21 | 8.2 | 2.6 | 16 | 7.3 | 2.0 | 12.9 |
| TOTAL | 320 | 100 | 39.8 | 259 | 100 | 32.2 | 225 | 100 | 28.0 | 100 |

*A = percentage share of the patriots of the age group.
†B = percentage share, in the total group, of each occupation in each age group.

| OCCUPATION OF PARENTS | Per cent born up to 1810 | Per cent born 1811–20 | Per cent born 1821–30 |
|---|---|---|---|
| Merchants, artisans, millers | 21.7 | 16.0 | 12.7 |
| Peasants | 4.5 | 4.2 | 6.1 |
| Officials, professional occupations | 3.1 | 6.4 | 5.2 |
| TOTAL | 39.8 | 32.2 | 28.0 |

generation, of those who reached maturity after the revolutionary years 1830–1, and the youngest generation, of those who had already begun their studies during the decline of phase B.[15] The social composition of the members of these three, numerically roughly equal generation groups, set out in Table 8, shows an interesting and rather pronounced trend of development.

Although from the end of the eighteenth century artisan production developed significantly and the towns grew along with the growth in the non-agricultural population, the number of patriots increased through an influx of those who came from peasant families. From the older generation, in which only a little over one-tenth of the patriots came from peasant families,[16] to the youngest generation, their proportion almost doubled. The increase in the proportion from the ranks of the officials and from the ranks of the professional occupations, especially in the older and middle generations, is even greater. An over-all trend emerges more clearly when we combine the data in larger social groups, as shown in the tabulation above.

It is of interest to see how the proportions of those joining the patriotic ranks from towns and countryside correspond to this picture. Table 9 confirms a growing influx of patriots from the countryside and a decrease in the proportion of patriots from towns – with the exception of Prague, whose proportion, on the contrary, grew. This trend is exactly the opposite of that revealed by the analysis of the social composition of the patriotic community. As a result, although the number of patriots domiciled in Prague increased considerably more slowly than the number domiciled in other towns, the number of patriots born in Prague increased, whereas the number born in other towns decreased relatively. The number of patriots who came from small towns with over 1000 population fell especially sharply.

The picture of the social origin of those participating in the Czech national renascence corresponds, then, less and less to traditional conceptions. On the basis

15 When dividing into generation groups we have also tried to arrange that the individual age groups are roughly equal numerically; this demand is met by taking as dividing line the years 1810 and 1820.

16 The relatively high percentage of persons whose type of employment in this age group is unknown is to a large extent made up of those born in towns who studied before 1815, i.e. before the column on parents' employment was in general use in university catalogues, and whose birth-place was determined from other encyclopaedic and biographic manuals. The real proportion of patriots from peasant families in this age group should, therefore, be under 10 per cent.

I

TABLE
Place of origin of patriotic intelligentsia according to date of birth
(column percentage in parentheses)

| | Born before 1811 | Born 1811–20 | Born 1821–30 | TOTAL |
|---|---|---|---|---|
| Prague | 44 (13.8) | 47 (18.1) | 41 (18.2) | 132 (16.4) |
| Towns with pop. over 4000 | 57 (18.2) | 46 (17.8) | 31 (14.0) | 134 (16.6) |
| Towns with pop. 1500–4000 | 93 (29.2) | 59 (22.7) | 51 (22.6) | 203 (25.4) |
| SUBTOTAL | 194 (61.2) | 152 (58.6) | 123 (54.8) | 469 (58.4) |
| Small towns | 51 (16.0) | 35 (13.6) | 24 (10.8) | 110 (13.6) |
| Villages | 75 (22.8) | 72 (27.8) | 78 (34.4) | 225 (28.0) |
| SUBTOTAL | 126 (38.8) | 107 (41.4) | 102 (45.2) | 335 (41.6) |
| TOTAL | 320 (100) | 259 (100) | 225 (100) | 804 (100) |

of these conceptions we would assume that the patriotic spirit expanded from the countryside to the towns; in reality, however, our figures show a decline of the originally very high proportion of patriots from the urban environment and a growth of the originally small proportion from the villages. Similarly, until now, we have assumed a large proportion of patriotic men of education coming from families of the intelligentsia in the older patriotic generation and a decline of this proportion in later generations in favour of patriots of popular origin (artisans and burghers). However, we now find the exact opposite: the proportion of patriotic intelligentsia coming from small urban artisan families declined, while the proportion of patriots coming from families of men of education (doctors and officials) increased considerably. It would seem that here, in the middle and in the youngest groups, the effect of the ascendence of the third generation, for whom there was a growth in the proportion of officials during phase B, has been felt.

Of course, the results of the study of the social origin of the patriots need verification and refining. To do this, the extent to which the social origin of the patriots and the changes in it over the course of time reflected only the social origin of Prague students in general would have to be considered. But this would require a systematic elaboration of the social origin of all students – a sufficient topic for an extensive and independent study. Let us be satisfied, therefore, with a random comparison of some years in various faculties.[17]

These comparisons showed that the proportion of students of peasant origin was generally higher, especially in theological seminaries, than that of the intelligentsia of peasant origin among the patriots: the proportion fluctuated between 15 and 20

17 A comparative analysis was done with students of philosophy and theology in 1819 and 1823, with theologians in Prague in the year 1831, in Hradec Králové in 1834–5, and in the law faculty in Prague in 1827.

I

per cent in philosophical faculties and between 20 and 30 per cent in theological faculties. The proportion of students from artisan and merchant families fluctuated considerably between 40 and 60 per cent, but there is nothing to support the view that it fell so distinctly that we could deduce any over-all trend of development from the declining influx of patriotic intelligentsia from these strata. Students from the ranks of the intelligentsia were found in theological seminaries only in very small numbers (about 10 per cent), but in the medical and law faculties their number was, understandably, considerably higher (about 40 per cent) and higher proportionally than the number of patriotic doctors and lawyers coming from the ranks of the intelligentsia. Roughly then, the social origin of patriots corresponded to the over-all picture of social origin of the university-educated intelligentsia in Bohemia during the pre-March period. Any deviations from the basic ratios are generally in just the opposite direction from the one we would expect on the basis of the summary estimates: the percentage of intelligentsia from peasant strata who joined the patriots was smaller than that of students of peasant origin in the whole student body; the percentage of patriots from the ranks of the intelligentsia (with the exception of doctors and lawyers), on the contrary, was above the over-all average. Our data, then, underline the significant role played by the artisan and urban environment in the birth of the Czech patriotic intelligentsia.

Another useful check will be a comparison of the social origin of the patriots with the social origin of a group of students – on the basis of a criterion close to, but not identical with, the criterion of patriotism. Such a group were the students of the Czech language in the philosophical faculty of the University of Prague. We certainly cannot consider as patriots even those among them who successfully passed the examinations, although we can, of course, consider the passing of these examinations as a criterion of Czech nationality in most cases. However, the environment in which these students moved was saturated with patriotic impulses and was the optimal environment for national awakening.[18] Hence we are interested not only in the over-all percentages on the basis of social origin but also in their evolution during the 1820s to 1840s (cf. Table 10). This table confirms the results of the analysis of the patriotic intelligentsia only in that it also registers the decrease in the proportion of students from artisan families. By contrast, the proportion of students from families of the intelligentsia increased, but that of students of peasant origin did not. This finding is also confirmed by the basic percentages of students of the Czech language according to their birthplace:[19]

18 The lists of students of the Czech language are in the catalogues of the so-called liberal philosophical studies. From 1826 all those who sat for examinations were listed in these catalogues, and before this date all those who registered for lectures. The numerical difference is considerable.

19 Here we omit the detailed tables for each year, but choose the totals for six-year periods roughly corresponding to the above-differentiated age groups.

I

50

| PLACE OF BIRTH | 1826–31 | 1832–37 | 1842–47 |
|---|---|---|---|
| Prague | 19.5 | 18 | 22.5 |
| Towns and small towns | 41 | 43 | 40 |
| Villages | 39.5 | 39 | 37.5 |

The proportion of village students did not therefore increase, but was from the beginning considerably higher than that of the educated of village origin among the members of the national renascence. As with the patriotic intelligentsia, here too the (somewhat smaller) growth in the 1840s of the proportion born in Prague is partly a reflection of the increase in the proportion of students from the families of officials.

On the basis of both sets of data, we can now state that the intelligentsia coming from villages and from peasant families were, in the older generation (i.e. those born before 1820), relatively more immune to patriotic agitation and, in general, to a patriotic environment. Only after the national awakening spread and the social prestige of the patriot increased did the nationalistic activity of the intelligentsia of peasant origin increase to the point where they were reasonably represented among the educated. No less explicit resistance to the patriotic environment was shown – but only in the older generation – by the educated from the families of officials and from the families of doctors and lawyers, but for them the situation was already changing during the 1830s. Therefore, it is still valid to say that the educated from the ranks of small artisan manufacturers and tradesmen were relatively more sensitive to patriotic impulses and participated in the national movement considerably more vigorously than one would have expected, judging by the over-all picture of the social origin of students.

Of course, we do not intend to exaggerate the significance of social origin, but it is of interest to know the environment that produced those of the educated with the highest qualifications who participated in the national movement and who were relatively most receptive to national interests. Because of the incompleteness of material we unfortunately cannot construct a table showing the relation between the social origin of the intelligentsia and the place where they received their high-school education, but we can make some use of the location of the birth-places on the "map" to obtain further information. First of all, we can already state that a considerable part of the patriots (also of those who came from places other than Prague) graduated from Prague high-schools. Furthermore, many were graduates from high-schools in Slaný, Rychnov, and understandably in Hradec Králové, where there was also a lively activity in the theological seminary, but in the seminary in Litoměřice we find only a few patriots, and the seminary in České Budějovice became activist only in the 1840s. Indeed, only in the case of České Budějovice is the traditional notion which we have subjected to criticism valid: namely, that those students who came from the villages to the German urban environment became

TABLE 10
Social origin of students of the Czech language at the University of Prague
(column percentage in parentheses)

| OCCUPATION OF PARENTS | 1826–31 | 1832–37 | 1842–47 |
|---|---|---|---|
| Landowners | 4 (0.8) | 8 (1.6) | 2 (0.2) |
| Merchants | 27 (5.3) | 25 (4.9) | 40 (4.3) |
| Artisans | 202 (38.3) | 191 (36.8) | 249 (28.8) |
| Professional occupations | 13 (2.6) | 10 (1.9) | 52 (5.6) |
| Officials | 58 (11.2) | 71 (13.6) | 129 (13.2) |
| Teachers | 11 (2.1) | 30 (5.8) | 26 (2.8) |
| Millers | 20 (3.8) | 22 (4.2) | 22 (2.4) |
| Peasants | 69 (13.3) | 67 (12.8) | 144 (15.4) |
| Servants and workers | 14 (2.8) | 23 (4.3) | 32 (3.4) |
| Other and undetermined | 103 (19.8) | 72 (14.1) | 212 (22.9) |
| TOTAL | 521 (100) | 519 (100) | 908 (100) |

nationally awakened. The majority of patriotic theologians in České Budějovice came from peasant families.

In regard to the school and living environment in which the patriots moved during their youth, we can also make a contribution by projecting their birth-place on the "map." These places were not distributed at all equally over the territory of Bohemia. The places from which most patriots came are to a large extent identical with the places where we found the largest patriotic groups and their thickest network. This is especially true of Polabí and northern Bohemia, while in western Bohemia the birth-places of a larger number of patriots reached farther south and southeast. The distribution of birth-places follows the network of high-schools only to the extent that all places with high-schools were also at the same time birth-places of the larger groups of patriots. National activation of those born in towns, near a place with a high-school, clearly depended on other factors as well, however. The area with the largest density of village birth-places roughly corresponds to the area of largest density of urban birth-places.

Let us finally ask at what average age the patriots began to support the Matice. We have ascertained that the average age of the groups of patriots clearly differed according to the social environment from which they came. Even if we could theoretically assume that the wealth of parents played a decisive role here, we still could not but be satisfied with the finding that the patriots who came to study from families without higher education merged into the national activity faster and at an earlier age than the patriots who came from educated families. An explanation on the basis of parents' wealth would give exactly the opposite result.

In conclusion, let us summarize the results of our analysis of the social composition of Czech patriots in Bohemia as follows:

1  The largest patriotic group at the beginning of phase B was composed of the

clergy; towards the end of phase B, however, their proportion decreased and became nearly equal to that of the students and officials (of the latter, one-half were seigniorial officials).

2  The proportion of small merchants and small artisan manufacturers among the contributors to the Matice followed only behind that of the intelligentsia. Control analyses of the social composition of participants in other patriotic activities or in activities close to the national movement have drawn attention to the fact that the participation of artisans among the patriots equalled that of the secular intelligentsia, and that the decrease in the participation of the clergy towards the end of phase B should have been more pronounced than numbers in the basic table indicate.

3  The largest proportion of patriots was active in the towns; the proportion in Prague was higher at the beginning of phase B, but decreased towards its end.

4  The distribution of patriotic activity over the territory of Bohemia was very uneven. It was strongest in central Polabí and adjacent regions of eastern and northern Bohemia. In contrast, we find a very weak participation (on the basis of contributions to the Matice) in the southern parts of Bohemia, roughly behind the line of the river Sázava to the Brdy mountains.

5  Patriotic groups with a high proportion of artisans and merchants were concentrated especially in the nationally active region of Polabí and they combined with the influential secular intelligentsia among the patriots of western and northern Bohemia. Clergy predominated in most groups in southern Bohemia and in the southeast (with the exception of towns with high-schools).

6  Most patriots came from an urban environment, and from the point of view of social origin sons of artisans and merchants formed the largest group. The proportion of patriots from peasant families and from families of the intelligentsia, however, grew significantly in the youngest generation.

7  Birth-places of the patriotic intelligentsia were concentrated roughly in the regions where the network of patriotic communities was thickest and also in the towns with high-schools.

A more thorough explanation and interpretation of the results of our analysis can, of course, only be given by a comparative analysis, by a consideration of these results in the light of what we know about the social composition of analogous patriotic communities in other small nations of Europe. In this sense, the present article is only a preparatory and partial study.[20]

20 Cf. M. Hroch, "Die Vorkämpfer der nationalen Bewegung bei den kleinen Völkern Europas. Eine vergleichende Analyse zur gesellschaftlichen Schichtung der patriotischen Gruppen," *Acta Universitatis Carolinae, Philosophica et Historica, Monographia* XXIV (Prague, 1968).

# II

# From ethnic group toward the modern nation: the Czech case

The Czech national movement is generally regarded as a 'success story'. The ethnically defined Czech national identity received, during several decades of national agitation, general acceptance from the masses of the Czech-speaking population. This happened under the conditions of the oppressive Metternich regime and against German cultural and social superiority. In my earlier comparative research, it was demonstrated that this success can be explained neither by the Herderian influence (as the traditionalist, above all German, historians supposed), nor by the force of the idea of 'nationalism' as a free-floating actor. At least, the oft-quoted author of the concept of nation as the product of nationalism, Ernest Gellner, proved that successful 'nationalism' had its deep historical roots in the social and cultural process labelled by him erroneously 'industrialization'. According to my earlier research, the transition from the Phase B of national agitation to the Phase C of mass movement was possible only under several conditions, which were independent of the wishes of its actors, the 'nationalists': firstly, strengthening social communication and mobility; secondly, a coincidence of national demands and social (political, cultural) interests, i.e. under conditions of a nationally relevant conflict of interests; thirdly, the pre-existing linguistic and cultural community, sometimes accompanied by a memory of old 'national' statehood.

This contribution does not intend to repeat earlier published results and recall generally known data on the transition of the national movement from Phase B to Phase C, i.e. to the mass movement. It aims to go one step back and try to interpret the transition from the learned Phase A dominated by nationally 'neutral' scholars to the nationally engaged, agitating Phase B. This article offers an attempt to explain motives: why some intellectuals decided to construct a new national identity and to propagate it among the members of their ethnic group. Expressed in the terms used by Anthony Smith, we try to explain the decision to transform the ethnic community into a modern nation. For good or ill, the actors of this procedure understood themselves as protagonists and 'awakeners' of the real existing nation and they regarded the non-existence of statehood in most cases (except the Balkans) as unimportant or as not decisive.

This turn to national agitation occurred in the Czech case (and above all in Bohemia) in the period between 1790 and 1815, contemporaneous with similar developments in Hungary, Norway and Greece, and much earlier than most other European national movements.

Our analysis chooses as its point of departure a hypothesis proceeding from social psychology that the need for a new identity has to be understood as a result of the crisis or loss of old identities, as an answer to the dissolution of old values and social ties, under conditions of uncertainty caused by social and political changes and transformations. This hypothesis will be verified through the analysis of empirical data from Czech history.

Our procedure follows three steps, answering three questions:

1. 'the constants': what were the basic factors of stability under the conditions of the old regime?
2. What changes and reforms destabilized or eroded old factors of stability?
3. 'the answers': How did members of the Czech ethnic community react to these changes?

During the second half of the eighteenth century, the way of life of the inhabitants, their beliefs, habits and identities were formed and maintained by several constant relations and institutions. These invariables or 'constants' had survived without significant change since the seventeenth century, in some cases even since the Middle Ages.

The medieval Kingdom of Bohemia gradually lost its independence under the rule of the Habsburgs, but it did not disappear: its name, its borders, its capital Prague survived, and also some institutions, like the Landtag, Court of Justice and even the constitution from 1627. Most aristocratic families were not Czech by origin (they usurped the confiscated lands of Protestants, who were expelled after their defeat in 1620), but their later members accepted an identity with the 'Lands of the Crown of Bohemia'. A new feeling of identity emerged among many members of the nobility in opposition to the centralist policy of Vienna and they tried to retain old privileges: the 'Landespatriotismus'. As a part of this process, the memory of old statehood of the Crown was retained. Nevertheless, for the most part, the majority of this nobility regarded the Austrian dynastic identity as the dominant one and many aristocrats supported Habsburg centralism.

Since Protestantism in Bohemia had been defeated, the Catholic Church had controlled all the religious, spiritual and cultural life in the country. Its organization corresponded to the old political structure: Bohemia remained an autonomous ecclesiastical unit with the archbishop in Prague as its head. Similarly, Moravia was an archbishopric with its capital in Olomouc. The Catholic hierarchy kept elements of the 'land'-identity and some among its members (and above all among the lower clergy) developed a Bohemian baroque patriotism, as a positive attitude to the land, and even regarded the Czech language as a symbol of Bohemian or Moravian individuality. The cult of St.Vaclav (Wenzel) I as 'Protector' of the Crown of Bohemia and of other 'national' saints represented an important element of this patriotism. Naturally, the Church asserted until the middle of the eighteenth century, beside its monopolistic control of education and all spiritual life, a privileged position in the economy and politics.

The most expressive social constant was signified by the rigid system of serfdom in the countryside and guilds in towns. Aristocratic domains, still strongly influenced by their feudal origins, created the basic unit of administration, taxation, and jurisdiction. All individuals were firmly included into the more or less effective system of Church and state administration. This meant that inhabitants of non-noble origin were subordinated to the state, to the Church and to their lordships. They had no right to self-administration and at the same time, they were the only tax-payers. Nevertheless, the inequality of human beings, predestined by birth, was still generally accepted by all strata of the non-privileged population as a self-evident feature of their life.

What about the ethnic constants? Since the Middle Ages, both Bohemia and Moravia were inhabited by a majority Czech-speaking and a minority German-speaking population. The written Czech language developed during the fourteenth century and remained, until the seventeenth century, the official language of administration. The new constitution of 1627 gave the German language an equal position with Czech, but in reality German became the dominant language in administration, the economy and cultural life. The Czech-speaking population was aware of its language, at least, since it remained the language of the Church. We have proof for some degree of ethnic identity, which – with very few exceptions – did not include xenophobia or spontaneous patriotic enthusiasm. The social structure, the 'Stand', was still decisive. An example of this was the fact that the Czech- and German-speaking peasants participated side by side in the great peasant war in northeast Bohemia and there is no evidence of any relevant conflict between insurgents from these two *ethnies*.

In general, one could gain the impression that this society was stabilized and based on currently accepted inequality, religious legitimacy and everyday oppression. Nevertheless, this was only on the surface. Within society, immanent tensions and signs of crisis increased. To prevent conflicts, to ameliorate the situation and to avoid a crisis, the enlightened absolutist rulers initiated efforts to modernize society through reforms. These famous reforms, introduced by the late Maria Theresa and above all by Joseph II, brought significant changes which brought old constants into question.

Their impact can be summarized in five points:

1. The hitherto monopolistic and uncontrolled power of the Catholic Church was limited not only by the introduction of religious tolerance and by diminishing its intellectual control, but also by the reduction of Church property by the state.
2. The state decreased the power of landlords, above all through the abolition of serfdom and through increasing state control in local and state administration.
3. The progress of jurisprudence and the reform of legislation, based on principles of equal value of all citizens, was the first step to abolish – at least in the theory – the inequality of classes.
4. The new concept of education and the school system tried to spread elementary education to all and to open higher schools to all inhabitants.
5. The state administration increasingly supported the spread of enlightened principles and scientific research, diminished the rights of censorship and contributed to the creation of a new secular public.

All these reforms, even though not generally welcomed, influenced sooner or later everyday experience, but their immediate importance was larger: they demonstrated not only to the educated classes, but also to the people that the conditions and circumstances of their life were not unchangeable and that they could be ameliorated.

Naturally, an opposition emerged against these reforms, led above all by a part of the nobility and by the Church hierarchy. This opposition – irrespective of its reactionary character – included a mobilizing impact: it demonstrated a phenomenon which seemed until this time unthinkable, i.e. public opposition against the will and the orders of the ruler and of the state authority. The image of the inviolability of the ruler's will was impaired. All this played a role as a factor which started to disturb old constants and old identities.

Beside this general impact, each of the five groups of reforms included changes which influenced – usually without having intended to – the preconditions for the strengthening of a new national identity.

The religious tolerance brought an end to more than one hundred years of persecution and ostracism of the Reformation tradition in Czech cultural life: non-Catholic books written in Czech and published before the triumph of the Counter-reformation had until this time been forbidden and destroyed and their authors had to be forgotten as 'heretics'. Only now was it possible to offer a full picture of the history of Czech-written literature since the fifteenth century. The religious tolerance allowed now even reprints of some important works written by Czech non-Catholics. In this context, some new historical sources could be published and this contributed to a better knowledge of the country's past, understood sometimes as 'national history'.

The abolition of serfdom was regarded by traditional historiography as the starting point of the migration from the Czech-speaking countryside to the German towns. Recent research has revised, this opinion in two respects: firstly, the immigration from the countryside had already started before the abolition of serfdom; secondly, the towns in the core territory of Bohemia were ethnically not as strongly Germanized as in Moravia. Nevertheless, more important from the point of view of identity crisis was the difference in the experience of personal freedom between the Czech-speaking and the German-speaking peasant. The German peasant entered a society whose official language was similar to his local dialect. The Czech peasant entered a society whose official language he was unable to understand. The difference in possibility of social advancement – and also in the search for a new identity – became apparent.

The reform of jurisdiction was discussed but not finished until after 1800. For this reason, it had a limited impact on the masses of people. Nevertheless, the educated public, partially Czech by origin, was well informed and accepted the principle of equality of human beings. The abolition of serfdom itself was regarded as a great demonstration of the principles of equality, which opened the possibility of new social relations (and identities).

The new school system was also an expression of this trend towards equality. From the point of view of the change of identities, its impact was ambivalent. In theory, all higher schools and the university in Prague were open to everyone regardless of social origin. On the other hand, the replace-ment of Latin by German as the language of instruction created a new inequality. German native speakers and also sons from bilingually educated families were in a more advantageous position in comparison with those who were born in Czech-speaking families.

The elementary schools received – unlike all higher schools – the 'local language' as the language of instruction. This was an important point of departure not only for the improvement of alphabetization, but also for the awareness of ethnic identity. Somehow, it could also be regarded as an important sign for the prestige of the Czech language.

While the elementary schools remained under ecclesiastical control, the majority of higher schools became secularized: the proportion of secularized themes increased and new scientific knowledge was allowed to enter education. Themes from history and geography achieved an unintended importance for the awareness of the specificity of one's own region, country, and nation.

The secularization of education together with the liberalization of intellectual and scientific life influenced the profile of the new emerging social strata – the secular 'intellectuals' (or better 'intelligentsia') who lived off con-tracted work or through free professions and who became partly independent of the state and religious control, even though the degree of independence of various professions differed from a totally loyal clerk in state service to a relatively independent attorney or surgeon. Naturally, this new category of educated people, without the disadvantage inherited in their birth, sometimes had difficulties in the search for a position which would correspond to their qualifications. It is not surprising that some of them defined a new understanding of social and material interests and were strongly interested in the search for identity.

That is to say, most of these new intellectuals did not belong to any established estate or self-conscious traditional professional group. Even those who were originally educated as priests or friars did not regard their affiliation to the Church as a decisive identity. Some of them identified with their aristocratic sponsors (and with the Bohemian nobility), with a limited chance to be accepted as members of this noble class. Some of them identified with the modernizing centralist state, in so far as they found jobs in state services. It was difficult for them to accept other traditional identities and so the search for a new identity seemed 'inevitable' for them.

The internal and institutional reforms of social and cultural life were only one part of the changes that shook the traditional social relations and identities of the old regime in the Habsburg monarchy. The other category of shocks were external in origin, did not depend on the state policy, and came from outside.

The most famous and influential among them originated from the French Revolution and were strengthened by the interventionist wars against it. In these wars, the Habsburg armies played the central role and could not be omitted in the system of communication in their Empire. Given the conditions of Central Europe, it was impossible to introduce a total blockade of information on the French Revolution, as was realized, with some success, in Russia and in Spain.

Since revolutionary terms like 'liberty' and 'equality' could not be ignored because they were an integral part of daily news, the governmental ideologists tried to adopt them and use them as positive values – naturally, not to announce the fall of the old regime, but on the contrary, as natural features of this regime. 'True' liberty and equality is realized not in the 'falsified' sense in France, but in the Habsburg lands. Later, the revolutionary term, 'la patrie', was adopted as 'Vaterland'. On the other hand, the term 'la nation' did not become an object of dynastic revaluation – maybe because it was not regarded as a danger to the stability of the old regime.

Even though the wars against revolutionary France affected the lands of the Crown of Bohemia only marginally, the German and Czech reading public was regularly informed about the battles and military campaigns and the 'French danger' was present, at least indirectly. The psychological and educational impact of these reports was immense: never before had the population received such detailed information about the war. Reports presented the war not only as the ruler's war, but also as 'our war', a war against a common enemy and this enemy was often defined ethnically: 'the French'. War reports were in some sense an instrument of identification, but they also offered a schooling in imagination: you never knew the consequences of military operations, of battles won or lost – the only thing you could do, was to imagine the different alternatives.

Beside this, the reading public – and indirectly also the people – received through war reports an immense amount of geographical information about foreign countries, peoples, towns, rivers etc. Some of these names the Czech and the German reading public had never heard of and, above all, this was a practical training in imagination: imagining the existence of 'the other', people could imagine their own group, their own country.

Later on, especially during the Napoleonic wars, another factor of identification was offered by military billeting and transits. For the first time, Czech peasants and urban inhabitants met others who spoke a language different from the usual Czech or German: French, and also the Slavic languages, like Russian. We know from contemporary comments that the Czech people oscillated between sympathy with soldiers who spoke a similar language, and aversion against the parasitic demands of foreign (and not only foreign) armies.

It is significant that all other innovations happening in the neighbourhood were overshadowed by the Revolution and wars. The process of dissolution of the Old Empire received only a marginal place in newspapers and contemporary comments. We can interpret this marginalization of the Reich as a partial success of the efforts of the Viennese government to strengthen the Austrian identity of both Czech and German speakers in contrast to the identity based on the Old Empire. The events in the 'Reich' were interpreted as events which happened abroad, in foreign countries.

In the end, we have to mention some events which did not change the life and institutions in the Empire, but mobilized the attention of the broad masses insofar as they also influenced the search for identities. Three great political festivities at the beginning of the 1790s played this role. Chronologically the first was the public transfer of the Bohemian Crown Jewels to Prague from Vienna, where they had been kept since the time of Maria Theresa. The transportation of the Crown Jewels of the Kingdom of Bohemia was accompanied by festive processions and meetings, where the feeling of Landespatriotismus were demonstrated, sometimes explicitly as a reaction to Viennese centralism.

The reason for transportation was the second festivity: the coronation of Leopold II as king of Bohemia in 1791 and one year later – after his unexpected death – another coronation, that of his son Franz. Both coronations were opportunities for great ceremony not only for the nobility but also for the people. Thousands of peasants and artisans were invited to come from the provinces to Prague for this occasion.

While these three festivities corresponded to the traditional patterns of the old regime, the attempt to awaken Bohemian patriotism in 1808 intended to mobilize all strata of society, aiming to strengthen the people's will to resist an eventual French invasion of Bohemia. As part of these patriotic activities, the old medieval Kingdom was celebrated and even the Czech Hussites were presented as an example of bravery and of the love for fatherland. After the defeat in 1809 patriotic agitation was stopped. Nevertheless, this short period offered to the small group of Czech patriots an opportunity to strengthen the arguments for, and to improve instruments and forms of, national agitation.

At least one negative experience with governmental 'innovations' has to be mentioned: the catastrophic failure and bankruptcy of state finances in 1811, which struck almost all inhabitants of the Monarchy. The loss of savings through the decision of the state did not provoke any larger social unrest, but it affected the search for identities, because it urgently reminded all state subjects that they lived in the same country and shared the same fate.

In the last part of this contribution, we ask, how did people respond to the challenge of all these historical events? How did all these changes and innovations influence the identity crisis and the search for new identities?

We have to resist a simplifying temptation to draw a teleological line from the identity crisis provoked by enlightened reforms to the creation of the modern Czech national identity. During the critical period, we distinguish several activities based on different and mutually overlapping identities. The aristocratic Landespatriotismus survived as an activating medium of scientific research on history of the kingdom, its old literature and the Czech language itself. Analogically, baroque patriotism, with strong religious affiliations, also survived the period of enlightened absolutism, stressing the traditions of the autonomous kingdom. Although both variants of old patriotism were based on anti-modernist feelings, they were partially compatible with the new identity which emerged with enlightened regional patriotism. This enlightened patriotism regarded the patriotic individual (usually an intellectual) as responsible for the wealth and prosperity of the region and its population: he had to improve the situation through school education, scientific research, and cultural activities.

During the last decade of the eighteenth century, this regional patriotism, originally intellectual, exclusive and in most cases German-*writing*, diverged into several streams. One of them kept the concept of a purely economic improvement of the country, disregarding linguistic aspects. Another integrated into the learned activities of Landespatriotismus. The third regarded its main responsibility as improving the cultural standard and education of the most neglected part of the population – the Czech-speaking part. This patriotism started to support Czech publishing not only on economic matters but also on the past of Bohemia, on its heroes, on the present situation and also descriptions of foreign countries as 'other'. A specific component of these educational efforts offered to the Czech public were translations (and increasingly also original works) of fiction, mostly 'popular' reading and in some places (above all in Prague) Czech-speaking theatre, with both translated pieces, and pieces from the history of Bohemia. This was the environment in which some intellectuals wrote enthusiastic 'defences' of the Czech language.

The enlightened patriotic activities were in most cases written in German, as it was the usual language of communication in the Habsburg monarchy at the end of the eighteenth century. The minority of Czech-*writing* enlightened patriots demonstrated that they accepted – beside a regional and professional identity – some kind of ethnic identity. Nevertheless, the use of Czech language was also compatible with baroque patriotism and eventually also with aristocratic Landespatriotismus. In spite of this overlapping of identities, they evidently differed in their social background. The Czech-*writing* patriotism of that time could hardly count on material or moral support from the ruling elites. The Czech-*writing* engagement could, in other words, bring no profits to the patriots. Some degree of selfless enthusiasm was a necessary precondition of this branch of patriotism and the activists could at best earn their reward in the immaterial field of prestige.

However, this patriotic attitude expressed the heritage of the basic moral principles of enlightened patriotism: self-denying and active love for the fatherland without regard to any material profit. Prestige was then regarded as some kind of moral, spiritual substitute for profit. Symptomatically formulated on the threshold of the nineteenth century by Bernard Bolzano, Professor in Moral Philosophy at the University in Prague, was a concept of regional patriotism, where the enlightenment and religious traditions were combined: patriotism was an expression of Christian charity imposed upon the people by God. In his understanding, all kinds of patriotic activities were fully in accord with religious moral principles.

Beside this combination of the enlightened and baroque patriotic traditions, another combination emerged at the very same time, Austrian state-patriotism, proposed in the above mentioned crisis year of 1808. The love for the fatherland was presented as an integral part of the love for the Emperor, who was presented as 'father' of his subjects. The official propaganda offered a twofold identity: the broader one with the Emperor and his Empire, the narrower one with the concrete historical Land. The new identity, offered by official Austrian state-patriotism, was accepted as a central one by a very small stratum of the state bureaucracy in Bohemia and partly among aristocrats. Nevertheless it was immanently or explicitly accepted also by the broader masses of population but not as their central identity.

For those patriotic intellectuals who tried to define their 'national' or regional identity in a new way, one central question had to be answered: how to define and describe the fatherland, 'patria', as an object of care and love? Where is the homeland of one's fellow-countrymen? Three answers can be distinguished at the threshold of the nineteenth century, corresponding to different types of old patriotism and to their modified versions.

The surviving concept of regional patriotism was related to a region, defined by political (or historical) borders, without regard to its internal structure and also without regard to the ethnic borders. Ethnic identities of the inhabitants were respected as a specific feature of the region. This old concept implied some overlapping with Landespatriotismus and with baroque patriotism and its linguistic or ethnic 'neutrality' meant that German was its basic language of communication and that its impact was limited and acceptable above all for

German-speaking enlightened elites, while the Czech-speaking population remained almost untouched.

Those intellectuals, ethnic Czechs by origin, who felt responsible to their ethnic countrymen, defined the 'patria' in a different way. The most important among them, Josef Jungmann, defined the fatherland (for the first time in 1806) as a territory, where people speak the same language, 'my' language. In this context, they used as synonym of fatherland the term 'narod' – nation. This term was not a neologism invented by them, but an old term used in the Czech language since the sixteenth century and understood at least since the seventeenth century as a community characterized by common history, living place and also by common language.

The third concept of fatherland was formulated at the same time by Professor Bolzano as a vision of one nation comprising all the inhabitants of Bohemia, who would be able to use or understand both Czech and German, i.e. a bilingual society. This vision seems to be very up-to-date, even fashionable today; nevertheless, the future proved, very soon, that it was only a utopian vision. Even if Bolzano was in his time more popular (above all among students) and influential than Jungmann, it was not his, but Jungmann's vision, which was accepted by young educated men in their search for a new group identity.

If we ask why this linguistic concept of national identity became the most attractive one, we have to take into account that these newly educated intellectuals and students proceeded from the lower middle classes; they were sons of artisans, small shopkeepers and peasants. Most of them kept in contact with their families and the localities where they were born, and were well aware about their way of life and about the impact of enlightened reforms.

The Czech-speaking artisan or peasant was, thanks to these reforms, personally free and regarded as an equal human being, he was often wealthy enough to acquire some degree of self-consciousness and for this reason he realized a humiliating fact, which was not relevant for his parents or grand parents: that he was excluded from the new emerging society of 'equals' because the language he spoke was rejected by this society as inferior. As long as the horizon of Czech-speakers was limited by the feudal estate, this inferior status of his language played no important role: the only linguistic difference he experienced as 'naturally' inferior to him was that in relation to the German-speaking landlord and his servants. As soon as he or his son overstepped the bounds of the local estate, he experienced his Czech ethnicity as a handicap or even as a source of humiliation. 'We are foreigners in our own land', commented one educated peasant as early as the 1780s.

It is evident that among those who experienced this inequality were young sons who started on the difficult process of achieving higher education. Even though they were personally able to learn German sooner or later, the only language of education, they were not able to achieve better social positions and jobs. This feeling of injustice provoked in some of them a need for total assimilation, but another reaction became increasingly frequent: the decision to struggle for linguistic equality in Bohemia, i.e., to accept and support the ethnic concept of national identity and of the nation, proposed by Jungmann.

The traditional historians regard this programme as Herderian and 'romanticist' – and for the same reason, some social scientists denounce it. Naturally, Herder played an important role as inspiration and as a source of arguments and similarly, German Romanticism was welcomed by Jungmann as validation of his concept, which was, however, formulated and written earlier than the famous 'Reden' of Fichte and the pamphlets of Ludwig Jahn.

There is no doubt that there were also emotional motifs behind the decision to accept an ethnic national identity. The 'irrational' love for language was derived from the more understandable love for his countrymen, for those inhabitants of the country he felt identity with. In this respect, Jungmann's proposals represents rather the heritage of enlightened patriotism than the influence of 'romanticism'.

Very soon, this ethno-national identity started to diverge into a moderate and a consistent stream. The moderate patriots regarded the Czech language as a loved symbol of community, they enjoyed using and developing it, but they regarded the demands for its equality with German as utopian and even as unnecessary. To adore the Czech language and to be proud of Czech national history did not negate their pessimisim concerning the chance of the Czech language becoming a modern written language. For this reason, German had to maintain its domination in Bohemia.

The consistent stream aimed to achieve a real and not just formal equality between both languages. Sooner or later, the Czech language had to be able to express all modern feelings and thoughts and to describe complicated connections. For this reason, it had to be accepted as a language of instruction in schools and as a language of communication in public life. Even if this vision seemed to be a utopian one in the eyes of contemporaries, these claims cannot be interpreted as a mere project of romanticism. Neither can they be explained as a tool in the struggle for political power, as was the case a century later.

The interpretation has to take into account that the enlightened concept of equal human beings was later accompanied by the proto-liberal concept of equal opportunities for every man. These principles, however, could not be fulfilled – at least according to the opinion of these patriots – under conditions of differential prestige and unequal possibilities of different languages. So far, the decision to embrace the linguistic national identity had not been very far from the emerging ideas of civil society and equality of its members. Additionally, the struggle for equality of languages (and their speakers) has something to do with the need for prestige and acknowledgement felt by the Czech-speaking intellectuals.

For a better understanding of this attitude, let us exemplify it by comparing the arguments used in favor of the Czech language by enlightened patriots in their 'Defences' from the 1780s and 1790s, with the arguments used by Jungmann in favour of the Czech language in 1806. In the eighteenth century Defences the Czech language was celebrated above all for its beauty, rich vocabulary and its age (as a language spoken by medieval Czech kings, etc.). Its practical use was recommended to the elites of that time: the landlord needs it for better understanding of his (Czech) servants or serfs, the officer can better understand his soldiers, the surgeon his patients. The general position of these Defences was a call addressed from below to the higher classes of Bohemian society.

Jungmann also praised historical and aesthetic values of the Czech language, but his most important argument was that it was above all the Czech people who needed the improvement of their language. It was not important to him which language was used by the nobility; what was important was that the Czech speaker, if he did not know German, had no chance for any social advancement.

The search for new identities proceeded in Bohemia at the time around 1800 in different ways and offered different identities. Naturally, it was always a matter of individual decision, which alternative was preferred, or how the hierarchy of old and new identities was constructed. To avoid the criticism of being under the influence of the concepts of 'teleolology' and 'ethnicism', let us put the concluding question, concerning the chances of different alternatives to be realized as the generally accepted modern national identity.

The non-ethnic regional patriotism kept its position as an identity accepted by German-speaking and bilingual intellectuals for several decades. Nevertheless, since it did not aim at any mass-mobilization, it was unable to compete with other identities, but could survive as a marginal identity in connection with another one. The same could be said about regional identity as a component of a national one, even though the regionalists tried to mobilize the population. So, for example, the Moravian regionalists opposed, until the second half of the nineteenth century, full integration into the Czech nation with the result that the national identity of the Moravian population existed alongside the regional identity not as an alternative but as an additional identity.

The alternative of the 'Bohemian' bilingual nation had a real chance of success only if accepted not only by Czech but also German speakers. Czechs, so far as they achieved higher education, fulfilled the claim for bilinguality, but only a few Germans by origin did the same by learning the Czech language so as to become consciously bilingual 'Bohemians'. Nevertheless, with the emerging national movement in German states, an increasing number of German intellectuals in Bohemia decided to accept the linguistic concept of German identity and regarded themselves as members of the German nation. This decision was for the first time demonstrated in 1848 in the dispute about participation in elections for the parliament in Frankfurt. Once this decision was taken, a bilingual nation in Bohemia ceased to be an alternative.

The old surviving Landespatriotismus also rejected Frankfurt and German identity, but it was socially exclusive and its aristocratic representatives only in very few exceptional cases supported the efforts to improve the Czech language as an integral part of their identity with the land. The decisive part of the nobility did not renege on their German language – not as a symbol of their national identity but as a symbol of their social superiority.

Consequently, the linguistic definition of a new national identity in Bohemia was the victorious alternative, because it was the only real way, which could integrate an intellectual patriotism with the Czech- (but also with the German-) speaking population. This does not mean that this population inevitably followed the 'national' call. Only if several conditions were fulfilled, could the real possibility of Phase B turn to the reality of Phase C. This is, nevertheless, already another problem.

## Bibliographical note

English historians writing on the Czech national movement were mostly interested in the period of political conflicts, but there are very few contributions to its initial phase. The best analysis is that of Hugh LeCaine Agnew, *Origins of the Czech National Renascence*, University of Pittsburg Press (1993) (with a rich bibliography). Among earlier authors, relevant is Robert Joseph Kerner, *Bohemia in the Eighteenth Century. A Study in Political, Economic, and Social History with Special Reference to the Reign of Leopold II., 1790–1792*, New York: Macmillan, 1932. More specialized is Janet Wolf Berls, *The elementary school reforms of Maria Theresia and Joseph II in Bohemia*, PhD. diss. Columbia University (1975); Paul P. Bernard, *Jesuits and Jacobins: Enlightement and enlightened despotism in Austria*, Urbana, Chicago 2nd London, University of Illinois Press, 1971; Joseph F. Zacek, 'The French revolution, Napoleon and the Czechs' in *Proceedings of the Consortium on Revolutionary Europe 1750–1850, Tallahassee*, Florida: Florida State University Press, 1980, pp. 254–63. The same author gave a general view of this period in 'Nationalism in Czechoslovakia', in Peter F. Sugar and Ivo John Lederer, *Nationalism in Eastern Europe*, 3rd ed. (1994), pp. 166ff. For the linguistic aspect, see George Thomas, *Linguistic Purism*, London: New York (1991).

# III

## ZIONISM AS EUROPEAN NATIONAL MOVEMENT*

The purpose of this paper is to categorize Zionism in the context of the European processes of national formation. In order to do this, it is first necessary to transcend the somewhat alibi-like perception that in the case of the Jews, national formation is to be regarded as "the unique destiny of a unique people" (Ben-Gurion) which hence defies comparison. Not only is this myth of "incomparability" widespread among nationalist politicians, but in addition, according to my admittedly limited knowledge, it is shared implicitly or even explicitly in the specialist literature about Zionism.

For this reason it may be foreseen that viewing Zionism as a national movement, i.e. in the context of and in comparison with other European national movements, will in no way meet with general agreement or approval. Hence in order to give reasons for my procedure, attention should be drawn to two circumstances.

First, I regard all phenomena which belong to one and the same category as being comparable in principle. What this means specifically in the case at hand is that if Zionism declared the existence of a Jewish nation, then it entered thereby (in conceptual terms too) an area which was "settled" or "inhabited" by nations or national movements already in existence, and hence accepted comparability, even if by implication.

Second, one of the basic insights (or rather, methodological principles) of research into nationalism is that in every nation's process

* Translated from the German to English by Ruth Morris.

of formation, in every national movement, one can observe both singular and generally occurring phenomena, attitudes, and connections. As far back as 100 years ago the classicist Ernst Bernheim recommended[1] the comparative method as being applicable to all research which sought to distinguish the general and the singular in every historical process. Only through knowledge of what is general and what is unique does it become possible to categorize every historical process, every phenomenon.

In my paper I shall try to examine Zionism (in its early phase, approximately up to World War I) as one of the national movements, and ask to what extent the general essential traits and connections which I have observed in these movements are also applicable when analyzing Zionist activities.

In order to be better understood, I should like to make it clear that I consider myself neither a "primordialist" nor a "modernist." I do not regard the nation as an eternal creation of God, nor as an artificial product of the imagination of a handful of intellectuals, but rather as a result of prolonged historical development. In this development I distinguish two stages. In the first one, a medieval (and early modern) stage, the preconditions were created for the second, decisive modern stage. The modern stage of nation-forming began in two different typologically basic situations: that of a nation-state, as in the case of the French, the Dutch, or the English, and in the situation of a "non-dominant ethnic group."

The second situation differs from the first in that the ethnic group had neither its own statehood, nor its own ruling class with a secular advanced civilization in codified written language. In this situation the path to the modern nation proceeded along the lines of an endeavor to overcome all the missing attributes of a complete national existence — an endeavor which we can describe as a national movement. This corresponds to Zionism's fundamental typological classification: its characteristic traits are analogous to those mentioned here, allowing us

---

1    See Ernst Bernheim, *Lehrbuch der historischen Methode und der Geschichtephilosophie*, Leipzig 1906.

to categorize it in the category of national movements. Within this category, it is fully comparable.

As in all national movements we can distinguish three phases in the Jewish counterpart. The first, the phase of academic interest (Phase A), which lasted a very long time (and can probably be dated from the Haskalah), was fairly heterogeneous, albeit mainly in the wake of the tension between the Orthodox and Enlightenment-influenced views of Jewish identity. The phase of national agitation (Phase B), beginning in the 1880s (i.e., later than in most of the European national movements) must be divided up into two stages: first an agitation without marked attainments, then with increasing effectiveness and a stable core of followers (such as in inter-war Poland). The Jewish national movement, however, failed to attain the mass-movement phase proper (Phase C) prior to World War II: only 3% of Jewish immigrants from Eastern and Central Europe went to Palestine before 1929. On the other hand, if we restrict the geographical area for a mass movement to Palestine, then there is no doubt at all about Phase C: in other words, a geographical transfer of Phase C — certainly a peculiarity of the Jewish national movement, perhaps with a parallel among the Armenians.

As in the other movements, the demands of the Jewish national movement were oriented in three directions which were both complementary and competitive. The linguistic and cultural goals were represented by the formation of a modern standard language (and a secular literature written in that language), and here the researcher must not underestimate the disintegrating factors, such as the competition between the Hebrew and Yiddish variants, as well as the antimodernist opposition of the Orthodox rabbis.

The political goals, represented first and foremost by Herzl and his supports, won acceptance albeit with certain difficulties, and ultimately gained the upper hand. The political demand for a polity in Palestine also implicitly contained the social demand generally present in the national movements: viz., a complete social structure of the nation-in-being. However, this was not the sole variant of the social program: in this connection, note the concept of Hibbat Zion, where the emphasis was on the social equality of the settlers, not on social hierarchy.

Significantly enough, Zionism's social goals, where they existed, were fairly heterogeneous, especially before World War I.

The Zionist program clearly differed from most other national movements in its use of nationally relevant conflicts of interest for political goals, while making less use of them for social demands in the interest of the Jewish population. It is here that the basic difference between Early Zionism and the Jewish Workers, Union, the Bund, would appear to lie.

Far be it from me to limit this comparison to a listing of similarities and differences. Every comparison should above all be applicable on an explanatory, explicative level. In every national movement the question first arises as to its causes (why did the movement start its activities?), and, secondly, as to the factors behind its success (why were they successful?). Such will be the case here also. I will start from the results of my comparative investigations of the European national movements, and ask to what extent these results are applicable to Zionism. Naturally this should all be understood as a working hypothesis or an intellectual exercise.

The first question concerns causes, and concentrates in practical (and chronological) terms on the beginning of national agitation (Phase B). What led to the fact that — independently of each other — the intellectuals in so many countries decided to initiate national agitation? Current research sees the most important condition as being constituted by a crisis of the old system of values and identities, a crisis which reacted in a variety of ways to the crisis of the *ancien régime* and the successes of the process of modernization. This connection is also identified in the specialist literature about the beginnings of Zionism[2]: the fact that the Talmudic tradition became increasingly out-of-step with the times, the new possibilities for social mobility (urbanization, access to higher

2    Jaacov Shavit, "The 'Glorious Century' of the 'Cursed Century': Fin-de-Siecle Europe and the Emergence of Modern Jewish Nationalism, J. Reinharz and G.L. Mosse, eds. *The Impact of Western Nationalism*, Sage 1992; David Vital, *The Origins of Zionism*, Oxford 1975; David Vital, *Zionism: The Formative Years*, Oxford 1982; Nathan Weinstock, *Zionism: False Messiah*, London 1979.

education, and so on), and professional activities all called into question the old Jewish identity which was defined in religious terms, and at the same time stimulated a quest for new identities. The alternative of a modern, secular Jewish national identity was contrasted with the overwhelmingly prevailing trend to assimilation with the specific dominant nation-state.

The effort to diffuse and disseminate a new national identity in no way meant the complete abandonment of earlier identities. Consciously or unconsciously the champions of the European national movements integrated elements of the older ethnic identity, as well as (where present) of a country-based patriotism (*Landespatriotismus*), enlightened regionalism, local identities, and so on. In the Jewish case both Landespatriotismus and regionalism were out of the question. This imparted even more significance to ethnic, cultural identity, based on an extraordinarily strong, religiously based collective memory. And it is also from this that the difficulty with the modernizing and reshaping of this historical tradition results: how is the ancient history of the Jewish nation (understood in primordialist terms) to be integrated into a secularized, modern national identity?

Another impetus to the quest for a new identity mentioned in the specialist literature is the rise of anti-Semitism and its specific version, the Russian pogroms in the 1880s: in other words, outside pressure, the clearly defined external enemy, as a stimulus to the reaction in the form of an independent national awareness. Their brutality undoubtedly made the pogroms a specific circumstance, but in the nineteenth/twentieth century, discrimination and harassment by foreigners, sometimes with racist overtones, constituted part of the frequently occurring concomitants of national movements (Germans to the Slavs, Swedes to the Finns, Magyars to the Romanians in Transylvania, English to the Irish, etc.). In other cases also they accelerated the decision to seek for new identities in these non-dominant ethnic groups.

The second complex of questions concerns the causes and prerequisites for the success of national agitation. I have summarized these nationally integrating factors on the basis of my researches, dividing them into five groups:

1. A successful, consensus-oriented Phase A
2. Progress in social mobility, especially the possibility of social advancement for some members at least of the non-dominant ethnic group
3. An increasing level of social communication
4. A strong, nationally relevant conflict of interests
5. Favorable external circumstances (political system, international relations, and so on).

Before I try to apply these factors to the case of Zionism, I would like to note that the success of national agitation (i.e. a mass movement) was not a historical necessity and that in the context of European national movements, Zionist agitation belongs to those movements which did not achieve this goal. Thus here the question posed is not only about the factors behind successes, but also about the factors behind failure.

1. These also specifically include Phase A which, as has already been stated, proceeded in an ambivalent fashion, without achieving any consensus between the Orthodox tradition and the Haskalah concerning the nature of the Jewish nation or of Jewishness. As a result, the new Jewish national identity was not required to define itself fully until the eve of or during the national agitation (Lilienblum, Pinsker), and was never capable of replacing the ethnic-religious identity by a modern national identity accepted by their own ethnic group to the extent that occurred in most other European national movements.

2. On the other hand, the possibility of social advancement (or of access to academic education) corresponds to the advent of national agitation to the same degree as in the other national movements. However, there is an important difference in the fact that, in the wake of the ambivalent Phase A, these possibilities of social advancement for the Jews opened up earlier than any definition of the nature of Jewish national identity. As a result, in the case of the Jews, social advancement was one of the factors of assimilation, not only in the ethnic but also the religious sense of the word. We can also identify certain parallels, even if less striking, to this phenomenon among other European national movements.

3. Social communication also played a rather ambivalent role in the

Jewish case. While all other national movements in Central and Eastern Europe were able to use the advantages of clearly intensifying communications (market relationships, literacy, journalism, etc.) for the goals of their agitation, which was directed horizontally, all of this progress worked only partially in favor of Zionist agitation. Above all, Zionist agitation did not work horizontally: in other words, in social terms its dissemination came "from above," making it extremely hard for it to get through to the regular channels and achieve communication with Jewish communities and the workers' movement alike. Thus in Eastern Europe, Zionist agitation remained permanently in the shadow of the Bund and Orthodoxy. Additionally, the distances were too immense to be overcome, even in the age of railroads and telegraphs: viewed from a purely territorial point of view, Zionist agitation had to contend with an incomparably larger area than any of the other national movements. The only analogy that can perhaps be found that is the early phase of the Greek movement at the beginning of the nineteenth century. The inner structure of communication was also disadvantageous. Although there was a center in Vienna (and a center was very important for all national agitation), this center was remote from the actual areas to which the agitation was addressed.

4.   When I refer to a nationally relevant conflict of interests I mean those stresses and conflicts which coincided with an ethnic (linguistic, religious) difference. The ability to exploit such conflicts of interest for national agitation was very important for the commencement of national agitation and the transition to Phase C. Now, in the Jewish case we are confronted by a problem, which I would not venture to attempt to resolve on the basis of my imperfect and incomplete knowledge: why was the mass poverty of the Jews not used as a practicable instrument of Zionist agitation? Generally it appears to me that this agitation did not emphasize the nationally relevant contrasts and conflicts (and perhaps did not wish to highlight them). For the poor and the poorest in Eastern Europe, the way out constituted by emigration was oriented far more markedly toward America, as well as Central and Western Europe than Palestine. What specific economic or social arguments could really be used for emigration to Palestine of all places? For the Jewish

entrepreneurial class, the Ottoman Empire had few attractions, as the agitators found all too often.

5.   The success of all national movements was more or less dependent on the "external" factor. This means firstly the support they receive from neighbors, the Great Powers, and so on. In the case of Zionism, dependence on the external factor was particularly extreme: the whole concept of the Jewish State was unthinkable without the consent (and support) of the politically powerful forces and great powers. Of course a national movement which mobilized broad masses always had a greater chance of finding support and being respected. Until the interwar period, Zionism did not belong to this category.

Nevertheless, the external factor was also represented massively by enemies (oppression from outside), although not everywhere. In Russia the role of the external factor differed from the situation in Germany or France. However, the intensity of the oppression does not appear to have been decisive for the successes of agitation. In fact, relatively few of the victims of persecution found their escape route in Zionism.

In conclusion, let us consider the typological classification of Zionism within the European national movements. This classification cannot be unequivocal, since Zionist agitation took place under basically different political and social conditions: on the one hand in Russia with its semi-feudal, absolutist system, and on the other hand in states where civil rights had long since been guaranteed and where clashes of interests could be addressed by political programs.

Thus in my typology, Zionism belongs both to those national movements which had long been forced to vegetate under the *ancien régime* before they achieved a mass base (the "belated type," such as the Ukrainians, Lithuanians, Latvians), and also to those which only started their agitation under the conditions of constitutionalism and found it difficult to make a mark for themselves among the existing political programs (the "western" or "disintegrated" type, such as the Flemings, Welsh, Catalans). It was most probably this peculiarity — of appearing under two essentially different typological conditions — which contributed to the fact that in many places Zionist agitation failed utterly to get through to the broad masses of the Jewish population, and even where it did this was a very slow process indeed.

To sum up, Zionism can rightly be regarded as one of the European national movements. Its roots are connected with the crisis of old identities and ties, its vision is a national one, its demands reveal an analogous structure to that of the other national movements. Even the fact that Zionist agitation was unsuccessful in mobilizing the masses of the Jewish population cannot be called a unique exception. In the comparative investigation of the causes of this relative failure, the following connections can be identified as disintegrating, again on the basis of the comparison with other national movements: the incompatible and antagonistic results of erudite interests during Phase A, the marked competition of other comparable identities (assimilation with the surrounding nation-states, like the Bund), and the particularly arduous and unfavorable external conditions. Naturally in considering all of this it is necessary to apply the reservation that Nazi Germany deprived Zionism in an utterly brutal fashion of the possibility of continuing its agitational activities.

Further references:

Aberbach David, "Hebrew Literature and the Jewish Nationalism in the Tsarist Empire 1881-1897", *Nations and Nationalism* 3 (1997) pp. 25-44.
Ben-Sasson H.H., ed., *A History of the Jewish People*, Cambridge, MA 1976.
Bodenheimer H.H., ed., *Im Anfang der zionistischen Bewegung*, Frankfurt (M.) 1965.
Frankel Jonathan, *Prophesy and Politics: Nationalism and the Russian Jews, 1862-1917*, Cambridge 1981.
Frankel Jonathan, "Assimilation and the Jews in Nineteenth-Century Europe: Toward a New Historiography?" J. Frakel and St. J. Zipperstein, eds., *Assimilation and Community*, Cambridge 1992, pp. 1-37.
Meyer M., *Response to Modernity: A History of the Reform Movement in Judaism*, Oxford 1988.
Reinharz J., ed., *Living with Antisemitism: Modern Jewish Response*, Hanover, NH 1987.

# DE L'ETHNICITÉ À LA NATION
## Un chemin oublié vers la modernité

La revendication généralisée de l'autonomie étatique à laquelle nous assistons depuis quelques années dans les pays « postcommunistes » est trop souvent désignée, avec quelque arrogance méprisante, de « nationalisme » et considérée par conséquent comme dépassée, irrationnelle et orientée vers le XIXᵉ siècle. Une telle accusation peut à l'occasion avoir un fondement ; elle ne contribue cependant guère à l'explication du phénomène. Et c'est de cela dont il s'agira ici : interpréter et comprendre plutôt que moraliser et accuser. De plus, le premier pas d'une explication rationnelle doit tenir compte de la dimension historique du processus de toute construction nationale.

### L'État-nation : une construction historique récente

Commençons par décrire « généalogiquement » la carte politique de l'Europe contemporaine. La plupart des États européens, à l'Est comme à l'Ouest, sont des États-nations, c'est-à-dire des États où n'existe qu'une nation, incluant souvent (mais pas toujours) une minorité dont les membres appartiennent à une autre nation qui détient souvent son propre État limitrophe. Des « empires multinationaux » où coexistent plusieurs nations ne se maintiennent qu'exceptionnellement : la Grande-Bretagne, l'Espagne, la Russie.

Les États-nations qui ont connu une continuité de leur autonomie étatique ethnonationale depuis au moins le XVIᵉ siècle sont en nombre limité. Ce sont premièrement les Français, les Portugais et les Néerlandais mais aussi les anciennes nations qui dominaient les empires multiethniques : les Anglais, les Danois et les Suédois. Les autres nations n'ont pas construit leur État en se fondant d'abord sur une tradition médiévale, mais tirent leur existence d'une communauté ethnique plus ou moins clairement circonscrite.

Si nous regardons la carte de l'Europe, il y a deux siècles, nous constatons qu'à côté de quelques rares États-nations existent plus d'une vingtaine de groupes ethniques vivant sur les territoires des Empires multiethniques. Ces groupes ne jouissaient pas d'une autonomie étatique, d'une maîtrise de leur propre langue écrite (et guère de tradition continue d'une littérature nationale), ni de classes au pouvoir appartenant à leur ethnie. Ils peuvent donc avec raison être décrits comme « groupes ethniques non dominants » (*non-dominant ethnic groups*[1]).

---

1. En anglais dans le texte (N.D.T.). Selon le terme utilisé par Alderman *et al.* (1993).

72

Toutefois, à l'intérieur de cette catégorie « groupes ethniques non dominants », on note des différences considérables. Certains pouvaient se référer à un État médiéval (les Tchèques, les Croates, les Catalans, les Norvégiens), d'autres possédaient leur « propre » aristocratie (les Polonais et les Magyars). La majorité cependant constituaient des groupes sans tradition étatique, tels les Estoniens, Finlandais, Lettons, Slovènes, Slovaques, Bretons, etc., ou au plus leur autonomie étatique passée ne jouait désormais qu'un rôle mythique (Lituaniens, Ukrainiens, Serbes, Grecs, Gallois, Islandais, etc.). L'étude de la transformation de tous ces groupes ethniques non dominants en nations modernes est parmi les tâches de recherche les plus importantes de notre époque. Cette courte contribution ne peut en analyser que quelques aspects. Elle vise à compléter de manière critique les riches travaux de chercheurs comme Hobsbawm (1990), Smith (1986), Lemberg (1964) ou Kohn (1967). Il est d'ailleurs regrettable que la recherche actuelle se concentre sur le XXe siècle, les conséquences dramatiques du nationalisme semblent plus attrayantes que ses modestes débuts.

Préalablement quelques remarques sur la sémantique s'imposent. Dans la littérature scientifique anglo-saxonne notamment, plusieurs malentendus proviennent du fait que le terme central de nos recherches, « la nation », condense des connotations différentes selon les traditions linguistiques[2]. En anglais, la notion est clairement liée à celle d'État, comme c'est d'ailleurs le cas, bien que dans une moindre mesure, en français. En langue allemande, comme dans les langues slaves, la « nation » s'articule plutôt en fonction de caractéristiques ethniques et linguistiques. Ceci a des conséquences non négligeables sur la formulation de notre problème. Posé en anglais, le chemin du groupe ethnique vers la nation traduit une relation entre deux catégories qui sont en principe distinctes et qui ne deviennent compatibles qu'après transformation du fait ethnique. Exprimé en allemand, il s'agit, au contraire, de deux phénomènes « généalogiquement » liés, de deux stades du développement d'une même entité.

Selon l'usage allemand et slave, la formation d'une nation moderne est entendue comme un passage du fait ethnique à la nation, c'est-à-dire un mégagroupe qui possède sa propre culture et langue. Ce processus de formation est conçu comme naturel et organique, en raison de la frontière fluide entre le groupe ethnique et la nation. Dans un sens figuré, s'abrite derrière cette sémantique la représentation que les nations sont, à l'instar des cultures, équivalentes et égales en droit.

D'un autre côté, la construction de la nation, telle qu'exprimée en anglais, est liée à la représentation d'un particularisme politique. Elle évoque l'idée d'autonomie étatique et donc de la sécession politique d'une entité d'un ensemble plus vaste. Les caractéristiques du groupe ethnique et les traits politiques de la nation appartiennent à des catégories distinctes et sont incompatibles, comme nous l'avons noté antérieurement. Pour la même raison, l'équivalence des cultures et l'égalité en droit des nations sont deux problèmes tout à fait différents.

Une autre complication que nous ne pouvons écarter réside dans notre appréhension du passé ethnonational non selon ses propres termes mais plutôt grâce à des

---

2. Voir l'analyse terminologique toujours valable de Kemiläinen (1964).

concepts nouveaux créés par des chercheurs contemporains. Concrètement, nous devons être conscients que nous n'utilisons pas la notion de « nation » dans le sens que lui prêtèrent les participants des mouvements nationaux, mais bien dans le nôtre. Ceci n'est toutefois pas une invitation à réouvrir la discussion sur le concept de nation[3].

Une autre notion exige quelques clarifications. On utilise souvent le terme « minorité » (*minority*[4]). Il s'agit en fait d'un terme polysémique désignant au moins quatre groupes différents :

(1)  une minorité ethnique d'immigrants qui appartiennent à une autre nation et qui se sont fixés sur le territoire d'un État-nation étranger, sans former une population compacte ;

(2)  une population autochtone vivant de manière dispersée sur un territoire national étranger, soit

   (*a*)  comme classe dominante (les barons allemands dans les pays baltes) ;

   (*b*)  comme groupe marginalisé et inégal en droit (les Tsiganes ou les Juifs) ;

(3)  un groupe vivant sur un territoire déterminé, à l'intérieur des limites d'un État-nation culturellement étranger et faisant partie d'une « nation » autonome possédant son propre État (la « nation mère »). Dans ce cas aussi, on distingue deux variantes :

   (*a*)  une minorité de frontière (*border minorities*[5]) établie à la frontière de l'État de leur « nation mère » (les Allemands de la Prusse occidentale polonaise, les Magyars en Slovaquie) ;

   (*b*)  les « îles ethniques » (les Magyars en Transsylvanie, les Allemands en Slovaquie, les Serbes en Croatie) ;

(4)  un groupe ethnique vivant sur un territoire situé dans les limites d'un empire multinational et qui se transforme en « nation » sans avoir de « nation mère » (les Estoniens et les Lettons en Russie, les Slovènes en Autriche, les Bulgares dans l'Empire ottoman). Dans ce cas, le concept de « minorité » peut induire en erreur et l'on devrait éviter de l'utiliser, du moins dans l'histoire récente. Le concept de « groupe ethnique non dominant » sied mieux.

## Nation étatique et État-nation

En étudiant la transformation d'un groupe ethnique en nation, nous devons distinguer ces deux catégories, pour tenir compte du moins de ces difficultés terminologiques. En quoi la nation se distingue-t-elle du groupe ethnique ? Il est peu satisfaisant de se suffire du dicton maintes fois répété selon lequel la nation se distingue d'un groupe ethnique par la conscience nationale qu'en ont ses membres. Nous allons d'ailleurs déconstruire cette proposition de manière critique. Elle est inacceptable pour au moins trois raisons :

---

3.  Voir par exemple Neumann (1988), Meinecke (1907), Bauer (1907), Hayes (1931), Hertz (1945).
4.  En anglais dans le texte (N.D.T.).
5.  En anglais dans le texte (N.D.T.).

(1) elle souligne les sentiments subjectifs, sans tenir compte des relations et liens objectifs (c'est-à-dire de ce qui est indépendant de la perception et des désirs des individus);

(2) elle passe sous silence la dimension « généalogique » : même si nous acceptons qu'une nation se distingue d'un groupe ethnique par sa conscience nationale, nous ne pouvons ignorer que cette conscience n'est pas immanente, qu'elle a pris du temps pour se répandre et être acceptée;

(3) elle suggère l'idée erronée que les membres d'un groupe ethnique n'avaient pas originellement une identité, une conscience collective, avant de former une nation.

Bien sûr, il semble que l'être du groupe ethnique fut caractérisé surtout par des relations objectives, telles que les mœurs, une religion, un dialecte, un territoire, etc. Chacun de ses membres avait plusieurs identités, sans que l'une ne soit prédominante. La conscience de former un groupe ne fut pas toujours présente. Nous y reviendrons.

Dans une perspective « idéale-typique », la nation se distingue du groupe ethnique non seulement par la conscience nationale qu'en ont ses membres, mais aussi par au moins cinq caractéristiques :

(1) une structure sociale hiérarchique, comprenant des élites éduquées qui participent au pouvoir politique;

(2) une administration interne institutionnalisée et une autonomie de gestion du territoire national;

(3) la qualité de sujet dans les relations internationales;

(4) une culture homogénéisée acceptée par tous qui s'appuie sur une langue unifiée sinon codifiée;

(5) une mémoire collective liée à l'identification d'un passé commun de la nation « personnifiée ».

Ce n'est pas un hasard si le problème fondamental de ces distinctions typiques renvoie à celle entre sociétés traditionnelle et moderne. Dans ce sens également, comme nous allons le voir, la transformation du groupe ethnique en nation s'inscrit dans la transition de la prémodernité vers la société moderne.

Sans doute, les groupes ethniques existaient durant la période féodale alors que la frontière politique était plus importante que la différence ethnique. Les modifications de la frontière politique comme la distribution des fiefs féodaux ne tenaient que rarement compte des distinctions ethniques. En dépit de cela, des régions ethniques se formèrent dans nombre d'États, déterminées par l'appartenance ethnique de la noblesse. Bien des groupes ethniques furent partiellement ou complètement assimilés comme conséquence de la constitution de telles régions ethniques « centrales ». La stabilisation de la frontière politique ne fut pas le seul facteur d'assimilation : il y eut aussi les migrations, telles que les colonisations allemande à l'est de l'Europe et suédoise de la côte finlandaise.

Au début de la période moderne, la frontière politique s'est solidifiée, tandis que l'État absolutiste exerçait un effet unificateur, notamment en termes linguistiques. La majorité des États européens de l'époque étant multiethniques, le croisement des frontières politiques et ethniques fut cependant particulièrement compliqué. Existaient les frontières politiques de l'État, les frontières historiques de l'entité médiévale désormais autonome (c'est-à-dire les frontières des régions historiques), les frontières ethniques face à l'État-nation dominant, les frontières ethniques face à un autre groupe ethnique non dominant.

La formation des États au Moyen Âge a été le fait, dans un premier temps, des membres de la classe dominante et de la mince couche des instruits. Sans égard aux termes utilisés — *natio, gens, lingua* — les documents conservés nous fournissent une abondante information traduisant une forte conscience « nationale »[6]. Certaines expressions nous rappellent les stéréotypes et slogans nationalistes modernes. Il serait toutefois déplacé d'utiliser le terme « nationalisme » dans le contexte du Moyen Âge.

Outre des identités nationales liées à une appartenance politique, nous connaissons dès le début du Moyen Âge des exemples d'identités définies sur une base linguistique; elles se manifestèrent notamment en situations de conflit. Des exemples d'amour de la langue maternelle remontent au IXe siècle (Ottfrid von Weissenburg, Gottschalk von Fulda et d'autres; voir Rexroth 1978). Par ailleurs, la langue servit d'argument dans la quête d'une autonomie étatique, par exemple au Pays de Galles, au XIIIe siècle, ou en Bohème, au XVe siècle[7]. Or, ceci ne devrait pas servir la thèse « primordialiste ». De la même manière que nous distinguons entre le groupe ethnique et la nation moderne, il faut opposer la nation étatique (*Staatsnation*) de la société féodale et l'État-nation (*Nationalstaat*) moderne. Si la nation moderne et l'État-nation sont congruents, la même affirmation ne peut être faite pour la « nation » monarchique du Moyen Âge. Certains groupes ethniques dont la noblesse devint « fondatrice de l'État » se transformèrent en nations médiévales et survécurent pour devenir des nations modernes. Il s'agit cependant d'un développement qui ne nous concerne guère dans cette contribution comme nous l'avons noté initialement.

Nous nous intéressons plutôt aux groupes ethniques non dominants. Ils eurent au Moyen Âge des destins très variés. C'est pourquoi l'intensité et la qualité de la conscience collective de leurs membres furent tout aussi variables. À ce propos, Anthony Smith (1991 : 20 *sq.*) distingue deux types : la « catégorie ethnique », dont les membres n'avaient aucun sentiment d'appartenance, et la « communauté ethnique », dont les membres développaient la conscience d'être un groupe historique.

Une telle distinction ne devrait pas être considérée absolue. Ces deux types constituent plutôt deux étapes consécutives dans le développement d'un groupe ethnique non dominant. La recherche arrivera peut-être, dans un proche avenir, à décrire de manière comparée le développement de la « catégorie » ou de la « communauté » chez des groupes ethniques concrets. La même typologie s'applique aussi à l'intérieur de chaque groupe ethnique, car ses membres étaient conscients de leur appartenance de manière variable. Disons finalement que le processus de reformation nationale, dans les conditions du groupe ethnique non dominant, ne

6. Voir les exemples chez Armstrong (1982), Werner (1970), Tripton (1972), Szücs (1981), Dann (1986).
7. Voir Richter (1976), Smahel (1969a et 1969b).

pouvait aboutir que lorsqu'au moins une partie du groupe percevait son identité ethnique, sa spécificité et sa différence. Or, même dans ce cas, parler d'une conscience nationale serait une simplification : la conscience ethnique ne fut à l'origine que l'une des formes de l'identité (Ross 1979).

Le rapport au passé — *pastness* dans les termes de Wallerstein (Balibar et Wallerstein 1991) — était une autre condition du processus de formation nationale. Cet auteur considère le rapport au passé comme un élément central de la socialisation des individus et du maintien d'une solidarité de groupe. Il ne s'agit point d'une conscience historique au sens moderne, mais plutôt d'un mythe collectif d'une origine commune, d'un destin partagé, de normes éthiques communes fondées sur l'habitus.

Avant de nous pencher sur l'analyse de la transition du groupe ethnique vers la nation, distinguons deux étapes fondamentales dans le processus de construction des nations modernes. La première comprend le Moyen Âge et le début de la modernité, la seconde, décisive, commence durant la deuxième moitié du XVIIIe siècle. Peu de cas se prêtent, dans la première étape, à l'examen des contours de la nation moderne, mais on peut néanmoins parler d'un processus de construction nationale au Moyen Âge, même quand le statut du groupe ethnique non dominant ne fut pas surmonté. En effet, les liens primordiaux (*primordial ties*[8]) furent renforcés tout autant que les relations de langue et de religion. Le réseau des liens primordiaux se solidifia au fil des siècles au point de dessiner des frontières claires entre les groupes ethniques, des frontières pas seulement tribales[9].

## Du groupe ethnique à la communauté nationale

De la même manière que les États du Moyen Âge n'accédèrent pas par la voie rectiligne à la nation moderne, on observe chez les groupes ethniques des développements alternatifs, des involutions, des assimilations, etc. De nombreux États médiévaux connus ont disparu comme de nombreux groupes ethniques. C'est dire qu'il n'y eut pas de développement téléologiquement orienté d'un groupe ethnique particulier à la nation moderne. Or, lorsqu'un groupe ethnique se maintint jusqu'au seuil du XIXe siècle, il devint tôt ou tard l'objet de la quête patriotique et forma dans ses rangs un groupe porteur du mouvement national. Tant la période que la force initiale de ce groupe dépendirent de la transition de la « catégorie » vers la « communauté », autrement dit, de la présence plus ou moins forte de l'idée de l'appartenance parmi ses membres. Il va de soi que cette idée trouva un terrain plus fertile là où le groupe ethnique pouvait renouer avec les vestiges d'une ancienne tradition étatique, mais également là où la pression extérieure créait une démarcation claire face à une « nation » dominante.

Il est empiriquement démontré qu'à l'intérieur de tout groupe ethnique non dominant quelques membres éduqués concluaient tôt ou tard que leur groupe était une « nation » opprimée, négligée, « dormante », et qu'il était de leur devoir patrio-

---

8. En anglais dans le texte.
9. Balibar parle dans ce contexte d'une longue préhistoire de chaque nation, une préhistoire réelle qu'il ne faut pas confondre avec le mythe national (Balibar et Wallerstein 1991 : 88 *sq.*).

tique de la revivifier. Dans la pratique, cela signifiait que ces intellectuels instauraient une agitation nationale qui visait à convaincre chaque membre du groupe d'être fier de son identité nationale. Le point de départ de cette agitation variait chronologiquement : dans certains cas, notamment chez les Norvégiens, les Tchèques, les Magyars et les Grecs, l'agitation nationale débuta vers 1800 ; dans d'autres cas, elle ne commença que vers le milieu du XIX$^e$ siècle (Finlandais, Estoniens, Slovènes, etc.) sinon plus tard (Lituaniens, Biélorusses, Catalans, Basques)[10].

Dans la plupart des cas, quoique pas toujours, l'agitation était couronnée de succès et réussissait à mobiliser les masses. Le processus de formation nationale devint alors irréversible. Le mouvement national a pu certes être freiné, interdit, ses porteurs persécutés, mais nous ne connaissons aucun exemple d'un renversement total du processus. Il faut donc considérer comme décisifs deux points tournants sur le chemin du groupe ethnique vers la « nation » : le début de l'agitation nationale, d'une part, et celui du mouvement national de masse résultant d'une telle agitation réussie, de l'autre. L'interprétation et l'explication de ces deux événements fournissent la clé pour comprendre l'ensemble du processus de construction de la nation, notamment en Europe centrale au XIX$^e$ siècle ainsi qu'en Europe de l'Est et du Sud.

Le dénominateur commun à ces événements est un changement d'identité. Comment cela arriva-t-il ? Dans le premier cas, au début de l'agitation nationale, il faut savoir ce qui a incité quelques intellectuels à rechercher une nouvelle identité. En examinant les faits empiriques, nous constatons que le déclenchement d'une agitation nationale coïncida toujours avec une crise ou un bouleversement social, politique ou éthique. Pour de nombreux mouvements nationaux, ce furent la Révolution française et les guerres napoléoniennes, pour d'autres, la révolution de 1848, la grande crise russe de la fin des années 1850, etc. Avec l'aide de la théorie sociopsychologique nous constatons que, selon plusieurs auteurs, tout changement fondamental des conditions sociales rend les identités existantes précaires[11]. Autrement dit, la quête d'une nouvelle identité nationale s'enracine dans la crise des anciens systèmes de valeurs, de l'ancien ordre social et des anciennes légitimités politiques et religieuses. C'est à travers des changements, comme ceux de l'affranchissement des paysans, de la sécularisation de la pensée par les Lumières, des réformes sociales et administratives, de la marchandisation croissante que les anciens liens, loyautés et certitudes furent ébranlés. Cette incertitude fut perçue d'abord par ceux qui, grâce à leur éducation ou leur profession, étaient plus proches du noyau du changement, plutôt que par les masses.

Toute modification de l'identité semble, du moins théoriquement, une décision individuelle. Dans la pratique toutefois, le choix d'une identité était « prédéterminé » sinon discipliné socialement par de nombreuses circonstances extérieures. Le concept de la nation ethniquement définie qui se réveille était simple, circonscrit, compréhensible de tous, car il correspondait à l'expérience quotidienne de chacun, qui pouvait communiquer au-delà des frontières de son village.

Quelles alternatives s'offraient à cette identité nationalement définie ? Ce fut surtout l'identité étatique, sous les deux variantes qui correspondaient aux stades

---

10. Sur la périodisation du mouvement national, voir Hroch (1985).
11. En résumé dans un livre récent de Bloom (1993).

du développement social. L'identité dynastique de l'État, legs de la dernière période de l'absolutisme, eut un succès variable et ne put survivre aux transformations bourgeoises même là où elle s'imposa. Dans le contexte de l'empire multiethnique, cependant, elle ne s'éclipsa pas face à l'identité nationale montante. En effet, l'agitation nationale pouvait souvent obtenir quelque succès durant la dernière période de l'absolutisme, à condition de savoir intégrer l'identité dynastique.

Après le succès des révolutions bourgeoises, l'agitation nationale était dans ces cas si avancée que la variante citoyenne de l'État multiethnique fut moins effective et fut « adoptée » comme un complément de l'identité nationale. Cette dernière était alors en même temps citoyenne, alors que le territoire ethnonational remplaçait celui de l'État multiethnique. Ainsi fut le chemin vers l'identité nationale emprunté par les Norvégiens, les Magyars, les Catalans, les Irlandais et, avec un certain décalage, les Tchèques.

La situation fut différente là où l'agitation nationale débuta dans un contexte de constitutionnalisme et de droits civiques. Le concept d'identité du citoyen nanti d'un État, indépendamment de son appartenance ethnique, concourut avec succès au concept ethnonational en Belgique (l'identité flamande), en Grande-Bretagne (les identités écossaise et galloise) et plus tard aussi dans l'Empire allemand (les identités polonaise, danoise, sorbe). Dans le cas allemand, les identités citoyenne et dynastico-étatique se superposaient d'ailleurs clairement.

## Du régionalisme au nationalisme

À part l'identité étatique, une autre identité joua un rôle considérable dans le processus de construction nationale, dont nous n'avons pas encore traité. Il s'agit de l'identité régionale dont le rôle sera analysé de manière plus détaillée. Une remarque préalable s'impose quant à la distinction des identités régionale et locale. Contrairement à l'identité locale qui est certes parmi les plus anciennes, l'identité régionale englobe un espace plus grand, d'une part, et ne fait pas référence à la position de chacun (« mon » village, « ma » ville), mais plutôt à l'existence d'une région. Les caractéristiques objectives de la région sont le plus souvent administratives, mais également historiques, géographiques ou économiques.

L'importance accrue de l'identité régionale dans toute l'Europe du XVIIIe siècle est sans doute articulée au patriotisme des Lumières. Ce patriotisme était d'abord orienté régionalement : l'identification avec le pays. Peu importait si le patriote était né dans la région ou s'il appartenait à la même ethnie que les habitants de la région. L'identité régionale signifiait pour le patriote des Lumières la responsabilité de servir « son » pays et de lui être utile. C'était une identité très intellectuelle qui devait encore rester étrangère à l'homme simple. Pour cette raison, elle ne pouvait guère devenir une alternative efficace à l'identité ethnique. Ceci n'exclut pas que d'aucuns parmi les premiers protagonistes de l'agitation nationale eurent comme point de départ l'identité régionale plutôt que l'appartenance au groupe ethnique non dominant. Si un groupe ethnique isolé vivait sur le territoire de la région, il était intégré naturellement dans l'identité régionale. Les deux identités ne s'excluaient donc nullement.

Ce fut surtout durant la première phase, intellectuelle, du mouvement national que l'activité des patriotes était animée par une identité régionale : on voulait être utile à « son » pays et à ses habitants, éventuellement aussi en étudiant la langue, la culture et le passé du groupe ethnique non dominant. Dans la phase subséquente de l'agitation nationale, le rapport entre les identités régionale et nationale fut à la fois compétitif et cumulatif.

En simplifiant, nous pouvons dire que l'identité nationale émergente se nourrissait de deux sources : la conscience d'une appartenance ethnique et d'une appartenance régionale. Dans chaque mouvement national, toutefois, le rapport réciproque et le poids de ces deux composantes — et donc aussi leur influence sur l'identité nationale — étaient distincts. Même si en fin de compte l'identité nationale s'imposait comme dominante, elle était accompagnée, complétée et parfois affaiblie par des identités régionales différentes et d'intensité variable. Quelques exemples de l'interaction entre l'ethnique et le régional illustreront ces recouvrements.

En Lituanie, une conscience régionale renouvelée régnait au début du XIX$^e$ siècle. C'est par l'expression *gente Lithuanus, natione Polonus* que la noblesse polonophone lituanienne désignait son identité. Le groupe ethnique lituanien demeura fermé sur lui-même, sans trace d'une conscience nationale jusqu'aux années 1860-1870. C'est seulement à ce moment que l'identité régionale d'une partie des intellectuels lituanophones trouva une connexion avec la conscience ethnique du groupe et instaura une agitation nationale dont l'aboutissement sera, un demi-siècle plus tard, la diffusion générale de l'identité nationale chez la population lituanophone.

La situation était différente chez les Lettons et les Estoniens avoisinants. L'identité régionale y était affaire exclusive des barons et des littéraires germanophones, tandis que parmi les ethnies lettonne et estonienne des identités locales prédominaient. Le mouvement national estonien et letton s'affirma indépendamment de l'identité régionale et les distinctions régionales n'eurent guère d'effet désintégrateur. La séparation de l'ethnie slovène en plusieurs pays, avec une identité régionale de la noblesse et de la bourgeoisie allemandes, fut même plus prononcée. Dans ce cas, la transition de la conscience ethnique à l'identité nationale fut plutôt stimulée de l'extérieur : conséquence de l'« illyrisme » selon lequel les Slovènes étaient perçus comme une partie de la nation slave du sud. Les identités régionales rejoignaient partiellement l'ethnie slovène et jouèrent parfois un rôle désintégrateur.

En Bohème et en Moravie, le patriotisme de la noblesse se renforça durant la seconde moitié du XVIII$^e$ siècle, en réaction au centralisme habsbourgeois. La particularité ethnique de la majorité de la population servait alors de contre-argument. La forte identité régionale influença la première génération des patriotes tchèques. Lorsqu'après 1800 l'agitation tchèque débuta, on tenta de transformer l'identité régionale en activité nationale, avec plus ou moins de succès. Plus tard, l'identité régionale servira d'argument pour appuyer les demandes de pouvoir de la nation tchèque en Bohème. Le développement de l'identité régionale en Moravie se fit d'abord de manière indépendante ; pendant longtemps, elle fut assez forte pour freiner un rayonnement de l'agitation nationale tchèque de la Bohème vers la Moravie. Ce ne sera que pendant le dernier tiers du XIX$^e$ siècle que l'identité nationale tchèque prendra le dessus en Moravie, sans toutefois enrayer l'identité régionale moravienne.

En Catalogne, la conscience régionale était affaiblie par l'absolutisme espagnol, au point d'être réanimée durant la seconde moitié du XIX^e siècle seulement. La quête de l'identité nationale était accompagnée d'une référence à l'identité catalane, et l'identité régionale considérée comme substitut de l'identité nationale, même après les premiers succès de l'agitation. C'est ainsi que le mouvement catalan se reconnut pendant longtemps comme « régionaliste », tandis que le qualificatif national ou nationaliste n'apparaîtra qu'après 1900. Il semble bien que, dans ce cas, identités régionale et nationale se soient épanouies parallèlement.

Ces quelques exemples démontrent la variété des rapports entre l'ethnie et l'identité régionale. De manière générale, on pourrait dire que l'identité régionale a pris une certaine importance surtout dans les cas où il s'agissait d'anciennes entités politico-administratives. Dans ces contextes, le mouvement ethnico-national du groupe non dominant pouvait renouer avec l'ancienne autonomie politique, perdue depuis ou affaiblie. L'identité régionale avait un rôle intégrateur à la nation là où le territoire de la nation était ethniquement homogène, peuplé majoritairement par les membres d'un groupe ethnique non dominant. Il en fut ainsi en Catalogne, en Norvège, en Finlande, en Bohème et en Croatie. Par contre, lorsque le groupe ethnique non dominant vivait en même temps dans d'autres régions (peut-être en tant que minorité), l'identité nationale ne s'y imposa que difficilement, avec un certain retard ou même pas du tout. Tel fut le cas en Moravie ou en Dalmatie.

La formation de l'identité nationale relevait d'un autre type quand le groupe ethnique non dominant ne pouvait se référer à une région ou à un pays historiquement circonscrit, comme chez les Ukrainiens, Slovaques ou Russes blancs en Galicie. Aucune identité régionale intégratrice n'émergeait alors. La séparation du territoire ethnique en plusieurs régions eut un effet clairement désintégrateur chez les Slovènes (Carnioles, Steiermark, Carinthiens, Istriens, etc.) ou les Sorbes (Saxons et Prussiens de Lusace). Vu le territoire de ces groupes ethniques restreints, l'identité locale (la vallée, les alentours d'une ville) put se substituer à l'identité régionale.

Bien que les identités régionale et ethnico-nationale ne soient pas contradictoires, il ne faudrait pas les confondre. Leurs fonctions respectives pour le processus de construction nationale sont distinctes. Si les deux identités se référaient à un territoire compact, les représentations du territoire étaient différentes. Tandis que le territoire national tend à établir une frontière exacte entre « nous » et « eux », ce trait ne désigne pas les caractéristiques centrales de la région. Le territoire national est habité par les membres de la nation, alors que celui de la région peut être ethniquement mixte. Dans un contexte de mobilité sociale, les émigrants qui appartenaient à une nation gardaient leur identité nationale, tandis que le fait de quitter une région pouvait être accompagné d'un changement complet d'identité.

Sur le plan culturalo-linguistique, la différence est évidente. L'identité nationale se fonde sur l'existence d'une culture et d'une langue littéraire autonomes et distinctes. La culture régionale fait partie d'une ou de plusieurs cultures nationales et même si elle a ses particularités, celles-ci s'inscrivent dans un ensemble national plus large. Les deux identités peuvent se compléter culturellement. Il y a d'ailleurs compatibilité sociopsychologique : l'identité nationale renvoie à la représentation de la nation « personnifiée », d'un corps, alors que l'identité régionale ne se rapporte toujours qu'à une partie de ce corps, sinon à des parties de plusieurs nations.

Le rapport au pouvoir central constitue une différence essentielle. La définition même de la région comporte l'appartenance à la périphérie, alors que le rapport de l'identité nationale au centre est différent dans les empires multinationaux : en cas de conflit, il ne s'agissait pas d'obéissance de la périphérie au centre, mais de volonté de s'établir comme centre, éventuellement de se séparer de l'ancien ensemble. Le pouvoir politique dans la région était toujours partiel, subordonné ; l'identité nationale ouvrait la porte à l'épanouissement des demandes de pouvoir à l'intérieur du territoire national. Les buts politiques liés à l'identité nationale pouvaient aller jusqu'à l'autodétermination, tandis que l'identité régionale visait dans le meilleur des cas l'autonomie.

En résumant : alors que l'identité nationale se présentait comme conséquence du mouvement national instauré par le groupe ethnique non dominant, l'identité régionale avait plutôt une fonction médiatrice entre l'ethnie et le mouvement national. Formulée dans une perspective « généalogique », l'identité nationale constituait un stade d'évolution plus avancé de la formation de l'identité moderne, comparé à l'identité régionale et au sentiment d'appartenance du groupe ethnique non dominant. Dans ce processus, l'identité régionale était une médiation utile sur le chemin du groupe ethnique vers la nation.

Jusqu'ici nous avons traité du groupe ethnique non dominant sans considérer ce qui fait la différence ethnique. La « base ethnique » (selon Smith 1991) de l'identité nationale était certes très complexe mais, sur un plan typologique, deux critères fondamentaux déterminaient tant la spécificité ethnique que les différences entre nations : la langue et la religion. Les deux critères ne s'excluaient pas mutuellement, mais l'un d'eux était dominant. Quand les deux coïncidaient, la route du groupe ethnique vers l'identité nationale (c'est-à-dire la phase de l'agitation nationale) était d'autant plus courte. Ainsi les Grecs et les Serbes face aux Ottomans ; les Irlandais face aux Anglais. Or, ces cas étaient rares.

Même si l'agencement dans le temps du programme politique pouvait avoir d'autres causes (notamment la structure sociale du groupe ethnique non dominant), on ne peut ignorer que, dans le cas des groupes ethniques fondés sur une distinction religieuse de la nation dominante, il agissait souvent dès la phase de l'agitation nationale. Était-ce dû au fait que le programme linguistique devait d'abord trouver sa stabilité par la construction d'une norme unifiée de la langue, tandis que la religion était déjà là, un critère « préfabriqué » et généralement accepté ?

La délimitation entre groupes ethniques et nations était d'ailleurs plus nette lorsque le critère de la religion les distinguait. La raison simple en est que des groupes entiers de populations pouvaient devenir bilingues mais non « bireligieux » et que l'assimilation linguistique — individuelle — était plus simple que la conversion religieuse. Contrairement à l'assimilation linguistique, les conversions religieuses étaient toujours contrôlées par l'administration.

## Conclusions

En terminant, nous considérerons le rapport du processus de construction nationale à la modernisation. Rappelons d'abord l'ancien débat entourant les conséquences de la « division sociale du travail[12] » sur les transformations ethniques. Alors que la théorie fonctionnaliste (Hechter 1971 : 21 *sq.*) voit comme conséquence la destruction des solidarités ethniques, la théorie réactive (« *reactive theory*[13] ») souligne son effet stimulant sur le renforcement des liens ethniques. En oubliant la théorie pour chercher des données empiriques, nous en trouvons qui confirment tant l'une que l'autre approche, bien que celles qui appuient la théorie réactive soient plus nombreuses. Quoi qu'il en soit, les deux théories ont en commun la position selon laquelle les membres de groupes ethniques se sentent menacés et insécurisés par les processus de la modernisation — une situation qui de toutes façons devait influencer le processus de construction nationale. Il s'agit donc de savoir si ce processus faisait partie de la modernisation.

La réponse devra qualifier ce rapport selon les phases du mouvement national. Dans la première phase, savante, le mouvement national naissant était clairement en accord avec la tendance générale d'une expansion des connaissances scientifiques et de l'instruction populaire. Afin d'éduquer et de former le peuple, il fallait d'abord mieux le connaître : l'étude de la langue et de la littérature populaires, des coutumes et du passé était donc loin d'être une fin en soi. Les nouvelles connaissances des patriotes ne concernaient toutefois pas seulement le fait ethnique mais également le social et l'économique. Il est symptomatique à ce titre que la personnalité du patriote des Lumières fasse partie des traditions positives tant des grandes nations établies que de celles des nouvelles et « petites ».

Le rapport à la modernisation était plus compliqué dans la phase de l'agitation nationale. Le succès des agitateurs parmi les membres du groupe ethnique non dominant n'était pas automatique, « préprogrammé », mais dépendait de plusieurs circonstances. Mis à part l'intensité croissante de la communication sociale et de la mobilité verticale et le succès de la première phase, c'étaient surtout les confrontations d'intérêts d'importance nationale qui prévalaient[14]. La relation au processus de modernisation est ici évidente, dans des conditions de ruptures sociales et de nouvelle division sociale du travail.

Nous avons constaté, dans les premières parties de cet article, qu'il y avait de toutes façons un lien causal entre le début de l'agitation nationale, la quête d'une nouvelle identité nationale, et la transformation de la société, la crise des valeurs et des anciennes certitudes. La réponse nationale au défi de la modernisation se voulait subjective et antimoderniste, ce qui est également vrai des premiers succès de l'agitation nationale. En voici quelques exemples : l'artisan tchèque craignait le grand commerce allemand naissant et la production industrielle des régions germanophones ; le prêtre lié à l'ancienne société sentait un malaise face à la sécularisation josephiniste ; le paysan lituanien, ukrainien ou slovène était mécontent de

---

12. En anglais dans le texte (N.D.T.).
13. En anglais dans le texte (N.D.T.).
14. Concernant ce conflit d'intérêts, voir Hroch (1993).

l'importance croissante de la ville germanophone ou polonophone; le propriétaire d'un domaine catalan voyait d'un mauvais œil les progrès de l'industrialisation capitaliste de plus en plus centralisée. Les exemples pourraient être multipliés.

D'autres confrontations d'intérêts d'importance nationale progressiste émergeaient. Ainsi, le commerçant norvégien voulait se libérer du contrôle de l'État étranger (d'abord danois, ensuite suédois); le paysan ukrainien luttait pour l'abolition de ses charges féodales contre le propriétaire polonais.

Avec les succès de l'agitation nationale et notamment dans les conditions de mouvement de masse, les confrontations d'intérêts d'importance nationale se multiplièrent, alors que les antimodernistes devinrent plus rares au sein du mouvement. Une partie des artisans des guildes et des petits commerçants devinrent eux-mêmes entrepreneurs et grands commerçants, le paysan affranchi s'intégra aux relations du marché, devint un concurrent du grand propriétaire et participa aux mesures de modernisation, ce qui apporta une autre couleur au rapport ville-campagne. La lutte pour les positions dans l'administration, les écoles et la politique fut intégrée au combat pour la démocratisation de la société et l'égalité des citoyens. Ceci se passait cependant dans un contexte où la nation était plus ou moins formée et est au-delà de notre propos ici. Il est toutefois établi que la modernisation pouvait apporter plus d'avantages à chacun, dans les conditions d'une nation en émergence plutôt que dans celles d'un groupe ethnique non dominant. En ce sens également, la distinction entre identité nationale et régionale est significative.

Ce fut donc au détour de l'antimodernisme patriarcal que le mouvement national devint un facteur important de la modernisation et qu'il acquit sur ce chemin la réputation d'avoir protégé, du moins partiellement, le territoire de l'ancien groupe ethnique d'un destin provincial (dans le sens du colonialisme interne) ou rétrograde.

*(Texte inédit en allemand traduit par Ruth Murbach)*

# Références

ALDERMAN G., J. Leslie et K.E. Pollmann
1993    *Governments, Ethnic Groups and Political Representation. Comparative Studies on Governments and Non-Dominant Ethnic Groups in Europe, 1850-1940.* Darthmouth : European Science Foundation.

ARMSTRONG J.A.
1982    *Nations before Nationalism.* Chapel Hill : University of North Carolina Press.

BALIBAR E. et I. Wallerstein
1991    *Race, Nation, Class : Ambiguous Identities.* Londres et New York : Verso.

BAUER O.
1907    *Nationalitätenfrege und Sozialdemokratie.* Vienne : Wiener Volksbuch, Marx-Studien 2.

BLOOM W.
1993    *Personal Identity, National Identity, and International Relations.* Cambridge : Cambridge University Press.

DANN O.
1986    *Nationalism in Vorindustrieller Zeit.* Munich : R. Oldenbourg Verlag.

HAYES C.J.
1931    *The Historical Evolution of Modern Nationalism.* New York : Smith.

HECHTER M.
1971    « Towards a Theory of Ethnic Change », *Politics and Society*, 2, 1 : 5-27.

HERTZ F.
1945    *Nationalism in History and Politics.* Londres : Kegan Paul, Trench, Trubner.

HOBSBAWM E.
1990    *Nations and Nationalism since 1780.* Cambridge : Cambridge University Press.

HROCH M.
1985    *Social Preconditions of National Revival in Europe.* Cambridge : Cambridge
        University Press.
1993    « From National Movement to the Fully-Formed Nation », *New Left Review*,
        198 : 3-20.

KEMILÄINEN A.
1964    *Nationalism. Problems Concerning the Word, the Concept and Classification.*
        Jyväskylä : Studia Historica Jyväskyläensia III.

KOHN H.
1967    *The Idea of Nationalism.* New York : Collier Books.

LEMBERG E.
1964    *Nationalismus* (tomes I et II). Hamburg : Rohwolt Taschenbuch Verlag.

MEINECKE F.
1907    *Weltbürgertum und Nationalstaat.* Berlin et Munich : R. Oldenbourg Verlag.

NEUMANN F.J.
1988    *Volk und Nation.* Leipzig.

REXROTH K.H.
1978    « Volkssprache und Werdendes Volksbewusstsein im Ostfränkischen Reich »,
        in H. Beumann et W. Schroeder (dir.), *Nationes. Aspekte der Nationenbildung
        im Mittelalter.* Sigmaringen.

RICHTER M.
1976    *Giraldes Cambrensis. The Growth of the Welsh Nation.* Aberyswyth.

ROSS J.A.
1979    « Language and the Mobilization of Ethnic Identity », in H. Giles et B. Saint-
        Jacques (dir.), *Language and Ethnic Relations.* New York : Pergamon.

SMAHEL F.
1969a   « The Idea of the Nation in Hussite Bohemia », *Historica*, 16 : 93-199.
1969b   « The Idea of the Nation in Hussite Bohemia », *Historica*, 17 : 143-249.

SMITH A.D.
1986    *The Ethnic Origins of Nations.* Oxford : Blackwell.
1991    *National Identity.* Londres : Penguin Books.

Szücs J.
1981     *Nation und Geschichte.* Cologne, Vienne et Budapest : Corvina.

Tripton C.L. (dir.)
1972     *Nationalism in the Middle Ages.* New York : Holt, Rinehart and Winston.

Turczyński E.
1976     *Konfession und Nation.* Düsseldorf : Schwann.

Werner K.F.
1970     « Les nations et le sentiment national dans l'Europe médiévale », *Revue historique,* 496 : 285-305.

# V

# The Social Interpretation of Linguistic Demands in European National Movements

The modern nation-forming process in Europe followed two typologically different paths. This contribution will deal with just one of these, namely that taken by non-dominant ethnic groups, the one which constituted organized and deliberate efforts at achieving the status of a fully developed nation, in all its attributes. This process is illustrated by comparison with the contrasting, more important and better known type of nation-forming process, which was based on the state nation that had been developing since the Middle Ages.[1]

I prefer to use the term *national movement* to characterize these projects rather than the nebulous and misleading term of 'nationalism'. The 'missing attributes' of a full national existence consisted of three features: a national literary language and culture, political autonomy (or in some cases, independence), and a social position equal with the ruling nation in terms of social structure and the division of wealth.

---

1    On the general concept of the nation-forming process, see M. HROCH, 'From National Movement to the Fully-formed Nation. The Nation-building Process in Europe', *New Left Review*, no. 198, April 1993, p. 3-19.

# V

Three distinctive groups of goals and demands, corresponding to these three 'deficits', can be identified in the programme of European national movements:

1. The creation of a national community, which would be equal to the ruling one, and which would also include a completed social structure (i.e. a structure sufficient for the creation of its 'own' ruling classes);

2. The achievement of some kind of self-administration, initially in the form of local or territorial autonomy, and ultimately (but not everywhere) the realization of independence;

3. The improvement — or even the establishment — of a national high culture based on the written national language, and the use of that language within the territory inhabited (or claimed) by the members of the non-dominant ethnic group.

There are of course some transitional cases, where completion of a full national existence was marked by only two missing attributes, and where the national programme was limited to just two groups of demands. To give one example: the Magyar national movement developed under the conditions of a full social structure, corresponding to a given stage of economic development.

Certain other irregularities and differences have to be taken into account, above all the very different timing of the groups of demands made by the various national movements. We also have to distinguish between the relative importance of linguistic, social or political demands during the different phases of national movements:

Phase A
where a small group of intellectuals devoted themselves to scholarly enquiry into the language, history, traditional culture and so on, of the non-dominant ethnic group;

Phase B
where a new range of activists emerged, who now began to agitate for their compatriots to join the project of creating a fully-fledged nation;

Phase C
where a majority of the population responded to the patriotic call and formed a mass movement; during this Phase C, the full social structure of the nation would usually come into being, and political differentiation begin to emerge.

In examining the strength of the linguistic and political programme produced during the 'B Phase' of different national movements, we can distinguish two types:

1. National movements where *political demands dominated Phase B,* accompanied by weaker and / or later developed linguistic and social demands, as was the case in the Polish, Norwegian, Irish, Greek and Scottish national movements;

2. National movements *dominated by linguistic and cultural demands* during their Phase B, with political demands following later, during Phase C. This was true of almost all national movements, except those belonging to the first type.

Even if a significant majority of national movements preferred to make linguistic demands in their Phase B, they did not define themselves exclusively in terms of a common language. They did not prioritize the linguistic argument because it was the only goal of which they could conceive, but because they regarded these demands as the most urgent.

This paper does not pretend to explain the nation-forming process in all its complexity, nor to discuss the concept of a nation. Its aims are instead limited to an interpretation of the demands and programmes elaborated by the protagonists within the national movements, and most attention will be given to linguistic demands, their structure and the role played by them in the nation-forming process.

When trying to explain and interpret the extraordinarily important role played by language in so many different national movements, it is first of all necessary to remember that language was not something that existed 'outside' of time and space. We have to begin with a consideration of the chronological and territorial dimensions to the role played by language during the centuries preceding the emergence of modern national movements in the l9th century.

Too many current theories of 'nationalism' ignore the fact that language difference had been perceived to be a criterion of diversity

V

since the Early Middle Ages.[2] During the 9th and 10th centuries, the linguistic difference between 'Franci' and 'Germani' or 'Teutoni' was more or less self-evident, and we know that conflicts occurred between groups and individuals based on differences in language. It is possible to find the term *amor linguae*, and mention of a *laudatio* for the popular tongue, or reflections on the role of the language, as for example: '*ex linguis gentes, non ex gentibus linguae exortae sunt*'.[3] In this last instance, the inspiration of the 'Tower of Babel' is clearly evident.[4]

The linguistic argument was used in politics, even though not as a central one, and many examples of this happening can be seen in both the West (France, Flanders, Wales, and England), and the East (Poland, Bohemia, Hungary).[5] During the Middle Ages, language became important as a component of identity, but the primary criterion was that relating to the state and its political institutions, such as the Diet.[6]

The emergence of the absolutist state constitutes the territorial dimension to the prehistory of our problem. We can observe absolutist policy — in so far as it deals with questions of language — in two different ways: *from above* (from the perspective of the state and its government), and *from below* (from the perspective of the region, the provincial elites or even, of all its inhabitants).

The absolutist principle of homogenization sooner or later involved issues of language. From the perspective of an absolutist state and its ruling elites, it was irrelevant whether or not the linguistic homogenization of a territory, which they regarded as being on the periphery of

---

2   The best contributions on this problem have been published in Central Europe, and in Germany in particular. For bibliographical information, see O. DANN (Hg.), *Nationalismus in vorindustrieller Zeit*, Munich, 1986.

3   See W. SCHLESINGER, 'Entstehung der Nationen', p. 57 ff., and K. H. REXROTH, 'Volkssprache und werdendes Volksbewusstsein im Ostfrankische Reich', p. 296 ff., in H. BEUMANN and W. SCHRODER, *Nationes. Aspekte der Nationenbildung im Mittelalter*, Siegmaringen, 1978.

4   A. BORST, *Der Turm von Babel: Geschichte der Meinungen* vol. 1-4, Stuttgart, 1957-63.

5   E. LEMBERG, *Nationalismus I.*, Hamburg, 1964; J. ARMSTRONG, *Nations before Nationalism*, Chapel Hill, 1982; A. D. SMITH, *The Ethnic Origins of Nations*, Oxford, 1986.

6   J. ARMSTRONG, *ibid.*, p. 279.

the state, concerned dialects of languages spoken in other states, dialects of the ruling state-language, or even regions with a tradition of their own literary, printed language.

Historians cannot pretend to solve the problem of identifying the boundaries separating high languages from dialects, nor those between dialects belonging to different high languages, during the centuries preceding the emergence of linguistic codification. However, it can be provisionally suggested that the use of a 'print-language' within the territory of an absolutist state seems to be a sufficient criterion for distinguishing the written language from dialects, patois and so on.[7] It is significant that medieval literary languages which did not become state-languages (or which lost that status) disappeared, or became marginalized during the period of absolutist rule (as was the case with Norwegian, Catalan, Czech and Welsh).

The cleavage between rural speech and the norms of the nationally accepted, 'high' written language used by the power elites was interpreted by enlightened aristocrats as being indicative of the degeneracy of the 'vulgar' speakers. Dialects were sometimes used for the amusement of the elites, who were 'marking their superiority over the lower classes'.[8] This attitude partially changed during the 'Age of Revolution' and was reversed during the 19th century, when patriots turned dialects into objects for admiration.

Generally, the Revolutions took over the homogenizing attitude of the absolutist state, as is indicated by the campaign against patois during the French Revolution and the stance of the German Left towards Slavic languages during the Revolutions of 1848-49. Nevertheless, two important differences suggest that the times were changing radically:

1. Absolutist attitudes were based on the concept of a homogeneous state, whereas revolutionary politics were based on the concept of the nation as an organic body, usually incarnated in the state: this

---

7   B. ANDERSON, *Imagined Communities. Reflections on the Origins and Spread of Nationalism*, rev. ed., London, 1991, p. 45.

8   E. HAUGEN, *The Scandinavian Languages*, London, 1976, p. 361 ff.

'personality-nation' should only use one language, because the use of any other language would weaken the state.

2. Revolutionary homogenization did not aim to preserve old mentalities and traditional values, but on the contrary, the use of a unified language was regarded as an instrument for the '*reproduction de l'homme nouveau*' and as a '*réformation des structures mentales*'.[9]

This perspective 'from above' needs to be completed by a consideration of the *perspective from below*, i.e. from the periphery. Homogenizing state policy affected many areas of life on the periphery, and its linguistic aspect was only one of many, and perhaps not the most important. Absolutist, centralist measures provoked opposition and discontent in almost all provinces, but the strength and success of this opposition was not the same everywhere,[10] and the arguments used by provincial representatives against centralism were also quite different. It would in fact be an exciting task for future research to make a comparative analysis of responses by the peripheral nobility and bourgeoisie to the centralist challenge. Given the current state of research in this area, we can only present here a few examples to illustrate the extreme diversity of reactions.

The centralist policy of the Prussian state did not meet with any significant opposition amongst the Sorbian population in Lusatia, or on the part of Polish speakers in Upper Silesia. The linguistic homogenization attempted by Joseph II, however, provoked a strong reaction from the Hungarian and Belgian Estates, and a moderate one from the Bohemian, with all of them partially expressing their opposition in linguistic terms. Russian centralism did not provoke any opposition amongst the population who spoke Ukrainian dialects, but on the other hand did produce a strong reaction in the Baltic Provinces, amongst local landlords and the German-speaking elites.[11]

9   P. BOURDIEU, *Ce que parler veut dire. L'économie des échanges linguistiques*, Paris, 1982, p. 31. The 'linguistic terror' accompanied the political one, see J.-Y. LARTICHAUX, 'Linguistic Politics During the French Revolution', *Diogènes* no. 97, 1977, p. 65 ff.

10  W. BLOOM, *Personal Identity, National Identity, and International Relations*, Cambridge, 1990, p. 143.

11  Originally, they argued in the name of the regional identity of the Baltic Provinces, but changed this into a German one during the 19th century.

When looking at the role of linguistic developments within the first, medieval stage of the nation-forming process, we can often distinguish two opposing trends: one tending towards an assimilation of ethnic groups, the other maintaining, and perhaps strengthening, ethnic diversity. The first 'Western', trend relates above all to France and England, and the second, 'Eastern' one, to the three Empires — Habsburg, Russian and Ottoman. Why were these Empires unable to assimilate their various populations? There are usually two basic answers to this question: it is argued that firstly, whilst the nation-state was able to assimilate marginal ethnic groups, this was not true of the multi-ethnic Empires, and secondly, that the ruling elites in the Empires did not try hard enough to assimilate and homogenize the population.

Neither answer is incorrect, but they are unable to fully explain the general phenomenon. We also have to look for more profound reasons, which can be found in five groups of factors.

1. The *level of economic integration* and economic growth during the Early Modern period was higher in France, England and the Netherlands than in the rest of the continent. It was only economic growth that enabled people from the periphery to achieve a higher level of prosperity, by migration into the core area and assimilation.

2. Uneven economic development also influenced the level of social communication: in the more advanced countries, communication functioned at a higher level, and the ruling state-language was the dominant language of communication, as it constituted the language of 'progress'.

3. The comparatively uneven level of *administration* in the Western and Eastern absolutist systems.

4. Assimilation was more effective where the ruling elites did not use ethnic difference as a social barrier. There was no effective assimilation in societies where ethnic groups were *strongly marginalized* and isolated as an 'out-group' by the ruling elite (e.g. in the Ottoman Empire, or Baltic states).

5. The *importance of time* cannot be neglected: whereas the process of assimilation in the West had already begun within the feudal system, the Eastern Empires emerged much later, and thus their attempts at assimilating ethnic groups did too. In the Habsburg Empire, this process really only began during the 18th century, and in Russia

during the l9th century, so the period available for assimilation was much shorter. This was nonetheless also a question of social formation, as well as chronology: assimilation had a better chance of success under feudal society, as it was more difficult to assimilate peasants after their liberation than it had been before.

The linguistic situation under Eastern late absolutism can be characterized as three types of *diglossia without bilingualism* (following the model of Joshua Fishman):[12]

1. Where elites spoke a high version ('H'), and the general population spoke a local version ('L') of the same language, the relationship can be described as 'H - L';

2. Where elites spoke an 'H'-language and the population partly spoke an 'L'-language, and partly a dialect belonging to another language ('L*'), the relationship can be given as: 'H - L - L*';

3. Apart from the 'H'-language, another print-language ('H+') was used within the territory of the state, which was obviously accompanied by a corresponding ('L+')-language.

Even though the absolutist state neglected these differences, they determined the point of departure for the early stages of national movements and the structure of their programmes.

The above arguments have tried to suggest and illustrate to what extent national development — the *nation-forming process — is a distinctively older phenomenon than the modern nation and nationalism:* any interpretation of modern national identity cannot ignore the peculiarities of pre-modern national development, or degrade it to the level of a mere myth.

The collective phenomena coming under the general heading of linguistic programmes cannot simply be analyzed as a homogeneous and unchanging complex of attitudes. In practice, they consisted of five stages, which emerged gradually and cumulatively, that is to say

---

12  J. FISHMAN, *Language in Sociocultural Change,* Stanford: University Press, 1972, p. 135 ff.

that the intensifying level of demands did not cancel out previous ones, but usually integrated them into the new programme, even if sometimes in a modified form. Unless we differentiate between these various levels and locate them within the concrete historical context of each national movement, any generalizations about the linguistic programmes will only cause confusion.

A. — In the first stage, *the language is celebrated and defended.* All kinds of arguments were used to support its claim to be accepted into the family of high languages — its aesthetic value, its ability to express all manner of feelings or convey information, its historical merits; but celebrations of this type were in no way specific to non-dominant ethnic groups. A *défense* of the French language was published in France in 1549 by the bishop Jean du Bellay.[13]

During the second half of the 18th century, defences of the German, Magyar, Czech, Slovak and Greek languages appeared. Chronologically later, but still coming during the same Phase A, nostalgic celebrations of the national language were written in Wales, Brittany and Flanders. All of these celebrations had one feature in common: they always concerned languages that had a Medieval or Early Modern tradition of literary activity.

During the emergence of Phase B, language celebrations turned into a fashionable form of agitation in almost all national movements, and from then on, language became a part of the national message. However, these celebrations had a different function from their former one, because they were primarily addressed towards their own ranks. Members of the non-dominant ethnic group were encouraged to love and defend their language — as one Czech *dictum,* published in 1824 in a translation from the German, put it: 'Who does not love his language, is an enemy of his own fatherland'.

---

13 A. DUPRONT, 'Sémantique historique et analyse de contenu : culture et civilisation', in M. CRANSTON and P. MAIR (eds.), *Langage et politique,* Bruxelles, 1982, p. 86 ff.; E. LEMBERG, *Nationalismus I, supra,* note 5, p. 128. See also N. MACHIAVELLI, *Discorso o Dialogo intorno alla lingua nostra,* (modern edition), Torino: B. T. Sozzi, 1976.

V

Related to this shift in the audience for national agitation, it is necessary to include a general proviso. National demands were generally targeted in two opposite directions:

(i) '*upwards*', towards the state administration, local authorities, educated ruling elites, etc.;

(ii) '*downwards*', towards their own peer group, trying to mobilize the members of the non-dominant ethnic group for participation in patriotic activities.

This dual perspective — from below and from above — was variable, and we have to take that into account when analyzing the structure of all the different types of national aims.

B. — The second stage: *language planning and codification*. This was an intrinsic part of cultural standardization.[14] Before codification was achieved, the language existed both as a group of dialects and also as a 'print-language', which already began to influence linguistic norms in the decades before the literary language was codified. These norms were based on the experience of the production of a print-language, and on the terms used in administration, trade relations, and public life. 'Language planning' included a simultaneous process of linguistic organization, popularization and standardization[15] — it would have been paradoxical to celebrate a vague complex of spoken dialects, without having a unified orthography or distinct language borders. But language planning was not just limited to cultural standardization: it also fulfilled an important social function and purpose. It was the only way of clearly distinguishing one's own national group, i.e. of drawing a clear and comprehensible border between the in-group and out group, particularly where there was a fluid transition between related dialects.[16]

---

14   E. GELLNER, *Culture, Identity and Politics*, Cambridge: University Press, 1987, p. 24; P. BOURDIEU, *Ce que parler veut dire..., supra*, note 9, p. 29.

15   J. A. FISHMAN, *Language and Nationalism. Two Integrative Essays*, Rowley/Mass., 1972, p. 61.

16   B. B. KHLEIF, 'Insiders, Outsiders and Renegades: Towards a Classification of Ethnolinguistic Labels', in H. GILES and B. SAINT-JACQUES (eds.), *Language and*

Learned linguistic disputes had emerged almost everywhere during Phase A, accompanied by the publication of grammar books and dictionaries, but the research of individual scholars was something altogether different from the evolution of a generally accepted codification. Voluntaristic decisions about codification and attempts to 'create' a new literary language were usually unsuccessful. Codification was generally related to the previous development of linguistic norms and occurred as a result of long-term, and often very heated, scientific discussions. The central — but by no means the only — topic of discussion and controversy tended to be whether the modern language was to be based on its older, printed (literary) form or on the current spoken language.[17]

The timing of language standardization varied greatly and reflected the asynchronical character of national development in different parts of Europe. The Czech and Magyar languages were codified during the first decades of the 19th century, whilst the codification of Slovak, Serbo-Croatian and Slovene came around the middle of the century. During the second half of the century, Finnish, Estonian and Latvian were codified, followed after 1900 by the Lithuanian and Ukrainian languages.[18]

This second stage in the linguistic programme was primarily directed towards the ethnic group itself, defined as an in-group, and offered a unified way of writing and speaking.

C. — The third stage: *the intellectualization of the national language* was closely connected to the earliest attempts at codification, and usually, worked against it — learned discussions on linguistic matters were unable to prevent the patriots concerned from improving their

*Ethnic Relations*, Pergamon, 1979, p. 159 ff.; F. BARTH, *Ethnic Groups and Boundaries*, Bergen, 1969, p. 8 ff.

17    R. AUTY, 'The Linguistic Revival Among the Slavs of the Austrian Empire 1780-1850: the Role of Individuals in the Codification and Acceptance of New Literary Languages', *Modern Language Review*, LIII, 1958, p. 392 ff.

18    A. SCAGLIONE (ed.), *The Emergence of National Languages*, Ravenna, 1984.

literary creativity, even though they were using different linguistic norms. As in the second stage, progress was rather asynchronical.

The development of literary creativity, as expressed in the evolution of different genres, occurred quite independently of this asynchronical course, and its pattern can be summarized as follows:

*a*) the earliest form of intellectualization was represented by journals and educational literature;

*b*) poetry, and translations from foreign literatures — above all from that of the ruling nation;

*c*) the collection and imitation of folk-songs;

*d*) the writing of theatre pieces;

*e*) the writing of short stories or tales, which was the archetypal prose genre of Phase B, with novels being written more commonly during Phase C;

*f*) the language of scientific literature tended to be the last to be improved, 'invented' or included in the national culture.

Some of the later national movements doubted if it was necessary to advance from the first sequence on to the higher ones, suggesting that the remainder could be filled in by translations. In one extreme example, a few national leaders in Russian Ukraine recommended — as late as 1905 — using the newly codified literary language exclusively for the writing of educational literature, journals and light novels for popular consumption.[19]

In comparing national and regional identities, it could be asked at this point to what extent the model of genres outlined above could also be used in the case of the development of regional cultures within the territory of larger national cultures.

---

19  G. SHEVELOV, *The Ukrainian Language in the First Half of the Twentieth Century (1900-1941): its State and Status,* Harvard: University Press, 1989, p. 98 ff.

D. — The fourth stage: *introducing the language into the schools.* The codified literary language could only fulfil its social mission once it had been mastered by the members of the non-dominant ethnic group — it had also to be 'consumed' by them, even if under conditions unlike those of a 'free market'. Patriots developed several modes of transmitting the language, which differed according to local traditions and the level of social organization achieved during Phase B. These included popular song-festivals (as in Estonia, Wales or Latvia), different forms of dancing (as in the Czech, Magyar and Catalan cases), reading circles (almost everywhere), cafés and so on. Nevertheless, the most powerful instrument for language dissemination was undoubtedly the schools.

The central demand put forward at this stage was for the 'nationalization' of schools,[20] which was directed both 'upwards' towards the ruling state administration, and 'downwards' towards members of the same ethnic group:

*a*) State authorities were to permit and support schools where children would be instructed in their mother tongue, or — at the very least, and as a provisional compromise — where they could learn it;

*b*) Where such schools existed, parents were asked to send their children for instruction in their mother tongue, rather than to schools where the ruling state-language was the means of instruction.

In this way, the struggle for national schools became an effective component within national mobilization during Phase B, though its effects went much deeper. Introducing the new language of instruction into school education was the only way of strengthening the ties which bound together the members of the nation-to-be. The importance of these schools thus exceeded that of supplying the needs of communication: through linguistic education, the school created a *'communauté de conscience'*. The children not only learned the emerging literary language there, but also an ability to describe, observe and perceive reality in the same, or nearly the same, way.[21]

---

20 E. BALIBAR and I. WALLERSTEIN, *Race, Nation, Class: Ambiguous Identities,* London/ New York, l991, p. 98 ff.

21 G. DAVY, *Éléments de sociologie,* Paris: 1950, p. 233; P. BOURDIEU, *Ce que parler veut dire...*, *supra,* note 9, p. 32.

V

From this point of view, an ambiguous situation was created in the school systems of the multi-ethnic states possessing one ruling nation, such as Germany or Russia. Both the ruling elites and the patriotic movements tried to use linguistic education in formulating their understanding of the world, society and national identity.

The results achieved during this stage of national demands depended on the attitude of the state administration to a greater extent than at previous stages. Some states, such as the Habsburg Empire or Sweden, permitted the use of local languages as the language of instruction in elementary schools even during the period before the emergence of Phase B. By contrast, other national movements were helpless against the all-powerful unilingual state education policy — this was true for Ukrainians and Lithuanians in Russia, or Slovaks in Hungary after 1870.

The fourth stage produced an important change in the character of the linguistic programme: *it entered the field of politics.* The struggle for 'national' schools continued into Phase C as well, and in so far as this occurred under constitutional conditions, it became a part of political disputes, and was discussed by political representatives at all levels.

E. — The fifth stage: *the realisation of the full equality of languages.* The most advanced stage in the linguistic programme was achieved when national leaders asked for the introduction of their language into the administration, courts of justice, the postal system, the railways, trade and politics. If this stage was reached at all, it was achieved during Phase C, but the complexity and radicalism of demands, as well as their results, differed chronologically and spatially even more than in all the previous stages. The most successful example was the Magyar national movement in the Compromise of 1867, whilst the Czechs advanced to some degree of linguistic equality in the Czech-speaking territories of Bohemia and Moravia, and similar results were achieved by the Croatians. In Russia, only the Finns were to achieve a degree of success, before the last wave of Russification at the end of the 19th century. The Flemish in Belgium also achieved a measure of equality, but the majority of national movements remained unsuccessful during the fifth stage of linguistic demands.

## Social Interpretation of Linguistic Demands

In cases where the fifth stage was successful, two levels of demands can be observed, corresponding to two ways of interpreting linguistic equality. The first concerned the equal use of both the ruling state-language and the minority language within the ethnic territory of the emerging small nation. The second step formulated the demand that only the language of the local inhabitants should be permitted within the ethnic territory, limiting the use of the state-language to contacts between the provincial and central administration. Escalation of conflicts of this kind only occurred in a few cases: the Czechs, Croatians, Finns and even the Flemish, created a model which was later accepted by almost all national movements.[22]

The same question could also be posed the other way round: why did the ruling elites even try to defend the primacy of their language on the territory of the non-dominant ethnic group, where this language was neither used nor known? The crucial point was that the call for the equality of languages in administration and political life endangered the monopolistic position of the state elites in this area.[23]

Naturally, linguistic demands entered the field of politics during the fifth stage and were included in the political programmes of national movements, and furthermore, were also included within their *social programmes*. Sooner or later, the call for full linguistic equality turned into a struggle for positions in the administration. The newly-created Czech, Croatian and Finnish elites observed with growing indignation the continuing occupation of well-paid positions by elites belonging to the ruling state nation. In these circumstances, the call for linguistic equality expressed much more than just national prestige or a symbolic value: it contributed to the emergence of a nationally significant conflict of interests. These kinds of conflicts were an

---

22 The Magyar claims for a unilingual Hungary after 1867 illustrate the ambiguities in the escalation of linguistic demands.

23 One of the founders of the Czech political programme asked in 1848:
'What good will freedom of speech and the press bring us, if our language is henceforth to be excluded from administration and public life? This will once again put the ruling power into the hands of a small group of privileged individuals'.

V

intrinsic part of the nation-forming process, and have been analyzed in another context.[24]

The second part of this paper deals with the social interpretation of linguistic programmes. We may well regard all these linguistic quarrels as infantile, or be ironic about the 'artificiality' of new languages, but we cannot ignore the political and social importance of this phenomenon, which requires a historical explanation. Any such explanation should keep in mind the long-term historical dimension to the nation-forming process in Europe: was the correlation between the primacy of the linguistic programme and the development of the social structure of purely marginal significance?

As far back as the Middle Ages, language was accepted as an instrument of group solidarity, though not everywhere and only by a rather limited part of feudal society: either those who,

*a*) were in power and could use language as an argument for their aims and goals, directed both at their neighbours and their own population; or

*b*) occupied a particular place in the system of communication — priests and later, in certain circumstances, merchants and even craftsmen.

For the most part, the mass of the rural population accepted as part of their fate the linguistic rules of the game that came from above. Spontaneous changes in the spoken language were conditioned by the need for survival, communication, or state interests, but this changed with the process of absolutist homogenization mentioned above. Opposition to homogenization only rarely used linguistic arguments, mainly in the Habsburg Empire. This opposition had one feature in common: a social background formed by the nobility and part of the clergy, who were defending the remnants of medieval privileges. They originally used linguistic arguments as a cover for their more

---

24 See M. HROCH, *Social Preconditions of National Revival in Europe*, Cambridge, 1985, 'Conclusion'.

important particularist political and social interests. Only in Hungary — where this kind of aristocratic opposition immediately stimulated the emergence of Phase B — did the switch from the linguistic to a political programme occur. In all other states apart from the Habsburg monarchy, the non-dominant ethnic groups accepted linguistic centralism with remarkably little resistance, e.g. Catalans under Bourbon absolutism, Norwegians under Danish rule, Ukrainians under both Russian and Habsburg rule, and so on. The social explanation for this seems to be quite clear: all these ethnic groups lacked a cohesive elite that was interested in political opposition to absolutist homogenization.

As a result of this development, most of the European national movements started their Phase B later, in the situation of a (just recently introduced) linguistic homogeneity within the administration of a state ruled by established elites, speaking and reading the state-language.

It is not the aim of this paper to explain why Phase B started, as this is a change which should be analyzed in all the complexity of its cultural, economic and socio-psychological context. Here, we can only outline some of its more important aspects. The emergence of national agitation was connected to important processes of modernization, which produced feelings of social, intellectual, and sometimes even political and moral, crisis. These changes stimulated a *need for some kind of new group solidarity* and identity, and produced dissatisfaction among educated members of the non-dominant ethnic group, who were motivated in part by the impression that the linguistic homogenization introduced by the absolutist state brought no benefits to the group to which they belonged.[25] On the contrary: they did not participate in any upward social mobility from the periphery to the centre, and they noticed that the increasing contacts with the linguistically different administration were becoming ever more difficult. Under these circumstances, they accepted the idea of defining their nation-to-be primarily in terms of its language.

25   W. BLOOM, *Personal Identity...*, *supra*, note 10, p. 143.

V

We can see that — in certain circumstances — their linguistic demands were usually successful. Even if it occurred before a full consensus on codification had been achieved, once a literary language had become established, *language — as an expression of national identity — could not be substituted* by anything else (there is no empirical evidence of any such case). This became even less possible at a later stage, after the transition to Phase C, as language had by then become a spiritual possession belonging to the masses.

In analyzing this occurrence, we first have to compare the other options available to the patriotic movement, which might have constituted *an alternative to the national language*. Was it possible to form a new identity in another way, without creating a new national language? In a very few cases, there was an alternative: the Flemish could choose a Dutch identity, Slovaks a Czech one, whilst the Croatians, Slovenes and Serbs were encouraged to accept Illyrism — all without success. In all cases an alternative existed, that of accepting linguistic assimilation, without relinquishing the new national identity, though there appear to be only two examples of this choice actually being made — the Irish and the Scottish cases.[26] However, these are such singular instances, that we can regard them as exceptions, rather than as a model for other national developments. The Swiss case is also exceptional, and is often recommended as an ideal solution to national problems, but none of these exceptions can really be accepted as cogent alternative models.

We have to acknowledge the fact that in some circumstances, *there was no alternative to the linguistic national programme*. The most important factor is illustrated by the remarkable correlation between national movements prioritising linguistic demands during Phase B and the existence of an incomplete social structure within the non-dominant ethnic group, and this is something that needs interpretation.

---

26   The Irish case proves that there was no need for a new 'H'-language, when the attempt to create it starts in the situation of a successful Phase C, and in a society where only a small minority were 'L*'-speakers.

After the literary language had become established, its acceptance or non-acceptance by the members of the nation-to-be became a matter of specific 'market-relations'. Here, it is necessary to ask who the audience for this message was, i.e. which social groups and classes were meant to become the 'consumers' of the new literary language, as a particular form of commodity?[27]

Contemporary sociolinguists argue that changes in the usage of language (and the acceptance of a new literary language was a change of this type) can be interpreted as 'the speaker's response to large-scale social processes'.[28] They also stress the need to take account of social conditions in research on shifts in language. Even if we follow this methodological approach, we still have to solve the central problem of how to explain the above-mentioned correlation between incomplete social structures and linguistic programmes during Phase B.

The problem cannot be solved simply by quoting J. G. Herder. Naturally, his arguments are often cited, but he was not some kind of 'Eastern thinker'[29] existing in isolation from the West. Nor should the importance of J.-J. Rousseau or German philosophers, such as Fichte or Schelling, be forgotten.[30] As an objection to these arguments, it can be asked why it was that the middle classes should have been more attracted to their (usually rather complicated) formulations, than were the ruling elites of national movements possessing a full social structure.[31]

---

27 P. BOURDIEU, *Ce que parler veut dire...*, *supra*, note 9, chap. 1.

28 M. MARTIN-JONES, 'Language, Power and Linguistic Minorities: the Need for an Alternative Approach to Bilinguism, Language Maintenance and Shift', in R. GROLLO (ed.), *Social Anthropology and Politics of Language*, London/New York, 1989, p. 118.

29 There are parallel thinkers in the West as well, e.g. H. Wergeland in Norway during the 1830s, or T. Davies in Ireland during the 1840s; J. A. FISHMAN, *Language and Nationalism...*, *supra*, note 15, p. 48.

30 A. COHLER, *Rousseau and Nationalism*, New York/London, 1970.

31 The explanatory capacity of K.W. Deutsch's model is also fairly limited: certainly, the growing importance of language is conditioned by more intense communication, but why were the lower and middle classes more strongly attracted to linguistic demands than the better educated elites?

V

Another standard explanation emphasizes *the influence of romanticism*. This can be partially accepted, in so far as it relates to the protagonists of those national movements in which Phase B started earlier, during the first half of the 19th century. This relationship cannot, however, be interpreted simply as being the one-sided impact of romanticism; it was instead a coexistence based on common roots. Both romanticism and the search for a new national identity tried to respond to the great crisis of legitimacy and social change, which had been provoked by the dissolution of the old feudal society, with its stable and transparent ties.[32] The upholder of these new values — the nation — had to be defined by stable and unchangeable features: language came to be of unique importance, as a stable and easy way of defining such ties.

A new concept of *the nation as a personalized body* emerged, based on this very coexistence and interconnection, and this metaphor was soon transformed into a basic conception, whereby the ethnic group was internally defined as 'us'. When seen as a personality, the nation could therefore naturally only use one literary language, just as it could only incorporate one common past into its 'memory'. The life of this personality-nation and its dissimilarity and differentiation from other nations, logically depended on the successful spread of the national language; if that failed, the personality-nation would 'die'. Being in fear of their nations' death provoked in the leaders of national movements during Phase B feelings analogous to those of fear for the loss of a loved person, or even of their own death. In this line of reasoning, every enemy of the new national language logically became a potential 'killer' of the nation, and incidentally, this sense of being in danger not only characterized national movements during Phase B, but formed one of their key stereotypes, sometimes right up to the present day.

The success of Phase B cannot be explained just by reference to the enthusiasm of the patriotic leaders, their mentalities and so on. It is necessary to take into account the ordinary members of the non-dominant ethnic group — the audience, whose decisions and behaviour played the crucial role in the nation-forming process. At this

---

32   E. J. HOBSBAWM, *The Age of Revolutions*, London, 1973, p. 312 ff.

## Social Interpretation of Linguistic Demands

point, we do not need to ask why the patriotic leaders made linguistic demands, but why the 'masses' accepted it.

Our point of departure is *the growing need for communication,* resulting from economic growth and the advance of innovations in the field of administration. With improving communication, a growing number of individuals became literate and receptive to the standardized presentation of information, and the volume and quality of language use was raised to a new level, in a similar way to what happened in school education.

However, it would be misleading to understand educational changes solely as an increase in literacy in its narrowest sense (knowledge of reading and writing). Oral education in the schools also attracted an increasing number of children aged ten years and over, the age when children can start to learn to think abstractly, not just in linguistic terms, but also in terms of an *ability to understand* phenomena such as the nation. Language could only take on the new qualities corresponding to the needs of communication through this new category of 'operational individuals'.[33] At the same time, it was only these operational personalities who were able to imagine large social groups or communities, such as the nation,[34] and understand that this group (as a personalized body) has similar needs, relationships and a common consciousness with other members of the community.[35]

For the growing number of individuals who achieved this degree of education, literacy became their *'real entrance-card to full citizenship and human dignity'.*[36] Nevertheless, this 'entrance-card' was accessible only to those whose mother-tongue corresponded to the state-language, the one which also played the dominant role in the education of operational individuals. Expressed in the sociolinguistic

---

33  G. STOKES, 'Cognition and the Function of Nationalism', *Journal of Interdisciplinary History,* no. IV, 1974, p. 533 ff.

34  From this perspective, we can understand more easily the term 'imagined communities', as used by B. ANDERSON.

35  H. WEILENMAN, 'The Interlocking of Nation and Personality Structure', in K. W. DEUTSCH and W. J. FOLTZ (eds.), *Nation-Building,* New York, 1966, p. 37 ff.

36  E. GELLNER, *Nations and Nationalism,* Oxford, 1983.

V

terms used above, rapid social change and the growing communication between 'H'- and 'L'-speakers made the diglossia dysfunctional. State institutions tended to make individuals monolingual in a language other than their mother tongue, with the result that school children who spoke an 'L*'-language at home increasingly became bilingual. For the first time, this new challenge produced an ambivalent response, which on the one hand accentuated the advantages of the newly-mastered state-language, and on the other, attempted to replace the 'foreign' state-language with an 'elaborated version' of their 'own pre-industrial tongue'.[37]

The actual historical conditions were nevertheless not as harmonious as envisaged by Fishman's model. The 'H'- and 'L*'-languages were ' *not only separate but also unequal*', and so the degree of freedom of choice for 'L*'-speakers should not be over-emphasized.[38] It was unusual for all members of a non-dominant ethnic group to become bilingual. On the contrary, the majority did not, and had to communicate with authorities and individuals whose 'H'-language was only partially understandable to them. Coming from an inferior social *stratum* and at the same time using an inferior 'L*'-tongue, they ended up in the position of 'inferior human beings', with all the feelings of humiliation accompanying that situation. In such circumstances, language naturally played a specific role in their understanding of the world.

Again, we can imagine two responses to this situation: either they would feel ashamed of their inferior 'L*'-tongue and try to adopt the superior 'H'-language and assimilate, or they would feel a growing animosity towards the ruling 'H'-speakers and be *receptive to the call for a new literary language,* corresponding or being fully understandable to their mother tongue.

However convincing this model may appear, there are two objections to it, which need answering.

---

37  J. FISHMAN, *Language in...*, *supra,* note 12, p. 148; The first trend was directed towards the monoethnic state, the second at two nations defined by different languages.

38  M. MARTIN-JONES, 'Language, Power and...', *supra,* note 28, p. 109 ff.

A. — The situation of linguistic inferiority described above had existed since the Middle Ages, without having caused any noticeable national mobilization amongst the mass of 'L*'-speakers. So of what precisely did the difference consist? It had been part and parcel of the feudal system that individuals were unequal from the moment of their birth; just as they were born serfs, so they were born as 'L*'-speakers, and this was accepted as a given reality. The process of modernization contributed to the spread of a new concept of human dignity and equality, and at the same time, a growing number of the members of the non-dominant ethnic group achieved an elementary level of education and / or became independent participants in a system of market relations. For these people, the medieval structure of unequal social relations was no longer self-evident.

B. — Why would this unequal social situation come to include the need for the formation of a new ethnolinguistic, national identity? Why did assimilation fail as a solution? The alternative to assimilation was far from being dependent on individual decisions; *access into the ranks of the ruling nation was not automatic everywhere.* As long as the number of individuals with a higher education increased, and exceeded the (limited) amount of 'acceptable' individuals moving from the lower linguistic strata to the centre, they could not be absorbed into the state elite, even if they adopted the ruling state-language and changed their identity: they remained an out-group (the Irish are a good example of this). The national agitation of Phase B offered to the educated individuals among them the opportunity to create a new in-group based on a common language, all of whose members could be equal and hope for better opportunities for social advancement without having to assimilate.[39] This prospect was at least more appealing than that of remaining an assimilated periphery. Even if we take into consideration the fact that in many European states differences between centre and periphery strengthened regional identities, this was not usually the case where the differences between the periphery and state-elites were not only regional and social, but also linguistic.

---

39   G. STOKES, 'Cognition and...', *supra*, note 33, p. 536.

V

Using these observations on the effects of modernization, we can return to the question of *the correlation between an incomplete social structure and the* charisma *of language.* The explanation can be summarized into three points.

A. — As modernization proceeded, vertical social mobility increased, but did not create equal opportunities for all individuals. This was the case where the remnants of feudal conditions and mentalities impeded social advancement, even for those members of the non-dominant ethnic group who became bilingual.

> The more difficulties they had in moving from the lower to the higher classes, the more significant the association between the language they spoke and the social position they occupied.[40]

This relationship seemed to be less important where:

*a*) the non-dominant ethnic group had a 'full' social structure, i.e. it possessed its own elites, and

*b*) Phase B started under the conditions of developed capitalist society. In both these situations, difficulties in social advancement could scarcely be explained other than by social conditions.

B. — Let us suppose that we are observing an advanced social situation which made vertical social mobility possible for everyone who managed to learn the state language. Becoming bilingual was nevertheless not just a matter of financing school education: it was also related to *the individual's linguistic aptitude,* which does not necessarily correspond to their intelligence quotient. In addition, it was connected to the intellectual level at which the mother-tongue was heard at home, as this was a precondition for any later ability to express abstract concepts. Even if their linguistic aptitude were the same, however, the results of linguistic instruction could differ according to the social environment from which children came.[41]

---

40   G. WILLIAMS, 'Language Group Allegiance and Ethnic Interaction', in H. GILES and
      B. SAINT-JACQUES (eds.), *Language and Ethnic Relations, supra,* note 16, p. 58.

41   See, among others, G. H. MEAD, *Mind, Self and Society,* Chicago, 1934, p. 135 ff.;
      E. HAUGEN, 'Bilinguals Have More Fun', *Journal of English Linguistics,* no. 19, 1986,

Many historical examples testify to this situation, as was observed by contemporaries during Phase B.[42]

C. — An incomplete social structure also had its impact on political culture. The national agitators of Phase B came predominantly from the lower strata of the population and addressed their appeals to the same strata. Whether this primarily related to small artisans and craftsmen, as in Bohemia, or farmers, as in Lithuania and Estonia, it always *involved social groups and classes, who at the time Phase B emerged, possessed neither political experience nor political education;* in fact, it was these very concerns that motivated patriotic leaders. The members of the non-dominant ethnic group needed to define group characteristics, which could be recognized in the easiest possible way.[43] They were hardly likely to become inspired by (or identified with) a programme of civil rights and political liberty. 'Freedom' for a peasant meant freedom from feudal oppression, while freedom of speech, association and so on, remained an uninteresting idea.[44] Linguistic group-characteristics were basically closer and more understandable to the lower classes. Recognizing these characteristics, the structure of the national programme implicitly accorded language the highest value, and passed this on to subsequent generations, even though they later earned a better political education, under changed conditions.

We have seen how linguistic demands became integrated into the political programme. Even during Phase C, this made them for several decades the most effective means of articulating different group

---

p. 106 ff.; J. HERMANN, 'Bilingualism Versus Identity', *Multilingual Matters*, no. 43, 1988, p. 227 ff.

42  In a memorandum of 1832, leading Czech patriots argued that Czech-speaking young men only attained a mechanical knowledge of subjects taught in schools where German was the (obligatory) language of instruction, and that their German was insufficient for better jobs or university studies. On the other hand, they were unable to use their mother-tongue either, because they had not learnt its written form.

43  H. WEILENMAN, 'The Interlocking of Nation...', *supra*, note 35, p. 37.

44  Analyzing the semantics of the French *Cahiers de doléances*, A. DUPRONT demonstrates that the only form of 'culture' familiar to peasants was the *culture des champs* [=agriculture], 'Sémantique historique...', *supra*, note 13, p. 87.

conflicts within the advancing modern society, though this did not necessarily mean that in these conflicts, the language of the non-dominant ethnic group represented a 'progressive' trend. Quite the reverse: it was sometimes used during Phase B as an anti-modern argument, expressing the fears of an old middle class (or part of it) that felt threatened by modern industrial development.

After analyzing the reasons for the priority of linguistic demands during Phase B, we have to ask why they retained *such an important position in the national programme during Phase C as well,* when the social structure of the national group was completed, and political experience became a part of everyday life. The answer to this question concerns the most striking social, political and socio-psychological peculiarities of national movements.

*Unequal opportunities for social advancement did not disappear with the transition to Phase C.* Even if the social structure of the new nation was sooner or later completed during this phase, the inferiority of the lower-middle classes did not disappear. During the preceding Phase B, these classes only became partially and gradually aware of the fact that their inferior social position was connected to differences in language, but this link was more fully experienced with national mass-mobilization. In other words, the inferiority of the non-dominant ethnic group, which had been identified by the patriotic leaders in Phase B as a disadvantage that was to be expected, changed during Phase C into a disadvantage that was actually experienced, and thus influenced the spread of linguistic demands, which were understood as a substitution for, or supplementation of, social ones.

As mentioned above, the linguistic programme entered the arena of politics during its fourth and fifth stages: it could be used as an argument in political disputes with the ruling state-elites, and also as an argument in the internal political disputes among the national leaders themselves. *Anyone who intended to become a successful politician, had to support linguistic demands:* to propose compromises or concessions with the ruling state nation in linguistic matters was tantamount to political suicide. Under the conditions of political differentiation existing during Phase C, both liberals and clericals, and even agrarians and most socialists, included linguistic demands in their political programme. Nevertheless, this did not mean that linguistic demands determined the structure and dimension of all political goals.

## Social Interpretation of Linguistic Demands

We often find one new political aim that was closely linked to linguistic demands: a modified understanding of *the equal rights of languages,* which emerged during Phase C. National leaders defined the ethnic territory of their nation as a territory where their own language was to be the dominant one, a demand which seems in part to be a response by the lower-middle classes to their experience of social disadvantage.[45] This demand obviously caused a sudden escalation of the political struggle, and it is precisely at this moment that it becomes appropriate to use the term 'nationalism', and that it takes on a real interpretative value.

The socio-psychological factors were more complex and heterogeneous, the most prominent among them being the *feeling that the existence of the emerging nation was endangered* by the loss of its language. This was a sentiment that had survived from Phase B, where it had been well-founded, and had then been carried on into the mass movement, where it became a fiction or myth. Both intellectuals and politicians continued to believe that their language would become extinct, unless they paid careful heed to linguistic demands.

This myth could only seem convincing to the broader public if it were combined with other psychological features. The most important of these seems to have been the fact that 'contrastive self-identification' (J. Fishman), which for centuries had been a typical pattern of behaviour limited to the ruling classes, came to be something generally accepted by a growing number of the members of the emerging nation during the transition to Phase C.[46] Complementary to this development was the tendency of operational individuals to feel comfortable and satisfied in a community, if it was based on a common interest in language,[47] though this could obviously only be the codified, standardized one, as using a correct high language formed part of the self-image of educated participants in Phase C.[48] The emerging elite of the nation acquired prestige from the correct use of their literary language, and by exerting pressure on the

45   E. J. HOBSBAWM, *Nations and Nationalism since 1789,* Cambridge, 1990, p. 116 ff.

46   J. A. FISHMAN, *Language and Nationalism..., supra,* note 15, p. 54.

47   G. STOKES, 'Cognition and...', *supra,* note 33, p. 537.

48   P. BOURDIEU, *Ce que parler veut dire..., supra,* note 9, p. 64 ff.

V

co-members of the national movement to use this literary language, they were able to *encourage a 'disciplinization' of the nation.*

However, even when standardized, intellectualized and used by a part of the elites, the new language still had a lower status than the ruling state-language — Russian, German or later, Magyar. Given that the status of the national group was also determined by the prestige of its language, the protection and upgrading of this language likewise became *a matter of prestige.*[49] This issue also involved the struggle to introduce the equality of languages into administration and public life, and in this situation, language therefore became 'highly ideologized',[50] which helps explain why the whole of the nationally mobilized population — and not just the emerging elites — accepted and supported the symbolic value of their language, as a pillar of the newly-formed ethno-national community.[51] This was still the decisive criterion for belonging to the group, and for distinguishing between 'Us' and 'Them'. Simultaneously, language retained the highly emotional potential that it had possessed since Phase B: it could serve not only as an instrument of social communication, but also as an 'outlet for intense feelings'.[52] It would, however, be an exaggeration to suppose that the symbolic significance of language generally prevailed over its actual use.[53]

Lastly but by no means least, language became a *criterion of the equality of all citizens* under the conditions of a modern, constitutional civil society and capitalism. It was inherent in the principles of this modern society that each citizen should learn the standardized language and use its spoken version, thus suppressing the dialect form, at least in the public sphere.[54] Since the language of the newly-formed nation was standardized, intellectualized and even accepted

49  G. WILLIAMS, 'Language Group Allegiance ...', *supra*, note 40, p. 62 ff.

50  J. A. FISHMAN, *Language and Nationalism...*, *supra*, note 15, p. 61.

51  J. A. ROSS, 'Language and the Mobilization of Ethnic Identity', in H. GILES and B. SAINT-JACQUES (eds.), *Language and...*, *supra*, note 16, p. 10.

52  O. JESPERSEN, *Mankind, Nation and Individual from a Linguistic Point of View*, Oslo, 1925, p. 5; J. A. ARMSTRONG, *Nations before...*, *supra*, note 5, p. 242.

53  E. J. HOBSBAWM, *Nations and...*, *supra*, note 45, p. 116 ff.

54  E. GELLNER, *Culture...*, *supra*, note 14, p. 17.

by the state authorities, learning and using it was also understood as a specific form of expressing civil rights.

The aim of this paper has not been to present a general 'theory' of the nation-forming process as a whole. It has instead concentrated on one particular and important problem: why was the significance of linguistic demands so 'disproportionately' high in most European national movements? Our explanation has suggested that linguistic demands and their success cannot simply be interpreted as a result of the voluntaristic activities of a small group of ambitious intellectuals. Even if these individual factors cannot be ignored, the extraordinary appeal of the linguistic programme was founded in deep-rooted transformations in society and mentalities.

Comparative research on the empirical data has shown that the primacy of linguistic demands was not a general feature of all national movements, even if it was characteristic of the majority. *The primacy of linguistic demands in Phase B correlated with the social structure* of the non-dominant ethnic group at the given stage of social and economic development. This correlation can be summarized in two sentences:

1. Where the social structure was obviously incomplete, the programme of the national movement was dominated by linguistic and cultural demands, while the political programme was formulated later, during Phase C.

2. Where the social structure of non-dominant ethnic groups included members of the ruling classes when on the threshold of its Phase B, the national movement's programme consisted of predominantly political goals, accompanied by social and linguistic ones.

In other words: the importance of linguistic demands was inversely proportional to the participation of ruling classes in the B Phase of national movements.

This was not an accidental correlation, but a causal one. Under given social circumstances, the nascent national movement had no alternative other than to emphasize linguistic demands during its Phase B. For important social and psychological reasons, the language fulfilled a non-linguistic, supra-communicative function in the

V

national movement, and later also influenced the political programme that emerged during Phase C.

The choice of a linguistic programme and linguistically defined nation was the response of a more or less peripheral population — the non-dominant ethnic group — to the challenge of modernization. In the general crisis of legitimacy and the feudal system, educated members of this group began to sense their inferiority because of their linguistic difference. Their success — the acceptance of their message by the general population — was primarily conditioned by factors other than just linguistic and cultural ones: above all, the structure of social communication and vertical mobility, and *the intensity of nationally significant conflicts of interest.* In this 'linguistic' type of national movement, language played a substitutional role in expressing nationally significant conflicts of interest.

This paper steers clear of the temptation of defining the nation by language, or of constructing a monocausal linguistic explanation for the success of national movements. Independent of agreement or disagreement with the explanation presented here, it cannot be disputed that language played an important role as a factor in the foundation of national consciousness and national traditions, nor that it ranked very high in the system of values of the majority of national movements. It became a symbolic expression of strategies of exclusion. In comparing the emergence of national and regional identities, it can be seen that the role played by language related more specifically to the *national* identity, and can be regarded as one of the features which distinguished between these two types of identity.

# Social and Territorial Characteristics in the Composition of the Leading Groups of National Movements

Every national movement took place in real space and was supported and directed by actual persons. In evaluating the transformation of non-dominant ethnic groups into nations, territorial distribution of national activities and the association of their leaders with specific social forces cannot be ignored. This is one of the reasons why the social origins of the leaders and the territorial distribution of their activities is of historical interest. Far from being an end in itself the comparative study of both phenomena sheds light on basic causal relations.[1]

The social characteristics of the leaders of Phase A (according to the periodisation proposed in chapter 1) are predetermined by certain pecularities. They were predominantly scholars, earning their living as university professors, librarians, members of religious orders and others who were close to the ruling classes – the 'elites' of the ruling nation. During the period of national agitation – Phase B – a more complex situation developed. Two questions, above all, should be considered. First how to interpret the motivation underlying the patriotic activities of the leaders and second why the rates of success of their agitation differed. Motivation was not restricted solely to individual decisions, which might have happened fortuitously. Accident, it can be argued, ends where several hundreds – even thousands – of individuals strove at the same time for similar goals and responded to identical or analogous slogans. In this state influences, interests and contexts might be involved which were, perhaps, not fully or consciously reflected by those taking part.

Unreflected motivation is also important in the second question raised. Enthusiasm and readiness for sacrifice undoubtedly played an important part. They were supposed to be subjective pre-conditions for the success of a national movement. The actual success (or failure) of these endeavours, however, was not determined solely by the personal endeavours and good intentions of the leaders. Broader contexts determined success or failure. The transition from Phase B to Phase C (the mass movement) was neither a mechanical certainty nor the result of subjective decisions taken by a small group of leaders. A different goal needs to be set for enquiry into Phase C. At that point national consciousness already had spread among the broad masses of the population. It is still important to find out what animated the leaders but the topical question is now how this motivation was related to the social interpretation of the national programme.

It is not vulgar economic determinism to claim that value systems and behaviour norms have been formed differently in separate social conditions. An activist from the administrative class probably lived and reasoned differently from one with peasant origins. This also meant they held distinctive views on what were the crucial interests of the people of the emerging nation and about the methods of struggle which should be employed. Social diversity within the group of leaders who shared the same national ideas can be seen as showing several variants during Phase B. To a large extent these differences were, however, restrained by the common purpose of agitation. Their importance increased parallel to the advancing political differentiation which affected political goals and pro-grammes.

Comparative analysis will not only define those characteristics and contexts shared by all (or most) national movements but also their distinctive features, and permit interpretation of these using social criteria. Differing levels of development make it desirable to conduct separate analyses of the social origins of the leaders for Phases B and C. Absence of uniform data for all non-dominant ethnic groups, though, inhibits comprehensive comparative treatment. A further difficulty, particularly for quantifying comparisons, arises from the shifting boundaries of the activist groups in the various national movements. The problems make essential a broader definition of the term 'activists' (as already characterised in the introduction). A narrow definition including only the leading personalities within the movement would be too limiting.

## The Representation of Specific Classes, Strata, and Professions

Involvement of certain social classes, strata and professional groups has been analysed across a range of different experiences. It is essential to stress that the social structure of Phase B activists differed in the various national movements. Though they came from a variety of strata and social groups they had one thing in common: in every case the intelligentsia was strongly represented. This fact however already has been recognised by numerous historians.

*The Upper Classes*

Apart from the Polish and Catalan movements, the number of noblemen and landed proprietors taking an active part was very small, sometimes nil, not only during the *ancien regime* but also after the capitalist upheaval. They were not a central feature of the movement. Some landed proprietors had a small share at the beginning of Phase B in the Ukrainian and Czech movements, for instance, or even in the initial stages of Phase C in Ireland. They did not however have a lasting influence on the course and the programmes of the national movement. In the Slovakian and the Croatian movements (not treated in this study) some landed proprietors of noble origin were present but also without marked importance. At the beginning of Phase C – if not earlier – activists of certain national movements tried to win over the local nobility. The Czechs and Irish in particular made this attempt but the results were disappointing. The Ukrainians in Russia, the Croats and the Slovaks did not have any greater success.

The nobility, or rather their mentality, played a certain part in the early stages of Phase B only in those regions where the non-dominant ethnic group, fully or partially, could claim a political identity (autonomy, existence as a state) dating from the feudal epoch. This does in fact denote a certain ambiguity on the part of these national movements. They were, as shown above, a component part of the anti-feudal bourgeois transformation (modernisation) but this did not preclude them from holding a jaundiced opinion of some results of the change. This was particularly true of those regions where modernisation first took place in the territory of the dominant nation, making the subject ethnic group feel threatened. The Polish movement in the Grand Duchy of Poznań, the Irish and Czech national movements fall into this category.

Activists coming from the new capitalist entrepreneural class (the bourgeoisie) were even more differentiated. It is generally supposed that the bourgeoisie, as a class engaged in capitalist enterprise, developed earlier and more strongly in the territories of the ruling nation. An implication of this might mean also that members of the non-dominant ethnic group rising as manufacturers or entrepreneurs found it convenient to change their ethnic affiliation (their

national identity) in order to exploit fully new economic opportunities. Membership in the ruling nation through assimilation or
integration proved a powerful attraction. Among movements
considered in the case studies the bourgeoisie was probably
represented most strongly in the Catalan instance, though only
towards the end of Phase B. But in Catalonia the bourgeoisie as a class
tended to support the idea of a unified Spanish nation. The
bourgeoisie, of course, took a prominent part in the German national
movement in Schleswig. It seems to be typical of most other national
movements however that the first bourgeois activists appear during
Phase C. This was true in the Czech and Polish cases though the
occasional entrepreneur can be found among the activists of both
movements, during Phase B. The Finnish movement (not treated
here) showed a comparable development. As for the Estonians, the
Ukrainians in Russia and Danes in Schleswig, their movements took
place almost without bourgeois participation. A special feature of the
latter movement was the numerous entrepreneurs domiciled in the
kingdom of Denmark (important civil servants, large scale
merchants, landed proprietors) taking part. It does not appear to be
important for the course of Phase B whether the leaders could count
few or any bourgeois members among their numbers.

Motivation for the participation of the noble landed proprietors
was clear: they had been the ruling class of the previously autonomous state now under alien rule. In the case of the Czechs and, to a
lesser degree, the Ukrainians of Russia, they were isolated relics from
a late feudal, anti-absolutist territorial patriotism. Similar anti-
centralist patterns were of some importance in Catalonia and Ireland,
where in the latter case landowners though being frequently of
dominant ethnic origins were alienated by treatment as colonial
subjects. The question of bourgeois participation can be put in a
negative manner. Why was their share in Phase B usually so
negligible? Much is explained by the social structure of the non-
dominant ethnic group and the desire to hasten economic success by
identifying with the ruling nation. Sometimes this was even a
precondition of social advancement. Only after the success of the
national movement and the transition into Phase C did an alternative
to assimilation (though this still remained a possibility) become
feasible: in such a case a new enterprising bourgeoise confronted (as a
weaker partner) the new dominating class of the ruling nation. In this
situation national tensions became exacerbated; this only ceased
when the bourgeoisie of the emergent (newly formed) nation also
started to become internationalised.

*Self-Employed Small Scale Producers in Town and Country: Artisans and Peasants*

Urban or at least rural artisans and small scale merchants had been present in the social structure of most non-dominant ethnic groups even before the beginning of the national movements. During Phase B they can be found taking part in patriotic meetings, subscribing to patriotic periodicals and joining patriotic organisations and clubs. An exception to this rule were the Ukrainians in Russia (and to some extent the Lithuanians). In both cases the artisans and merchants predominantly were Jews. Estonians were an intermediate case because artisans, though not permitted to work in the towns, were present in the villages. The Macedonian rural merchants and artisans were of some importance. In the national activities of the Danes in Schleswig artisans participated less, being dependent on the German speaking citizens of their towns. Only among the Czechs during Phase B were artisans decisive activists, real leaders in the sense of being strongly represented and influential.

Where the national movement succeeded in attaining Phase C urban artisans and small scale merchants nearly always contributed to its success (though probably to a lesser degree in the Czech movement). But even after that time they did not necessarily attain leadership positions. This was particularly the case in the Czech movement; also at a later date in the Irish and Catalan examples. In the Irish movement artisans were very strongly represented in the Fenian movement which corresponds approximately to Phase B. In the mass movement they were no longer overrepresented. Small scale merchants, though, had considerable importance and some leadership functions as well.

Motivations for artisan activism could be ambiguous where the conditions of a feudal society still existed. Their participation enabled a political opposition to raise its voice against the surviving *ancien regime* and a feudal absolutism. Yet through them a strongly surviving guild mentality could be moblised as discontent with the beginnings of modernisation, industrialism and free competition. After all this modernisation came from the centre – the ruling nation. Ambiguity was less apparent in most cases were the old order was abolished and bourgeois reforms had been realised, though in Ireland such change further inflamed discontent. During Phase C the significance of the petit bourgeoisie rose as they became the most important exponents of national self-assertion, even of nationalism. They were responsible for spreading national consciousness among the working classes. The bourgeoisie of the newly forming nation was recruited mainly from their ranks. Myriad circumstances must be taken into account in analysing the programme of every national movement.

As already mentioned the participation of peasants was negligible during Phase B. Only in the Estonian national movement and in that of the Danish minority in Schleswig, and that of the Germans in northern Schleswig were there numerous peasant activists. In both instances they subscribed to periodicals, attended meetings and also took part in political decisions. For the rest the interest of peasants in the national movement only rose during Phase C, mostly in the Czech, Irish and Catalan movements. Even then generally there were no peasants among the higher echelon of the national leadership. Peasant participation in leadership only assumed importance during Phase C and largely in the Estonian and Irish movements from the 1880s. In Ireland they were prominent as local leaders. Contrary to hypothetical conjecture national activity of peasants during Phase B was very small even in those cases where they formed the overwhelming majority of the non-dominant ethnic group as they did in the Russian Ukraine and Ireland. But without the participation of peasant groups the national movement could not achieve the transition to Phase C – the mass movement.

In other cases, too, peasants were only converted to active national consciousness during Phase C with hesitation. Acceptance and involvement were stronger in those countries where the Church sided unmistakably with the non-dominant ethnic group or/and where the national programme was unequivocally in favour of the social demands made by the peasants. This was true for the Irish, the Estonians and the Lithuanians. This rather reluctant attitude of the peasantry towards the national agitation of Phase B and the nationalism of Phase C does not alter the fact that the rural population of all groups supplied an 'ethnic substratum' for the activists: the village was the guardian of folk culture, of the vernacular language and as such it was admired and celebrated as the healthy nucleus of the emergent nation. Peasants however did not accept this role with instant enthusiasm, sometimes they even refused cooperation.

*The Secular Intelligentsia*

Among the activists of Phase B the high percentage of members of the learned professions is apparent everywhere. The extent to which certain professional groups took part in the activist movement differed widely in the various national movements. To avoid misunderstanding, a definition of 'intelligentsia' in this context is vital. Included in this stratum are all those who attained a certain (not necessarily academic) advanced education and earned their living by intellectual activities. It is a definition which encompasses a broad spectrum of professional groups, from poor village teachers to wealthy lawyers. Thus different professional groups have to be examined separately.

The so-called liberal professions (above all lawyers and physicians) increased in number parallel to society's push towards capitalist development. As these were professions needing an academic education and resulting in great financial independence, their members played an important part in every reformist social activity. Among these the national movements are undoubtedly to be counted. At the top physicians, lawyers, independent scholars and, in some cases, university professors affiliated with the liberal professions are nearly always to be found. Journalists and (very few) writers, later evident among the leaders, had independence in common with the liberal professions but not always an academic education. Of all social groups actively taking part in the national movement, members of the liberal professions were the only ones more or less equal to the 'elites' of the dominant nation. Social proximity did not lead automatically to a readiness for compromise among the activists of the national movement. One thing is certain: if there were any direct social relations between the activists of Phase B and the 'elites' of the ruling nation these nearly always occurred in professional circles.

The proportion of professionals in the leading groups differed widely. During Phase B their share was tiny in Estonia where ethnic and social boundaries coincided even after the abolition of serfdom. There were also few of them in the Schleswig movement though Danes were free to engage in the liberal professions. The percentage of professionals in the Catalan, Polish and Irish agitation was very high – these were territories where the social structure of the non-dominant ethnic group was nearly complete or as in the instance of Ireland advancing swiftly towards that position. Between extremes are the instances of the Czech, Macedonian and Ukrainian national movements. Only in the Russian Ukraine did the proportion of professionals rise during Phase B; in other movements they declined. Members of these professions however played an important part in the movements, even during Phase C, though their percentage was small.

Whereas the role of the liberal professions within the national movements was determined by their comparative political and social independence, the opposite was true of the national activities of civil servants employed by public bodies or the state. It is not surprising that their numbers and influence among the activists in most of the national movements was minimal. During Phase C their numbers increased in places, but even then they rarely aspired to, or achieved, influential positions. In some national movements administrators were activists during Phase B; their material situation was similar to that of civil servants. These were particularly numerous in the Czech national movement: they were the so-called patrimonial (serving landed proprietors) and municipal civil servants. Moreover in the Estonian and Ukrainian movements also there were a number of clerks among the activists, such as scribes, and *Zemstvo* employees. After the abolition of the feudal system this group, naturally, diminished in number. The percentage of clerks in municipal and state employment, and in the emerging trade and industrial enterprises, rose proportionally. The high percentage of estate officials, except in Ireland, and clerks resulted because these employments were open to members of the non-dominant ethnic groups. On the other hand the professionalisation of civil servants could lead to a hardening of conflicts and linguistic barriers – as was, for instance, the case in Schleswig.

Two categories of activists among teachers have to be distinguished: those in institutions of secondary education, and primary school teachers. The former shared characteristics with the liberal professions: though few in number they were very influential among the activists. This pertained only in territories where the institutions of secondary education were open to members of the non-dominant ethnic group, which was not the case everywhere during Phase B. Teachers in secondary schools were, then, important among the leaders of the Czech, Polish, Ukrainian and Estonian movements though in the latter country their number was very small. In Ireland their participation was never extensive and their attitude usually tentative as education, even in national schools, was controlled by the clergy.

It is often stated that primary school teachers took an important part in all national movements. Among the cases examined teachers played an important, perhaps even the most crucial, part during Phase B in the Macedonian and the Estonian movements. They also had some importance in the Danish and German cases in Schleswig but in all other movements their participation was minimal and did not correspond to their numerical size. They were even rarely found among the more broadly defined sympathisers. However during Phase C the number of teachers taking an active part rose perceptibly.

How can these impressive differences in the national activities of teachers be interpreted? Not by seeking contrasts in their status, incomes and educations. In these respects there were few differences between the Macedonian, Czech, Catalan and Estonian cases. They have played an important, even dominant, part among the leaders only in those territories where the teaching professions were a decisive, sometimes the only, means of social advance for members of the non-dominant ethnic group. For instance during Phase B becoming a teacher was the only way for an Estonian to achieve a higher education without shedding ethnic identity. It also is significant that teachers had always been very politically and materially dependent. In the various countries they depended on different institutions. Teachers had distinct experiences and opportunities depending on whether they were controlled by Church authorities, the state or the village community (for example Danes in Schleswig). A special position was occupied by the teachers of German and Danish minority groups after 1918 which were supported by state authorities of their respective mother countries.

Students from groups which had access to academic education were a driving force in most national movements though naturally they were rarely its actual leaders. Their percentage in patriotic activities and organisations rose significantly during Phase B but declined again with the emergence of the mass movements. Students from non-dominant ethnic groups who did not have a university in their native territory and therefore had to study abroad or at the universities of the ruling nation provide special cases. These students also sometimes formed patriotic groups but these were of differing importance. They were quite strong among the Poles in the Grand Duchy of Poznań, weaker in Estonia, and negligible among the Danes in Schleswig. Except in Ireland, where universities were situated in the ethnic territory, they were an important integrating factor for the intelligentsia and the whole national movement.

*The Clergy*

Differences in confession did not cause any fundamental distinctions of clerical participation in national movements. The Catholic clergy in the Czech and Irish Phase B, and partly in Phase C, took a leading role while priests hardly participated in the Catalan patriotic organisations. A high percentage of Protestant pastors were in the Finnish and Slovak movements though not conspicuous as activists among the Danes and Germans in Schleswig, nor in Estonia. Orthodox priests took a leading part in the Macedonian national movement and among the Ukrainians in Austria but were largely absent among the Ukrainian activists in Russia. These differences obviously were not determined automatically by the confession as such. They were, however, related to special conditions within specific national Churches, their organisation and the political position of the ecclesiastical hierarchy.

The small percentage of clergy taking part in the Catalan organisations is explained by the fact that the Catholic Church there was under the strict control of a unitary Spanish state and did not favour ethnic demands. The same applied in the Russian Ukraine, where the official position of the Church was 'all Russian', not Ukrainian. By contrast the Catholic Church in Bohemia was a territorial Church, identifying with the Bohemians, and had supported a territorial patriotism since the seventeenth century. The Bohemian Church did not prohibit national activism as long as such ambitions were formulated along linguistic and cultural lines. This accounts for the extraordinarily high percentage of priests in the Czech Phase B. It was only when the liberal political programme was formulated during Phase C that conflict arose. The Church was not prepared for such demands and developed over time a national–conservative clerical programme. Though this did not play an important part in Bohemia it had some significance in Moravia. It is easy to explain the higher percentage of priests in the Polish and Irish national movements where the ethnic and religious frontiers were identical. In many cases the seminary was for the sons of peasants the only way of rising socially. In Estonia and Lithuania conditions were entirely different. There a clerical career was a preserve of the ruling Germans and was for a long time closed to the Estonian speaking population.

Even where priests were numerous among the leaders of the movement they were unable to exercise a decisive influence in the formulation of national demands. Their influence on objectives were somewhat greater in those territories where the non-dominant ethnic group belonged to a different confession from that of the ruling nation – as in Prussian Poland, the Balkans and in Ireland. Where differences in confession coincided with the ethnic division it was of national relevance. Without this knowledge it would be hard to comprehend why the influence exercised by the numerous Czech priests active in the movement was much less than that of the (comparatively few) priests among the activists of the Polish movement in the Grand Duchy of Poznań. Priests, particularly in rural society, had a dual role. They exercised ecclesiastical and spiritual functions but were also often the most educated men in the region. Cultural functions, which might easily include national components, were in their hands. These two roles were combined or continued along parallel paths, depending on local circumstances.

*Common and Specific Features in the Social Composition of Leading Groups*

An attempt to formulate a generalising summary has to begin with a negative statement. Social (and even less, professional) groups were not represented equally in the leading circles of national movements. A group might be represented strongly in one movement and hardly visible in another. Even those national movements which took place contemporaneously differed markedly in the social origins of their leaders. Chronology, however, was crucial. National movements which started earlier (such as Czech, Irish, Polish) had a larger percentage of urban activists, while those movements entering Phase B later (about the second half of the nineteenth century) found more support in rural communities (such as Estonians, Macedonians, Ukrainians). The former experienced less difficulty in penetrating the rural population with the beginning of Phase C than the latter had in gaining a foothold in the towns. Nevertheless the leading groups of those national movements starting within the conditions of a bourgeois society already had an urban structure in spite of having begun later.

Despite enormous regional variations a further generalisation can be made. The national movements of Phase B were above all carried by members of those social groups and professions standing at the threshold of spontaneous linguistic assimilation. Social groups particularly were active which were on a level that could just be attained by a member of the non-dominant ethnic group which did not want to take the final step of assimilation. For the Poles in Poznań this might mean all strata; for the Czechs, the liberal professions and the lower administration; for the Estonians, the teaching professions. Another general conclusion appears to be that with the transition to Phase C members of the higher strata of the intelligentsia were represented more heavily than during Phase B.

## The Social Origins of the Leaders

Social characterisation of the leading groups has to consider the environment from which the future activists sprang and how they were educated. The question of social origins is particularly important because of the extended drive towards nationhood. It took several generations for a non-dominant ethnic group to become a fully formed nation and some never reached that stage. Research into social origins is difficult because source material is incomplete. It is easier to reconstruct the social origins of the intelligentsia, the stratum from which the majority of the leaders was drawn. Marked differences can be seen in the social origins of the leaders.

The upper social strata, the ranks of the old dominant class of landed proprietors and leading civil servants, was well represented among the Catalan leaders. But this class provided only a small number of Polish activists in the Grand Duchy of Poznań during Phase B. In the Russian Ukraine there was a larger percentage of activists coming from noble landed proprietors while in Ireland their number was small. Activists of urban origin were represented strongly in several national movements. About half of all Czech leaders of Phase B were artisans or in trade. The percentage was somewhat lower among the Poles in the Grand Duchy of Poznań and in the Irish, Macedonian and Slovak national movements. In the German movement in Schleswig and in the Finnish movement (not treated in this study) fewer activists came from this strata, though the number was not negligible. Activists of urban origin were quite insignificant in the Ukrainian and Estonian movements.

Activists of peasant origin were less evident. It is obvious that they were most numerous in those movements having a low percentage of urban activists – mostly in Russian Ukraine, Estonia and Schleswig (Danish activists). In the case of Polish activists in the Grand Duchy of Poznań the peasant class was largely represented by Catholic priests. In the Finnish and, probably, the Catalan group of leaders in Phase B there were hardly any descendants from peasant families. In the case of the Irish, Czech, Ukrainian and Slovakian activists from peasant families made up about ten to 20 per cent, showing a tendency to rise during Phase C. This tendency does not however apply to all of the national movements treated.

Only in those national movements where the intelligentsia already had been represented among the members of the non-dominant ethnic group before or at the beginning of Phase B, can there be found a higher percentage of activists from this stratum. Above all the cases of the Polish, Irish, Catalan and Finnish movements illustrate the point. The percentage was somewhat lower among the Czechs (and Slovakians) at the end of Phase B. A significant number of Ukrainian activists in Russia came from the noble intelligentsia. But the largest leadership group in Estonia had its origins in the families of rural teachers and sextons.

Sons of pastors were represented very unequally. Their share was negligible in the Danish and wholly absent in the Estonian movements. Generalisation remains an elusive possibility however, as sons of pastors formed an important section of both Finnish and Slovakian activists. In both countries pastors were represented in the social structure of the non-dominant ethnic group. Among sons of the Orthodox clergy a difference is discernable between the Ukrainian national movement, where they were represented strongly, and Macedonia where only a small share was evident. The high percentage of the sons of clergy in the leading groups undoubtedly reflected the fact that most of the ministers lived in the countryside and were in close contact with the peasant people but also had sufficient means to send their sons to university.

A closed model showing the social origins of the leaders is impossible, but one fact is certain – that most of the leaders of Phase B came from the traditional middle classes and lower and middle strata of the intelligentsia. It may be taken for granted that most of these leaders occupied a higher position than their fathers, particularly in the Czech, Estonian and Irish movements, though in the Catalan,

Polish and Ukrainian groups, this is less apparent. Actual social recruitment of the leaders can be shown by defining three different categories: first national movements drawing leaders mostly from the towns, especially among the urban artisan and trade classes (such as Czechs); second those with most of their leaders coming from the countryside, from landlord or peasant families or from the petty village intelligentsia (such as Catalans, Russian Ukrainians, Danes in Schleswig or Estonians); third those with a majority of leaders from intelligentsia families (Poles of the Grand Duchy of Poznań, Catalans and Irish).

## Comparison with the 'Elites' of the Dominant Nation

To date little attention has been given to the question of how the social composition and origin of the leaders differed from the 'elites' of the ruling nation. It raises the problem whether the national movement can be described as being a conflict between different ethnic groups (nationalities) representing the same social strata or a clash between distinct classes. It is therefore necessary to compare the social characteristics of ethnic leaders to those of the leading strata of those states against which the national movement was directed. Once again the results are not uniform.

In the Grand Duchy of Poznań members of the dominating Polish class confronted their Prussian social equivalents. Both consisted of landed proprietors belonging to the nobility, bourgeois entrepreneurs and industrialists (the latter being, of course, not as numerous as in the *Ruhrgebiet* (Ruhr region)). However the social structures of the two sides differed significantly in one point: civil servants, who played such an important part in the Prussian state, were not represented among the Polish leaders. Prussian civil servants were hostile to the Polish national movement. A similar feature can be detected in Spanish–Catalan relations. Members of the dominating class stood at the head of both camps, with the difference that the Catalan bourgeoisie joined the movement at a later date. Again it is possible to define the conflicts between different members of the same dominant classes and strata, but separated by ethnic loyalties. Though a large number of the activists were of noble birth in the Russian Ukraine they were drawn from the intelligentsia within the sector rather than from the landed proprietors. Nevertheless a certain analogy to the social characteristics of the Russian intelligentsia can be put forward. As in the Grand Duchy of Poznań there were no civil servants among the Ukrainian activists in Russia.

Fundamental differences existed in other cases between the social characteristics of patriotic activists and the 'elites' of the ruling nations. Generalisations are elusive. In Estonia peasants and petty intelligentsia challenged the German privileged class of landed proprietors and the academically educated. Macedonian activists were led by the middle class and the petty intelligentsia in opposition to the dominant privileged strata of civil servants and landlords. The German speaking 'elite' of landed proprietors, state officials, and bourgeois entrepreneurs were distinguishable from the Czech rural artisans and the middle and lower strata of the intelligentsia. Activists in the Danish movement in Schleswig belonged to a very different social stratum from the German 'elites' in Schleswig. But the Germans' resistance to Danish rule pitted two analogously structured dominating classes against each other.

Even when the differences during Phase C were no longer as significant as they had been earlier their results were of lasting importance. How did these distinctions influence the course and goals of different national movements? One way of interpreting these phenomena can be found by looking at the different conceptions concerning civil liberties and how these were applied. In territories where the leaders were associated with lower and middle classes having no political experience and sometimes lacking interest in politics, demands for civil liberties were represented weakly or, at the beginning, not at all in some programmes (such as Czech, Macedonian and Estonians). The greater the similarities between the social characteristics of the leaders of national movements and those of the 'elites' of the ruling nations, the more those leaders stressed political demands in their programmes (as in the case of Poles, Irish and Catalans). In the latter situation there was also an early differentiation of political ideas within the national movement. In both situations there was a conflict between moderate and radical activists. On the threshold of the mass movement or in its first decades the radicals represented, at the same time, the democratic wing whereas the moderates made up the rather conservative–liberal wing of the national movement.

Differences in social characteristics were of crucial importance in the formation of the national programme. When disparities between leaders of the movement and the ruling 'elites' were particularly great during Phase B, as in the case of the Czechs and, even more, the Estonians, social demands were more strongly represented in national programmes than, for instance, in those of the Polish and Catalan movements, where those differences were less strong. Social demands at the beginning were concerned with the liberation of peasants and sometimes also with obtaining better working conditions for artisans and craftsmen (or in Estonia with obtaining permission to join these trades at all). When these demands had been met, however, there survived in these national movements, even during Phase C, the stereotype of the national cause being a fight for social justice, for the rights of the weak and oppressed.

## The Territorial Structure of National Activity

It is vital to examine where the agitation and organising activities of the leaders were located and the extent to which they succeeded in penetrating various sections of the ethnic territory. The results illuminate the deeply rooted causes leading to the success (or failure) of a national movement. Territorial characteristics of the activists – where they were born, educated, worked and secured followers – may be treated as symptoms or circumstantial evidence for the general receptiveness of all strata of non-dominant ethnic groups towards national agitation.

*The Centres of National Movement*

From the beginning of Phase B every national movement had a traditional stronghold or strove to establish a new territorial base. Leading personalities and the organisational headquarters were concentrated in the chief national centres. From such points patriotic intensity rose and pleas for action were directed towards the provinces. Such places were also crucial as collecting stations for information from the provinces. Because of their special situation the border minorities of Schleswig did not have a centre (or only an insignificant one) in their territories. They might have several provincial centres but the actual centre was situated in the 'mother country'. In most cases the national movement was located in the regional centre, the city within the territory of the non-dominant ethnic group where the administration of the ruling nation was domiciled. For Czechs Prague was the centre; Poznań for Poles in the Grand Duchy of Poznań; for the Catalans Barcelona; Kiev for Russian Ukrainians; Dublin for the Irish; and somewhat later Tallinn for the Estonians. Only the Macedonians had a certain provincial 'poly-centrism' rather analogous to the border minorities. There were rare, usually unsuccessful, attempts to create an alternative national centre which did not coincide with that of the ruling state adminis-tration. The concentration of the national life in Viljandi attempted by the Estonians was one such case. Other instances in areas not covered here can be cited. For example Slovakian patriots tried to establish an alternative centre to the Magyar–German administrative centre of Bratislava/Pressburg, first in Trnava and then in Martin.

Sometimes the non-dominant ethnic group was in fact a numerical minority in the chief city of the national movement as, for instance, the Ukrainians in Kiev and the Estonians in Tallinn. At times a number of leaders and their offices were located in the capital of the dominant state thus forming a 'supplementary centre'. A number of Macedonian leaders, for instance, were in Istanbul or Salonika; some Ukrainians in St Petersburg or Moscow; Slovaks in Budapest; and Irish in London. When the centre was situated within the territory of the non-dominant ethnic group, in a favourable position both for administration and communication, the influence of the leaders and the prospects of success rose. From the beginning of the respective national movements Prague, Barcelona, Kiev, Dublin and Poznań provided examples of this kind.

*The Territorial Distribution of National Activity*

Finally it is essential to reconstruct how the leaders and, above all, their activities were distributed within the territories of the non-dominant ethnic groups. Unfortunately the information available on this is neither comprehensive in scope nor complete. Though sources are often incomplete two factors stand out:

- National activity was distributed unevenly within the territory of the non-dominant ethnic group. Different regions did not contribute an equal number of leaders to the movement nor were activities distributed in equivalent density throughout the territory, and the results of these endeavours were not identical everywhere.
- This territorial inequality usually relates to whole regions rather than sub-regions. One or more compact territories usually stand out by being more active, others marked by a rather passive role.

Investigation of the characteristics of the active regions can provide evidence about social, economic and cultural factors leading to national integration. Regions with above average national activity, where a proportionally larger number of leaders were domiciled, sometimes formed the hinterland of the centres of the national movements, as for instance in Catalonia or the Grand Duchy of Poznań. More often, however, these regions were only a small section of the hinterland, such as in the environs of Prague, Kiev and Tallinn, where nationally passive regions can also be seen.

Did a relationship exist between industrialisation (as a dominant agent of economic prosperity and social mobilisation) and the distribution of national activities? The answer is in the negative. These regions were never congruent though sometimes their boundaries overlapped, and a certain correspondence existed in Catalonia. But it should not be concluded that the nationally active territories were economically backward. Industrialisation either took place in the territories occupied by members of the ruling nation (such as Bohemia, Ireland and Prussia) or by encouraging territorial mobility, it brought about a high degree of ethnic intermingling, allowing little scope for non-dominant ethnic groups. This was the case in the southern Ukraine, in Tallinn and Narva, Mährisch-Ostrau as well as in other instances.

Obviously in the determining characteristics of nationally active regions neither backwardness nor industrialisation predominated. Which, then, were the characteristics furthering national activity?

- They were regions having better than average school networks or conditions generally favouring education, so the number of illiterate people was comparatively low.
- They were market orientated regions; that is areas which regularly produced goods for the market and where urban and rural producers (artisans, craftsmen and peasants) took an active part in economic life. Sometimes the regular selling of a rather specific kind of wares – the export of labour into remote regions (such as seasonal workers from the Macedonian mountains) – played a part. The accompanying phenomena can only be touched upon briefly; an expanding monetary economy, horizontal social mobility and social communication extending beyond the traditional forms.
- They were regions of comparative ethnic purity, populated only or mostly by members of the non-dominant ethnic group. In these cases it was not only the compactness of the ethnic territory which was decisive but also the fact that in these regions the social structure of the non-dominant group was nearly complete, or that the incompleteness of the social structure had a less disintegrative effect than in places with an ethnically mixed population. The nearness of the ethnic boundary was not necessarily significant though it had importance in those regions where a political or social challenge radiated from the other side of the linguistic boundary.

Specific traditions could also be important. In the Russian Ukraine, for instance, the old tradition of the Cossack *Hetmanate* (autonomous area) proved to be vital. Later on growing railway construction and the resulting changes in population density and market structure formed an integrating (or, under certain circumstances, a disintegrating) factor. In regions having an extraordinarily low degree of social communication and mobility the activities of the national movements also were weak even if some of the leaders lived in this territory. Chance also played a part. A certain level of social communication and mobility was undoubtedly necessary for the advancement of national agitation but it was not the cause of success. Leaders were welcomed most warmly in those parts of the territory where education, social communication and mobility were high. This characteristic can be demonstrated from data on school provision and attendance, literacy, transport networks and market relations. There was however no compelling causation: there were regions where all these characteristics applied and which were, nevertheless, nationally passive.

A high level of social communication or of social mobility, however, was not decisive for the activism of the national movement and the success of agitation. More important were the matters of the nature of the message content transmitted and the conditions which existed within different social situations. The same is valid for social mobility. How often and under what circumstances members of the non-dominant ethnic group engaged members of the ruling nation was crucial. Empirical research has demonstrated that horizontal and vertical social mobility could facilitate assimilation but it also might provoke or deepen national tensions and conflicts. Which social groups and classes of the ruling nation and the non-dominant ethnic group met and how they reacted to the entire social context, was decisive.

Members of different or equal professions, social groups and classes whose interests partly coincide with, or contradict, each other are pertinent factors. Major antagonism could develop when rival individuals or social groups were reinforced in their hostility by ethnic differences. 'Antagonisms of interests with national relevance' could exist, as for example between the Ukrainian peasant and the Polish or Russian landlord, or as in the case of the Czech craftsmen and the German merchant or entrepreneur. Antagonisms of interests with national relevance could also rise among members of the same social group or class, as with competition for employment as officials, or between merchants. Unfortunately little is known about antagonisms of interests of national relevance within the 'old middle class' or among farmers or craftsmen who belonged to different ethnic groups. The antagonism of interests with social relevance thus made possible the national articulation of social and other matters. Such an antagonism in combination with nationalist agitation even could become an independent phenomenon. Fictitious, stereotyped antagonisms of interests were spread as national ones by social communication. As this is a field not yet examined thoroughly any suggestions must remain hypothetical.[2] Yet it is essential that the force animating non-dominant ethnic groups is analysed in the context of the social backgrounds of activists.

## Notes

1 This comparative chapter is based primarily on the case studies. All the other material utilised is taken from the studies of the author cited in the introductory chapter.
2 In his classical work (1953), *Nationalism and Social Communication*, Cambridge, Mass., K.W. Deutsch, has underestimated this connection. It was only later that he considered the antagonism of interests at least partly as a driving force of nationalism.

# VII

# Real and constructed: the nature
# of the nation

When, thirty years ago, I began to write my book about the social composition of the leaders of national movements, it was not my intention to present a 'theory' of the origins of nations.[1] My aim was far more modest: to determine just which social circumstances were favourable for the successful spread of national consciousness among the broad mass of the population – in other words the conditions for the success of those activities which I grouped together under the term 'national agitation'. At the same time I hoped to clarify the place of the Czech 'national revival' in the European context. If I had any ambitions beyond the realm of empirical research, these lay in the field of methods rather than theory: I tried to demonstrate the utility of comparative methods at a time when their use was not yet a commonplace in European (and even less in Czech) historiography. I also aimed to investigate the possibilities of quantification as a modified form of 'Namierism'.

In order to apply comparative methods, it was first necessary to select an approach which would exclude voluntarism and above all avoid the error of attempting to compare things that are not comparable. Therefore it was necessary to define the subject of comparison (the 'nation' or 'nationality') and to choose a set of processes involved in the formation of nations that have enough features in common so as to be brought together under a single type. My definition of the 'nation' at that time was thus a wholly provisional one intended to promote a better understanding of the issues. Behind all this of course stood a certain theoretical conception: the view that the great social group known as the 'nation' was formed in historical time, that it really exists in the present and may thus serve as an object of empirical research far more conveniently than the irrational and foggy notion of 'nationalism'.

As the objects to be compared I chose only those which belonged to one of two basic types of processes of national formation, the one which I called the 'formation of smaller nations' – in traditional terminology a 'national revival'. Here the adjective 'smaller' had a qualitative rather than quantitative connotation. This consisted in the fact that, at the beginning of its development towards a modern national state, the 'smaller nation' lacked its own ruling classes, while its language had been significantly weakened, so that it possessed only an enfeebled or interrupted literary tradition. Its leaders were just launching their efforts to gain the sympathy of the people for their idea of the nation and to win recognition from the ruling state-nation. I called this twin effort a 'national movement'.

In order to compare national movements it was necessary to establish a periodisation which would not only permit a synchronic comparison but also one according to analogous situations. Of the three phases of the national movement I chose the second, 'Phase B', that of national agitation, in which the decision was taken to proceed to a mass-based national movement. The criterion of comparison, then, was the social and territorial composition or origin of the national leaders, the 'pioneers' of the agitation in Phase B of the national movement. This composition was not limited to a consideration of professional grouping but also included the wider context of property, relation to the state, position in the distribution of goods, and varying life-styles – in short membership of classes (landlords, yeomen, urban middle class) and social groups (various categories of officials, professionals, craftsmen, students, clergy).

The English translation of the book was prepared at the end of the 1970s, at a time when publication in western Europe, even of an old manuscript, carried the risk of repression at home. For a number of reasons publication was delayed, so that the book appeared only after the new and significant theoretical works by Anthony Smith, Benedict Anderson and Ernest Gellner, but too soon for me to be able even to refer to them in the preface or notes.[2] It therefore appeared in the context of those studies which attempted a comprehensive theory, and so it was judged in a context which its author had not anticipated when it was written twenty years earlier.[3] This explains, among other things, why the book devotes scant attention to analysis of the relationship between the 'revival' of the nation and the social transformations during the transition to modern society, even though the author, inspired by historical materialism, considered this relationship to be of decisive importance and practically self-evident.[4]

At the time the book was written, the problems of the formation of nations were considered to be outdated, and 'nationalism' itself was studied as an antiquated deviation, a historical error.[5] This represented an advantage for scholarly analysis: it was possible to work free of ideological constraint, independently, especially when the chief object of analysis was quantification of social and geographical structures. Practically no models existed, and thus it was not difficult to choose path-breaking procedures and to open new horizons.

Since the 1960s, of course, conditions have changed: new researchers appeared on the scene, and the informational base expanded. The need to explain and clarify the process of the formation of modern nations took on the aspect of a currently relevant task for the social sciences, and the study of 'nationalism' was raised to a political and ethical duty. In these circumstances it was necessary to reckon with a scholarly boom in the field and with the advisability of presenting as quickly as possible the most original and effective results. The social sciences saw an over-production of new theories; on the other hand, historians recognised that they could not limit themselves to mere empiricism. They were also obliged to take into account the findings of the social sciences, at least at the level of middle-range theories.[6]

With the growing number of studies, a certain terminological poverty became increasingly widespread – especially the monotonous and unreflected repetition of the term 'nationalism' in the most varied contexts and applied to the most varied phenomena. Sometimes an individual state of mind is meant, sometimes that of a certain group or even of an entire society. Sometimes the term is applied to the activities of individuals, sometimes to that of groups.[7] The result is frequent misunderstanding and an inability to provide explanation. If we regard 'nationalism' as the prime mover, then we merely shift the explanation from the level of empirically grasped social activity to that of a 'state of mind', which is not susceptible to historical investigation. This is perhaps the reason why contemporary historical research on 'nationalism' has yielded so few relevant (i.e. generalising) results. I do not presume to pass judgement on the results of research in the social sciences.

As long as the historian has not given up on perceiving development in causal contexts, then the notion that the nation is a mere myth or construct will be of little help, as will the authoritative *a priori* thesis that the conflict of nations is unrepresented in history.[8] Even if national identity is not the sole determinant of an individual's place in society, one cannot ignore the fact that from a certain point in the history of modern Europe there have existed large groupings of people who are integrated by a combination of several kinds of relationships (economic, historical, political, religious, linguistic, cultural, geographical, etc.), and by their subjective perception of a collective consciousness of belonging together. Many of these ties could be mutually substitutable, but among them, three stand out as irreplaceable: a memory of a common past, treated as a destiny of the group; a density of linguistic or religious ties enabling a higher degree of social communication within the group than beyond it; and a conception of the equality of all members of the group organised as a civil society. The fact that members of these groups term themselves as a 'nation' – a term whose equivalents in different languages have varying connotations – is no reason to doubt the existence of such groups. These, or similar groups, would still exist if they were assigned another verbal designation or some sort of code.

This does not mean that nations should be regarded as eternal categories. In this connection it is necessary to note that I have used the term 'revival' in a metaphorical sense, though it is a term which comes from a vocabulary characteristic of the primordialist vision of the nation and was a typical commonplace for the national movements of the nineteenth century. But if we wish to analyse the processes of national formation, we must take into account the fact that objective relationships and ties, which were characteristic of the coherence of a large group (the nation), took centuries to be formed.[9] The process whereby nations were built was not preordained or irreversible. It went through two distinct stages, of unequal length and intensity. The first stage had an extensive character and began during the Middle Ages. The second, which was intensive and decisive, took place during the nineteenth century and was a part of that basic social transformation referred to above.

The relation between the formation of nations and this transformation occupies a key place in our discussion. Some authors, such as Hans Kohn and his followers, limit this relation to the diffusion of the ideas of the French Revolution. Sometimes greater emphasis is placed on other intellectual currents, such as the influence of Herder or of German Romanticism. But the origin of nations cannot be satisfactorily explained without reference to the changes in the spheres of society, politics and economics. The fact that the rise of modern capitalist society comes in the same period as the rise of nations is not merely a chronological coincidence. At the same time I think it is unimportant whether we call the great social transformation a transition from feudal-absolutist society to capitalism, a process of modernisation, or (in Gellner's usage) a process of industrialisation.[10]

Two basic types of nation-forming may be distinguished, according to the starting-point of the second, decisive stage. The first was that in the early modern state-nation, as in France, the Netherlands or Sweden. The second type, which I first called the 'smaller nation', began under conditions of a non-dominant ethnic group, i.e. a group which formed an ethnic community and whose members possessed a greater or lesser degree of ethnic identity.[11] The non-dominant ethnic group was distinguished from the state-nation by three deficiencies: it lacked 'its own' nobility or ruling classes, statehood and continuous literary tradition in its own language.

Sooner or later a group of educated members of these ethnic communities reached the conclusion that their group also belonged to the category of the 'nation', but that it was still an 'unconscious' nation which needed to be awakened, revived and made aware, but also required recognition from the other, already established nations. In time there began a purposeful activity aimed at achieving all the attributes of a fully formed nation: they started a 'national movement'. The success of this movement was by no means preordained. My research was focused on this second type of nation-forming process, the national movement. Therefore the central role was occupied neither by the ideas of the French Revolution, nor by the theories of Tocqueville nor by the politics of Bismarck.

In a historical explanation, the term 'national movement' has a significant advantage over 'nationalism' in that it refers to empirically observable activity by concrete individuals. We can analyse their goals and demands, their forms of organisation, their numbers and their social composition. At the beginning of the national movements there was activity which was above all devoted to scholarly inquiry into and propagation of an awareness of the linguistic, cultural, social, economic and historical attributes of the non-dominant ethnic group (Phase A). In the ensuing period, Phase B, a new range of activists emerged, who now sought to win over as many of their ethnic group as possible to the project of creating a modern nation, by patriotic agitation. Once the major part of the population came to set special store by their national identity, a mass movement emerged – Phase C.

This periodisation, originally worked out in order to compare analogous stages of various national movements, has met with the approval of many researchers. It gradually became clear that its usefulness extended beyond its original role as a purely working approach; it can be used for the measurement of national territory, for codification of language and for determining the basic components of national identity. The attitude of the patriots, their relation to the state and to power – and also the response they elicited from within their ethnic group – varied according to which phase the national movement had attained. The same holds true for the national programme.

The essence of national agitation, which arose with Phase B, was the effort to spread the idea of national identity in an environment which until that time recognised several distinct identities. As has been mentioned, ethnic identity was stronger wherever it was supported by institutions – ecclesiastical organisations, parliaments, armies and so forth – in which a 'memory' of political or cultural uniqueness survived. However, national identity cannot be reduced to a mere transformation of ethnic identity. With varying strength and social results, other identities were represented in the territory of the non-dominant ethnic groups: those defined by the state or dynasty, in a multiethnic monarchy focused upon the ruler; by the land or country, sometimes in the form of 'land patriotism'; by the region, in the sense of enlightened patriotism; and finally by social group or religion.

In what ways did national identity differ from these older identities? In contrast with ethnic identity, national identity expressed a relationship to a large social group which (1) possessed, or should possess, a fully formed social composition, including an educated elite and an entrepreneurial class; (2) was at the same time a community of citizens enjoying equal rights; (3) acknowledged a body of 'higher culture' in the national language; (4) combined an awareness of a common origin with an awareness of a common destiny, to create a historical 'personalised' collectivity.

The relationship between national and state identity depended to a decisive degree on the level of modernisation attained during Phase B of the national movement. Wherever the idea of the state was still formed by the dynastic identity of the absolutist monarchy, the efforts towards a new, national identity could focus on a combination of the civic principle and cultural uniqueness. Wherever a constitutional system and civic society had appeared before the inauguration of Phase B, it became far more difficult to make national identity independent of state identity, as for example in Catalonia, Scotland or Slovakia.

In contrast to the premodern state identity, regional identity was compatible with national identity and in certain situations could act as a preparation for it. The difference lay in the fact that enlightened regional patriotism was based chiefly on the idea of the responsibility of the educated elite for the life of the people of the given region and on the moral obligation to be useful for these people. Its goal, then, was not the mobilisation of the mass of the people. What is now regarded as regionalism already posits the existence of a mass regional identity and depends upon it. This identity is of course based on vaguely defined borders, it usually lacks a firm awareness of ethnic community and a personalised conception of a common past.

The national movement did not operate in a social and political vacuum. Members of non-dominant ethnic groups lived in multiethnic states which had their ruling elites, administrations, and their fully developed social composition. The leaders of the national movements therefore had to adopt an attitude towards the internal conditions of the given state and participate in its internal conflicts. The basic problem was the process of social transformation and modernisation mentioned earlier. Wherever the national movement began under conditions of late absolutism, it was obliged to take up a stance towards that system, and its social and cultural demands, whatever the intentions of the movement's leaders, were inevitably aimed against the old regime, even when their goal was only modernisation through reforms.[12]

The structure of the demands of national movements corresponded roughly to those missing elements which excluded them from the ranks of the fully-fledged nations. We may divide these demands into three groups:

(i)   Cultural and linguistic demands: the development of a national culture based on the local language and its normal use in literature, education, administration and political life.

(ii)  Political demands: the achievement of civil rights and political self-administration and participation; later also autonomy and independence.

(iii) Social demands: here the specific demands varied according to the prevailing social and economic situation – emancipation of the peasantry, better conditions for the crafts, access to education, and so forth. However, all national movements endeavoured to attain a complete social structure within the ethnic group, including an educated elite, an entrepreneurial and sometimes a landowning class.

The combination of groups of demands varied, as did their timing, but it was not random, and certainly it cannot be inferred from the arbitrary decisions of the 'nationalists'. On the contrary, we can observe a remarkable correlation between the character of the demands and the social structure. Most of the national movements pursued cultural, linguistic and social goals during Phase B, while political demands were formulated only at the beginning or during the course of Phase C. However, some national movements already formulated political demands during Phase B, sometimes demanding complete independence (the Greeks, Norwegians, Serbs, Poles), at others only aiming for autonomy (the Irish, Hungarians). If we ask what these national movements had in common, the answer is clear: they were movements of ethnic groups which possessed 'their own' elites including 'their own' nobility or bourgeoisie. A second common feature is that these ethnic groups could point to the sometime existence of 'their own' state and demand its renewal.[13]

As mentioned earlier, the process of nation-forming acquired an irreversible character only once the national movement had won mass support, thereby reaching Phase C. This is a fact which has escaped most contemporary theoreticians of 'nationalism'. We know of a number of cases in which the national movement remained in Phase B for a long time, sometimes down to the present: here we may point to Wales, Brittany, Belarus or the eastern Ukraine. How can these differences be explained? Certainly not by reference to 'nationalism': for if we wish, we can find it everywhere.

The question of the 'success' of the national movement cannot be posed in the abstract, but concretely within the individual phases of the national movement. Three analytical levels need to be distinguished:

(i) Why did some of the patriots from Phase A decide to begin national agitation? In other words, why did Phase B begin?
(ii) Why did their national agitation win a mass response, and why was the national movement able to proceed to Phase C?
(iii) Why and in what circumstances did the national movement achieve its cultural, social and political goals?

The first level of the problem has so far been accorded scant attention in empirical research.[14] But we may infer the basic connections by evaluating the conditions in which the decision in favour of a new national identity was taken. This always occurred during a crisis of the old regime (whether we choose to emphasise its absolutist or its feudal character) at a time when the old relations and ties were disrupted and opened to doubt, and when the old religious legitimacy was challenged. The ruling elites – or more specifically some of their members – reacted to this crisis of the old regime with efforts at reform from above, at a systematic modernisation by decree. The immediate outcome of these reforms was of course a further disruption of the existing relations and certainties, and hence also of identity.

We may recall for example, that Phase B of the national movements in the Hapsburg monarchy began with reaction to the Josephine Reforms and to the shocks of the Napoleonic wars, which also certainly resulted in the turn towards the official Austrian state identity. The national movement in tsarist Russia reacted to the crisis of the monarchy in the 1850s and the ensuing reforms of Alexander II. The beginning of the Serbian and Greek struggles for independence followed immediately upon the political tremors within the Ottoman empire, which were preceded by Selim III's efforts to reform the backward system and which continued during the Napoleonic period.

Of course it must be admitted that in the beginning the weakening of old certainties and the old system of values was only perceived by those who possessed a certain breadth of outlook and education; they concluded that it was necessary to search for new certainties and to create a new system of values which would correspond to the modern age. For some of them the solution was to look for new certainties in a new type of identity: by identifying with a group of equal citizens bound together by a common culture, destiny, social position, language and so forth.

For this new type of group solidarity the term 'nation' offered itself, and in many cases it echoed an analogous historical community to which it was possible to subscribe. Thus the term 'nation' was able to take on a new connotation, sometimes (though not always) under the influence of the French Revolution, which imparted to it the attributes of a political programme. The comparative study of the different connotations which the term 'nation' had at the beginning of Phase B (or also during Phase A) in the varying linguistic contexts of the European national movements would be an attractive theme for future scholars.[15]

The success of national agitation during Phase B, as has been mentioned, was a basic factor in the successful outcome of the nation-forming process within the non-dominant ethnic group. If national agitation is evaluated in this way, then the question arises of whether the modern nation cannot be regarded as the result of a wilful decision on the part of the 'nationalists'. Is it not possible to agree with Gellner's view that a 'rival conclusion' may be drawn from my analysis – that it was 'nationalism' that created nations?[16]

If this were the case, we would have to explain why it occurred to nobody at the beginning of the nineteenth century to launch a campaign to persuade, for example, the Irish that they were in fact Germans, or to win over the Hungarians to the notion that they were actually Chinese. What explains the failure to create a Slavic nation, as the Pan-Slavists attempted, or an Illyrian nation? Why did the idea of a united Czechoslovak nation fail among the Slovaks, even though in the interwar period the Czechoslovak Republic possessed all the necessary means of effective agitation to put across this view of state and national identity?

The answer is simple. The basic condition for the success of any agitation (not only national agitation) is that its argument at least roughly corresponds to reality as perceived by those to whom it is directed. National agitation therefore had to (and normally did) begin with the fact that, quite independently of the will of the 'patriots', certain relations and ties had developed over the centuries which united those people towards whom the agitation was directed. They formed a community united by inward ties, and they were at least vaguely aware of this. There was of course a further psychological condition that was not entirely evident: this was the ability of the targets of national agitation to conceive of the existence of 'their' group outside the framework of their everyday experience.[17] This conception in turn depended on the degree of education and the personal experiences of individuals. These were not circumstances which the agitators could themselves create or influence; they were results of the process of modernisation.

Along with these elementary and general conditions for successful agitation, four further factors must be mentioned, for taken together they were of decisive importance. The first was the successful course of Phase A: successful in so far as it clearly distinguished the nation-to-be from its neighbours, codified the language, provided basic information about the 'national' past, and so forth. The second was a basic level of vertical social mobility: some educated people must come from the non-dominant ethnic group without being assimilated. The third necessary condition was an increasing level of social communication, including literacy, schooling and market relations.

While these three conditions are more or less generally accepted as necessary to the nation-forming process, the fourth factor in national integration was more controversial. I have termed this factor a 'nationally relevant conflict of interests', i.e. a social or professional tension or collision that could be mapped onto linguistic divisions. Although I emphasised that these nationally relevant conflicts of interests 'definitely cannot be reduced to fundamental antagonisms' such as those between tenants and landlords, Gellner based his criticism of my book on the assertion that I had reduced history to the history of class conflicts and had explained the formation of nations as a result of such conflicts.[18] In any case, among the examples of nationally relevant conflicts of interests I pointed chiefly to conflicts which *cannot* be classified in the repertory of class conflict.[19]

Especially it was the conflict between new university graduates coming from a non-dominant ethnic group and a closed elite from the ruling nation keeping a hereditary grip on leading positions in the state. Further, I pointed to the tension between craftsmen belonging to the non-dominant group and the large traders and manufacturers belonging to the dominant nation.[20] To these instances may be added the tension between the towns and the countryside, between the centre and the provinces, and so forth.[21] Ultimately the struggle for positions of power may also be considered an interesting conflict.

In any case, I always used the phrase 'classes and groups' (i.e. social groups) in order to distance myself from a simplistic class 'reductionism'. On the other hand, I have searched the text in vain for the term 'class struggle' ascribed to me by Gellner.[22] Nor did I ever assert that the origin of the nation depended *exclusively* on the existence of nationally relevant conflicts of interests (they were only one of four factors), and in this connection I certainly never emphasised the class interest. Twenty-five years ago I considered 'the most outstanding and obvious result' of my empirical analysis to have been that 'no class or social group had a stable place in the structure of the patriotic communities'.[23]

In interpreting the response to national agitation, I do not consider it to be of fundamental importance whether we refer to artisans or officials as 'classes' or 'social groups'. What is important is to demonstrate that national agitation was more effective wherever the conflict of interests could be articulated in national terms. And conversely, wherever the issues were only those of language and culture, or where conflicts of interests were articulated not in national, but in political terms, national agitation encountered marked difficulties, and Phase B lasted much longer, as in the case of the Flemings or Welsh.

I fully agree with Gellner's view that history 'is rich in countless kinds of conflict', and that it cannot be reduced to class conflicts.[24] But unlike him I believe that conflicts between classes (that is, those social groups which are distinguished by the nature of the ownership of productive forces) also have their place among these 'countless' conflicts. This difference of opinion is only a nuance in the interpretation of nation-forming and without any fundamental importance. What is important, however, is that nationally relevant conflicts of interests can only be applied as a factor in nation-forming in the case of national movements, and not in the type of nation-forming which began in the context of the nation-state. Here – in France, England, Sweden and so forth – conflicts of interests did not acquire a national relevance: they were firmly confined to the social sphere and were sometimes articulated in the political sphere. Since Gellner failed to take account of my typological distinction between two basic processes of nation-forming, it is perhaps possible to accept his criticism of the relation between class and nation in conditions of 'industrialism' as far as the first 'French' type of nation-forming is concerned, but not for the type which was the object of my analysis and which I designated as 'national movements'.[25]

While Phase B of the national movement was chiefly a struggle for the very existence of the nation, Phase C decided the form that the emerging nation would take. This form was not defined merely by the political programme worked out by this or that national movement, which in Phase B inclined towards linguistic and cultural aims. For it was only in Phase C that most of the national communities achieved a fully formed social structure. National elites appeared: industrialists, financiers, large traders, high officials, scholars. Meanwhile, at least a part of the peasantry or yeomanry had been won over for the national community, and there were efforts to integrate the national working class. Phase C, then, was marked by three significant novelties: first, a political programme was formulated, in which nationalism (in the proper sense of the word) was established; secondly, the nation acquired a fully-formed social composition; and third, the working class – or more precisely, an organised socialist movement – appeared on the scene.

In my view, the rise of a working-class movement was not significant, as Gellner supposes, because it signalled the end of capitalism and the rise of socialism,[26] but rather because the socialists offered the only relevant alternative to a national identity and nationalism, namely, a class identity and internationalism. For the study of the factors which influenced the process of nation-forming – and especially for the study of the spread of a national identity among the popular masses – the fact that this alternative did not ultimately win out is completely irrelevant.

If class identity did not in most cases replace national identity, this has its reasons which are susceptible to analysis, though this theme exceeds the scope of the present chapter. Apart from this, the rise of the socialist workers' movement is also of significance for the study of the nation-forming process itself. The Austro-Marxists (above all Otto Bauer) were the first to criticise the myth of the eternal nation, and the Marxist discussion concerning the relation between the working class and the national movements set the agenda for the ensuing discussion of the phenomenon of 'nationalism'.[27]

That which we characterise as the political programme of the national movement contained several elements which emerged gradually and in connection with broad political changes within the given multiethnic state. The demand for local self-administration emerged quite early: the struggle for influence in 'City Hall' provided the first political school for most of the national movements. Another level of political demands was participation, which of course was only practicable within a constitutional regime. The demand for participation was followed by that for autonomy, that is, the possibility to take decisions within territory which the leaders of the national movement considered 'their own'.

If we accept Balibar's view that 'the bourgeoisie was always the state bourgeoisie',[28] it is logical that the demand for automony or statehood could appear in the programme of the national movement only after the social composition of the emerging nation had been completed, i.e. that it also included the bourgeoisie (or some parts of nobility as its substitute – as in the case of Hungary). Also connected with the completion of the social composition was the internal differentiation of political programmes, which found its institutional expression in the appearance of political parties. It is symptomatic, and part of the nature of national movements, that all the political parties emphasised general national interests along with their particular party demands.

When can we consider the national movement to have been finished? On the plane of theory, the usual answer is: after it has achieved all attributes of a fully-fledged nation. But on the concrete plane, the question remains of what we consider to be the fulfilment of the individual elements of the national programme. This is especially important for the political programme. While full linguistic equality and cultural emancipation can be achieved in conditions of political autonomy, it remains debatable whether we can consider autonomy to be the 'fulfilment' of the political demands. Surely much depends on the degree of autonomy. With Dualism, Hungary practically became a national state, so that here we may speak of a completion of the national movement. On the other hand, Finnish or Galician autonomy was far from being able to create the conditions for a full national self-administration.

Full independence in the form of a nation-state, then, was part of the political programme of only some of the European national movements (Norwegian, Polish, Irish), while in most cases the right of self-determination was limited to autonomy. If in spite of this most of the national movements in fact ended with the formation of a nation-state, this was not the fruit of a deliberate and long-term effort on the part of the national leaders; rather it was a consequence of external events. The disintegration of three multiethnic empires at the end of World War I (together with the policies of the Allied powers) opened the way to national independence. Therefore it is a mistake to project the outcome back into the past and assign credit for eventual state independence to all political programmes of the nineteenth century.[29]

In conclusion, I do not believe that my explanation of nation-forming was merely an unintended 'alternative vision' to Gellner's theory. On the contrary, it seems to me that our approaches to the basic question are concurrent: our shared view is that nation-forming must be explained and understood in the context of the great social and cultural transformation that ushered in the modern age. As a historian I cannot conceive of this transformation in the abstract but rather as a shift in relations among real, actually existing people, who had their specific interests and concrete social background, while their social and economic interests cannot be trivialised as a fiction or 'stereotype'. I also agree with Gellner that it would be a mistake to reduce the social and cultural situation to relations between the classes. However, such a reduction cannot be ascribed to me. The basic difference of opinion lies elsewhere: I cannot accept the view that nations are a mere 'myth', nor do I accept Gellner's global understanding of nationalism as an all-purpose explanation including categories of which the nation is a mere derivative.[30] The relation between the nation and national consciousness (or national identity, or 'nationalism') is not one of unilateral derivation but one of mutual and complementary correlation, and the discussion about which of them is 'primary' can, at least for the present, be left to the philosophers and ideologues.

NOTES

John A. Hall encouraged me to contribute to this collection an explanation of my conception of nation-forming, in part as an answer to Gellner's recent critique of my work. I complied only after hesitation, and I regret that my reply appears after the death of this outstanding scholar.

1 The book appeared in German in Prague in 1968: *Die Vorkämpfer der nationalen Bewegung bei den kleinen Völkern Europas. Eine vergleichende Analyse zur gesellschaftlichen Schichtung der patriotischen Gruppen*, Acta Universtatis Carolinae Philosophica et Historica, Monographia XXIV.

2 *Social Preconditions of National Revival in Europe: A Comparative Analysis of Patriotic Groups among the Smaller European Nations*, Cambridge, 1985.

3 Thus it is flattering but chronologically inaccurate for Gellner to see – as he does in *Encounters with Nationalism*, Oxford, 1994, ch. 14 – my book of 1968 as 'an alternative vision' to his own 1983 monograph.

4 Whether we apply to this process of transformation the term 'transition from traditional to modern society' or 'transition from agrarian to industrial society' is not, I think, of any great importance.

5 Typical in this respect is E. Kedourie, *Nationalism*, London, 1960.

6 The most noteworthy result of this trend in recent years was the interdisciplinary conference held in Santiago de Compostela in 1993, the papers of which appeared in two volumes as J. G. Beramendi, R. Maiz and S. M. Nunez, eds., *Nationalism in Europe: Past and Present*, Santiago de Compostela, 1994.

7 Gellner's characterisation of my book as a study of nationalism suggests a serious misunderstanding. I never used the word 'nationalism' because I do not consider it an appropriate tool for scholarly analysis. Nor does the content of my book deal with an attitude that I would characterise as 'nationalist'.

8 Gellner, *Encounters with Nationalism*, p. 199.

9 Ibid., pp. 185–6. Gellner's presupposition that I do not recognise the 'earlier roots' (i.e. the pre-modern stage) of national development is again the result of misunderstanding. In a book about the social composition of nineteenth-century patriots, which did not aim at developing a general theory, there was no reason to discuss earlier developments, except for occasional remarks at

the beginning of particular case studies – on which, see *Social Preconditions of National Revival*, pp. 33, 44, 86, 98, etc.

10 Gellner's understanding of the terms 'industrialisation' and 'industrial' differs from that of most historians. In his text they do not refer to the age in which machine production was introduced in the factories but to the appearance of new forms of enterprise, social mobility and shifts in ownership patterns – in other words, roughly the sense of the category 'transition to capitalist society'. This is also the source of his mistaken impression that I did not place the process of nation-forming in the context of this great transformation. This context was for me self-evident: the difficulty lies only in the fact that Gellner's term 'industrialisation' was not applied to the transformation. In fact, one result of my analysis was that industrialisation (in the sense of the introduction of machine production, the rise of a modern proletariat, etc.), as far as it coincided with Phase B of the national movement, had no demonstrable influence on a positive response from the masses to national agitation. On this see *Social Preconditions of National Revival*, pp. 169ff.

11 I originally used the term 'smaller nations' for this type of development but now prefer the more precise 'non-dominant ethnic group', the term popularised and in a way codified by the European Science Foundation's 'Comparative Studies on Governments and Non-Dominant Ethnic Groups in Europe, 1850–1950', whose results were published in a six volume series under the same title by New York University Press, Dartmouth, 1990.

12 To Gellner's remark that I have assigned feudalism and absolutism to one period (*Encounters with Nationalism*, p. 183), I can only note here that I analysed the relations between the two in a book co-authored with J. Petráň, *Das 17. Jahrhundert – Krise der Feudalgesellschaft*, Hamburg, 1981. Decisive for my not very different approach towards the problem of the formation of nations as part of the rise of modern society was that the absolutist system had more features in common with classical feudalism than with civic society.

13 I have analysed these and other elements of national demands in my latest study *V národním zájmu. Požadavky a cíle evropských národních hnutí v komparativní perspkktivě*, Prague, 1996.

14 This is a serious weakness of my work of 1968 – which, however, Gellner overlooks. But even from this model we cannot explain why some individuals decided in favour of the new identity and embarked on national agitation.

15 On this subject there is a suggestive book by the Finnish historian A. Kemiläinen, *Nationalism: Problems Concerning the Word, the Concept and Classification*, Helsinki, 1964, which of course limits itself to the 'major' languages.

16 In this modification I locate the rational nucleus of Gellner's suggestion (*Encounters with Nationalism*, pp. 195ff.) that 'rival conclusions' may be drawn from the empirical data that I collected.

17 Benedict Anderson's metaphor of 'imagined community' must also be interpreted in this sense. In accord with this is the concept of operationalisation formulated earlier by Gail Stokes in 'Cognition and the Function of Nationalism', *Journal of Interdisciplinary History*, vol. 4, 1976, pp. 530ff.

18 *Social Preconditions of National Revival*, p. 188; *Encounters with Nationalism*, pp. 196ff.

19 In any case, Gellner's critique contains no concrete examples of the class conflicts that he has in mind when labelling their role as a 'myth'.

20 *Social Preconditions of National Revival*, pp. 188ff.

21 M. Hechter, *Internal Colonialism: The Celtic Fringe in British National Development, 1536–1966*, London, 1975.

22 I never wrote the sentence 'Class struggle on its own led to no revolution . . . was similarly ineffective' which Gellner cites (*Encounters with Nationalism*, p. 197). The quotation from my book (p. 185) actually begins 'Conflicts of interest . . .' Nor can the sentence 'It is the presence . . . ' (cited by Gellner on the same page) be found in my book.

23 *Social Preconditions of National Revival*, p. 129.

24 *Encounters with Nationalism*, p. 199.

25 Ibid., pp. 198ff. In this connection should be considered Gellner's claim that I 'map' class and cultural differences as if they were 'really independent'. I am not sure what the term 'independent' signifies in anthropology, but from a historical perspective the two phenomena cannot be regarded as 'independent', since in that case we would be unable to explain the dynamic of their change. On the contrary, the concept of 'nationally relevant conflicts of interests' is based on their functional interdependence – or, in Gellner's phrase, on the assumption that 'class and cultural differences overlap'.

26 If, as Gellner correctly asserts (*Encounters with Nationalism*, pp. 194ff.), I never mentioned the 'victory of socialism' or a 'socialist nation' (though both phrases would have been welcomed by the regime at the time), this surely had its reasons.

27 O. Bauer, *Nationalitätenfrage und die Sozialdemokratie*, Vienna, 1907; E. Nimni, *Marxism and Nationalism: Theoretical Origins of a Political Crisis*, London, 1991, pp. 50ff.

28 E. Balibar and I. Wallerstein, *Race, Nation, Class: Ambiguous Identities*, London, 1991, p. 91.

29 The opinion that Gellner attributes to me (that national movements had to 'create their high culture before they could even strive for a state . . . ') seems somewhat teleological. In any case, I mentioned several examples of national movements beginning to strive for a state prior to their formation of a high culture (Norwegians, Greeks, etc.).

30 I believe that this brief contribution convincingly shows that Gellner's critical objections to my book are based partly on misunderstanding and partly on an inadequate interpretation of my terms and concepts. I consider some of them as a demonstration of his efforts to distance his explanation from Marxism, to which in his historical materialism he was methodologically (though not politically) closer than most of the authors who have dealt with the problem of 'nationalism'. In any case, on the level of methods and working procedures, the distinctions between Marxism, 'semi-Marxism' and historical materialism are matters more of definition than principle.

# VIII

## NATIONAL MINORITY MOVEMENTS AND THEIR AIMS

The problem of non-dominant ethnic groups and national movements is usually and often contemporarily characterized as being part of the broader issue of national, ethnic minorities. This is usually explained with the reasoning that these groups have a common trait: they form a numerically large minority on the territory of a state from whose ruling nation they differ by language, religion, as well as identification.

This sort of quantitative characteristic may be of some sense to contemporary experts in the field of minority rights, but for historical analysis it is rather more misleading, as it throws into one category such disparate groups as small nations on the one hand, and scattered immigrants on the other. Nevertheless, the use of the term „national minority" makes sense in an historical account only if it is used to designate a group that differs from the „majority" not only numerically, but rather and above all in terms of its qualitative characteristics: it was of course numerically „smaller", but more to the point it was „disadvantaged". At times the „majority" need not even have had a numerical advantage: it was enough that it held a decisive position, that power, prestige, etc. was concentrated in its hands.

Therefore, the term „minority" is unsatisfactory unless it is defined more precisely in a temporal and terminological sense. For our subject the temporal designation is especially important, as minorities and their activities became historically relevant precisely in their relationship to the national movement and eventually also in their relationship to its success in the form of the nation-state. We can, therefore, leave aside the situation of minorities in the period prior to the emergence of the national movement: we have already dealt with this issue to some extent in Chapter I in connection with ethnic identity. Moreover, for that earlier period it is more suitable to make use of the term ethnic group, or ethnic minority.

The issue of minorities itself involves two stages: the period of national movements, when the delimitation of minorities vis a vis the forming nations need not have been precise and enduring, and the period after the rise of nation states, which rounded off the nation forming process. In concrete terms, this means that it is necessary to differentiate between the problem of national minorities in the period leading up to World War I, and in the period between the two world wars (and as the case may be even after the Second World War). The interwar period is for understandable reasons of more peripheral significance for the problem of national movements, as it represents a time when the majority of these movements had already achieved their aims. Within the context of the theme of minority movements themselves, the exact reverse is of course true: it was in the interwar period that the national minorities moved into the forefront of political events and into the sphere of international relations.

It will be useful to at first leave aside periodization and to recapitulate the connections in which the term minority is used. In this way we determine which of these connections is substantial and relevant for comparison with the national movement. The term minority denotes significantly different groups and shared communities which we can break down according to four basic situations that also have their own subvariants:

1. The furthest from our subject is the interpretation of minority as a category for ethnic **migrants**, individuals who have come from abroad into an environment which is alien to them in ethnic, religious and cultural terms. These immigrants could have been integrated into society at various levels of the social ladder, from top academics to assistant labourers. Usually, however, they were unable penetrate the administrative system of the given state, or to participate in the political power struggle.

2. Ethnic groups whose members had for centuries lived **scattered** throughout territories that were inhabited in the majority by another ethnic group. This type includes two substantially different variants:

a) The minority was a **ruling elite** that in relationship to the majority ethnic group held a privileged position: German landowners and urban elites in the eastern Baltic, Ottomans on Greek territory, the Polish nobility in parts of Belorussia and the Ukraine. In this case, the national movement created a sort of „reverse situation" as the ethnic majority was mobilized against a numerical minority in the struggle for equality.

b) Conversely the scattered minority was formed of **groups without equal rights** who could not or did not wish to accept the identity of the majority: Jews, Roma. Sooner or later the activities of this minority began to acquire some features analogical to the national movement.

3. The minority inhabited a **compact territory** within a state from which the inhabitant substantially differed in ethnic terms. This group acknowledged during the period of the national movements a „mother nation", which inhabited the territory of another state, and there it formed either a state-nation or was forming itself through the national movement. Here we can also distinguish two variants that are not different typologically but rather in terms of their external, „technical" circumstances:

a) Minorities that lived along political borders separating them from their „mother nation". These **border minorities** fall among the classic examples of minorities in the interwar period, but we also have examples of them already in the period of the national movements: for example, Germans in Denmark, Romanians in Hungarian Transylvania, Serbs in the Hungary, Italians in Austria. A specific coincidence between this type of minority and the national movement is the case of the Polish national movement, which took its course as a parallel struggle of „minorities" on the territory of three foreign states.

b) Minorities that formed **linguistic islands**, whether in the form of towns or compactly distinct countryside (Germans in Hungary). Minority movements in the circumstances of linguistic islands appeared relatively rarely, perhaps for the reason that linguistic islands in multiethnic empires were common, and that the multiethnic empires were permeated both with islands inhabited by members of the state-nation and islands inhabited by members of the minorities.

In both variants the existence of a „mother nation", or its national movement, played a decisive role in activating minorities and their demands.

4. Ethnic groups inhabited a compact territory within a state to whose majority population, or ruling elites, they did not belong. They could not however acknowledge any „mother nation" outside the borders of this state. Of course, it is possible to characterize the position of most of the **non-dominant ethnic groups** in this way during the period prior to the rise of the national movements, but it is also the situation of the national movements themselves. At times this term is inappropriately applied to national movements that have already reached Phase C and acquired a complete social structure - thus for the stage when it is already possible to speak of a formed nation. So it is not a matter of a minority in the real sense of the word, and for this reason we are limiting ourselves to those ethnic groups whose members only weakly identified with one other (on the level of Smith's „ethnic category"), such as the Frisians, Sami and Galicians. It is also possible to include here groups whose Phase B had not been successful, that is to say those ethnic groups that initiated the national movement quite late, temporally falling rather into the period between and after the wars, and also groups whose national movement had indeed been active, but given their small numbers had no hope of success (Sorbians in Lusatia, Brittons etc).

For the period of the national movements, the minority movements that come into consideration are only those which fall within the third type - the border minorities and linguistic islands. „Minorities" included in the fourth type fall within the category of national movements, and that holds true even for the period after the First World War: even as such we must distinguish, in order to avoid a methodological error, the minority movements of Germans and

Hungarians in the newly emerged states, from the national movements of Croatians, Ukrainians or Slovaks. This is not to say that the organizational forms and demands of the minority movements essentially and substantially differed from the demands of national movements: the difference was in their political function and especially in the role in the process of the formation of modern nations. The similarity has its roots in the fact that ethnic minorities were actually a specific type of non-dominant ethnic group, so that in their further development they reacted to external impulses in a similar way.

For this reason, the analysis of minority movements and the issue of minorities in the period before World War I, will at the same time be an account of the roots of later minority movements: many of the demands and stereotypes of minority movements in the interwar period tied onto demands and stereotypes that were formed by national and minority movements in the preceding period. In this respect it is not possible to draw a precise temporal dividing line between both periods, so a series of connections and relationships will be derived also from development in the interwar period.

At first, however, it is necessary to characterize the **genesis of the situation of minorities**. Its starting point is the existence of the non-dominant ethnic group in a situation where the difference between 'H-' language and 'L\*'-language (in Fishman's terminology) became a matter of importance to the everyday lives of members of the non-dominant ethnic group. The position of the minority in the typological, and by no means the numerical, sense may here be applied from the beginning to all ethnic groups who used 'L\*'-languages, but who did not have their own literary 'H\*'-language. A national minority in the real sense of the word was realized of course when members of the non-dominant ethnic group whose 'H\*'-language had already been codified, but was applied as a state or at least established language **outside** the territory of the state in which they lived: in this sense, for example, Danes in Schleswig, Germans and Romanians in Transylvania, Slovenians in Italy, all became national minorities.

Given that this was a question of groups which belonged to an established, or forming, nation it will be suitable to here use the term **national** minority as a designation for that group which alongside the 'L\*'-language sooner or later began to rest their identity on the literary 'H\*'-language as well, which was used by their „mother nation". In this way the national minority differed from a minority that can be designated as **ethnic**: members of the latter group did not use nor even claim a codified 'H\*'-language. This was either because such a language had never emerged or because knowledge of it had never reached them: for example, Ruthenians in the Hungarian lands, non-Russian ethnic groups along the Volga, and Frisians etc. Also, at times the ethnic minority could be defined in religious terms, in which case the language factor was not decisive (Pomaks in Bulgaria, Muslims in Bosnia).

A basic difference between the ethnic and the national minority, expressed from the point of view of identification, lay in the fact that members of the national minority identified with the community of the „mother nation" that existed or took shape outside the state territory on which they lived. Conversely, members of ethnic minorities lacked (whether temporarily or permanently) such a national identity.

It is clear that the national minority (or its leaders) formulated demands that went beyond the framework of the state on whose territory they lived, and as a result it became the „subject" of international relations. The minority issue from this point of view was born only where and when this difference between the national minority and the „majority" nation became a subject and argument of political debate. The minority movement, its character and aims, should be analysed on three levels:
1. the degree of self-awareness and identification among the members of the national minority themselves,
2. the stance taken up by members of the state elites toward minorities, or by the politicians of the ruling nation of the very state on whose territory the minority lived,

3. the stance of politicians and intellectuals from the ranks of the „mother nation" toward the existence of the national minority which they considered as „their own", that is to say as a part of the community with which they identified.

These three levels at the same time represent three basic approaches that qualified the position and at the same time determined the fate and demands of the national minority.

1. An analysis of the process of **identification of the members of the national minority** must take into consideration above all the fact that no one is defined by one identity alone. Each individual has several identities that need not necessarily rule each other out, but instead form a sort of hierarchy. In it, some identities may be entirely compatible, among others there may exist to a greater or lesser degree some rivalry or tension. Concretely stated, the identification of members of a national minority could oscillate between a broader statewide identity and a narrower ethnic, or regional land one. In this the situation does not differ from the situations of members of non-dominant ethnic groups in the period of the national movement. A difference can be noted above all in the fact that the national minority did not strive to create its own independent nation, but identified themselves with the nation or the nation forming process that had its centre outside the territory of the state where the minority lived. By way of illustration we can introduce several examples.

Around the year 1900, the Czech-speaking inhabitants of Moravia had several identities. They were citizens of Austro-Hungary, members of the Czech nation, and they were Moravian, that is to say the inhabitants of an administratively and historically defined region, Moravia. These three identities were not mutually exclusive on condition that there were no external pressures in effect, such as the discrimination of Czech-speaking citizens on the statewide level, or phenomena such as Prague centralism and paternalism. Developments after 1918 showed that of the three identities here mentioned, national identity was the most stable, but that does not justify us in extrapolating back into the nineteenth century. The ultimate success of

Czech identity cannot be considered as sufficient evidence for the opinion that the Czech national identity occupied the highest position in the hierarchy of identities in Moravia throughout the nineteenth century. It does, however, demonstrate that during the nineteenth century (or earlier) there had already formed strong objective ties and relationships that prepared the way for the successful assertion of the Czech national identity.

Slovak-speaking inhabitants of the Hungarian lands could, as citizens, identify with the historical state of Hungary, but that did not prevent them from ethnically identifying with either the Slovak or the Czechoslovak nation. There also existed for a long time an eastern Slovak regional identity that was based on the specificity of local dialects, but this did not of course grow into a national movement. Slovak identity corresponded to the context of the national movement in order to obtain all the attributes of national independence for the Slovak nation. The Czechoslovak identity put the Slovak-speaking citizen, in the period before World War I, in the position of being a member of a minority that had its Czech „mother nation" in existence outside the boundaries of the Hungarian lands. After the emergence of an independent Czechoslovakia, the new state offered these citizens a new, Czechoslovak state identity that was, or should have been, a national identity at the same time. The Slovak identity was shifted into the position of being a regional identity and both national identities competed together. Over the course of the successful national movement the Slovak national identity took over, as we have seen.

The Lithuanian-speaking inhabitant of the former Polish state, who lived under Russian rule, preserved as a part of his collective memory the historical identity of the Polish-Lithuanian state, but at the same time maintained the no less historical, regional land consciousness with a Lithuanian orientation. To this was added the ethnic identify, which relatively late on - during the last third of the nineteenth century - began to take on the form of a national identity. At the same time, the Tsarist government demanded of him a state, or dynastic identity that was Russian. The Polish national movement offered Lithuanians the preservation of the priority of Polish state-nation identity, and relegated the identification with Lithuania to the sphere of regional identity. Unlike Czechoslovakism, however, this variant was unsuccessful from the very beginning of Phase B of the national movement. A strong national identity among Lithuanians already existed and prevented the renewal of the Polish-Lithuanian state.

In the case of Romanians and Serbs in the Hungarian lands, just like the Danes in German Schleswig (after 1864), a „true" minority situation was nonetheless born: two „national" identities clashed here, of which one was identical to the state identity and did not correspond to the ethnic identity, while the second was in opposition to the state identity but corresponded to the ethnic identity, and as long as the latter was accepted by at least part of the inhabitants, it became the basis of the minority movement. The minority movement exhibited characteristics similar to those we know from the national movement. It had a Phase of national agitation (Phase B) and a Phase of the mass movement, while the „mother nation" had usually already stood in for Phase A, a number of years earlier. This movement also formed its aims in the political, social and linguistic spheres, the difference being that these aims were not directed at forming an independent language and nation. Instead it aimed, in the linguistic sphere, toward the acceptance and preservation of the language of the „mother nation". In the political sphere the level of self-determination was not directed at creating an autonomous territory, but - insofar as objective circumstances allowed for it - at joining the „mother nation". This difference remained preserved also in the minority programmes during the interwar period.

In the creation of the minority programme and in the identification with the minority, the **picture of history** played a significant role: how was the past of the minority to be defined? Had the minority a history in common with the state or land, on whose territory they lived, or was its history in common with the „mother nation"? The inhabitants of the upper Hungarian lands could at the outset of the twentieth century consider their „national" history to be

Czech history, as long as they identified with the Czechoslovak nation. They could also, however, seek their history in German history, as long as they had already accepted the German identity. If they spoke Slovak, but identified with the Hungarian state, they could consider their history to be Hungarian history, and Slovak history as one of its parts. If in the hierarchy of identities the Slovak national identity was dominant, then it was necessary to yet define their national history and its territorial dimensions.

Historical consciousness helped the minority to bridge the social, political and at times also territorial distance separating them from the „mother nation". It perhaps had a decisive share in helping members of national minorities to often (though not always) identify with a personified nation, that is to say that they considered themselves a part of the „personality" of the „mother nation", and were accepted in this sense also by the „mother nation". Slovaks were (in the spirit of Czechoslovakism) supposed to consider the Premyslids as „their own" national kings, just as German barons in the Baltics were supposed to consider the Prussian kings as „theirs".

The basic precondition for the emergence of each movement of a national minority was the latent discontent of a part or all of the members of the minority, and the willingness (or opportunity) to seek the causes for this discontent in ethnic, national differences. Thus it was the feeling of being overlooked, discriminated against, and of being without rights on the basis of nationality, as was also typical for nationally relevant interest conflicts and their role in the national movements. At the forefront of these conflicts was - and more noticeably than in the national movements - the conflict between the centre and the provinces. The geographical position of the minority territory itself usually carried with it the possibility of it becoming an „internal colony" - whether in reality or only in the imagination of the leaders of the movement. Where there were no conditions for the emergence of nationally relevant interest conflicts, the minority movement was also relatively weak: the situation of Sorbians in Lower Lusatia, the Mazurs in Eastern Prussia, Ukrainians in the Hungarian lands. An important factor here was of course the level of intensity of social communication and the place occupied by the minority territory in its system.

2. National minorities did not of course inhabit a vacuum space. Of great importance was what kind of information actually entered into the system of social communications. The **stance of the ruling elites** was as equally important as the stance of the relevant „mother nation", and the position of the latter toward „its" national minorities was not in any way unambiguous or consistent. That portion of the ruling elites who had during the nineteenth century adopted liberal ideology and a liberal conception of the nation, viewed the assimilation of minorities as the best route to civic integration and providing equal rights for their members. It was through assimilation that equal opportunity for social ascendancy was to be guaranteed for all. At times the policy of assimilation was successful - especially in cases where it offered clear advantages, and where the opportunity to raise nationally relevant interest conflicts was weak. However, the pressure of assimilation sometimes had the reverse effect and instead provoked the activation of the minority movement.

Quite unlike this was the „tolerant" way in which conservative politicians approached minorities: the ethnic barrier ought to be preserved because it acted at the same time as an effective social barrier. This fact explains the compromises made in education and cultural policies. There was also of course a difference in the very idea behind state identity. While liberals appealed to statehood defined in national terms, conservatives remained true to a dynastic conception of the state, thus to a multiethnic empire that takes into a account the existence of national minorities and non-dominant ethnic groups as one of its obvious components.

The situation of minorities did, however, significantly change once nationalism penetrated into state ideology; in general this occurred around the end of the nineteenth century. In the name of national homogenization of the state, assimilation often became state policy, while liberal slogans of equal chances for all were at times still to be heard in the background. However, the idea predominated that in a strong nation-state there should be only one nation. It is enough to recall the assimilation policies of the Second German Reich, Tsarist Russia, the Hungarian lands, France and Italy.

How did the stance of the state-nation influence the programmes and demands of the minority movements? Liberalism did provide national agitation with space to move among the members of minorities, but it limited the response to this agitation in advance by offering the members of minorities advantages that would stem from their assimilation. Conservative governments limited the space for activities of minority movements (just as in the case of the activities of national movements) to a sphere outside of politics, that is to say that they were limited to demands in the linguistic, cultural and social spheres. The rise of nationalism did not automatically indicate the general assimilation of minorities. The success of assimilation policy depended on several circumstances that the government itself had no influence on: above all the degree of national mobilization that had already been achieved among members of the minority, the level of social communication as well, and finally the stance of the „mother nation".

Also of importance was the eventual difference in the cultural advancement of members of the minority in comparison with the ruling state-nation. If the culture of the state-nation significantly predominated over that of the members of the minority then assimilation was probable, especially if the national minority did not have its own educated elites. Conversely, if education, or the cultural level of the minority, were higher (which was conditional on the inclusion of higher social strata and the intelligentsia) then assimilation could not assert itself even under force. This explains why the Russification policies from the 1880s achieved few results in Finland and the Baltics, in comparison with German and French assimilation policies. It also helps us to understand why the Magyarizing policy in the Hungarian lands after 1870 was more successful among the Slovak than the German ethnic group.

It is sometimes claimed that the main precondition for solving the minority issue is the process of persistent democratization. This claim is only substantiated if a democratic constitutional regime does not subject members of minorities to forced assimilation and the restriction of human rights. The principle of parliamentary democracy itself of course has from the viewpoint of the minority a disadvantage in that it assumes that each minority can potentially, with the decision of the electorate, turn into a ruling majority. This of course is not true in the case of national minorities if their participation in politics is above all defined in terms of national identity. Moreover, if the minority had no constitutionally embedded protection against the danger of the long-term „majoritization" of the state-nation, then the political programme became radicalized. Therefore, the introduction of a constitutional regime was not an automatic „solution" for the position of national minorities, as neither it was in the case of national movements.

3. The third decisive factor was the **stance of the „mother nation"** toward the national minorities that identified with it. This stance transformed itself over time and was also dependent on the degree of development of the „mother nation" itself. If the nation forming process had achieved that degree of development where the nation became in the eyes of the majority of its members a personalized authority, it was possible for the position of national minorities to be interpreted as a part of the fate of the nation itself. They were adopted, so to speak, and support of them could be reasoned as a „national interest". Such a stance could be a part of inner state or even foreign policy when the formation of the nation had already reached complete statehood: therefore, in the case of state-nations in the nineteenth century, and in the case of nation-states only in the following century. Particularly in German and Italian foreign policy the protection of minorities became a pretext for aggressive expansion. To a limited extent we can say the same about Serbian, Greek or Bulgarian policies.

The stance of the „mother nation" toward the minorities abroad, as well as its stance toward foreign minorities living on „its" political, or state, territory, was influenced by one other factor: this was the concept of national affiliation. What criteria prescribed this national „belonging"? If the criterion for belonging was a fictitious blood tie, that is to say ethnic origin, then even a minority living on a very distant territory was considered as part of the nation, thus as a group that required support. This was so in the German, Hungarian and Serbian cases. If the criterion was membership in the state and place of birth, then the relationship to their own minorities abroad was much more restrained.

We can note this difference even in the relationship to foreign minorities living on the territory of the „mother nation". Affiliation determined by „blood" inevitably led to the opinion that foreign minorities constituted an uncomfortable heterogeneous body that interfered with national integrity, and therefore, it was necessary to assimilate them. Conversely, national affiliation defined in state terms de facto did not recognize longstanding ethnic minorities: if someone was born in France, according to this conception they were French. This is the source of the urgency and explosiveness of the problem of national minorities in Central Europe.

It was that region which became in the interwar period a sort of „laboratory" for finding solutions to the ethnic problem. If this problem is to be systematically analysed it is necessary to start with an assessment of the ratio of power between the state-nation, the „mother nation" and the national minority. If we assume that the national minority had been activated and had formulated its cultural and political demands, the degree of its success also depended on what was the **proportion of strength** between its „mother nation" and the state on whose territory it lived. For this there is a valid and simple model for three possible situations:

- the „mother nation" was clearly stronger than the state-nation on whose territory the minority lived
- the „mother nation" was clearly weaker than the nation state, either because it was numerically weaker, or because it had not yet achieved complete national existence
- between both units there was a rough balance in the ration of power

For the rise and radicalization of minority movements the first situation was quite favourable and facilitated the formation of extreme political demands, even for secession, which is to say, for the revision of state borders (understandably in the case of „border minorities"). The activity of German minorities in Poland and Czechoslovakia fall into this category.

For the second situation, the opposite holds true. The minority movement was unable to count on any significant help from the „mother nation", and had difficulties already in its agitation Phase. The national identity of the minority at times remained indefinitely formed and opened the door to assimilation. Such was the development of the Slovenian minority in Italy, the Ukrainian in the Hungarian lands, the Flemish and Basque in France. Elsewhere, solid support for the developed but oppressed minority movement was impeded by a simple power imbalance: an example could be found in the Danes in Schleswig (after 1864), or the Irish in Ulster. A noteworthy variant is that of the development, when over time the power relation was reversed: until World War I, the Italian-Austrian conflict over the southern Tyrol favoured the stronger German „mother nation" (even though it was a question in state terms of Austrian territory), but after the war it became an affair between a stronger Italy and a weaker Austria.

The third situation was probably the most complicated. The success of the minority movement depended on how the state and „mother" nations came to terms with each other. A solution through compromise was quite rare. We know of this as a lasting state in the example of the Swedes in Finland. In the majority of cases however, the question of minorities became a source of chronic tension, whether between Hungary and the successor states in the interwar period, or between Austria and Yugoslavia, between Czechoslovakia and Poland, between Greece and Bulgaria.

It would, however, be a mistake to restrict the analysis of the issue of minority movements and their demands to the question of power relationships. A consequential factor was also that of **mentality**. A minority that identified with its „mother nation" usually also gained its culture, but also its history and the stereotypes and prejudices along with it. The burden of history was particularly heavy where members of a former state-nation became the national minority in the nation-state, and the former members of the non-dominant ethnic group became the state forming power. After 1918, Germans in Poland and Czechoslovakia, just like Hungarians in Romania and Yugoslavians in Czechoslovakia, were unable to come to terms with this reversal. A certain analogy can be found contemporarily in the stance of Russian minorities throughout the former Soviet Republics, and the Serbian minorities in Croatia and Bosnia.

It generally holds true that the problem of national minorities as being politically relevant really emerged only as a „side product" of the success attained by the national movements at the end of World War I (an analogous situation emerged for the second time after 1989). It would however - for reasons we have already presented - be a mistake if we were to approach them as a phenomenon of our century. These minority movements inherited the spirit of the previous century, and more than once directly linked themselves up with the national movement of their „mother nations". An essential difference was that to a much greater extent than before they became the subject of Great Power interests.

The mentalities of national and ethnic minorities were not conditioned only historically but also socially. Similarly to the case of the non-dominant ethnic group, in the case of minorities the shape of the social structure was also very important. Minorities primarily made up of rural inhabitants were relatively difficult to mobilize for national aims, and long remained on the level of Phase B, while they were often left to the agitators who came from the ranks of the „mother nation". If the minority movement arose at all, it pursued social and linguistic aims above all. National minorities that had a complete or near complete social structure were mobilized very quickly. Their programme often included quite radical political demands, including even secession, obviously on condition that the minority could count on sufficient support from its „mother nation", as was the case with the German and Hungarian minorities mentioned above.

For the time being we have occupied ourselves with national minorities whose aims and activities are comparable to those of national movements, and which became an important factor in political history. To be thorough it is also necessary to mention minorities that in no way participated significantly in shaping the political or cultural profile of their time. These were especially those minorities that we categorized as scattered minorities. Their members also reacted to their own minority situation, but this reaction was in no way uniform.

Some minorities protected their individuality by isolating themselves from their surroundings, without their leaders organizing any movement: this was especially the case with the not very numerous clear cut minorities such as, for example, Armenians in Galicia or Vlachs in the Balkans. Other minorities opted for the strategy of living in two worlds: their members preserved their cultural specificity and internal ties with the group, but at the same time participated in the life of the state-nation and partially accepted linguistic assimilation. This was the approach of the majority of Jews before the emergence of Zionism. The third type of minority stance was closest to ethnic minority movements: it was an effort to preserve linguistic and cultural independence within the framework of the give state unit (Sorbians in Lusatia, Turks in the Balkans, Tatars in Russia, etc).

* * *

By way of conclusion we will try to characterize the specificity of the programmes and demands of the national movements of minorities. As has already been said, these movements were in many ways analogous to national movements, they ran their course along the lines of an analogous periodization, but it is also necessary to take into consideration differences stemming particularly from the fact that the national minority did not claim the right to become a nation, but rather strove to acquire certain group rights, especially in the cultural and political spheres.

Given that the aim of the minority movement was not that of obtaining all the attributes of national existence - these were gained or striven for by their „mother nation" - we cannot expect that their demands, or more precisely the demands of the leaders, will present a true copy of the programme of the national movement. Even among these demands we can nonetheless distinguish linguistic, political and social demands. Where did their specificity lie?

In the case of the linguistic programme, the task of codifying and intellectualizing the national language was dropped: it was enough to accept this language from the „mother nation". In return however, the struggle to get the language into schools and administration gradually came up on the agenda. In both instances of course, the language question on the territory of the national minority was interlocked with the question of the ruling language and also with the historical background of the minority. When it was a matter of a minority movement that had grown out from the roots of a local ethnic minority with an incomplete social structure, the national movement satisfied itself with the demand for language rights on the local level - in schools and local administration. When the minority was made up of members of the former ruling nation, linguistic equality was demanded for the entire territory they had formerly dominated (Swedes in Finland, Germans in the Czech lands).

Among political demands, the most frequent concerned the level of participation, especially in local and regional self-administration. The demands of made by representatives of the national minority to decide themselves on their own affairs opened the way to a programme for political autonomy. Minorities, however, up until World War II were not permitted this - usually on the grounds that it would interfere with the integrity of the nation-state. A serious argument against permitting political autonomy was the fear that the „mother nation" could make use of the autonomous territory of „its" minority to strengthen its power influence. The demand for self-determination had of course also its own extreme form: understandably in favour not of independence, but secession, annexation to the territory of the „mother nation".

This brings us to the most relevant difference between the demands of national and minority movements: **the role of the external factor**. The structure of demands of the minority movement as well as the path to meeting them was markedly determined by the stances and the ratio of power outside the minority itself - by the bilateral interest conflict of the „mother nation" and the interest of the nation-state. The significance of minority movements in international relations was rather low, and can be compared only to the significance of the national movements in the Balkans.

# IX

# How Much Does Nation Formation Depend on Nationalism?

Roman Szporluk's book touches on a sensitive issue in the history of Marxist thought. Because of this, and because it is based on a broad knowledge of Marx's and Engels's works, it enhances the already rich literature dedicated to the problem of nations and nationalism. In the contrast between the views of Marx and Engels on the one hand and Friedrich List on the other, Szporluk sees a concentrated form of the tension between internationalism and nationalism. He convincingly discusses the historical development of nations in the second half of the nineteenth century as being more consistent with List's ideas than with those of Marx and Engels in 1848, but he is less convincing in discussing why Marxist theory and practice allegedly abandoned an internationalist position in favor of "nationalism."

Szporluk's book has three components: a comparison of the views of Marx and List; a study of the mechanism of the rise of modern "nationalism"; and the present state of views on the nationality problem in the Soviet Union. In the following I shall deal only with the first of these, since the third abandons the field of history in favor of politics, for which I lack the knowledge and qualifications. In this instance, I believe the author also lacks some of these prerequisites.[1]

There is no point in enumerating here the things with which I agree and in developing at length my opinion that the book is inspiring,

1. I have two critical comments concerning the last chapter. 1) We can not reach reliable conclusions if we analyze the nationality problems in Russia and the USSR without analyzing more deeply Lenin's view on this question, particularly his contributions from pre-revolutionary times (e.g., his discussion with R. Luxemburg, "The Right of Nations to Self-Determination," in V.I. Lenin, *Collected Works*, 4th ed. [Moscow, 1964], p. 20). Had he done so, the author would more likely have come to the view that Marxism-Leninism used the national movement as an ally, and would not have stated that "Marxism-Leninism became a variant of nationalism" (p. 225). As a matter of fact, E. Lemberg expressed this view twenty years earlier: "Stalinismus als Wiedergeburt des Nationalismus," (*Nationalismus,* Vol. 1, *Psychologie und Geschichte* [Hamburg, 1964], p. 232). 2) It would be useful in analyzing the contemporary nationality problem to distinguish between theory and practice, which, although they influence each other, are not identical.

intelligently written, and well founded, at least the first three-quarters of it. Instead I shall concentrate on the central points of Szporluk's analysis that I consider debatable and on views I do not share with Szporluk, or, better said, views that are not entirely clear to me.

It is clear why Marx and List would differ in their attitudes toward social reality in the 1840s. Whereas List considered the rise and permanent existence of big national states a historical necessity, even the optimal type of development, Marx and Engels were concerned with the transformation of capitalism as a class society. Marx and Engels regarded the creation of national states as an unnecessary detour on the path to a universal society. Still, where national states already existed, Marx and Engels considered them historical givens with which one had to reckon. For example, even when Engels in 1849 unambiguously rejected the right of small "non-historical" nations to a future independent existence, he also spoke about the "free development of all the reserves of the big nations." For this reason Szporluk errs by attributing to Marx the view that the state and the nation form an entity which cannot be analyzed "within itself" (p. 49). One need only recall *Class Struggle in France, 18th Brumaire,* and Engels's studies on Germany and Poland to realize that Marx and Engels could analyze issues in national frameworks. Furthermore, their predictions about the fate of the nation after the proletarian revolution are not unequivocal either. They expected the end of hostility among nations, and they projected the merging of nations at some time in future, but in many places where they spoke about concrete developmental issues, they recognized that nations would exist in the future. Therefore, even in the period prior to 1848, I cannot accept without reservation Szporluk's assertion that Marx and Engels assumed that "hostility between nations will disappear together with the nations themselves" (p. 68). They unambiguously rejected a national future only for one group: nations under foreign political and economic rule. But we shall return to this question.

It seems to me that Szporluk overemphasizes the antagonism between Marx and List. I see no basic difference between the young Marx saying, "What the nations have done as nations they have done for human society" (p. 32), and List saying that the nation stands between the individual and humanity. Similarly, where Marx says the German philistine "puffs himself up into being the 'nation' " (p. 34), this is not to say Marx negates the nation. He was only criticizing the fact that the bourgeoisie passes off its interests as those of the whole nation while at the same time sacrificing the interests of the nation's other components (p. 40). Furthermore, in later life Marx and Engels revised their negative attitude towards nation. Whereas Szporluk takes note of this shift, his desire to exaggerate the contrast between Marx and List leads him to devote far more attention to the radical views of the young Marx.

One of the difficulties of Szporluk's interpretation involves terminology. Szporluk is right when he states that Marx "never found time to present his understanding" of the term "nationality." We might add that the same thing could be said about the terms nation, peoples, and *Völker*. But a good deal can be inferred from the context in which these terms are used, as the classic work of S. F. Bloom did so well.[2] Let me give at least one example. Szporluk regards as incomprehensible the contradiction between the following two statements in *The German Ideology:* "Bid industry destroyed the peculiar individuality of various nationalities," and "The bourgeoisie of each nation retained national interests."[3] Yet an explanation is quite simple. Nationality (*Nationalität*), as used here, means the remains of ethnic groups that did not have their own state or even their own ruling class, whereas "Nation" indicates a great nation with its own state and a full social structure.

Another terminological problem centers on the term nation, which has a different meaning in French and English than it does in the German and Slavic languages. Unlike Marx and Engels, Szporluk, in the spirit of the English language, tends toward a spontaneous identification of the "state" and the "nation," although he is well aware of the difference. Thus, for instance, in his view "nationalist movements" endeavored to create their own states, and he uses the term "nation-building" as a synonym for "state-building" (p. 158). Such an identity, however, was not generally true in the nineteenth century.

One should approach the texts of Marx and Engels as sources, that is, in the historical context in which they appeared. It is understand-

2. S. F. Bloom, *The World of Nations. A Study of the National Implications in the Work of Karl Marx* (New York, 1941), chapter 2.
3. It would be useful if the author would analyze the German texts, not English translations. So, for instance, the above quotations in German: "[Die grosse Industrie . . .] erzeugte im Allgemeinen überall dieselben Verhältnisse zwischen den Klassen der Gesellschaft und vernichtete dadurch die Besonderheit der sinzelnen *Nationalitäten*. Und endlich, während die Bourgeoisie jeder *Nation* noch aparte nationale Interessen behält . . ." ("Deutsche Ideologie," in *Marx-Engels Gesamtausgabe*, I, Abt., Bd. 6 [Berlin, 1932], p. 50. There are further examples.

able that terms that were not precisely defined before 1850, such as nation, nationality, and *Volk,* might have been used somewhat differently in different situations. It is logical, for instance, that in addresses delivered at the Festival of Nations in London Marx and Engels would emphasize the prospect of a lasting fraternity rather than, say, economic and commercial antagonisms among nations. It seems to me that Szporluk does not give sufficient weight to the fact that opinions and judgements can have different relevances according to the situation. One cannot place views expressed in theoretical analyses on the same level as those aired in the heat of polemic, as was the case, for example, in Marx's criticisms of the political attitudes of the conservative leaders of national movements in 1848–49.

A more fundamental problem, perhaps, and one common to Western historians in general, is Szporluk's effort to contrast "nationalism" to "communism." I do not believe that the problem he wishes to attack can be expressed by counterposing these two phenomena so baldly, just as it cannot be personalized into differences between Marx and List. One way to understand the contrast Szporluk is interested in would be to contrast Marxism on the one hand and bourgeois protectionism on the other. Or to put it differently: in the relation between Marx and List the contradiction between the goal of liberating the proletariat and the aim of the bourgeoisie to establish a civil society is personalized. If in discussing this issue we use the term "nationalism," then we distort rather than clarify these relations.[4] The term is simply too ambiguous. Some of the views and opinions that are usually covered by this term are actually opposed to Marxism, but others are not. Especially after 1860, for example, we can hardly put the positive attitude toward their homeland among the leaders of a working-class movement in the same category as the "nationalism" of the bourgeoisie of the same country fighting against British commercial domination.

Similarly, one cannot draw a parallel between the class struggle on the one hand and the contradictions between nations on the other, if only because the theory of class struggle leaves no room for compromise and

---

4. Szporluk does not say which of the many meanings of nationalism he is using. Cf. A. Kemiläinen, *Nationalism, Problems Concerning the Word, the Concept and Classification* (Jyväskylä, 1964); H. A. Winkler, ed., *Nationalismus* (Königstein/Ts, 1985), 2nd ed.; E. Lemberg, *Nationalismus,* 2 vols. (Hamburg, 1964); O. Dann, ed., *Nationalismus und sozialer Wandel* (Hamburg, 1978).

friendship between antagonistic classes, whereas relations between nations can be either hostile or cooperative. Cooperation between nations was not only List's program, it was Marx's and Engels's as well, although theirs was based on a different type of social relations. In this instance, too, the contrast between Marx and List is not as striking as Szporluk claims. A clear contrast does appear, of course: Marx and Engels, in contrast to List, interpreted the conflict among nations as a conflict between the special interests of each nation's ruling class (bourgeoisie). What Szporluk terms Marx's internationalism is not the absolute negation of nation, nor does it exclude adherence to a nation or the existence of nations. One might better term the attitude of young Marx to the future of nations as ambivalent, or ambiguous, not simply negative. It was surely not the polar opposite of what Szporluk terms "nationalism."

I admit that I have a certain difficulty in understanding the term "nationalism" as it is used not only by Szporluk, but by most historians in the Anglo-Saxon tradition. Thus, for example, Szporluk states that "Marx failed to notice that nationalism already became a major force that mobilized masses around its goals and ideals." But what was "nationalism" in the period of Marx's youth? If Szporluk wants to say that Marx did not appreciate the importance and possible success of national movements prior to 1850, one could understand. But insofar as the author conceives "nationalism" as a historical force which "was changing actual social reality" (p. 75), then he is on uncertain ground. How is it possible to make an idea we cannot define the determining force of history? If we ourselves have difficulty with the term, we can hardly accuse Marx of not finding "nationalism" the moving force of social development. The problem here is epistemological: how are we to determine what was or no longer is "nationalism?" The classical thinkers in the nation-building tradition, such as Carlton J. H. Hayes, distinguished variants of "nationalism" by using adjectives (liberal, conservative, economic, integral). From these, at least, one can imagine what the author was thinking of when he used the term.[5]

Chronology presents another problem. Hans Kohn linked nationalism with the French Revolution.[6] But what is the difference between the set of stereotypes at the beginning of the nineteenth century that we

5. Carlton J. H. Hayes, *The Historical Evolution of Modern Nationalism* (New York, 1931).
6. H. Kohn, *Die Idee des Nationalismus. Ursprung und Geschichte bis zur Französischen Revolution* (Frankfurt, 1962).

106     *Nation Formation and Nationalism*

designate as "nationalism" and the stereotypes that characterized the mentality of Flemish burghers in the fourteenth century, the Czech Hussites, the Swedish fighters against the Kalmar Union, of the Dutch, Polish, and other patriots in the years before the French Revolution?[7] The difference—and this is fundamental—was not in the ideas and stereotypes, but in the social bearer of the ideas and stereotypes. From the time of the French Revolution this bearer was the nation "as a sovereign people," that is, an ensemble of equal citizens. If Szporluk notes that nationalism "gradually won approbation in the many parts of Europe," then one must ask why this occurred precisely in the nineteenth century?

The question of the emergence of the nation and its character is fundamental. Briefly, I regard as decisive these transformations that on the threshold of modern times led to the weakening and demise of patriarchal and feudal relationships. This was the result not only of the advance of capitalist enterprise and of industrialization, but of other encroachments as well, such as the reforms of enlightened absolutism. Whether one classified the overall phenomenon as the advance of capitalism or the process of modernization, new bonds among people and new views of society arose as an integral part of this process of social transformation. As far as "nation-building" goes, two factors were of particular importance:

1)  the subjective need of a growing number of individuals to find a new object of social identification after the loss of their traditional social and political ties to the village, to the feudal lord, or to the guild;

2)  the objective fact that the ever more distant regions were brought into contact with each other through advances in transportation, expanding markets, industrialization, and increased contacts with state authorities, producing greater territorial and social mobility and an increase in social communication.

7. E. Lemberg, *Wege und Wandlungen des Nationalbewusstseins. Studien zur Geschichte der Volkwerdung in den Niederlanden und in Böhmen* (Münster, 1934); J. Huizinga, "Aus der Vorgeschichte des niederländischen Nationalbewusstseind," in *Wege der Kulturgeschichte* (Munich, 1930); J. Tazbir, "National Consciousness in the 16th–17th Centuries," *Acta Poloniae Historica*, 46 (1982); H. Pietschmann, "Zum Problem eines frühneuzeitlichen Nationalismus in Spanien. Der Widerstand Kastiliens gegen Karl V.," in O. Dann, ed., *Nationalismus in vorindustrieller Zeit* (Munich, 1986).

Simultaneously with the rise in social communication, school attendance expanded, and, therefore, literacy. Language grew in importance not only as a means of understanding, but also as an elementary distinguishing criterion between "We" and "They." As literacy increased, so did the importance of a selected standard literary language. Of course, language was not the only distinguishing criterion. In Ireland and the Balkans, for example, religion was a differentiating factor as well.

The fact that some educated persons, officials, or politicians displayed a national awareness, however, cannot be regarded automatically as proving the existence of a nation, nor that the nation-building process was thereby predestined for success. Only if these patriotic individuals regarded the nation as a value sufficiently unique that they were willing to work to win others over to their conviction can we consider their identification as the beginning of the nation-building process. Even then, however, the result was not certain. What was decisive was that the people, and not just the ruling class, approved the new view and began to identify with the new community. The idea of nation had to correspond with the real possibility of the existence of the large social group, the community of the nation. That is, behind successful nation-building stands the reality of increased social communication that results from the development of capitalism. If such ties did not exist, and there were such cases, then what emerged was only a region within a larger political organism, the "big nation." A nation could not emerge without a previous and often long-lasting elaboration of linkages among the potential members of the nation; without a process of social communication and social mobility; and without a capitalist (*bürgerlich*) transformation of the old regime and the transformation of unfree serfs into free and equal citizens.[8] It is only in this sense that one can claim that without a national consciousness ("nationalism") of intellectuals a modern nation could not emerge.[9]

The underlying tempo of the transformation, that is to say, depended on economic development, but this was certainly not the sole determining factor in the pace of change, particularly in the process of

8. In this context, I accept Deutsch's model.
9. Here it might be possible to apply Gale Stokes's term "operationalism," which in a broader sense meant that certain groups of people were capable of expressing their really existing interests in terms of the "interest" of a broader community—a nation. Such group interests were articulated as demands intending to serve the success of a national movement. G. Stokes, "Cognition and the Function of Nationalism," *Journal of Interdisciplinary History* 4 (1975), p. 532.

identification with the new, national entity.[10] With gradual modernization there was a strengthening of linguistic, cultural and administrative
ties within certain territorial entities that might or might not be political or state entities. And this process was not simultaneous. The transformation was stronger in some states than others, later in some regions
than others. For example, changes in the capacity for communication
influenced the nation-building process faster where there had existed an
earlier identification with a feudal state. Feudal or territorial patriotism
(*Landespatriotismus*) was, of course, limited only to members of the
politically privileged ruling class and the educated people who served
them. Sometimes the term "proto-nationalism" is used to describe this
relationship, since it implies stereotypes that were later taken over by
members of modern nations.[11] The attitude of members of a modern
nation differs from "proto-nationalism," however, in that the object of
identification has become the collective, a community of equal citizens.
The great French Revolution was a milestone in creating this notion
(one should not overlook the American Revolution either), because
after it the new idea of adherence to a national entity did not have to
draw on a previous *Landespatriotismus* or proto-nationalism. Its source
also might have been an outside influence or model, especially where
the nation-building process took place later.

Nation-building went on in Europe, therefore, along two basic
paths. The first took the form of the transformation of a feudal state
into a modern civil (*bürgerlich*) state. The new ruling class, the "third
estate," worked against the *ancien régime* and proclaimed itself the representative of the entire nation. The new society of citizens was organized
as a national community with social interests in relation to other,
similar communities. In other words, development towards a modern
society went on parallel with development towards a modern nation.
This French model, or as I prefer to think of it, "ruling nation" model,
was often considered the sole, or better said, typical path of national
development, but in actuality it was not.

10. M. Hroch, *Obrozeni malych evropskych národů*, I (Prague, 1971).
11. About proto-nationalism in general see J. Huizinga, "Patriotisme et Nationalisme," in *de
    Europese Geschiedenis tot het Einde der negentiende Eeuw* (Haarlem, 1940); C. L. Tripton, ed.,
    *Nationalism in the Middle Ages* (New York, 1972); B. Zientara, "La conscience nationale en
    Europe occidentale au Moyen Age," *Acta Poloniae Historica*, 46 (1982); J. Szücs, *Nation und
    Geschichte* (Cologne and Vienna, 1981); O. Dann, *Nationalismus in vorindustrieler Zeit*, Intro-
    duction.

The second path took place in nations that did not have a proto-nationalist tradition. In this equally legitimate and typical process the creation of a nation and "nationalism" occurred, usually on the territory of an imperial state, not in a linear manner but in the confrontation of alternatives.[12] In this situation two and sometimes even three possibilities of national identification faced the inhabitants of what we have called "small nations." At the time they were formed into modern nations these peoples:

1) did not have a ruling class of their own ethnic group, so that the social structure of the nation was incomplete;
2) did not inhabit an administratively defined political subunit that matched the extent of their ethnic population;
3) lacked a continuous tradition of cultural production in their own literary language.

Because of these weaknesses, the rise of capitalism did not liberate these groups nationally, but placed them under the rule of a new foreign ruling class, the bourgeoisie of another ethnic background.

The nation-building process in this second type, the "small nation," took the form not only of agitation, but of a struggle by the patriots of the nation to provide the missing attributes of full national existence. We call this—the struggle for equal rights, for national language and culture, for a share in economic prosperity, for social liberation and for political autonomy—a *national movement*. According to the content of the demands and the level of response, we distinguish three phases of the national movement: Phase A, the scholarly phase; Phase B, the national agitation phase; and Phase C, the era of the mass national movement. Anglo-Saxon terminology would use "nationalist" for each of these phases of this one variant of nation formation, but subsuming essentially separate phases under the one term limits our ability to understand the considerable variety in the process of nation-formation.

There is a third model of nation-building beyond the two already mentioned (ruling and small nation), a situation in which only one of the three deficits mentioned above was missing, i.e., state unity and

12. For a more detailed discussion see M. Hroch, *Social Preconditions of National Revival in Europe* (Cambridge, 1985).

independence. Such was the case with Germany, Italy, Poland, and Hungary (in the last case cultural-linguistic background was missing as well). Still, these nations had their national movements, including a Phase B and a Phase C in which they won over the masses for the idea of a nation. But whereas one might have predicted success for these movements, the success of a small nation during Phase B was not self-evident. What did success or failure depend on? It cannot be explained simply by the personal abilities and enthusiasm of patriots, nor even solely on the extent of social communication. One must take into account in addition a factor that I term "a nationally relevant conflict of group interests." By this I mean social interest conflicts that coincided during Phase B with linguistic, or sometimes religious, conflicts. A frequent example of such a nationally relevant conflict is that between young academicians from a small nation, and therefore from lower strata, and the closed elite of the ruling nation that maintains itself in the most prominent social positions by inheritance. Another is the conflict between the peasant of the small nation and his feudal lord, who belonged to the ruling nation. Another is the conflict between craftsmen belonging to one national group and large-scale trade and industry in the hands of another.

I admit that it is not possible to find in the sources proof for every instance of a direct relationship between national activity and social interest contradiction. My evidence is mostly indicative. But neither am I merely speculating. By a comparative analysis of the social structure of national movements I came to the understanding that besides personal enthusiasm, mobility, and social communication there must also be another factor, an "x factor." This factor acted with different intensity and changed over time, and it was linked to various nations or social milieux, but the common feature of the groups that most actively accepted and supported national agitation was precisely this nationally relevant conflict of interests. Since this contradiction has its roots outside the sphere of national existence and "nationalism" we cannot speak here of a tautology.

I have written at length here about differentiation in the nation-building process for three reasons. In the first place I would like to maintain that the term "national movement" is more functional in analyzing the process than "nationalism." In the second place I would like to call attention to the differentiated reality that stood behind the views of the young Marx on the nationality question. And in the third place I would like to demonstrate that the term "nationalism" in the nineteenth century hides a dual content. I do not have in mind Kohn's dichotomy, but rather the difference between the national consciousness in a ruling class and in a small nation. When we speak of the process in small nations, national awareness has the function of an instrument in the struggle headed by the leaders of the suppressed nationality (ethnic group) for language equality and for cultural and administrative emancipation. And in this struggle for the rights of the weaker and the worse off the motive of political and social justice was not lacking. Therefore it comes as no surprise that this type of national movement, this type of "nationalism," was acceptable to many leaders of the working-class movement within the small nation, if only sometimes as an ally.

Another difficulty in determining the relationship between a nation and its "nationalism" (and their definitions) lies in the contrast between the changing character of the nation as a developing community and the static character of "nationalism." The nation's internal class structure changes, as does its cultural ties and relations with the world that surrounds it. In contrast, nationalism is a relatively stable set of stereotyped views and attitudes. Nationalism, even though the word ends in "ism," is neither a philosophical nor a political trend, as are, for example, liberalism, Marxism, or positivism. It takes its place, as Benedict Anderson says, "alongside such categories as kinship and religion."[13] Eugen Lemberg, whom Szporluk does not cite, defined nationalism as being "eine bedingungslose Hingabe an eine über individuelle Instanz."[14] Nationalism is a new concept, one of the twentieth century, and not really appropriate to the nineteenth. On the basis of the analysis given above, I prefer the term national movement, which expresses the purposeful activities of people and which can be internally periodicized and differentiated according to the objectives it pursues. There is nothing of this in the ordinary western use of the term.

For this reason too, Ernest Gellner's statement that nationalism

---

13. B. Anderson, *Imagined Communities: Reflections on the Origin and Spread of Nationalism* (London, 1983), pp. 14–15.
14. E. Lemberg, *Nationalismus*, I, p. 23ff. Nationalism is a "Bindekraft . . . die nationale oder quasinationale Gruppen integriert" (p. 20). For criticism of this concept see H. Mommsen, *Neue politische Literatur* 11 (1966), pp. 72–76.

112    *Nation Formation and Nationalism*

"invents nations where they do not exist" does not convince me. Nations were not a consequence of the decisions and activities of a group of intellectuals who turned a nation from "an sich" group into a "für sich" group. Szporluk may have good reasons to consider a nation the work of intellectuals, but I do not understand why he called on the results of my research in support of his view, especially since I arrived at a conclusion more or less opposite to his: a modern nation is not the product of "nationalism," but the consequence of long-term social processes in the transition from feudal to capitalist society.

If we are far from agreeing on what is meant by nationalism in the nineteenth century, then we can hardly agree with Gerschenkron's thesis, which Szporluk shares, that nationalism and Marxism were "competing theories" in the course of industrialization, all the more so since we are agreed that nationalism can hardly be termed a theory. If we consider nationalism as every manifestation of identification with a nation, i.e., national awareness or consciousness, then our two "theories" are not mutually exclusive. A worker who was not originally national-conscious might gradually identify himself with a nation, especially a small one, but this does note exclude his accepting a revolutionary ideology and Marxism. Of course, the tension between the two identifications would remain.

Szporluk rejects Marx's criticism that List, in his struggle for protectionism, expressed the interests of the German bourgeoisie, holding that the delayed development of German society, as compared with England, also affected the other classes, and that List wanted to benefit them all. Subjectively, List may well have thought this way, but on the objective level his demands supported the interests of the bourgeoisie. In this sense, Marx's criticism of List seems justified to me. Actually, Marx made a different mistake in his criticism of List: he underestimated List's teaching "linking culture, politics and economy in a single comprehensive world view," not realizing as yet the force of these ties, which were not a product of intellectual qualities but of civil society, and which corresponded to the reality of the nation-building process.

Perhaps there is some agreement between List and the young Marx in their common view that big state-nations swallow up small nationalities, but the socio-political implications of their views were quite different. List was concerned with the development of civil society, whereas Marx at first was interested in the process of transformation after the victory of the proletarian revolution. Later developments demonstrated that the defensive struggle of the oppressed nationalities against the big nations and their bourgeoisies, that is to say their defensive "nationalism," took on similar forms as the struggle of the oppressed proletariat against the ruling bourgeoisie and its state.

Wherein, therefore, lay that fatal underestimation by Marx and Engels of "nationalism?" I do not think they erred in their view that a nation is the product of civil society and that it is therefore essential to regard it as a "secondary phenomenon" in relation to that "civil society." Such a relation between the nation and society exists even today without calling into doubt the right of nations to exist. Marx's and Engels's view that the ruling class of a modern nation is the bourgeoisie is correct, that is to say, it corresponds to historical reality. The logical inference is that a nation cannot exist without its own bourgeoisie. It seems to me, therefore, that Marx had good reason to believe that what List presented as "national interest" was intended primarily to serve the interests of the bourgeoisie, which does not exclude the fact that the other strata of the nation may have shared to some extent in the prosperity of the bourgeoisie.

The error of the young Marx and Engels was that they anticipated an early victory of the proletarian revolution, which was expected to open the way to the extinction of nations, at least nations in the form in which they existed at the time. After the experience of the revolutions of 1848–49, however, they gradually revised their view, recognizing at least the prospect of the continuation of the already existing big (state) nations. But they did not revise their view that nationalities and ethnic groups that lacked their own bourgeoisie or their own states would gradually disappear. Still, they recognized the force of national activization ("nationalism") by these groups, or at least by their leaders. Engels rated the national movements in the Habsburg monarch and the Ottoman empire highly, but this did not prevent him from believing that these national movements had no hope of creating modern, independent nations.[15] This negative assessment grew out of his negative view of the antirevolutionary role some of these nations played in

15. F. Engels, for instance, expressed very positive views on the Czech national movement in June 1848. See his articles in *Neue Rheinische Zeitung*, no. 18 (June 18), no. 25 (June 25), no. 33 (July 3), and 42 (July 12). His and Marx's opinion changed after the fall of Vienna in November 1848.

114    *Nation Formation and Nationalism*

1848–49. But Marx's and Engels's negative position had deeper reasons than simply the search for a culprit in the immediate emotion of defeat.

What was the basis of their mistake? A contributing factor was their belief that the fate of the medieval peoples of Provence, Wales, and Brittany forecast the fate of small Slavic nations. This was a faulty historical analogy, because the assimilation of a large part of these peoples was decided under feudalism. After the emergence of civil society assimilation took place in a different context. More importantly, they were often partially and incorrectly informed about the social and political situation of the national movements. One has only to recall that in his article on "democratic Pan-Slavism" Engels regarded the peasantry as the main force in the national movements of the Habsburg monarchy, a view that was valid at best, perhaps, for the Ukrainians and Romanians.[16] Of course his view that the bourgeoisie did not head these movements was correct, and without a bourgeoisie one could not imagine a modern nation. Therefore these national groups had only one prospect: assimilation under the rule of a foreign, German bourgeoisie. Thirty years later Karl Kautsky shared that view, but by that time the assertion that the small peoples of the Habsburg monarchy did not have their own bourgeoisies was incorrect.[17]

Thus we come to the root of the erroneous view of Marx and Engels about the prospects of national movements. Their mistake lay in an incorrect estimation of the development of social structure. Marx and Engels believed that industrialization and the victory of capitalism would lead to the rapid disappearance of the lower strata of the middle class, which would sink into the proletariat, leaving only two classes to constitute civil society. But this proletarianization and impoverishment of craftsmen, small farmers, and merchants did not happen. Not only did the old middle class remain and adapt to capitalist conditions, but capitalism gave rise to a new middle class of white collar workers,

16. "Und da die Bewegung der Bauern, die überall die Träger der nationalen und lokalen Borniertheit sind, notwendig eine lokale und nationale ist, so tauchten mit ihr zugleich die alten nationalen Kämpfe wieder auf."

17. ". . . aber Bauern- und Kleinbürgertum sind dem Untergang geweiht, und mit ihnen die Sprache, die sie sprechen. Je mehr sie zurückgehen, je mehr der Kapitalismus sich entwickelt, desto geringer wird in Böhmen die ökonomische Bedeutung des Tschechischen, desto grösser die des Deutschen werden." K. Kautsky, "Die moderne Nationalität," *Die Neue Zeit* (Stuttgart, 1887), p. 447.

teachers, and similarly employed persons. It was precisely from this milieu that the bourgeoisies of the smaller, weaker, and dependent nationalities emerged. Since a universal bourgeoisie did not develop, "nationalism" was not overcome and nations and national awareness did not disappear. Instead, both the old and the new middle classes became the main champions of "nationalism," both in state-nations and in small nations that experienced the nation-building process. Only in this context can we understand why the proletariat, which originally really "did not have a homeland," also became nationally aware. The proletariat in capitalist society obtained access to education and therefore to the cultural community of the nation to which it belonged ethnically, thus ceasing to be only international and becoming integrated into national communities. We can hardly imagine that the workers identified directly with the bourgeoisie, although such cases did occur, but they could easily feel allegiance to a community to which their middle-class neighbors (e.g., small craftsmen) belonged and from whose families they came, as did the teachers of their children. Allegiance to a nation could, but need not, have automatically meant the abandonment of internationalism. Without question it became a lasting source of antagonism within the working-class movement.

# X

# Nationalism and national movements: comparing the past and the present of Central and Eastern Europe*

ABSTRACT. This article compares the 'new nationalism' in post-communist countries since the 1980s with the 'classical' national movements of the nineteenth century. Looking for analogies and differences between these two processes, it seeks to achieve a better understanding and more profound interpretation of contemporary 'nationalism'. Most important analogies are: both national movements emerged as a result of (and as an answer to) the crisis and disintegration of an old regime and its value system; in both cases we observe a low level of political experience among the population, the stereotype of a personalised nation, and of a defensive position. Similarly both movements define their national border by both ethnic and historical borders: in both cases, the nationally relevant conflict of interests plays a decisive role. Among the differences are: the extremely high level of social communication in the twentieth-century movements, combined with a 'vacuum at the top' (the need for new elites) and with deep economic depression. The 'contemporary' national movements fought for the political rights of undoubtedly pre-existing nations (above all, for full independence), while the 'classical' ones fought for the concept of a nation-to-be, whose existence was not generally accepted. Nevertheless, in both cases, similar specifics of the nation-forming process under conditions of a 'small nation' can be observed. The author does not view nationalism as a 'disease' or external force: but rather as an answer given by some members of the nation to new challenges and unexpected conflicts of interests, which could be interpreted as national ones.

The exciting experience of the current 'revival of nationalism' represents for a historian of nation-forming processes a kind of testing ground, giving him the opportunity to verify his theories. The primary aim of this article is to determine whether or not we could use the results of historical research on the nation-forming process in order to explain current nationalism, national movements and ethnic conflicts in Central and Eastern Europe.

* This article is an enlarged version of the paper given at the second ASEN Annual Conference in February 1992 at the London School of Economics.

Five or six years ago, when the first strong expressions of the 'new nationalism' emerged, the question was above all: how to explain the sudden emergence of nationalist feelings, proclamations and actions? The most frequent and 'fashionable' answer was the following: under communist rule, nationalism was forbidden, but it had survived from pre-communist times and it now becomes again the active ideology, because communism did not solve the 'national problem'. We could give some persuasive empirical and theoretical arguments against this 'fridge theory', but I do not think that it would be useful to present them here: this 'fridge theory' has been disproved by the experience of the last five years and has become a thing of the past.

Nevertheless, what survives is the concept of nationalism as some kind of epidemic disease, which can be and has to be treated: the only problem seems to be to find the right medicine and the proper method of treatment. At the outset I have to admit that I strongly disagree with this voluntaristic concept. We have to find a deeper explanation of this phenomenon. As a historian, I have tried to understand and interpret it in its ancestry, in its historical perspective.

First of all, it is necessary to say something about the term itself. I have my doubts concerning the explanatory competence of the term 'nationalism', which is used in so many different meanings that it makes mutual understanding difficult. For this reason, I use this term only in its limited sense, which is its original one, i.e. not as a synonym for national identity or a national programme, but as a state of mind (collective mentality), that gives priority to the interests and values of one's own nation over all other interests and values. Trying to interpret the national conflicts and changes of the last decade, I regard it as more practical to use the term 'national movement', understood as organised efforts to achieve all the attributes of a 'fully fledged' nation, i.e. to obtain all attributes characterising already existing nation-states.

To make my interpretations more comprehensible, it is necessary to formulate some premises, without attempting to give a detailed explanation.

1   We cannot interpret the phenomenon 'nationalism' without taking into account the real existing large social group 'nation', which emerged as the result of a long nation-forming process, which had its prehistory in Middle Ages.

2   The key element of the analysis of this nation-forming process is not 'nationalism', but national identity.

3   The nation-forming process, the emergence of modern nations during the nineteenth and twentieth centuries, was not an 'error of history', as some intellectuals suggest, but a natural part of the transformation of modern European society, parallel to industrialisation, capitalism, constitutionalism etc.

4   The emergence of nations, national identities and nationalisms is not a specifically Eastern development, but part of an overall European

development, naturally including some typological differences and a high degree of unevenness in time.

5  Analyzing nationalism in the proper, narrow sense of the word, we should prefer unbiased causal examination to moralistic preaching and denunciations.

Living under Soviet rule, nations in Eastern and Central Europe experienced limited independence or even total loss of independence. They lived not only under the political, but also under the cultural and economic rule of the communist nomenclatura. It was understandable that some members of these nations started a national agitation, trying to persuade members of their own nation that the time for a renewed full national existence was coming. This was the moment when new national movements started.

National movements are, nevertheless, a much older phenomenon. Originally, national movement was one of two main types (forms) of nation-forming process during the nineteenth century. To understand this view, I have to mention some actual dates. At the beginning of the nineteenth century, there existed in Europe only eight state-nations with a more or less developed literary language, a tradition of high culture and established ruling elites: the English, French, Spanish (Castilian), Dutch, Portuguese, Danish, Swedish and later Russian nation-states. The nation-forming process inclined in these cases towards a modern nation as a community of equal citizens and passed for an integral part of political modernisation of the state.

On the other hand, there existed at the very same time more than thirty ethnic groups (nationalities) without statehood, or with a weak or no continuity of literary language and without 'their own' ruling elites. All of them lived within the territory of multiethnic empires, e.g. the Habsburg and Ottoman empires, tsarist Russia, but also Great Britain, Spain and Denmark. This was the situation, which I called originally a nation-forming process under conditions of a 'small nation'. Today, I accept the more suitable term 'non-dominant ethnic group'. Sooner or later, some members of this group decided to start national agitation demanding all the attributes of a fully fledged nation: they started the decisive phase of their national movement. In some cases, this national agitation started very early, around the year 1800 (the Greeks, Czechs, Norwegians, Irish), in some others one generation later (the Finns, Croats, Slovenes, Flemish, Welsh etc.), or even during the second half of the nineteenth century (Latvians, Estonians, Catalans, Basques etc.). If national agitation was successful, it achieved the support of the masses and opened the way to a fully formed nation. Sometimes, national agitation did not achieve its goal or had to fight for mass support for a very long time (the Flemish, Welsh, Byelorussians). Nationalism in the narrow sense of the word was but an accompanying component of this process, not its main force. Its participation and influence in the national movement strengthened during the third phase (the phase of mass movement).

Is this type of national movement we know from the nineteenth century, comparable with those we have witnessed since the 1980s? My answer is affirmative: the points of departure of each process are analogous, as are their goals, which can be divided into three groups:

1   Political demands, which in contemporary national movements are strongly concentrated towards independence, while in the nineteenth-century in most cases self-administration and some degree of autonomy were preferred.

2   Cultural demands, which tried to establish and strengthen an independent culture and national literary language.

3   Social demands, which asked for a just division of national income and tried to achieve a full social structure in the emerging national society, corresponding to the stage of capitalist transformation of the multi-ethnic state.

If we compare the historical explanation of 'classical' national movements with contemporary developments, we find some significant analogies and, naturally, also some differences. Let me summarise them, illustrating the possibilities of interpreting current developments as part of long-term processes.

1 The transition to the decisive phase of national agitation occurred almost at the same time as the old regimes and social systems were in crisis. As old ties disappeared or weakened, the need for a new group identity brought together, under the auspices of one national movement, people belonging to different classes and groups. Similarly, following the breakdown of the systems of planned economy and communist control, old ties disappeared. Under conditions of general uncertainty and lack of confidence, the national idea assumed an integrating role. These were stressful circumstances, and people usually over-estimated the protective effect of their national group.

2 Identification with a national group includes, as it did in the last century, the construct of the personified and personalised nation. The glorious history of this personalised nation is understood as the, or a, personal past of each of its members. Its defeats are understood as personal failures and continue to affect their feelings. As a result of this personalisation, people regard their own nation – which they equate with themselves – as one body. If any misfortune befalls a small section of the nation, then the whole 'body' feels the pain of that misfortune. If a small group belonging to the ethnic group – even if living in a different state from the 'mother-nation' – is endangered by assimilation, the members of the personified nation interpret it as an amputation of a part of the national 'body'.

3 Like the classical national movements, the personalised and personified national body needs a distinct space. This space was – and is also today – defined in two different and controversial ways. First, it is defined in terms of its ethnic homogeneity, a homogeneity which is primarily delimited as a linguistically (or religiously) bound cultural space. Secondly, it is defined by

historical frontiers of 'national' territory, which could, in many cases, also include other ethnic groups and minorities. This second criterion is symptomatic of the so-called 'historical nations', for example, Magyars regarding the historical kingdom of Hungary as their own national body, Czechs similarly in 'their' historical Kingdom of Bohemia and Margravate of Moravia, Croats, who look upon all three parts of the medieval kingdom (Croatia, Dalmatia, Slavonia) as 'their own' etc. These situations have even more analogies today for, besides the established *historical nations*, we find a new group of nations – that is, nations which enjoyed their independence (including state borders) during the short inter-war period, for example, Estonians, Lithuanians, Latvians, and even those whose independence was only realised during the Second World War as Nazi 'protectorates', the case of Croats and Slovaks. Furthermore, in such cases, many leaders of national movements interpret state frontiers as national frontiers, and regard the ethnic minorities within 'their own' territory as outlanders, in the end worthless enough to be expelled or to have their national identity neglected.

4 National agitation began during the nineteenth century, usually in conditions when members of the non-dominant ethnic group did not have any political experience in civic society, nor any political education. For these reasons, they could hardly formulate political arguments and slogans for civil and human rights in the modern sense of the word. 'Freedom' for Czech or Estonian peasants meant the abolition of feudal domination and the free use of their farmland, not freedom of speech or parliamentary elections. The notions of common language and customs, however, were much more comprehensible to them. Having spent more than fifty (or even seventy) years under dictatorial regimes, the mentality of the people is once again such that in many countries, linguistic, cultural and social demands play a surrogate political role. Nevertheless, the importance of ethnicity is not equally prevalent in all modern day national movements. In some cases, especially under conditions of Soviet rule, the language of the ruling nation remained a symbol of political oppression in the eyes of, for example Estonians and Lithuanians, even when the character of political oppression differed from that of the nineteenth century. In these recent cases the language of a small nation fighting for independence was automatically viewed as the language of liberty.

5 During the nineteenth century, members of non-dominant ethnic groups were disadvantaged by the unwillingness of ruling nations to accept the real equality of all languages, that is, equality of the language of the ruling nation with the language of the non-dominant ethnic groups. The members of ruling nations, for example, Germans or Magyars (after 1867), refused to learn and use the language of ethnic groups living in 'their' territory. After the emergence of the new independent national states in 1918–19, members of the former ruling nations became national minorities in the newly formed states. Yet they remained unwilling to accept the equality of language of the small, but now ruling, nations of for example,

Czechs, Romanians, Serbs, Croats, etc., and this made for potentially explosive situations at the threshold of the Second World War. Currently, members of the former ruling nations, and particularly Russians (and also Serbs), have once again, as a result of successful national movements, become minorities in the newly emerged and emerging states, such as Estonia, Lithuania and Croatia. The parallel between the real fate and historical role of the *Volksdeutsche* and the potential role of the *Volksrussen* is striking.

6 National movements sanctified some national demands by the fact that their non-dominant ethnic group was endangered through assimilation: they emphasised their defensive character. Similarly today, the defence of 'national existence', of 'national rights' creates an illusion of moral immunity, which is stressed especially by the nationalist wing of the movement.

7 The overestimation of ethnic elements and linguistic demands is symptomatic of a specific feature of contemporary national movements. It is the illusion of a 'replay', of a 'repeat performance'. The leaders of the new national movements, believing that they could utilise the successful methods of their 'classical' national movements, hold that old ethnic values can be resuscitated. This 'replay' mentality makes it difficult for a researcher to distinguish between real and replayed needs, between stereotypes and sincerely formulated demands.

8 If we ask why national agitation during the nineteenth century achieved the support of the masses, we find everywhere (besides intensified social communication and mobility) one factor, which was undervalued in traditional research on 'nationalism'. This factor could be called 'nationally relevant conflict of group interests', which means social and political conflicts or tensions that coincided with linguistic (or eventually religious) differences. Let me illustrate this kind of conflict by some examples: a conflict between peasants belonging to the non-dominant ethnic group and the landlords from the dominant nation; between the 'centre' and the 'province'; between traditionalist village and the town; between new academics from the non-dominant ethnic group and the old elites belonging to the ruling nation. Nationally relevant conflicts of interests of today may differ in part from those of the nineteenth century, but they also play an important role as an integral element of new national movements.

There exist, nevertheless, not only similarities and analogies but also important differences. To mention them means also to take them into account as explanatory factors in recent research.

1 National movements during the nineteenth century constituted a part and a form of the nation-forming process – and the fully fledged nation emerged as a result, which was not at all a self-evident result. Contemporary national movements enter the battlefield in the name of a nation which came into existence just before they started. The goal in 1990 was not to create a new entity, but to restore the previously existing one.

2 There is an important difference caused by the immense intensity of social communication. For this reason, all the processes that we know from the nineteenth century are highly accelerated.

3 The modern mass media are now strong enough to manipulate populations, to distort or intensify in what they portray conflicts of interests where they do not exist, that is, to promote or diminish the danger of aggressive nationalism.

4 There is a difference in social structure. The present situation, marked by the 'vacuum at the top' as a result of the sudden disintegration of the system of planned economy and the nomenclatura ruling class, is unique in European history. New elites, educated under the old regime but belonging to the new national movements, are successfully trying to achieve the status of ruling elites. As the educated members of non-dominant ethnic groups tried to achieve ruling status during the nineteenth century, they had to fight for each single position among the established elites of the ruling nation. At the same time, they had to maintain the way of life and the value system of these established ruling classes. In the recent cases, there is no previous establishment and upward social mobility is not influenced by any surviving traditional systems or moral norms – except individual and national selfishness. I must point out that the disintegration of the old nomenclatura ruling class has not occurred in all the countries under survey. In countries such as Serbia nationalism has been manipulated by them in order to enable them to stay in power.

5 During the nineteenth century, nationally relevant conflicts were above all conflicts which resulted from modernisation and reflected the general trend of economic growth joined to social improvement. In the recent cases, these conflicts are instead a response to a short-term depression and decline, to the fact that the 'cake' has become smaller. Even though this does not imply that this decline is irreversible, the psychological effect is strong: events being condensed into a short period of a few years, allows short-term decline to act in the same way as long-term decline.

So much for the situation at the turn of the decade. What changed, however, during the last four or five years? Most national movements quickly achieved their principal goal: political independence. New nation-states are emerging in Slovenia, Slovakia, Byelorussia, Macedonia and so on. For this reason, national movements in most countries are disappearing, after having achieved their main goals. Nevertheless, what about nationalism and conflicts between nation-states? Let us start by giving some actual cases. Since the retreat of the Yugoslav army, we hear very little about Slovene nationalism; since the division of Czechoslovakia, nationalist groupings in Slovakia have become weaker and they have almost disappeared in the Czech Republic. In Poland, nationalist slogans get no real support. Nationalist parties lost in last elections in Lithuania and Hungary and similar developments seem to be happening in Ukraine and Bulgaria. The only regions where nationalism gained strength are those where national movements did not achieve their goals: in former Yugoslavia and in Russia. It would be too optimistic to say that nationalism in post-communist countries is definitely disappearing, but there is no doubt that it is weaker than it was five years ago when the national movements started.

This positive trend is not the merit of the 'European idea' or of anti-nationalist humanist intellectuals, but the result of social and political changes. In most of the cases mentioned above, the nation-states became independent without being seriously endangered from abroad. Social tensions and conflicts of interests are still strong, but those which are nationally relevant are rare, especially in monoethnic states, such as Poland, Slovenia or the Czech Republic. At the same time, the vacuum at the top in these states is filled and there are some signs of economic improvements for the future.

This is, nevertheless, only one side of the coin. On the other side, there are countries where nationalist conflicts ended in bloodshed. Remember Bosnia, Croatia, the Caucasus. How can we explain this difference?

If we accept the view that the nationalism is not an abstract disease but a state of mind of actual human beings, we are able to formulate the precondition for its strengthening, as occurs in some European regions. Favourable conditions for a growing force of nationalism can be sum-marised as follows:

1   The vacuum at the top is still not filled and the fight for political power and for leading positions in the economy are not limited by old value systems or by the 'rules of the game' of democratic civil society: the struggle for these positions becomes the nationally relevant conflict of interests.

2   The decline of the economy and the standard of living is hopelessly deep and the ethnic situation allows the agitators to denounce 'the others' as responsible for backward developments.

3   The difference between the nations is not defined primarily by differences of language, but by religion.

4   The political culture is forgotten or absent and is difficult to improve, sometimes being related to low levels of education.

5   The members of the former ruling nation were degraded to the level of an ethnic minority under the rule of the former oppressed nation.

6   The national tradition and myth, the 'collective memory', includes the tradition of fighting and dying for the nation as an extremely positive and morally binding value.

If we project these six points into concrete historical developments, we find without a doubt a striking and convincing coincidence of these factors only in one European country: in Bosnia. In other regions, we find only some of these factors, and on the other hand, these six destabilising factors are almost absent in countries with lower levels of the nationalist attitudes mentioned above.

To summarise, the first point of my conclusion is: the 'new nationalism' operates in different countries with rather different emphases. The explosion of aggressive nationalism that we are observing in former Yugoslavia is a rather unique case and cannot be generalised as the main trend in all former communist countries.

On the contrary, we are observing a retreat of nationalism in some of them, as a result of changing social and political realities. Even though this retreat cannot be generalised, it is an important sign for two reasons. Above all, it demonstrates the importance of the nationally relevant conflict of interests as a stimulating force of nationalism. Secondly, it allows us to put the phenomenon 'nationalism' into an appropriate framework.

Nationalism – this has to be stressed once more – is not a malady, not a virus which could be exterminated forever by an appropriate treatment. Nationalism is a potential function and product of actually existing national identities. As long as nations exist, nationalism will remain as a latent answer to problems and challenges. In this sense, it can be regarded as a latent danger – not only in Eastern Europe, but also in Western Europe.

Sometimes, the difference between the 'nationalist East' and the 'democratic West' is based to the concept of democracy as the best treatment which can be used to prevent or exterminate nationalism. The relation between democracy and the nation-forming process is, nevertheless, more complicated. Naturally, constitutionalism and democracy are an inevitable condition of civil society, but it would be a wrong deduction to say that national movements and democracy exclude each other. On the contrary, in many cases, the oppressed nations perceived democracy as a suitable instrument to be used by their national movement.

For this reason, democracy cannot be regarded as a universal treatment for nationalism. The decisive role that emerging or weakening nationalism plays, as in the past, is in response to nationally relevant conflicts of interests, conditioned by a high intensity of social communication and mobility. These conflicts of interests can under given conditions be either real or constructed. The emergence of nationally relevant conflicts of interests in reality is usually an answer to some social, economical or political crisis and, for this reason, cannot be prevented by learned arguments or humanist speeches. Nevertheless, its constructed form could be avoided by responsible mass media. Even though this sounds utopian, it is proven by experience that emergent nationalism will find it difficult to persuade a majority, if it happens under conditions of constitutionalism and high political culture.

The usual concluding question, addressed to 'experts', is: what must be done? I cannot escape this question, but I prefer its modified version: what can be done? Naturally, the historian is not qualified to recommend treatments: he prefers to summarise and generalise empirical observations. The utopian concept of creating a civil society as an alternative to the national one has failed. It is not the place here to analyse the reasons for this failure: one of these reasons is, nevertheless, its ignorance of reality, its neglect of actual nations and of existing conflicts of interests after the breakdown of Communism.

However, the central problem is how to prevent conflicts of interests expanding into nationally relevant ones. One way, as mentioned above, is to avoid artificially constructed conflicts 'produced' by mass media. Naturally, this is difficult under conditions of a free society. Even more difficult is to prevent real emerging conflicts: can it happen through social engineering or by improving the economic conditions? If we accept the fact that conflicts of interest are inevitable, then the only way seems to be – at least in theory – to avoid the transformation of these conflicts into national ones. This can only partially be influenced by moralistic preaching, but it can be proved by historical record that under conditions of political culture and the potency of political consensus, this transformation can be avoided or minimalised. In such cases, the conflict of interests would be expressed in political terms, instead of being translated into national terms. Nevertheless, all these considerations will remain merely as some kind of intellectual game, until we learn how to improve the economy and political culture of post-communist countries.

# An unwelcome national identity, or what to do about 'nationalism' in the post-communist countries?

This critical essay is addressed to those Western intellectuals who draw the conclusion that contemporary development in post-communist countries is dominated primarily by the growth of irrational and destructive nationalism. A number of terminological and methodological misunderstandings are pointed out. Nation-forming has occurred in the form of national movements, a type which started from a non-dominant ethnic group and not from an Early–Modern state-nation. Such development towards a modern nation was prevalent in Central and Eastern Europe, although it is also found in Western and Northern parts of Europe. This type of nation-forming resulted in some permanent characteristics and stereotypes which developed typically in the members of 'small nations'. It is necessary to discriminate in the use of the term, nationalism: we must recognize that national identity is different from nationalism. Ideas about real or partially imagined national interests accompany the existence of every (and hence also East European) nation. The process of education toward a European identity cannot ignore the existence of nations as a sociological fact with regard to the post-communist countries. The decision about the inclusion of these countries in the European identity does not only depend on the members of these nations, but also on whether the West will cease to perceive the small post-communist countries as mere accidental foci of 'nationalism' and the recipients of economic aid.

Whether one finds it exciting or distressing, it is an undeniable fact that 12 new nation states were formed over the last few years in the region formerly comfortably

XI

labelled the Soviet Bloc by Western Europeans. These states did not come into being by command from Moscow, but were (mostly) motivated by a spontaneous desire for national self-determination, by which most Western commentators unfortunately including social scientists were taken aback. Western commentators were used to the idea that constitutional changes in 'the East' happened by Moscow's orders, and that there was only one 'correct' way of resisting communism; adoration of the global market economy and a declaration of civil rights. They were almost uniformly horrified by the current development, Europe was endangered by a new kind of destructive nationalism! This paper does not want to increase the number of the moralizing accounts telling us what is correct, nor does it venture any fashionable forecasts. The primary task of a historian is to analyse and explain, not to judge.

## Points of departure leading to the deadlock of misunderstanding

Current studies on 'nationalism' in Central and Eastern Europe struggle with several methodological and terminological problems which are a handicap in capturing the essence of the current processes.

First is the semantic problem. Every specialist knows that the term *'nation'* has a different meaning in the English linguistic consciousness than the word's equivalent in German and most Slavic languages. Yet, we encounter opinion and attitude analyses of the members of these nations using the term 'nation' (which is connotative of 'state') in English texts unreflectingly. However, the agents of contemporary national movements in post-communist Europe strongly associate the term with ethnicity, language, and community of culture. The English linguistic context understands the relation between 'nation' and 'ethnic group' as two different categories, while the German, Czech, Croatian and other linguistic environments refer to two developing categories: a nation is a successor of an ethnic group, ethnicity is contained in national existence.

The danger of a bad misunderstanding is obvious. Even worse is the misunderstanding ensuing from the similarly reckless use of the derivative 'nationalism'. In English, this is again connotative of the strive for statehood or of the idea of the state interests, while its meaning is very unstable in the linguistic context of Central and Eastern Europe. The negative connotations of the term are prevalent there. This is reinforced by the official terminology of the Leninist theory considering 'bourgeois nationalism' corrupt.

The term *nationalism* is a relatively recent academic concept, it entered American research in the period between the World Wars, and appeared in Europe after World War II. Many social scientists have tried to use it as a neutral, technical term, but it has always depended on the linguistic consciousness of the particular nations whether it is accepted as neutral or negative. After all, even in American terminology 'patriotism' refers to positive manifestations of the relation to a nation.

Nationalism appears in so many contexts that we can characterize the situation as one of total confusion. Does it refer to the 'state of mind' as Hans Kohn understood it in his classic *The Idea of Nationalism* at the end of World War II? Does it mean a human activity, political struggle, or armed struggle? Is it to be understood as the reality of identification with the nation? Certainly all of this and much more. We can see the paradox even in the work of such a concise thinker as Ernest Gellner. He defines nationalism as a 'political principle asserting that the political and the national units must be identical', but he further speaks about nationalism in relation to already existing states, that is, where the postulate of nationalism was achieved and its effects *ex definitione* should therefore have ceased (E. Gellner, *Nations and Nationalism*, 1983). The same pertains to the thesis shared also by Eric Hobsbawm that 'nationalism created nations'. If this were the case, nationalism ought either to disappear or 'start creating' something else after the formation of fully-fledged nations.

The picture of confusion will be complete if we ask in reference of whom is the term used. This terminology makes a member of the SS a 'nationalist', as equally as a participant in the Norwegian or Polish resistance, a Medieval chronicle, Dostoievski, or Masaryk. The term is used also in the plural and some groups are labelled as 'nationalists'. Neither developmental no structural differences between these groups of 'nationalists' are taken into consideration. Even whole nations are now called 'nationalist': i.e. Serbians, Estonians, Macedonians, Russians. Only the Germans, who have recently united with such national enthusiasm, are spared this stigma.

The list of examples could continue. For now, I would like to add that the evidence of one person taking a 'nationalist' attitude to one nation and being sympathetic to another is quite common. One person or one group of people can take 'nationalist' attitudes at one time and depart from them later, and vice versa.

We can lessen the confusion at least to an extent, if we use 'nationalism' in its rather old-fashioned meaning, that is, in relation to an attitude of superiority of one's own nation and its interests over other nations and their interests. We can also add that, in many languages, the term 'patriotism' and its equivalents are the positive counterparts to 'nationalism'. The problem is that we may be able to draw a line between these attitudes (with some difficulty) in the analysis of an individual's attitudes, but it is impossible to apply it to group attitudes. It seems that academically the most productive solution is to avoid the term nationalism and replace it with other, less confusing terms, like national consciousness, national identity and identification, national movement, love for one's country, hatred toward the nation *N*, separatism, xenophobia, etc. As we will see later, the most important of these is the term 'identity'.

Another shortcoming of many studies on the nation-forming processes and national objectives in Central and Eastern Europe is that they take the 'French model' as their starting point for assessment of the development of the whole of Europe. Any phenomena which do not fit the model are considered 'deviations'. It is significant that Kohn's dichotomy of double nationalism is being revived (whether authors quote him or not), in that Western nationalism was bred on the ideas of democracy and liberalism, and Eastern nationalism based on the principles of ethnicity, that is, 'blood'. The former is, of course, progressive, because it is in accordance with the civil principle; the latter is reactionary and should be renounced, for it is associated with authority and dictatorship. The problem, however, is not so simple, since nations were formed as part of a historical process, and history did not unravel the way contemporary humanists had imaged it would.

This brings us to another defective approach, the lack of a historical approach to the contemporary processes in Central and Eastern Europe. For example, it is symptomatic of studies on nation-forming in the cases of France, Great Britain, or the Netherlands to reach as far back as the late Middle Ages, while studies on the European 'East' present the issue, as if current 'nationalism' came out of the blue in this region, or was a repetition of a 19th century phenomenon. The sheer ignorance of the history of nations which dared to form a nation state in the conditions of backward 'Eastern' society (whose languages and culture the Western authors usually do not know) is, of course, much at fault.

The most frequent interpretation of contemporary 'nationalism' in post-communist Europe is to blame Communism for everything. Nationalism was banned and suppressed under the dictatorships, therefore, it could not manifest itself. It emerged out of some tucked-away source like the genie out of the bottle with the fall of the dictatorships. This simple-minded, but effective theory presupposes that it is possible to freeze a state of mind for decades, and it will then arise afresh after defrosting. Unfortunately, the reality, which can be tested empirically, does not correspond to this theory.

Empirical evidence in support of the other part of the interpretation of nationalism as the work of communism is a bit better. Many former Communist leaders now use nationalist slogans to achieve their political objectives. This interpretation, however, also has a weak spot: it does not explain why, in some countries, the masses agree with these former leaders and support them, while in others, such argumentation is not successful. Should we not look for the causes of the success of nationalist slogans rather in the overall conditions of a particular country, in the context of its historical traditions, and international position?

The last element of the methodological confusion, which I would like to point out, could be called 'pars pro toto'. The fact that a strong wave of aggressive nationalism and mass xenophobia sprang out in one or two post-communist countries is only too often generalized in Western European studies (or rather, in current-affairs coverage) to the extent that they speak about nationalism in the whole of Eastern Europe. The same short cut occurs if several nationalist articles appear in the press of one of these countries, or if nationalist slogans win the support of a certain percentage of voters. The manifestation of nationalism of a part of society is then presented as 'nationalism' of the whole nation, as evidence of the absence of the civil principle in the whole society etc. I do not venture a guess as to how Western Europe would accept this interpretation, if someone concluded from Le Pen's election successes that all French are xenophobic, or from IRA activities that all Irish are terrorists.

## The specificity of 'small nations'

If we want to explain contemporary 'nationalisms' in Central and Eastern Europe, we have to take the fact that this region, just as any other part of Europe, has been subject to nation-forming processes as our point of departure. Historically, there are two basic types of this process: the first started from integrated state-nations, absolute or constitutional monarchies. At the end of the 18th century, these began to transform—either gradually or by means of a revolution—into communities of equal citizens sharing national consciousness. The state-nations had their own culture in the tradition of a literary language; the social structure of their members included all classes and social strata corresponding to the existing level of economic and social development. The modern French, English, Dutch, Portuguese, and Swedish nations followed this path, as with some modifications did the Spanish and Danish nations.

The second type of the nation-forming process gave rise to all other European nations. It occurred in the conditions of a non-dominant ethnic group, that is, '*an ethnie*' (A. Smith), which had a higher or lower degree of ethnic identity, but which lacked the following criteria of a full national existence: (1) statehood; (2) a complete social structure (that is, own 'national' elites); and (3) the tradition of a literary language. The development into a national community took the more complicated form of a national movement; that is, a purposeful effort to achieve all the missing attributes of full national existence. Such national movements occurred in the territories of multi-ethnic empires. The best known of these are the Russian, Habsburg, and Ottoman Empires, but Great Britain, Denmark, and Spain also belong to this category.

The programmes of these national movements included linguistic, social, and political demands. Both specific national (the use of the language in the state administration, political participation, complete social structure) and general modernizing (civil rights, democratic franchise, freeing of the peasantry, etc) objectives were included. The political objectives of these movements usually did not include the demand for full national independence. Only Balkan, Polish, and later also Hungarian national movements aimed at that. It is important for our argument that all nations in the post-communist part of Europe (with the exception of the Russians) were formed by this process, which means that they resulted from more or less successful national movements. It needs to be emphasized that the process was one of these two basic types of nation-forming and not a deviation, mistake, or artificial construct, as German Nationalliberalen and Russian Slavophiles asserted in the 19th century.

This typological differentiation was not included in order to preach about dead history, but because the forming of modern nations in the conditions of national movement has had far-reaching effects on the mentality of these nations and their specific stereotypes, and also on their relations with neighbours up to the current time. What is the essence of this specificity? We can sum it up as follows.

(1) Most national movements did not focus on forming a state and therefore, the tradition of modern statehood has only marginal importance in the underlying political thinking. This explains their weak interest in the discussions of Jacobinism or liberalism, and the fervent protection of their newly-gained statehood as a national value. This attitude certainly contains (and did contain in the past) the danger of establishing an authoritarian regime out of 'national interests'.

(2) The existence of nationally-relevant antagonisms—that is social antagonisms—in which members of the non-dominant ethnic group conflicted with members of the state-nation or ruling elites of a multi-national empire, was very important for the success of national mobilization. This bred a stereotype of nationalization of social conflicts and conflicts of interests in general. That which is addressed as a social antagonism and sometimes 'translated' into political terminology in state-nations becomes 'translated' into national terminology in the conditions of a national movement and later also in the nation-state. The old stereotype mixed with reality in this process.

(3) The national movements in all the three 'Eastern' empires, targeted directly or indirectly, the old system of absolutism and oppression, and its dynastic legitimacy. Disrespect for legitimacy and continuity often followed this attitude. Also, these movements started 'from below' and were directed up against the ruling elites. The image (and later the stereotype) of the enemy, thus, was not associated with the neighbour, as was the case with state-nations (for example, Germans in the view of the French), but with somebody 'at the top': Turks for the Serbs, Bulgarians, and Greeks; Russians and Germans in the case of the Poles; and Hungarians in the view of the Slovaks. This relation was then easily open to the idea of the national movement as a struggle in the interest of progress and against the forces of the old world; Tsarism, Ottomanism, the Habsburgs. It is possible that this idea still survives with some modifications; i.e. the Soviet system took over the role of Tsarism, Ottomanism was replaced by the Turks (or rather, with Muslims), and the Habsburgs with the Germans.

(4) It follows from these typological characteristics that national movements had to aim at winning the support of the masses, because the success of nation-forming depended on their mobilization. The quick integration of the masses in the national community (much faster than in the case of the state-nations) and the myth of the people as the preserver of ethnicity, and therefore, the core of the nation, followed from this premise. We can also deduce spontaneous democratism and egalitarianism, as well as the weakened resistance against populism.

(5) The national movements occurred in the ambience in which national existence was not taken for granted. The movements' leaders were rejected, humiliated,

sometimes even persecuted, and their objective was called fiction, a mistake, a crime. This gave rise to the ensuing feeling of permanent endangerment of the nation—which was later transformed into a lasting stereotype—as well as an urge to prove the legitimacy of one's own national existence. A member of a state-nation, who takes the existence of his or her own nation for granted has difficulty in understanding these feelings and stereotypes. The need to justify the grounds for one's own national existence has manifested itself in various and often controversial ways. On the one hand, it can stimulate innovation, the effort 'to catch up', but on the other, it can encourage looking for excuses for one's own shortcomings, and creating delusions of one's qualities.

(6) The feeling of endangerment also bred another attitude which has survived in stereotypes: the position of defence. The national movements started from the premise that they had merely defended the rights of their nations to existence, that they had not threatened the existence of other nations and had not intended to do so. The image of a peaceful and non-violent national character usually developed from the defensive complex: bravery and war qualities are appreciated in the historical consciousness only in relation to the defence against an external threat. While this stereotype could have positive educational effects (a plough is always a better national symbol than a sword), another stereotype is clearly dangerous: it is the moral exculpation from deeds committed in the defence of real or fictional national interests.

(7) The national movements were always movements of the province against the centre and, therefore, had great difficulties in overcoming the barriers determined by this peripheral position. The leaders often idealized 'smallness' and marginalization as specific virtues, to which evaluating criteria used by 'big' nations could not be applied. Hence there was strong provincialism, which has survived to the present day. This also explains why the national movements paid relatively less attention to international relations and contacts—at least in comparison with the state-nations.

National movements were not exclusively Central and Eastern European phenomena, nation-forming in Western Europe has also occurred in this way—as was the case in Germany and Italy where national movements strove to achieve just one attribute which they needed for full national existence: statehood. We can trace many German and Italian stereotypes similar to these we have just described.

## Lessons learned from the historical parallel

If we attempted an unbiased assessment of the events in the so-called post-communist countries over the last few years, we find that we can characterize only a fraction of them by the term 'nationalism'. The term 'national movement' will cover a much larger spectrum. Indeed, the development in many of these countries was, in a condensed form, what in historical terminology is called a *national movement*. The parallels are convincing, also in the present, the main objective of these nations was to achieve the attributes of a fully-fledged national existence, which they lacked—that is, full independence, a complete social structure corresponding to those countries with developed market economies, and an independent national culture. Although the basic elements of the national demands were the same, they differed in detail so that the political programme was dominant in the contemporary movement and the linguistic and cultural programme was also strong, especially in the territory of the former Soviet Union.

The question is whether the comparison with a historical parallel can help to explain the roots or at least more complex circumstances of contemporary national movements. The 19th-century national movements were responses to the crisis of the old system, to the disintegration of the old value systems. This determined the need for a new community, new relations, a new group identity. This is essentially similar to the present disintegration of established relations, uncertainties, and fears for the future that followed the collapse of the centrally planned economy, social security, and ideological control. In this situation, a national community constitutes a promise of tangible support, and a new and comprehensible value system. Unlike the 19th century, the idea of national solidarity was already in existence and could be adopted and modified.

In most national movements, agitation started in a situation when neither the protagonists nor the addressees had any political experience of life in a civil society, and therefore, national demands were more easily understandable and acceptable for them than abstract political programmes. A similar situation occurred in the late 1980s after the 50 or 70 years of authoritarian regime. National and social demands were more successful in mobilizing the masses than complicated statements about human rights and consensual democracy.

The national movements had to define the physical borders of their nations (the nations were seen in terms of a group personality) sooner or later. Two criteria were available for this process—ethnic or historical definitions. Neither criteria covered all the known consequences of minority movements in the period between the two World Wars in those cases in which a historical definition was possible. Nearly all contemporary national movements faced the same problem, and their leaders usually decided in favour of the historical border, although it would again creat ethnic minorities in Estonia, Latvia, Lithuania, Croatia, and Moldova. Nations are still personified, which increases the discordance between ethnic and political borders. It is still true that the situation of minorities consisting of the members of the former ruling (state) nation in the territory of the former underprivileged nation is particularly critical. The role that German and Hungarian minorities played between the World Wars is now played by Russian and Serbian minorities.

The defensive argument still dominates national stereotypes; a national movement defends rightful claims, which makes possible moral exculpation. This is usually complemented by the stereotype of peacefulness, the demand for the national unity, and the need to express the right to sovereignty.

The important role of the nationally relevant conflict of interests has shifted in comparison with the past: then the conflicts of interests occurred in the conditions of an ascending society, and of economic growth. The present conflicts, however, have been accompanied by economic depressions and crises and, above all, with a total change of the economic system and the ascension of new elites to the power vacuum that was left after the withdrawal of the Communist 'nomenclatura' elites.

If a certain level of social communication conditioned the success of national agitation in the past, the role of the mass media has now become the decisive force in the speed and intensity of national mobilization. This was a reason for a speedy mass response to national agitation. Nevertheless, not even the mass media can 'construct' a nation state if the conditions are not favourable.

The possibility of social advancement was another necessary condition of successful nation-forming. We can observe a significant difference in this respect. In the past, national movement leaders had to strive for each position and, if they managed to penetrate into the elites, they had to modify their lifestyle and moral code. Leaders of the contemporary national movements penetrate 'a vacuum' in which no traditional values exist. This contains the potential for abuse, but also for a fresh start.

After the 19th-century national movements rejected identification with a dynastically defined multi-ethnic empire, they had no supranational authority as a source of a higher identity. Today, the supranational identity is represented by the project of European integration. Even though almost none of the new national movement leaders question the prospect of 'Europe', it is not clear whether they will be willing to accept fully the Europe of regions.

## European, national and regional identities

The aim of the emphasis on the regional identity is to weaken national identity and nationalism to make way for the European identity. Although the idea was developed in the post-war period, it needs to be noted that the relationship between the region and the nation has a longer history. In the 18th century, the patriotism of the Enlightenment was based on identification with 'the country', which was defined in terms of a region. A national identity, or a national movement marginalized and eventually superseded this regional identity. The historical experience can be a useful lesson for the present. Let us focus on the points of difference. How did, and how does, national identity differ from regional identity?

Both identities are related to the population of a particular territory, but they differ significantly in defining the territory. A national territory does not have to be entirely compact (it can include minorities living in the territory of other nations or states) and it is determined by a strict dividing line between US and THEM, the two ethnically defined groups. A region is not so precisely defined, nor is it important whether the inhabitants of the region are ethnically homogeneous. A nation has members, a region inhabitants. This means different consequences of migration. The inhabitants of a region lose their regional identity by moving out of the region, while the members of a nation preserve it (at least for one generation). Similarly, immigrants easily accept a regional identity, but they have the status of foreigners in relation to the ethnically-defined members of a nation for a long time.

National identity is based on the existence of a distinctive culture, different from others, while a regional culture usually constitutes a part of a broader national culture or several national cultures, although it can have certain national specifics in this framework. From the perspective of cultural specificity, both identities are not mutually exclusive, but complementary.

National identity is associated with the idea of a personified nation (group personality) with its own history, with which an individual identifies. Regional identity has no such personification. This creates a difference which was more important in the Enlightenment than today. Regional patriotism was based on the idea of the patriot's responsibility for the people, for the inhabitants of the region, including the possibility of advancement. National activism aims at a fictional idea of a personality who has certain needs and articulates his or her demands. Regional interests are only the interests of the community of the inhabitants, and lack the charisma of a group personality.

The difference in the relation to state power is symptomatic. A region always evokes the image of a province, a territory within a larger whole. A multi-ethnic empire represented the larger whole in the period of nation-forming. If the regional identity was compatible with the national identity at the time, it was not the case with the relation between the national identity and the supra-national state. There, the effort toward the minimization of the peripheral position of the nation and the subsequent establishment of national territory as a sovereign centre within the state prevailed. In the changed conditions of the 20th century, this process results in the drive for nation statehood.

The most important advantage of a regional identity is that although conflicts of interests will still occur they will not become nationally-relevant, and therefore, will not be used in the interest of nationalism. The advantage might become merely relative if the concept of a region is substituted for the concept of a nation in our time, because antagonisms between regions could be 'translated' into the language of antagonisms between nations.

Here we arrive at an important relation to political power. While the politicians of a nation-state are more or less independent agents of power in their 'own' territory, regionalization presupposes dependence of the politicians in the region on the overarching state—or on Europe. Under what conditions will the ruling elites of the post-communist nation-states be willing to concede their position to regional politicians? Direct dependence on Europe seems to be, at least judging from verbal declarations, more acceptable than dependence mediated through a multi-ethnic state. From this perspective, the disintegration of federations and the creation of nation-states after 1989 appears to be a favourable starting point for European integration. Nevertheless, the dangers follow from a situation in which a nation with a low population will also be in a position of a region in relation to Europe, with all the risks of nationally-relevant conflicts. We should note that a weaker national unit always separates from a stronger one in secessions and not the other way round.

The acceptance of a European identity seems unproblematic, leaving aside the issue of political power, providing that we can assume that a European identity can be 'cultivated', just as nationalism can be cured. Such an approach, however, is too voluntarist, because the success of any education always depends on certain external determinants, and no identity, not even the European one, can be introduced by a decree without regard to them. Some of the determinants are that the citizens who are to accept the new identity share the same economic level, culture and value systems, and identify with the present and the past of the new unit. This is the crux of the problem.

The differences in the increase of economic level after 1989 can stultify the possibility of creating a West–East community based on shared interests (unless we call multinational corporations communities of shared interests). The prospect of a cultural community is no less dubious. The reason is that a possible pan-European and integrating impact is dominated by American (and possibly Japanese) imports. A visitor from another planet might say that the common features of the continent called Europe are primarily TV series like *Dallas* and catering of the McDonald's type! The historical dimension of the European identity is perhaps even more complicated since it seems that the 'West' is unwilling to integrate the past of the post-communist countries in the established image of European history, as can be seen in looking at any European history textbook published in France, Great Britain or Germany. The well-meant projects of the new concept of European history have had no impact on this fact yet.

The most often quoted issue is of the insufficient compatibility of the value systems as shown by the contrast of Western civil society and Eastern 'nationalism'. In this respect, the terminological arbitrariness, mentioned in the introduction, creates the largest problem. The abstract, undefined, but often repeated vision of the undifferentiated Eastern 'nationalism' blatantly overlooks the fact that separatism is gaining in force in many Western European countries and its agents are nationalists in the same way as, say, right-wing politicians in Hungary or Lithuania. The two groups, after all, share a positive relation to European integration. I have not mentioned the success of semi-fascist and racist political parties, for example, in France and Italy, because I perceive a fundamental difference in the differing levels of political culture, rather than in a qualitatively different 'nationalism'.

If we want to undertake a serious analysis (as opposed to statements consisting of journalistic clichés) of the issues concerning national identity of citizens of post-communist nation-states and the extent that this identity is a threat to civil values and a hindrance to the inclusion in Europe, we have first to put aside the abstract scarecrow of 'Eastern nationalism'. As long as we persist in using such unclear terminology, we cannot arrive at any concrete solution to the problem. Thus, we have to start with concrete analyses not at the level of grand ideas, but at the level of real life.

I can, therefore, imagine a coordinated research project focusing equally on Europe, West and East, and exploring the foundations of national (and regional) identities of the nation-states' nationals, and the existing stereotypes. From what traditions do these identities follow? What have been the 'nationalist' demands? What phase of the nation-forming process are all these particular communities going through? Such research would also have to include the historical dimension.

As long as the opinion that, from the historical point of view, the European 'West' and 'East' are and have been, two incomparable units prevails in the European Union, the discussions about European integration will remain mere propaganda. The Iron Curtain was created by Communism in defence against democracy. The historical irony is that, seven years after its fall, it still survives as a mental barrier, especially in Western mass-media, which helps 'the West' keep its exclusivity.

# XII

## EUGEN LEMBERGS „NATIONALISMUSTHEORIE" *

Jede wissenschaftliche Arbeit kann auf zwei Weisen analysiert werden: Man kann sie aus ihrer Zeit heraus begreifen und ihren unmittelbaren Einfluss auf die zeitgenössische Forschung untersuchen, oder ihrem Weiterleben nachgehen, ihre Wirkungsgeschichte nachzeichnen. Dabei zeigt sich, dass die meisten Werke mit der Zeit immer weniger rezipiert werden, bis sie schließlich zum bloßen bibliographischen Hinweis absinken. Das ist das Schicksal jeder wissenschaftlichen Untersuchung. Eugen Lembergs zweibändiges Werk über den Nationalismus aus dem Jahr 1964, dem ich mich im Folgenden auf beiden angedeuteten Ebenen nähern werde, bildet hier keine Ausnahme.

Zweimal habe ich mich mit Eugen Lembergs Nationalismustheorie auseinander gesetzt, allerdings immer mit jenen Abschnitten seines Werkes, die dem Prozess der Formierung moderner Nationen gewidmet sind, nicht mit seinen Überlegungen zu den in der Gegenwart politisch wirksamen Aspekten des Nationalismus. Das erste Mal befasste ich mich kurz nach dem Erscheinen von Lembergs Nationalismusbuch mit seinen Ideen, genau zu der Zeit, in der ich mich nach methodischen und terminologischen Inspirationen umsah, die mir den Einstieg in meine komparative Untersuchung nationaler Bewegungen erleichtern sollten. Anfang der 1990er Jahre, als ich mich mit der Entwicklung von Theorien und Konzepten zu nationalen Formierungsprozessen beschäftigte, las ich Eugen Lemberg zum zweiten Mal. Ich begegnete seinen Theorien also in unterschiedlichen Etappen meiner eigenen Forschungen und unter veränderten gesellschaftlichen Umständen. Und es waren zwei völlig verschiedene Motive, die mich zu Lembergs Werk führten.

Im ersten Fall sah ich, dass Lembergs Buch am Ende einer langen Reihe von Werken über die Nation und die Nationsbildung stand, von denen ein großer Teil einer primordialistischen Sicht verpflichtet und mit einem politischen Narrativ verbunden war, während ein kleinerer Teil wie die Arbeiten von Hans Kohn oder Elie Kedourie eher spekulativ vorgingen. Und schließlich arbeitete ich in einem Land, in dem noch immer das stalinistische Modell als verbindlich galt. Was konnte Lembergs Buch einem jungen Forscher damals bieten, der eine Alternative zu diesem Modell suchte und zugleich beabsichtigte, den damals als verdächtig geltenden Weg des historischen Vergleichs anzutreten?

Vor allem beeindruckte mich die Fülle des empirischen Materials, die Breite des Horizonts. Ermunternd wirkte der Mut und natürlich auch die Fähigkeit Lembergs, auf der Basis der empirischen Daten zu generalisieren, Fragen von großer Tragweite zu stellen und zu beantworten. In einer Atmosphäre, in der einerseits auf traditio-

---

* Dieser Text ist die leicht ergänzte Version eines Vortrages, der am 16. Januar 2004 im Collegium Carolinum gehalten wurde.

2

nalistischer Seite Generalisierungen als mit dem Metier des Historikers unvereinbar galten, andererseits nur solche Generalisierungen und Erklärungen erlaubt waren, die mit dem offiziellen begrifflichen und methodischen Kanon übereinstimmten bzw. diesem zumindest nicht widersprachen, war das besonders aufbauend. Zudem lieferte Lembergs Buch viele Denkanstöße. Die soziologische Terminologie, der er sich reichlich und wie selbstverständlich bediente, wirkte inspirierend und ich fühlte mich in der Verwendung einiger Termini unterstützt, wie z. B. des Begriffs der „Großgruppe" im Zusammenhang mit der Definition der Nation, oder des Begriffspaars (nationale) Integration und Desintegration. Bestätigt fühlte ich mich auch in der Ansicht, dass die „Kriterien" der Nation austauschbar sind, wenngleich mir der Begriff „Kriterium" zu statisch war und zu nahe an Stalins „Merkmalen" lag.

Die Formierung moderner Nationen im Kontext der gesellschaftlichen Umgestaltung zu beobachten, war zwar keineswegs eine Entdeckung Lembergs. Ich fand es aber wichtig, dass er den „Nationalismus" nicht im luftleeren Raum, sondern im sozialen Kontext der Veränderung vormoderner „feudaler" Gesellschaften untersuchte. Nicht zufällig gehörte Karl W. Deutsch zu den wenigen Autoren, auf die er sich nachdrücklich berief. In diesem Zusammenhang soll Lembergs programmatische Interdisziplinarität nicht unerwähnt bleiben. Obwohl er explizit vor allem die Verknüpfung der Geschichte mit der Soziologie forderte, stand er auch den Politologen und Ethnologen nahe, zumindest soweit es in diesen Fächern relevante Arbeiten zum Thema gab. Diese Interdisziplinarität demonstrierte er so überzeugend, dass sie mir ganz natürlich erschien. Erst später sollte ich die Erfahrung machen, dass sie keineswegs so geläufig war.

Andererseits hat mich vor allem das Moralisierende bei Lemberg gestört, besonders im zweiten Band des Nationalismusbuches, in dem er die nationalen Phänomene als Gegenstand der politischen Pädagogik unter die Lupe nimmt, also seine Überlegungen zum „ewigen Traum der Menschheit" von einer „Welt ohne soziale und nationale Schranken". Damals – und auch heute noch – war ich der Auffassung, dass man die kausale Analyse vom moralischen Urteil möglichst sauber trennen sollte, wenn man dem Vorwurf einer instrumentalisierenden bzw. ideologisierenden Geschichtsdarstellung vorbeugen will.

Was mich ausgesprochen irritiert hat, war Lembergs Umgang mit dem Begriff „Nation". Es erschien mir als ein Zeichen von Ratlosigkeit, wenn er diesen Terminus als undefinierbar zur Seite schob – allerdings, nachdem er vor allem im ersten Band seines Buches „Nation" und „Volk" auf vielen Seiten synonym benutzt hatte. Seine Wende zum Topos „Nationalismus" verstand ich daher als Notlösung, seine Definition dieses für seine eigene Arbeit zentralen Begriffs hielt ich für unbrauchbar. Damals – und im Grunde genommen auch heute noch – erschien es mir zu allgemein, und somit für die konkrete Forschung kaum anwendbar, den Nationalismus als bedingungslose Hingabe an das überpersönliche Ganze zu charakterisieren. Außerdem sah ich eine Spannung oder sogar Inkonsequenz in der Einschätzung des Phänomens, die sich bei Lemberg zwischen moralisch neutral (insbesondere in seinen theoretischen Überlegungen) und negativ (im konkreten historischen Fall) bewegt. Wahrhaft inspirierend war indessen für mich, dass Lemberg die sozialen Aspekte des

Nationalen betonte. Allerdings blieb er dabei auf der theoretischen Ebene stehen, was mich in meiner schon zuvor formulierten Überzeugung bestätigte, dass es sich bei der Frage nach den sozialen Bedingungen nationaler Bewegungen, der sozialen Struktur von Gruppen nationaler „Vorkämpfer", um eine echte Forschungslücke handelte, die nur durch konkrete und am besten komparative Untersuchungen zu schließen war.

Nur wenig konnte ich bei Eugen Lemberg für mein wichtigstes methodisches Problem, die vergleichende Analyse, lernen. Er demonstrierte zwar eine imponierende Faktenkenntnis, stellte die einzelnen Daten aber lediglich nebeneinander. Der Vergleich erschien mir unsystematisch, oft auch willkürlich und im Falle der Nationalismen neuester Zeit zudem ideologisch belastet.

So habe ich von Eugen Lemberg nur wenige Ideen übernommen, aber doch manche Inspiration gewonnen. Seine Interdisziplinarität und sein breiter Horizont haben mich ermutigt, seine Generalisierungen intellektuell angeregt, seine Begrifflichkeit zu erneutem Nachdenken herausgefordert. Doch viel mehr habe ich von Eric Hobsbawm und Karl W. Deutsch profitiert, obwohl ich Letzterem in seiner Überschätzung der sozialen Kommunikation nicht folge. Und im Grunde genommen schien mir damals, in den sechziger Jahren, auch Otto Bauers Begrifflichkeit und Arbeitsweise für meine Zwecke in mancher Hinsicht brauchbarer und methodisch inspirierender zu sein.

Später hatte ich dann Gelegenheit, Eugen Lembergs Werk mit anderen Augen und in einem anderen Kontext neu zu entdecken: nicht als eine mögliche Inspirationsquelle für meine eigenen Arbeiten, sondern als Teil der Geschichte der Forschung zum Problemkreis Nation, Nationsbildung und Nationalismus. Der Umfang und die Bandbreite dieser Forschungen sind seit dem Erscheinen von Lembergs Nationalismusbuch in mehreren Schüben gewachsen, was allerdings nicht bedeutet, dass die Originalität und Relevanz der Ergebnisse all dieser Studien ihrer immensen Zahl entspräche.

Die zentrale Frage bei dieser Wiederbegegnung war, wo Lemberg im Kontext der heute so reichen Nations- und Nationalismusforschung steht. Es galt dabei nicht allein, das Neue in Lembergs Werk zu identifizieren, sondern auch zu prüfen, wie stark er in der traditionellen Forschung verankert ist. Ohne diese traditionellen Elemente, die Lemberg natürlich vor allem mit der deutschen Forschungstradition verbinden, können wir auch das Neue seiner Ideen nicht richtig erfassen.

Das Traditionelle im Denken Eugen Lembergs über die Nation und den Nationalismus sehe ich vor allem in fünf Punkten: Erstens fällt ein starker Historismus auf, den ein Historiker natürlich immer spontan begrüßt, also die Neigung, die Wurzeln des Phänomens bzw. Problems in der Vergangenheit zu suchen, in der Entwicklung dessen, was die ältere Forschung als „Nationalgefühl" oder „Volksbewusstsein" bezeichnete. Mit anderen Worten: Die Formierung der Nation wird auch bei Lemberg als eine Entwicklung, die bereits im Mittelalter begonnen hat, beobachtet und kommentiert. Dadurch komplizierte sich allerdings die Aussagekraft des neu eingeführten Begriffs „Nationalismus".

Zweitens war sein Ausgangspunkt essentialistisch, wenn auch nicht ausgesprochen primordialistisch: Für Lemberg existierte die Nation nicht nur als Wort, nicht

4

nur als ein Idealtypus im Sinne Max Webers, sondern als soziale Großgruppe. Aus dieser traditionellen Herangehensweise leiteten sich auch die ausführlichen Überlegungen ab, anhand welcher „Merkmale" man diese Großgruppe Nation bzw. Volk bestimmen könnte. Auch wenn Lemberg bei der Antwort auf diese Frage letztlich resignierte, beharrte er auf der Vorstellung einer „an sich" existierenden Großgruppe „Volk" bzw. „Nation".

Aus der spezifisch deutschen sprachlichen Tradition stammt drittens diese Duplizität der Termini „Nation" und „Volk", die scheinbar synonym, aber dann doch in unterschiedlichen Kontexten benutzt werden. Es würde sich allerdings lohnen, zu untersuchen, welche Nuancen sich in Lembergs Texten im Gebrauch von „Volk" und „Nation" feststellen lassen.

Viertens war an Lembergs Überlegungen irritierend, dass er diese an vielen Stellen durch Einschübe zu dem damals sehr präsenten Thema Nationalsozialismus unterbrach. Diese Exkurse stören die sonst sehr ausgewogene Auswahl der untersuchten Nationalisierungsprozesse, die geographisch ganz Europa abdecken. Wiederholt greift Lemberg auf die für ihn offensichtlich schmerzhafte Erfahrung des Dritten Reiches und auf dessen Nationalismusvariante zurück. Immer wieder reagiert er auf Verzerrungen, die durch eine – seiner Ansicht nach übertriebene – Ablehnung all der Gedanken und Theorien entstünden, die zur Vorgeschichte der nationalsozialistischen Ideologie gerechnet werden könnten. Hier ist wohl der Grund für die spontane Übernahme des Volksbegriffs und für die Verteidigung von Herders Gedankengut gegen Vorwürfe zu suchen, dieser sei ein Wegbereiter bzw. Vorläufer der nationalsozialistischen Ideologie gewesen. Aus dem zeitgenössischen Kontext ist diese deutsche Traumatisierung durchaus verständlich. Heute wirken die entsprechenden Passagen seines Buches wie auch Lembergs Auseinandersetzung mit dem Stalinismus unorganisch und unangemessen politisierend.

Fünftens übernahm Lemberg aus der früheren Forschung auch den psychologisierenden Ansatz, den er weiter vertiefte und auf eine nicht traditionelle Art anwandte.

Viel wichtiger und interessanter sind aber die Kapitel seines Nationalismusbuches, die etwas wirklich Neues brachten und – um meinen Schluss gleich vorwegzunehmen – in mancher Hinsicht bahnbrechend waren. Manchmal antizipierten sie sogar Thesen, die erst viel später in der (vor allem der deutschen Literatur unkundigen anglo-amerikanischen) Forschung als Neuheiten präsentiert wurden.

Bahnbrechend war vor allem die Einführung des Terminus „Nationalismus" in die deutsche und eigentlich in die gesamte kontinentale Forschung. Natürlich war der Begriff in der Sprache der Politik und des Journalismus geläufig, und zwar eindeutig mit negativer Konnotation. Von der amerikanischen Forschung inspiriert, versuchte Lemberg, „Nationalismus" jedoch als analytischen Begriff, als einen Teil des methodischen Instrumentariums, zu etablieren. Er bekannte sich explizit zu der „distanzierten anglo-amerikanischen Betrachtungsweise", wie sie z. B. bei Carlton Hayes fand, der schrieb, solange der eine Nationalismus als gut, der andere als böse gelte, könne es nicht zu einer ausreichenden Theorie des Nationalismus kommen. Das „Neutrale" verstand Lemberg als die integrierende und zugleich nach außen abgrenzende Kraft, die der Nationalismus in nationalen oder quasinationalen Großgruppen entfaltet. Dieses Argument kehrt übrigens fast vierzig Jahre später in Dieter Lange-wiesches Kritik an Otto Danns Nationalismuskonzept wieder.

In diesen Zusammenhang gehört auch Lembergs Auseinandersetzung mit Hans Kohns Dichotomie des liberalen, progressiven (westlichen) und ethnisch-rassischen, reaktionären (deutschen bzw. osteuropäischen) Nationalismus. Allerdings erleich-terte sich Lemberg die Kritik an Kohns Konzept durch eine Sinnverschiebung bzw. Fehlinterpretation Kohns: Handelte es sich doch bei Lembergs Interpretation der Kohnschen Dichotomie um eine Gegenüberstellung von Zionismus und deutschem Nationalismus. Doch hat Lemberg durchaus Recht, wenn er schreibt, dass der Kohnsche Nationalismusbegriff den Leser im Unklaren darüber lasse, worauf er bezogen sei.

Natürlich musste sich auch Lemberg in der Mannigfaltigkeit positiver und nega-tiver Erscheinungen und Einstellungen orientieren, die er unter diesem Sammel-begriff subsumierte. Wie vor ihm bereits Hayes, versuchte Lemberg dieses Problem durch Adjektive zu lösen. Auch er unterscheidet – teilweise im Widerspruch zu sei-ner theoretischen Annahme der „Neutralität" des Begriffs – zwei Sorten von Natio-nalismus: den „primitiven", der egoistisch die Priorität des eigenen Landes betont, und den „ideologischen", in dem er den eigentlichen Nationalismus sieht. Dieser verlange vom Einzelnen die Unterordnung unter das Ganze und sei moralisch ambi-valent. Er trage sowohl negative Züge (Hass, Egoismus, Selbstüberschätzung) als auch positive, zu denen Lemberg – nicht besonders überzeugend – schöpferische Kraft und kulturelle Leistungen zählt.

Auch im „praktischen" Gebrauch des Begriffs „Nationalismus" war Lemberg also nicht immer konsequent, er schwankte zwischen einem neutralen und einem negati-ven Verständnis des Phänomens. Dieses Problems war er sich durchaus bewusst, in seinem abschließenden Exkurs zu Band zwei des Nationalismuswerkes thematisier-te er es ausdrücklich. Hier führte er auch terminologische Alternativen zum negativ konnotierten Nationalismus wie „Vaterlandsliebe" oder „Patriotismus" auf. Analog bemerkt übrigens auch Ernest Gellner zwanzig Jahre später auf den letzten Seiten seines Buches, der Nationalismus sei eine besondere Art von Patriotismus. Diese Schwankungen in Lembergs Nationalismusbegriff schmälern seine Vorreiterrolle auf diesem Gebiet aber keineswegs.

Wenn ich diese Pionierleistung hervorhebe, bedeutet das natürlich nicht, dass ich die Meinung teile, es sei nützlich und progressiv gewesen, diesen Terminus einzu-führen. Schließlich stehen wir heute vor einem begrifflichen Scherbenhaufen, einem Durcheinander, in dem alles, was mit der Nation zu tun hat, als Nationalismus ver-standen wird (natürlich mit Ausnahme der amerikanischen Nation, die den Begriff des „Patriotismus" für sich besetzt hat). Aber das konnte Lemberg Anfang der 1960er Jahre nicht ahnen, als er sich beklagte, es gäbe viele materialreiche Studien über Nationen, aber keine „Nationalismustheorie". Heute sind wir umgekehrt mit einer Überproduktion von Theorien konfrontiert, die mit der empirischen For-schung, ja überhaupt mit der Kenntnis von empirischen Daten, nur wenig zu tun haben.

Einer anderen methodischen Neuerung Lembergs kann man allerdings ohne jedes Zögern zustimmen: seinem Ruf nach einer interdisziplinären Forschung unter der

6

Beteiligung von Historikern, Ethnologen, Soziologen und Psychologen. Und Lemberg blieb nicht bei frommen Wünschen, sondern setzte seine Forderung in seiner eigenen Forschungspraxis konsequent um. Mit seinem Nationalismusbuch legte er ein für die Zeit sehr gelungenes Beispiel dafür vor, wie historische, soziologische und sozialpsychologische Betrachtungsweisen kombiniert und organisch verbunden werden können.

In der eigentlichen Analyse sollte vor allem auf Lembergs Erklärungsmodell für die Entstehung des Nationalismus eingegangen werden: Ein zentrales Element seines Modells ist die Auffassung, dass die neuzeitliche Entwicklung der Technik und der Produktion – kurz die Industrialisierung – auch soziale und kulturelle Veränderungen erforderte. Die Industrialisierung führte vor allem zu einer neuen Arbeitsteilung, einer neuen Abstufung von Abhängigkeiten, wodurch neue soziale Gruppen mit neuen spezifischen Interessen entstanden. Diese neuen Gruppen mussten sich integrieren und brauchten, um sich nach außen abgrenzen zu können, ein Kriterium, das sie von anderen Gruppen unterschied und ihre Gemeinsamkeiten betonte. In Lembergs Typologie war das im Falle des „Risorgimento-Nationalismus" das Bedürfnis, anstelle der alten, ständisch verankerten und auf Ungleichheit beruhenden Abhängigkeiten ein neues Kriterium der Bindung und der Gemeinsamkeit zu finden. Dieses wurde aus einem „kulturellen Merkmal" – d. h. auch der Sprache – abgeleitet. Damit war, so Lemberg, der Weg zur modernen Nation frei.

Wenn man sich hier an Gellners Interpretation der Genese des Nationalismus durch die Industrialisierung erinnert fühlt, ist das eine richtige Assoziation. Allerdings bezweifle ich stark, dass Gellner Lembergs Nationalismuswerk kannte, auf seiner Literaturliste für deutsche Leser fehlt es auf jeden Fall. Aber es gibt noch eine weitere Parallele. Wie Gellner bringt Lemberg den Nationalismus mit dem Zerfall der alten ständischen Bindungen in Zusammenhang. Auch hier ist Lemberg anderen Forschern voraus. In der deutschen Forschung steht er damit am Anfang einer Reihe, deren Ende vielleicht das zuletzt erschienene kleine Buch über den Nationalismus von Hans-Ulrich Wehler bildet. Natürlich argumentieren diese beiden Autoren raffinierter, auch ihr Vokabular ist zum Teil ein anderes. Das ändert aber nichts an dem zeitlichen Primat Eugen Lembergs. Allerdings war Lemberg selbst auch Teil einer Entwicklungslinie: Was die These von der Nationsbildung aus der Industrialisierung betrifft, war er stark von den Arbeiten seines um zehn Jahre älteren Landsmannes Karl W. Deutsch inspiriert.

Liest man das Kapitel über die Rolle der Romantik, fühlt man sich an eine andere aktuelle Diskussion über die Genese des Nationalismus erinnert. Heute ist es wieder Mode, auf die romantischen Wurzeln der Nation hinzuweisen. Die Vertreter dieser Auffassung sehen sich in der Tradition von Hans Kohn und versuchen, über eine idealistische Interpretation des Nationalismus aus dem Geist der Zeit die Realität der Nation und ihrer Mitglieder zu ignorieren. Obwohl er die romantischen Elemente im nationalen Denken nicht leugnete, wusste schon Eugen Lemberg, dass eine solche Vereinfachung nicht zulässig ist. Leider geht den neuen Anhängern der romantischen Interpretation auch jene differenzierte Betrachtungsweise ab, die wir bei Lemberg finden. Lemberg begreift die Romantik – den „romantischen Volksbegriff" – nicht nur als eine konservative, rückwärts gewandte Kraft, sondern auch als eine zukunftsweisende, mit demokratischen Elementen arbeitende Bewegung. Er spricht sogar vom „revolutionären Prinzip des romantischen Weltbildes". Verglichen damit ist – um nur ein Beispiel zu nennen – die einseitige, ideologisch voreingenommene Auffassung einer Liah Greenfeld vom deutschen Nationalismus, den sie für reaktionär hält, weil er dem romantischen Ideengut entsprungen sei, keineswegs als ein Schritt nach vorne zu betrachten.

Obgleich Lemberg die Definierbarkeit der Nation schließlich in Frage stellte, waren seine Überlegungen zu diesem Thema in seiner Zeit nicht zuletzt deswegen innovativ, weil er die Frage nach der „Austauschbarkeit der Kriterien" der Nation stellte. Seiner Auffassung zufolge konnte die Großgruppe Nation auch durch von Fall zu Fall differierende, nicht-ethnische Kriterien integriert werden. Damit signalisierte er die Loslösung von der dogmatischen Vorstellung, es könne eine allgemein verbindliche Definition der Nation durch eine feste Kombination von Kriterien geben. Diese Wende war nicht ganz originell, wir finden einen ähnlichen Hinweis z. B. bei dem Soziologen Pitirim Sorokin. Lemberg setzt allerdings voraus, dass die Merkmale oder Kriterien, über die sich eine Nation integriert, von den Mitgliedern der Großgruppe akzeptiert werden müssen.

Lemberg verfolgte diese Austauschbarkeit vor allem in diachroner Linie. Er ging davon aus, dass ein und dieselbe Nation im Laufe der Zeiten anhand ganz unterschiedlicher Merkmale charakterisiert werden könne. Ich würde hingegen die synchrone Perspektive stärker betonen, also die Austauschbarkeit im Sinne einer wechselnden Kombination von Merkmalen oder besser gesagt von Beziehungen und Bindungen verschiedener Nationen. Sehr modern und innovativ wirkt Lembergs These, die jeweiligen Integrationskriterien könnten ihre Rolle dadurch spielen, dass sie von den Mitgliedern dieser Nation selbst als ihre Gemeinsamkeit aufgefasst würden. Also ein Schritt in Richtung Diskursanalyse bei Eugen Lemberg? Man ginge zu weit, würde man seine Auffassung als vor-postmodernistischen Ansatz deuten. Schließlich waren für Lemberg bei der Integration von Nationen auch objektive Bindungen relevant – ohne das zu sehen, lässt sich seine Hochschätzung für die Theorie Karl W. Deutschs nicht nachvollziehen.

Die Schlussfolgerungen, die Lemberg aus dem Konzept der Austauschbarkeit der Kriterien zog, sind, kombiniert mit seiner breiten Auffassung des Nationalismus, ein Beleg dafür, wie fruchtbar der Versuch ist, auf den Begriff der Nation zu verzichten und sich konsequent auf den Nationalismus zu konzentrieren. Eugen Lemberg ging in seiner Suche nach einer Definition des Nationalismus sehr weit und gelangte zu einer mutigen theoretischen Innovation. Dadurch, dass er den Terminus „Nationalismus" als „Integrationsideologie" verstand, hob er ihn auf eine höhere Abstraktionsebene. Den Nationalismus charakterisierte er als „bedingungslose Hingabe" an eine „überindividuelle Instanz", also an eine Autorität, die mehr sein konnte als die Großgruppe Nation. Diese Hingabe war für ihn mit der „Preisgabe der individuellen Selbstbestimmung im Dienste einer Gruppe" identisch, wobei die Nation nur als eines der möglichen Bezugsobjekte erscheinen konnte.

Dieser Ansatz war seinerzeit sehr innovativ, hat sich aber als unproduktiv erwiesen. Denn versteht man den Nationalismus als die zentrale Integrationsideologie mit austauschbaren Kriterien, sind die Kriterien letztlich irrelevant, entscheidend ist

8

allein die Kraft der Integration. So gesehen, könnte jede Form „bedingungsloser Hingabe" als ein Anzeichen für Nationalismus identifiziert werden, unabhängig davon, ob es sich um das Ergebnis staatlicher, politischer oder konfessioneller Integration handelt. Und jede Integrationsideologie könnte als Nationalismus verstanden und bezeichnet werden. Lemberg illustrierte also unfreiwillig eine der Gefahren, die einem von der Nation getrennten Verständnis des Nationalismus immanent ist: Mit seinem Versuch, den Begriff auf höchstem Abstraktionsniveau zu definieren, geriet er im Grunde genommen in eine terminologische Sackgasse.

Trotzdem enthielten diese Überlegungen eine weiterweisende Perspektive. Lemberg reagierte mit seinem Ideologiebegriff auf das – im Grunde genommen bis heute bestehende – Desiderat der sozialgeschichtlichen und soziologischen Forschung an einem die Integration von Großgruppen subsumierenden Oberbegriff. Beschreiben wir diese Integrationsprozesse als Hingabe an eine überpersönliche Großgruppe – also an eine politische Partei, Konfession, den Staat oder eine Klasse –, erfassen wir sicher gewisse Analogien. Ein verbindlicher, allgemein akzeptierter Begriff für dieses Phänomen fehlt damit aber immer noch und es würde lediglich Verwirrung stiften, würden wir als Ersatzbegriff den des „Nationalismus" wählen.

Meiner Ansicht nach könnte die „Identität", ein Terminus, den Lemberg nicht kannte bzw. nicht benutzte, die Rolle dieses Oberbegriffs übernehmen, und zwar in dem Sinne, in dem dieser seit etwa zwei Jahrzehnten von Forschern wie Anthony Smith verwendet wird. Der Begriff „Identität" könnte die fragwürdige und belastete „Ideologie" ersetzen und wäre zugleich viel flexibler. Lemberg stand vor der Schwierigkeit, den Anspruch der Ideologie auf Exklusivität mit der empirischen Tatsache zusammenzubringen, dass Menschen stets in verschiedene Gruppen integriert werden. Dieses Dilemma ergibt sich bei der Arbeit mit einem Identitätsbegriff nicht, dem die Annahme zugrunde liegt, dass es stets eine Vielzahl von Identitäten gibt.

Man muss gerechterweise aber sagen, dass Lemberg die „Hingabe" nicht so idealistisch verstand, wie man auf den ersten Blick vermuten könnte. Im Gegenteil, er formulierte es als eine der nächsten Aufgaben der soziologischen Forschung, die sozialen Ursachen zu untersuchen, die sich im nationalen Formierungsprozess als gruppenintegrierende Kräfte erwiesen haben. In diesem Zusammenhang richtete er drei Forderungen an die Soziologie: Erstens sollte sie die Rolle der Ideologie, vor allem deren gruppenintegrierende Funktion, untersuchen. Zweitens sollte sie das Verhalten dieser Großgruppen selbst – ihr Entstehen und Vergehen – unter der Perspektive analysieren, welche Kräfte der Integration in ihnen wirkten. Und drittens sollte sie prüfen, unter welchen Bedingungen solche ideologischen Kräfte der Integration auftreten, einen bestimmten Grad und bestimmte Funktionen erreichen bzw. unter welchen Bedingungen sie wieder verschwinden und von anderen Integrationskräften abgelöst werden.

Es ist übrigens signifikant, dass Lemberg in seinem eigenen Werk die Ansicht, der zufolge der Nationalismus die alles dominierende Integrationsideologie darstellt, selbst nicht konsequent umsetzte. Dazu hätte er sein Buch auch von Grund auf anders konzipieren müssen. Zum Beispiel hätte er nicht die These vertreten können, dass die Nation und der Nationalismus spezifisch europäische Phänomene sind, deren äußere Merkmale im 20. Jahrhundert auch nach Asien und Afrika „exportiert" wurden. Von dieser Beobachtung ausgehend, skizzierte er eine Übersicht über diese Phänomene auf anderen Kontinenten, die schon deswegen interessant ist, weil sie uns zeigt, wie weit der Nationalismus vor dem Beginn der Entkolonialisierung in der Welt verbreitet war. Mit der Orientierung an systematischer Information hob sich Lemberg gegenüber vielen späteren Autoren wie z.B. Benedict Anderson oder Eric Hobsbawm, die Ereignisse außerhalb Europas nur am Rande erwähnen, positiv ab.

Zu den produktiven Inkonsequenzen in Lembergs Werk gehören auch seine Überlegungen zur historisch begründeten Typologie der Formierung moderner Nationen – also nicht nur der Nationalismen. Seine Unterscheidung zwischen der „Geburt der Nation aus dem Territorialstaat" und der „Geburt aus Sprache, Kultur und Idee" ist nur scheinbar selbstverständlich: Sie fehlt bis heute vor allem bei den zahlreichen, meist anglo-amerikanischen Autoren, die sich ausschließlich auf den Nationalismus konzentrieren. Formulierungen wie „Geburt aus der Sprache" klingen für uns heute zu „idealistisch". Solche Formulierungen waren, nicht anders als der Begriff „Risorgimento-Nationalismus", der uns vielleicht auch nicht sehr glücklich erscheint, vom damaligen Zeitgeist bestimmt. Auch spricht Lemberg in Bezug auf diesen Nationalismus vom „Minderwertigkeitskomplex" der kleinen Völker. Doch die Analogie zur Kohnschen Dichotomie ist nur partiell: Im Unterschied zu Kohn reduziert Lemberg seine Typologie nicht auf das Ost-West-Schema. Vielmehr arbeitet er mit den konkreten historischen Ausgangssituationen, in denen die jeweiligen nationalen Formierungsprozesse ihren Anfang nahmen.

Noch eine andere damals originelle Beobachtung Lembergs aus seinen historischen Überlegungen soll hier erwähnt werden, nämlich seine (übrigens komparativ begründete) Meinung, dass die Strukturelemente des modernen „Nationalismus" – wir können hier bei seiner Terminologie bleiben – seit dem Mittelalter mit dem bürgerlichen Milieu verbunden waren. Zu dieser These war Lemberg bereits in den 1930er Jahren gelangt, in der er einen für die damalige Zeit gewagten Vergleich des nationalen Gedankengutes in den flämischen Städten des 14. Jahrhunderts mit der hussitischen Bewegung unternahm. Diese Arbeit wurde zwar schon vor dem Krieg publiziert, blieb in Deutschland aber ebenso nahezu unbekannt wie im tschechischen Milieu.

Zuletzt möchte ich noch auf einen signifikanten Widerspruch in Lembergs Nationalismuswerk eingehen. Einerseits erwartet er von der soziologischen Forschung eine vertiefte Analyse des Verhaltens der Großgruppen und der sozialen Bedingungen für die Wirkung von Integrationsideen. Er spricht von Menschengruppen, die zu Trägern und Vorkämpfern bestimmter Ideen wurden. Andererseits findet man bei ihm ein überraschend geringes Interesse an der Konkretisierung der sozialen Träger des nationalen Gedankens. „Nationalismus" wirkte in seinem Text entweder als eine abstrakte Kraft oder als eine irgendwie von oben unpersönlich durchgesetzte Ideologie. Das illustrieren Wendungen wie „man hatte eine Sendung" bzw. „man liebte das Vaterland". Zwar finden sich in Lembergs Text auch konkrete Hinweise auf nationalistische Einstellungen oder Gedanken, diese werden aber ausschließlich großen Persönlichkeiten, bekannten Intellektuellen, Herrschern oder Politikern

10

zugeschrieben. Wie die Lage der national zu integrierenden Bevölkerung aussah, war keine Frage, die Lemberg interessierte. Mit anderen Worten: Es fehlt hier die Hobsbawmsche „Perspektive von unten".

*Fazit*

Wie ist also das Werk Eugen Lembergs in die Entwicklung der Nationalismusforschung einzuordnen? Indem Lemberg den Nationalismus als eine grundlegende Ordnungs- und Formierungskraft der Nation betrachtete, reihte er sich in die Linie der „subjektivistischen" Autoren ein. Zugleich war ihm jedoch bewusst, dass die Aufnahme bzw. Ausbreitung des Nationalismus kausal aus den sozialen und politischen Zusammenhängen zu deuten ist und der Forscher nach objektiven – d.h. von subjektiven Wünschen unabhängigen – Faktoren fragen muss. Insofern ist Eugen Lemberg, was die spätere Forschung angeht, in der Nähe von Ernest Gellner oder John Breuilly zu verorten. Er war zwar Subjektivist, aber zugleich auch Empiriker und Systematiker. Er gehörte nicht zu den radikalen Konstruktivisten, die der Nation überhaupt keine oder eine nur sehr kurze Vergangenheit zugestehen. Die objektiv existierenden Merkmale der Nation lehnte er nicht ab, vielmehr akzeptierte er sie als Bausteine des nationalen Bewusstseins. Auch war er kein Schwärmer, verstand die Nation nicht als Unglück oder Unfall der Geschichte. Die „Neutralität" des Begriffs Nationalismus bedeutete für ihn eher eine Anerkennung der Ambivalenz dieses Phänomens, das sowohl positiv als auch negativ wirken kann.

Lemberg zählt zu den wenigen Autoren, die sich nicht nur verbal zum Prinzip der Interdisziplinarität bekannten, sondern Interdisziplinarität auch praktizierten. Damit steht er unter den historisch orientierten Forschern in einer Reihe mit historischen Soziologen und Politologen wie Stein Rokkan, Charles Tilly oder Anthony Smith.

Bahnbrechend an Lembergs Denken war die Überregionalität seiner Perspektive. Im Unterschied zu den meisten deutschen Autoren begrenzte er sich nicht auf die deutsche bzw. deutsche und französische historische Realität, sondern führte den europäischen Westen und den Osten Europas zusammen – und das in der Zeit des Kalten Krieges und in einem Land, in dem der Blick nach Osten sogar institutionell von der gesamteuropäischen Perspektive abgetrennt worden war.

Auch mit seinem Versuch, die politische Pädagogik in die historisch orientierte Nationalismusforschung einzubeziehen, stand und steht Lemberg, obwohl sich seine Grundüberzeugungen durchaus mit denen der meisten Politologen der Gegenwart decken, ziemlich einsam da. Lemberg argumentierte, dass wir uns in der zivilen Gesellschaft mit dem Phänomen Nationalismus abfinden müssen. Keine Toleranz dürfe es allerdings für den integralen Nationalismus geben.

Die methodischen Ansätze wie das breite empirische Material machen Eugen Lembergs Nationalismusbuch von 1964 zu einer Lektüre, die auch heute noch inspirierend wirken kann, wenngleich uns manches methodisch inkonsequent und anderes voreingenommen erscheinen mag. Trotzdem ist dieses Werk nahezu vergessen. Dass Lemberg von der anglo-amerikanischen und französischen Forschung nicht rezipiert wurde, lässt sich mit der Sprachbarriere erklären. Doch dass seine

Nationalismustheorie auch in der deutschen Debatte keine Rolle spielt, sein Buch oft nicht einmal als bibliographischer Hinweis aufscheint, ist verwunderlich. Die inkonsequenten und mitunter veraltet klingenden Begriffe Lembergs bilden dafür sicher eine der Ursachen. Ich meine aber, dass Lemberg in erster Linie aufgrund der Interdisziplinarität und überregionalen Perspektive seiner Arbeit in Vergessenheit geraten ist. Für die Soziologen war er zu historisch, den Historikern schien er zu soziologisch und theorielastig. Den Spezialisten für die deutsche Geschichte war sein Blick zu übernational, Fachleuten für die allgemeine Geschichte wiederum zu osteuropäisch. Zwischen den Fächern und verschiedenen Strömungen stände Lemberg auch heute wieder; daher fehlen für eine „Wiederentdeckung" seines Nationalismuswerkes derzeit zumindest in der deutschen Forschung wohl die Verbündeten: Den Konstruktivisten wäre er zu essentialistisch, seine Sprache wäre nicht theoretisch genug, für die traditionellen Historiker wäre er zu stark generalisierend. So wird Eugen Lemberg ein Geheimtipp für Spezialisten bleiben.

### Zur Literatur

*Anderson,* Benedict: Imagined Communities. Reflections on the Origin and Spread of Nationalism. London 1983.

*Bauer,* Otto: Die Nationalitaetenfrage und die Sozialdemokratie. Wien 1924 (Marx-Studien 2).

*Breuilly,* John: Nationalism and the State. Manchester 1992.

*Dann,* Otto: Nationalismus. Hamburg 1978 (Historische Perspektiven 11).

*Deutsch,* Karl W.: The Integration of Political Communities. Hg. von Philip E. *Jacob.* Philadelphia 1964.

*Ders.:* Nationalism and Social Communication An Inquiry into the Foundations of Nationality. Cambridge/Mass. 1969.

*Gellner,* Ernest: Nations and Nationalism. London 1983 (deutsche Ausgabe: Nationalismus und Moderne. Berlin 1991).

*Giesen,* Bernhard (Hg.): Nationale und kulturelle Identität. Studien zur Entwicklung des kollektiven Bewusstseins in der Neuzeit. Frankfurt a. M. 1991.

*Greenfeld,* Liah: Nationalism. Five Roads to Modernity. Cambridge/Mass. 1993.

*Hayes,* Carlton J. H.: The Historical Evolution of Modern Nationalism. New York 1931.

*Hobsbawm,* Eric J.: Nations and Nationalism since 1780. Programme, Myth, Reality. Cambridge 1990.

*Kohn,* Hans: Die Idee des Nationalismus. Ursprung und Geschichte bis zur Französischen Revolution. Frankfurt a. M. 1962.

*Langewiesche,* Dieter: Nation, Nationalismus, Nationalstaat: Forschungsstand und Forschungsperspektiven. In: Neue politische Literatur 40 (1995) 190-236.

*Lemberg,* Eugen: Nationalismus. 2 Bde. Reinbek bei Hamburg 1964, 1968.

*Ders.:* Wege und Wandlungen des Nationalbewusstseins. Studien zur Geschichte der Volkwerdung in den Niederlanden und in Böhmen. Münster 1934 (Deutschtum und Ausland 57/58).

*Smith,* Anthony: National Identity. Reno/Nev. 1994 (Ethnonationalism in Comparative Perspective).

*Sorokin,* Pitirim: Society, Culture, and Personality. New York, London 1947.

*Wehler,* Hans-Ulrich: Nationalismus: Geschichte, Formen, Folgen. München 2001.

# XIII

# Historical belles-lettres as a vehicle of the image of national history

## Typologies of nation-building

National identity is unthinkable without a historical dimension. Differences do, however, exist in chronological distance (how far back in the past?) and the extent of the role of 'myth' (reality or fiction?). For many decades both questions have been the subject of debate sometimes scholarly, sometimes not. Almost all West European participants in this debate make the methodological error of treating images of all national histories by the same criteria. This means that, for example, the image of history in the Latvian or the Bulgarian national movement is judged by the same standards and viewed through the same prism as English or German history. In analysing the image of a national history, account has be taken of the fundamental typological differences present in the process of nation-building in different parts of Europe.

The essential typological difference is that a number of peoples had already established themselves as nation-states by the onset of the period of modern capitalist transformation (e.g. the French, English, Dutch, Portuguese), while others remained in the position of 'non-dominant ethnic groups'. The latter lacked three features characteristic of a fully formed nation: political autonomy; a standardised language used to express all forms of high culture; and an established class structure. It is clear that the image of history of an Englishman (together with his historical myths) was constructed in an essentially different way from that of a Finn or a Lithuanian. There are of course examples of nations of an 'intermediate' or 'transitional' type, falling somewhere between the nation-states and the non-dominant ethnic groups — such as the Germans, Italians or Poles. This chapter will focus primarily on the role of the image of history among non-dominant ethnic groups, although the image of history among nation-states cannot be overlooked when considering relations with neighbouring peoples or with the nation dominant in a given state. First, however, I must consider a number of theoretical and methodological problems.

Ever since the nineteenth century the central question which has divided scholars has been whether a non-dominant ethnic group, or the nation arising out of such a group, possessed a history of relevance to the nation. Those who denied the existence of any such relevant history concluded, utterly consistently, that the whole historical dimension of the given national identity was a myth, a fiction, an academically irrelevant invention.

Those who claimed a relevant history did exist (and the present chapter supports this view) assumed that the members of the non-dominant group out of which the nation was taking shape shared a common past. Consideration of this common past is important since only this can ascertain what had contributed to the strengthening of the group's sense of togetherness. It is possible to point to relationships from the Middle Ages onwards which have led to the cohesion and disintegration of such groups. According to this conception, 'having' a history means to have shared a common fate within a relatively coherent territory irrespective of whether this shared experience included a lack of political autonomy or an interrupted autonomy, or whether it did not. Some degree of social integration and education is a necessary precondition to the creation of a sense of shared identity with a given nation-state history. It is salutary to remember here that in the eyes of a nineteenth-century French peasant the history of medieval France had as little (or as much) to do with his 'national' history as the history of Hungary had in the eyes of a Slovak or Romanian peasant.

Thus the analysis of the historical dimension of national identity should not be restricted to the 'great' nation-states. Similarly we shall make no progress if we limit our conceptual framework solely to 'myth'. The concept of 'historical consciousness' is far more productive. I use this term to denote the totality of a group's (in the present case, a nation's) information about its past which has been stored in the consciousness of its members at a given time. A fundamental polarity dominates in this enormous stock of information, transmitted partly through social communication and partly through memory. This is on the one hand the polarity between the critically reflective reconstruction of the past (the approach of contemporary historiography) and, on the other hand, by superstitious, mythological, chronologically indeterminate 'unconscious' imaginings of a common past. Each individual's historical consciousness moves oscillates between these two poles, and, naturally, enormous differences obtain between individuals. Historical consciousness attaches itself to various objects and identities, some of which are decisive in shaping a perception of national history and are therefore central to the process of nation-building. Although the boundary between national and non-national history was never stable, and was constantly susceptible to modification, there always remained a historical 'core' locatable in the national past.

Hence it is not appropriate to see historical consciousness solely in terms of one of the two poles. Moreover, a one-sided emphasis on 'mythology' as part of the critique of the image of national history has inherent methodological weaknesses. First, the image was almost always originally formulated by the élites of the ruling nation-state. The pejorative description of the historical consciousness of 'small' nations as 'myth' appears suspiciously like prejudice. Secondly, such an approach is empirically unsound. In reality every social group has a common past from which differences in the structuring of individual elements of the past have originated. Thirdly, the widely disparate understandings of the term 'myth' incorporate a logical inconsistency which must be examined in greater detail.

While — to take a counter-example — the myths of the Greek gods cannot be linked to real people, what some call the myths of a national history are unambiguously founded on some element of reality. In speaking of a national historical myth, it is implicitly assumed that the myth in question has some relationship to reality and is to be measured against that reality. If such a historical reality existed, then it was and remains an object of scholarly investigation for an historian. Since the establishment of scholarly research methods and since the general acceptance of the argument of scientifically based truth, the emphasis on the relationship between the past and the present has changed into a search for the most objective possible historical facts. By this I do not mean that the academic historian can constructed a picture of history which corresponds wholly to reality. Historians were influenced by the lack of knowledge of sources and, above all, by their personal sympathies. Moreover, the results of historical research were popularised and reproduced in a distorted form.

As a result of these processes, there arose in the historical consciousness of each national community a polarity, a tension between the uncritical or ideologised myth on the one hand and the critical and, as far as it was possible, the exact product of scholarly research on the other. Thus present-day analyses of the image of a national history cannot be restricted solely to 'mythology'. In contrast to this, two approaches which have proved productive have been the analysis of the tension between the academic and the mythological poles of historical consciousness (including the relationship between myth and reality), and the testing of the social relevance of differing images of a given history and their mythological and critical components.

The investigation into the role of historical consciousness as a factor involved in the formation of nations should begin with the question: what had influenced and shaped that consciousness, and how had this been done? Historical research is, naturally, far from being the only factor involved in this process. Other factors include:

- family traditions and other forms of oral tradition in which the mythological component was strongly represented
- schooling, above all in history but also in related disciplines
- the plastic arts: monuments, paintings, book illustrations and so forth
- historical belles-lettres, e.g. novellas, short stories, tales, epic and lyric poetry, drama

The influence and the reception of academic history is present more or less intensively in all the above factors, and in a more or less distorted, mythologised form.

The present chapter is concerned with only one set of the factors listed above: the role of historical belles-lettres across the whole spectrum of literary genres. The term 'factor' describes only one aspect of the process. Historical belles-lettres must be investigated not only on account of their role in forming the historical image but also as a source of information about the perceptions of the past current among the readership of the emerging nation. The more a national movement advances and the larger a readership grows, the more dependable literature becomes as a source for the reconstruction of the image of a national history.

Certain basic principles have been developed for the analysis of historical belles-lettres, facilitating consideration both of the works' individual inner structures and their social role. Above all, it is not a matter of understanding historical belles-lettres as purely imaginative writings with no relationship to reality. This relationship has to be considered on two levels: on one level, historical reality, knowledge of the past transmitted, for example, through knowledge of specialist literature, of sources and education; on the second level, the contemporary reality of the author, contemporary political conflicts, interests and views. The fact that the role of the present is usually judged the more important should not lead us to disregard the relevance of historical reality.

Taking both levels into account, we must seek to reconstruct and understand better the impact of historical belles-lettres. Three questions (each of which may subsequently be sub-divided) must be asked:

1 How far are historical belles-lettres a medium of information about the national past? We need to know what actually happened in the past. Only then are we in a position to assess an author's choice and interpretation of facts. Naturally, we have to take into account what was available to the author from historical scholarship at the time of composition. In this connection we also have to ascertain the contemporary criteria by which events, personalities and achievements were judged to be 'national'.

2 What is portrayed in historical belles-lettres and what seems to have guided the choice of facts? This requires a systematic investigation of the problem based on a series of questions that have to be asked of each work of fiction. Of these questions the following are the most important:

    a Which periods of national history were preferred? How were individual periods represented?

    b Which themes and conflicts were used as examples of social, political, religious, national conflicts, court intrigues, private life, work, the family?

    c How powerful was the national component? Which concepts of the national history were predominant at the time of writing?

    d In which social milieu did the action take place? What were the social origins of the main characters? How are rulers, nobles and, for example, peasants portrayed?

    e How are members of other nations portrayed? To what extent was the nationality of the writer contrasted with that of foreigners?

3 Who made up the audience or readership? How large was it, and what was its social composition? The answers to these questions will inform us not only of the reception of the work but will also illuminate possible later impacts. In fact, many historical novellas became standard texts for whole generations, and many came back into favour after several decades — in different social and political circumstances.

The aesthetic value of historical belles-lettres is of interest for the purpose of this chapter only from the standpoint of a work's social relevance. There is no inherent correlation between artistic value and social and national relevance. Because *Trivialliteratur* had a wide readership, its projection of history is equally as interesting for us as works of 'high' literature. Nevertheless we must not overlook the general context of a given literary history. This applies equally to the literature of the dominant nation-state, which often served as a model for the emerging literature of a non-dominant group.

## Two case studies

In the second part of this chapter I shall present two case studies and subject them to the theoretical and methodological approaches I have set out above. The first case study is an exposition of the role of historical belles-lettres in the shaping of the image of Czech national history in the nineteenth century. The second case study will test the value of a comparative approach, comparing — and contrasting — in this instance points of contact between the Czech example and a similar development German historical belles-lettres.

## The Czech case

Czech writing has a continuous tradition of 'high literature' dating from the late thirteenth century. However, there is a general view, though it is not shared by many literary scholars, that Czech writing of the sixteenth century marked the zenith of the tradition of 'high literature' and that after 1620 a decline set in. By the mid-seventeenth century high literature was dominated by devotional poetry (some of it of high quality) and theological tracts and sermons. Popular literature continued to thrive in fiction, drama, broadside ballads and ditties, usually of a moralising nature. The language norms of modern Czech literature were established the end of the eighteenth century. In the nineteenth century, the new literature had to assume certain specific functions — especially in the field of popular enlightenment and education — which had been performed in the eighteenth century by literatures on which the Enlightenment had had an earlier impact.

Leaving aside the reprinting or first publication of Old Czech works (at the time the most influential chronicle was Václav Hájek z Libočan's Middle Czech *Kronika česká* of 1541), the past made its first appearance in modern Czech literature in *Trivialliteratur*. *Ritterromane* and cautionary tales, mainly translated from German, were ill-suited to the shaping of an image of national history. Historical narratives developed only slowly after the 1810s. Alongside the few attempts at novel-writing, historical plays were also written. Their number remained small, however, because of the very limited opportunities for having them publicly performed.

In the 1840s the historical novella and short story became the subject of debate amongst activist supporters of the national movement, who criticised the patriarchal world-view and the overwhelming concern with the Middle Ages characteristic of these works. 1848 marked an important turning point. Historical drama, in particular, enjoyed great popularity with the public. After 1860 historical fiction entered a transitional phase: while it put aside nostalgia for the Middle Ages, it did not advance any new concepts. It was not until the last thirty years of the nineteenth century that the historical novel and novella came into their own.

The sources to which Czech authors turned for their materials for historical fiction up to 1870 has been subjected to careful systematic analysis. Research shows that authors selected their materials almost exclusively from Czech national history. It is only in writing published after 1860 that we begin to find occasional signs of interest in non-Czech material. Until 1848, medieval themes dominated: a third of all historical fiction treated pre-1310 history (i.e. the period of the Přemyslids, the Czechs' own 'national' ruling dynasty — which died out on the sword side in 1306); a further fifteen per cent of publications were devoted to the fifteenth century (i.e. Hussitism). The attraction of medieval themes declined quickly after 1848 with the result that in the 1860s only ten per cent of historical writings were set in the period before 1400. The proportion of works based on fifteenth-century material increased markedly with one third concerned with the Hussite Revolution and the National Revival which soon became a stock component of the image of national history.

After 1870 the focus of emphasis was self-evident even though I cannot offer exact quantitative data. The interest of the leading writers focused on four periods of Czech history with the choice of material determined above all by theme rather than historical period. These were the period of the Hussite Revolution, the sixteenth century, the period of enforced Counter-Reformation after 1620 (the Battle of the White Mountain), and the National Revival. However, there was almost total agreement among writers in their evaluation of each period. The Hussite period and the National Revival marked the two high points of the Czechs' national history: for the sixteenth century it was above all the blossoming of culture that was thematised, while the period after 1620 was judged as a tragic age of national decay.

The chronological disposition of the material increasingly began to convey a clear concept of national history. What was considered nationally relevant did not, however, remain static. In the *Vormärz*,[1] the existence of a national monarchy in the Middle Ages was celebrated, although writers drew no political conclusions from the existence of the monarchy.

Not only during the *Vormärz*, but also later, Czech medieval history was represented overwhelmingly as the Czechs' struggle against the German threat. This struggle was understood as the nation's fight for survival. Although the later struggles of the Estates against the Habsburgs were less frequently portrayed in fiction (probably not least for fear of the censor), they were always interpreted from a national perspective.

National history was originally understood as the history of the Kingdom of Bohemia and the Margravate of Moravia. Around the middle of the nineteenth century this concept transformed into that of the history of the Czech nation on Bohemian and Moravian territory. Hence the concept of the Czech nation came to be understood as comprising not only the Czech-speaking population but also the Bohemian and Moravian Estates (i.e. the *natio*). The influence of the basic five-volume history written by a leading nineteenth-century historian and politician, František Palacký, under the title *Die Geschichte der tschechischen Nation in Böhmen und Mähren*, played an important role in the conception of national history.[2] Equally important, however, was the final split of the Czech- and German-speaking political camps in the 1848 revolution.

The image of the 'enemy' was also determined by the fact that throughout their history the Czech-speaking population had encountered hardly any other peoples than 'Germans' (i.e. of various tribes). Czech fiction recognised only one foreign and one hostile nation: the 'Germans'. The 'Germans' were also for the most part the bearers of negative character traits. This concept had, however, significant nuances. In the *Vormärz*, hostile 'Germans' were mostly from Germany proper (e.g. Saxony, Prussia, Swabia), that is 'foreigners'. It was only after the middle of the century that the local German-speaking population of Bohemia and Moravia was also included in the category of hostile Germans. The acceptance of the modernisers' retrospective linguistic definition of nationality had the effect of categorising practically all non-Czechs as 'Germans', including members of the imperial family as well as foreign mercenaries and princes. Sometimes peasants and a few intellectuals were considered exceptions, as not being hostile to the Czechs.

The antipathy to Germans, characteristic of Czech historical belles-lettres, was accompanied by a sceptical, often condemnatory attitude to the late medieval and early modern state. This state could not be identified with a Czech national state since it was a state in which a foreign dynasty and later a foreign nobility had ruled. This attitude explains why so little attention has been paid in Czech historical belles-lettres to international contacts and influences in the period after about 1500. It is in this attitude that the political provincialism of the Czech image of history has its roots. Socially important religious problems are scarcely reflected at all in the fiction of the *Vormärz*. People were avowed monarchists, Roman Catholics and loyal to the ruling house. For these reasons (and also because of the censor), the Estates' conflicts with the Habsburgs were celebrated just as rarely as the Hussite Revolution.

This opportunist attitude, however, underwent a radical change after 1870. The central model for integration was no longer sought in the Přemyslid state, but in periods when this state (or its territory) were no longer ruled by the aristocracy but by the burghers, or when the burghers ruled jointly with the aristocracy. The decisive influences in this transformation were the Hussite period, the Estates' opposition to the Habsburgs, and the national movement. Such an attitude was hardly compatible with loyalty to the Church of Rome.

Almost all important writers of historical works in the last third of the nineteenth century and at the beginning of the twentieth saw the Catholic Church, or its hierarchy, as the second most dangerous enemy of the Czech nation. The Hussites had fought against this Church and the great cultural flowering in the sixteenth century had occurred under the aegis of the Reformation. The decline after 1620 was a consequence of the Counter-Reformation. The seventeenth- and eighteenth-century Church of Rome was depicted as the arch-enemy of books written in Czech.

This anti-Catholic conception of history was set before a readership of whom more than ninety per cent belonged to the Catholic Church — the established church of Austria. These circumstances created a dichotomy between two competing versions of history: on the one hand, the version of history transmitted through the state schools and on the other, that advanced by the non-conformist, national image of history. Within the, now strong, national movement a bourgeois anti-clerical view of history emerged which was acceptable both to the Social Democrats and to a section of the Agrarian party.

This is linked to the treatment of the burgher theme in historical writing. Up to 1848, Czech historical belles-lettres had shown an interest in themes drawn from the lives of the nobility. After 1848, such characters became marginal. Centre stage was taken over by themes drawn from urban, burgher society and dealing with the lives of millers and farmers. In this connection the social conflicts in which the burghers were participating also became the subject of fiction. In such writings the members of the Czech nation are mostly placed on the side of rebels, the persecuted, nonconformists and the poor. This choice of theme was driven by a theoretical conception, again derived from Palacký. In his view of history, the 'Germans' in their endeavours represented the principles of authority and aggression, whereas the Czechs represented democracy and liberty. This conception became firmly anchored in the image of Czech national history, and remains so today.

The development of hero figures comported with this. During the *Vormärz*, as we have already seen, action centred on kings and nobles with the burghers confined to secondary roles. The image of the nobles, however, lacked for the most part any political content. In general they provided a vehicle for the expression of general, human behaviour (mostly protagonists of love stories). The vagueness with which the nobility was portrayed indicates that Czech authors had no direct contact with that world.

The 1848 revolution brought a radical change to the choice of heroes. The first of this new generation of heroes to appear on the scene were hitherto denounced characters from the late Middle Ages such as Jan Hus and the victorious Hussite military commander Jan Žižka. In the longer term, however, more was needed. Kings and princes — in so far as they could be accommodated to the requirements of the image of national history — remained convenient symbolic figures of national autonomy. The nobility was depicted as bearing a share of the responsibility for the fate of the nation. This allowed writers to distinguish between the patriotic national-minded and the 'alienated' anti-nationalist nobility. Burghers began to appear in fiction with ever increasing frequency.

From the 1870s onwards, the role of the burghers in historical writing became ever more prominent, while rulers and the higher nobility played secondary, marginal roles. A parallel was sometimes drawn between the lesser nobility and the burghers, while the higher nobility was represented as alien and hostile. In addition to the burghers and lesser nobles (both, naturally, Czech-speaking), we also find the role of the positive hero played by villagers who have made their mark in society such as millers, peasant-farmers and blacksmiths. An increasing number of heroes springs from those members of the intelligentsia who had close ties to the ordinary people. Out of such social choices emerged a retrospective image of a national community with markedly bourgeois characteristics.

## Image and reality

How far did this historical image correspond to historical reality? It will be useful to consider this question for a moment though without going into detail. Broadly speaking, the burghers played an extraordinarily influential role in the Hussite Revolution and in sixteenth-century Czech cultural life. The fact that the nobility played virtually no part in the national movement and the negative impact of the Counter-Reformation are generally recognised. Hence this historical image represents the critical-scholarly pole. However, we also have to take account of mythologising and ideologising elements in interpreting this standpoint. The important role of the burghers was reformulated in terms of national concepts. The positive image of the Czech lesser nobility was idealised. The negative role of the Counter-Reformation was one-sidedly emphasized; the early phases of the national movement were depicted as a harmonious idyll. Although the existence of a Czech national consciousness going back to the Middle Ages can be documented, the general basis and political relevance of this consciousness was in many cases exaggerated and anachronistically modernised. Thus the image of Czech history communicated through fiction is not wholly identical with historical reality. Neither can it be categorised however as mere fiction — myth with no connection to historical reality.

How seriously was historical fiction taken by its readers? In the *Vormärz*, the readership of Czech-language periodicals and books comprised mainly the lower levels of the intelligentsia such as priests, junior officials, some members of the professions, grammar school teachers together with a small number of urban craftsmen and retailers. In its social origins the Czech intelligentsia was linked for the most part to the old urban middle classes; links with the peasantry were fewer. In other words, it was a readership whose mentality may be described as patriarchal and loyally apolitical (*kaisertreu*).

The social structure of the readership changed hardly at all after the 1848 revolution and the introduction of a constitution. Nevertheless, a decisive social change in those groups making up the readership did begin to emerge in the form of a more developed political awareness which responded approvingly to liberal, democratic and nationalist ideas. This readership was therefore able to accept a revision of national history in which anti-feudal, anti-authoritarian and anti-clerical attitudes coalesced under the common denominator of anti-German attitudes. The growth in readership occurring through the expansion of social mobility upwards (into the educated bourgeoisie) and downwards (peasants, workers) brought no essential change to this image of history.

## A German model?

We must now turn to the image of history communicated through German historical belles-lettres and ask to what extent it differed from the Czech image. Comparison with the German image of history is important above all because in the German case we are dealing with a highly influential culture. How far was the Czech image of history 'translated' from the German?

In respect of the *Vormärz* it is possible to argue that this was indeed the case. German historical fiction also showed a preference for the Middle Ages with rulers and nobles leading the action. The parallels do not, however, continue after this period. After 1850, the interest of German writers shifted to the eighteenth century and to the wars against Napoleon. After the foundation of the Second Reich in 1871, interest in medieval German material, primarily from the early period, grew again. There was, however, a fundamental difference in the choice of themes. The depiction of social and religious conflicts (with the exception of the Reformation) received far less attention than in Czech fiction. The choice of hero manifests an even greater difference. After 1848, the shift in theme towards burgher life, characteristic of Czech writing, occurred only marginally in German historical writing. The overwhelming majority of German works retained their noble heroes and even more frequently portrayed the deeds of princely ruling families, above all the Hohenzollerns. This choice of heroes was in line with the strong preference for the portrayal of princely courts and families.

On to this image of the past — wholly different in its social structure from that of its Czech counterpart — German historical fiction projected, just as strongly as Czech, a set of national values. The outcome, however, was markedly different from the Czech case. The bearers of German national identity were, apart from scholars, the princes with an especially prominent role played by the kings of Prussia. The roots of German unity were to be teleologically traced to Prussian and even to Brandenburger history. In a national image such as this there was but little space for the anti-feudal and anti-authoritarian elements of the kind that played so important a role in Czech writing. On the contrary, the preference for descriptions of life at the feudal courts was linked to the tendency to idealise them.

Although themes from burgher life were less frequently represented in German historical writing, an important substitute for them can be identified from the 1860s onwards. This substitute was in the form of a growing interest in themes from cultural history. Books about writers and artists were mostly set in a burgher milieu. In this way, a model for national identification was offered to the educated German middle classes.

By analogy we also find in German fiction a 'substitute' for internal conflicts. This is reflected in the frequency of portrayal of conflicts with the outside world. Wars and battles, mostly against the threat posed by the French or their allies, signalled the identity of the national enemy: France was criticised for its disastrous role not only in international relations but also in its influence on culture.

It can also be said of German historical belles-lettres that the image of its national history corresponded in broad terms to historical reality. The process of mythologisation and ideologisation were, as with the Czech examples, shaped by the political and social conditions of the nineteenth century. However, since these conditions were fundamentally different in Germany (for example, a developed social structure, the cult of Prussia, unity under the Hohenzollerns, defeat of the liberals), the emphases on the mythologising standpoint of the German perception of national history were also quite different in nature than among the Czechs. Perhaps this, too, is one area in which to seek the roots of the specifically German course of development.

## Fact and fancy

In conclusion, it is necessary to ask how the relationship between the mythologising and scholarly poles should be interpreted. Leaving aside genre-specific manners of story-telling (e.g. love stories, modernised psychology), we can state that the images of national history transmitted by Czech and German fiction (with the exception of prehistory and early history) corresponded in its basic facts to historical reality. By and large, writers respected the results of historical research. In this sense the academic interpretation of the nature and tenor of the past was faithfully presented in the literary image of history. Historical reality was generally interpreted through the selection of facts and through moral judgements and modernising fiction in a form that corresponded to 'present-day' demands — that is to say the contemporary phase in the process of nation-building. In other words, the effect on the writers of contemporary conditions made itself felt not only through modernising love stories and psychological interpretations but also through the retrospective perception of national goals.

In the Czech case the mythological elements in the image of history corresponded to the three basic components of the programme of the national movement. National history was depicted as unambiguously ethno-linguistic, and aspects of autonomy — whether won or lost —

were strongly emphasized. The social perspective evolved symptomatically from a reverence for the Czech 'patriotic' nobility of the Middle Ages (especially during the *Vormärz*) into an *embourgeoisement* of the image of history, accompanied by an idealisation of the peasantry.

In short, the Czech image of history was — in step with the state of the national movement at any given time — overwhelmingly plebeian-democratic and provincial, whereas the German image of history was overwhelmingly focused on élites and therefore authoritarian, monarchist, missionary, and liberal-minded. Nevertheless, there are analogies. These can be characterised by three features: the ethnic determination of the national historical 'body' of the nation; a retrospectively projected demand for national discipline; and a hyperbolical emphasis on the threat to the nation's destiny from outside, wherein historical events are rendered topical.

## NOTES

[1]   The period between 1815 and 1848.
[2]   Czech translation: *Dějiny národu českého v Čechách i v Moravě* (1848-76).

## BIBLIOGRAPHY

Borová, V. 1988. Vztah Čechu a Němcu v české krásné literatuře s historickou tematikou v 1. polovině 19. století. In *Literární a publicistické zdroje národního historického vědomí* (ed.) M. Hroch. *Acta Universitatis Carolinae* 3.

Hroch, M. 1987. *Die historische Belletristik als Vermittlerin des bürgerlichen Geschichtsbewußtseins*. Zentrum für interdisziplinäre Forschung, 9. Bielefeld.

Hroch, M. 1988a. Historická beletrie a historické vědomí v 19. století. In *Literární a publicistické zdroje národního historického vědomí* (ed.) M. Hroch. *Acta Universitatis Carolinae* 3, 9-27.

Hroch, M. 1988b. Příspěvek k poznání ideové a tematické skladby německého historického románu a povídky v 19, století. In ibid, 115-35.

Nováková, M. 1988. Obraz národních dějin v českyàch časopisech let 1860-1867. In *Literární a publicistické zdroje národního historického vědomí* (ed.) M. Hroch. *Acta Universitatis Carolinae* 3.

Zítko, M. 1976. Obraz české minulosti v kulturních časopisech doby předbřeznové. In *Úloha historického povědomí v evropském národním hnutí v 19. století* (ed.) M. Hroch. *Acta Universitatis Carolinae, Philosophica et Historica* 5, 15-44.

# XIV

## HISTORICAL HERITAGE: CONTINUITY AND DISCONTINUITY IN THE CONSTRUCTION OF NATIONAL HISTORIES

MIROSLAV HROCH and JITKA MALEČKOVÁ

The creation of modern national identity has always involved a search for the historical dimension of that identity, but however much the protagonists of nation-building processes liked to present their people or nation as having existed from time immemorial and their current society as a natural outcome of its past development, they were in fact retrospectively deciding on the nature of the national past and the elements that did or did not belong in it. In other words, the construction of national histories played a fundamental role in the emergence of modern national identity, but conversely national interest, the actual situation of an emergent national community, and contemporary notions of the nature of that community, were all projected back into the picture of national histories.

In order to provide a better test of the mechanisms of this feedback, we have chosen to compare the construction of four national histories. Although occurring at different times and under different conditions these national histories – Czech, Norwegian, Greek and Turkish – nonetheless have certain common features. The Czech and Norwegian national movements were among the earliest and most successful movements of non-dominant nations of multinational empires in Europe, but there were fundamental differences between the social and cultural features of the two movements, and the contrast can be illuminating. The Turks and Greeks were linked by geographical proximity, overlapping territorial demands and above all the shared past of the Ottoman Empire, even if for the Greeks the Ottoman Empire remained a foreign state. The Turks are the only one of the foursome not to have been a subject (non-dominant) nation, but the formation of Turkish national identity followed a difficult course, and in this sense has a series of points in common with the non-dominant peoples of the multinational empires.

Despite the differences certain structural similarities can be found in the four cases, inviting comparison. All four historiographies had a common starting point in the sense that their modern nations had not emerged as a result of the continuous transformation of a "state-nation" existing since the Middle Ages. The formation of the nations was not something to be taken for granted, since their histories had been as it were "interrupted" or included a time of "darkness". At the same time, however, continuity could be claimed with objectively demonstrable earlier state formations definable as "fore-runners" or the historical basis of national existence.

In all the cases chosen, then, we find constructions of national history that had to cope with a discontinuity of historical processes, or more precisely had to ponder the relationship between continuity and discontinuity in the national past. The aim of our comparison is to cast light on how the national idea "appropriated" the past of the nation in the different cases, and so to contribute to a deeper understanding of the relationships that drove the formation of national identity.

In this limited space comparison will focus only on the formative initial phase of the construction of national histories (we shall leave aside the "revisionism" of the 20th century), and only on a few criteria, or angles of vision. Given that in all the cases chosen historians had to come to terms with the problem of historical discontinuity, the central question seems to us to have been "What do we draw on from the past?" Specific areas of comparison therefore include first the sources of information (and inspiration) for national history and second the historiographical tradition providing the material on which construction of national histories could be based, or could at least draw. A third area is the identification of the object of continuity/discontinuity, i.e. the historical periods and formations that patriotic historians regarded as part of "our" national history, or from which they wanted to distance themselves. A fourth area is that of the idealised values supposed to serve as inspiration or argument in the present day.

A second set of themes is linked to the question of "How to determine the form of the national community in the past?" We divide this into three aspects. First, there is the space regarded as the historical territory of the nation, the geographical framework of historical identity. Second, there is the question of who belongs to national history (and who does not) and third, the issue of the wider context to which constructions of national history refer or appeal. In order to make the comparison of four national histories comprehensible, we shall provide brief introductory information on the basic historical events and the relations with which constructions of national histories worked.

## 1. First Comparison: The History of the Norwegian and Czech Nations

### 1.1. Historical Development

Viewed from outside Czech and Norwegian history show a surprising number of similarities. Early medieval statehood emerged at roughly the same time in both cases and the rule of a "national", i.e. native dynasty lasted for roughly as long – in the Czech Lands to 1306 and in Norway to 1319. In both cases the domestic dynasty died out just at a time of a promising economic and political upswing for the state. In the Czech Lands and in Norway this was followed by long-term rule by a foreign dynasty.

In the Norwegian case, the dynastic change resulted in membership of the Union of Kalmar, which opened the way to full dependence on the Danish state. In the case of the Czech Lands, the process was more complex: the initially successful rule of the Luxemburg dynasty gave way to the Hussite Revolution, which actually increased a sense of distinctive Bohemian identity and even ushered in a short period of national monarchy. At this stage then, during the 15th and 16th centuries, the history of the two countries diverged strongly, but we can draw a certain parallel between the year 1536, when Norway was entirely deprived of statehood and fully incorporated into the Danish state, and the triumph of Habsburg power in Bohemia following the Battle of the White Mountain in 1620.

Although in the Czech case certain elements of statehood were preserved, the political status and fortunes of the two countries from this point followed very similar lines of development. Absolutism was imposed (in the Czech case with the maintenance of remnants of provincial rights), an alien linguistic culture was imposed (German in the Czech case, and Danish in the Norwegian case) and the local administration was controlled by a governing class of mainly foreign origin. Another similarity lies in the fact that subsequently the Danish and Habsburg monarchies encouraged economic progress and in the later 18th century implemented progressive reforms and modernising measures. In contrast to the situation in the Czech Lands the ruling class in Norway consisted of officials closely linked to the Absolutist court, but the peasants maintained their personal freedom and certain, albeit limited elements of communal self-government. The prosperity and trade turnover of Norwegian towns was incomparably greater than in Czech conditions, where no self-confident commercial bourgeoisie comparable to that of Norway emerged.

The beginnings of the two national movements fall roughly into the same period around 1800 and were preceded by several decades of intense academic interest in the past and present of the country and its inhabitants. The major difference was that the Norwegian national movement was quick to adopt a political programme. Its leaders succeeded in exploiting favourable external circumstances (by the Peace of Kiel of 1814 Norway was to be annexed to Sweden by decision of the great powers), meeting in the spring of 1814 to draw up a liberal constitution. Their attempt to declare independence failed, and Norway then became an autonomous part of the union with Sweden. The interest in specific linguistic and cultural identity that dominated the first decades of the Czech national movement, on the other hand, developed significantly in Norway only several decades after the adoption of the constitution. From the start it took the form of a struggle between those who proposed to create an entirely independent Norwegian linguistic culture, and those who wanted to build on the Danish cultural legacy and develop it further in a Norwegian spirit. The background to this struggle was the continuing linguistic division of the Norwegian population into Danish-speaking official and commercial elites on the one hand, and the Norwegian-speaking countryside on the other. This struggle was one factor in the political polarisation of Norway, with supporters of Norwegian independence gaining the edge at the end of the 19th century. They achieved their goal in 1905, but the supporters of a new Norwegian language never managed to win over the majority of the population.

### 1.2.1. Historiographical Tradition and Sources of Information

No construction of national history started "from scratch"; whether by rejection or by agreement, consciously or unconsciously, the architects of national history drew on traditional historical accounts and the results of earlier historical writings, whether chronicles or early modern historical works. Historians who identified themselves with the modern nation worked not just with information and value judgements, but also with the conceptual vocabulary that had come down to them in historiographical tradition. They were also addressing a public whose "collective memory" had been formed to a greater or lesser extent by a historiographical tradition.

The Czechs possessed a historiographical tradition that went right back into the Middle Ages, and had been weakened, but never severed. A living historiographical continuity had been maintained, particularly in the Chronicle of Hájek, and so at the end of the 18th century, it could easily be reinvigorated by re-editions of works like Dalimil's Chronicle or Stránský's Republica Bojema (of 1643). In Norway, there was almost nothing in the way of a Humanist or Baroque historiography; historiographical tradition was limited to medieval chronicles, with which sagas were also classified. In the first period of search for national history the chronicles and sagas also formed the main source of information, and were regarded as of central importance. This naturally meant that the first syntheses of national history were focused on the medieval Norwegian state, and only later did historians proceed to study later centuries on the basis of sources found mainly in Danish archives. In contrast, work on Czech history was from the outset based on critical consideration of the existing historiographical tradition and its modification on the basis of research on abundant sources. Criticism of the narrative sources from the early period and the study of new sources preceded the actual construction of the national history.

One specific element of historiographical tradition that we find used analogically in both Bohemia and Norway was the tradition of the national saints – St. Wenceslas and St. Olaf. Both were linked with the beginnings of Christianity and also the origins of statehood. Their cult survived right into the 19th century – in Catholic Bohemia rather more strongly than in Lutheran Norway – and so helped significantly to bridge the discontinuity of national history.

### 1.2.2. Continuity and Discontinuity

The differences in the approach to the phenomenon of discontinuity reflected the different degrees to which medieval statehood had been disrupted. In the Czech case discontinuity was interpreted as a partial suppression of political independence that did not exclude continuity in the survival of certain institutions and especially cultural continuity in the form of literature in the national language. The gap between Norwegian medieval history and the Norwegian present was wider, having affected not only political institutions, but also the tradition of a literary language.

In Bohemia, therefore, continuity was sought on the basis of study of everything that had in some way survived from the period of statehood, starting with the institution of the King of Bohemia, and moving on to Estates bodies and to administrative and church organisations. This went hand in hand with the revival of a literary heritage, or rather of Czech literature of the Humanist period. The continuity of Czech ethnic society appeared unchallengeable. The Norwegian search for national history focused, logically enough, on the medieval kingdom (including the Viking period), but in the construction of continuity historians had to face the question of who had actually been the subsequent bearer of the national tradition: had it been the "authentic" Norwegians, i.e. the peasants, who had maintained their dialects from the Middle Ages, or the Danish-speaking towns and officials as well?

At first the dominant view in Norway was that national history had been interrupted across the board, and it was necessary to draw on medieval statehood with a kind of "leap". This approach was expressed by the poet and historian of the Romantic generation H. Wergeland in his metaphor of two halves of a ring – the medieval and modern – that had to be put together. The idea also implied and involved an extremely critical view of the period of Danish rule; Norwegian patriots used stereotypes similar to those later employed by Czechs when they rejected the "time of darkness" and identified those to blame for the discontinuity, i.e. in the Czech case, the Habsburgs, and in the Norwegian case, the Danish kings. There was a subtle difference, however, since the Czech concept of "darkness" implied the sense of the diminished but still surviving continuity of the nation, whereas in the eyes of the Norwegian Romantics, the situation had been one of complete "emptiness" – a yawning chasm in national life.

This one-sided Norwegian view was not, of course, defensible in the long term and in the later 19th century it was replaced by a more balanced perspective, made necessary by the existence of two undeniable facts. First, especially in the 18th century, Norway had experienced an era of economic upswing and second, the architects of the renewal of Norwegian statehood on the threshold of the 19th century had actually been Danish-speaking patriots from the ranks of officials and merchants, who were Norwegian by sentiment and adopted Norwegian national identity without any appearance of strain. The rich merchants and ship-owners, like the Norwegian-minded official elites, thus became an acceptable link (in addition to the continuity of peasant settlements) with which to bridge the discontinuity of national history and make identification with it possible.

The question of the "culprit" was also revised. The fall of Norwegian statehood was no longer interpreted just as the result of the arbitrary will of the Danish king, but was also seen as a consequence of the extreme weakening of the Norwegian Kingdom, which had ceased to be viable. This shift certainly reflected contemporary political conditions. Denmark no longer presented any threat to Norwegian independence, since in the later 19th century the period of Danish oppression had been overlaid with the political struggle against Swedish oppression, i.e. against the dominant position of Swedish elites in the union.

In the Czech case there was to be no re-location of the political enemy. Instead the political urgency of the struggle against dependence on Vienna grew during the later 19th century. Emphasis on blaming the Habsburgs (who were ever more elided with the image of the main enemy, the Germans) for the disruption of national development remained a live issue in the political arena, and even acquired a social component in the fight against a "foreign" nobility. In Norway, by contrast, there were no classes that could come to be regarded as the embodiment of national humiliation.

### 1.2.3. History as a Source of National and Civic Values

A concept of national history fulfilled its nation-building function primarily to the extent that it sought or created positive values which the national movement could embrace, identify with, and under certain circumstances use as reference point for present endeavours. Czechs soon found simple pride in medieval princes and kings inadequate to their purposes, especially since it was hard to present them as models of identification for a modern civic society. Humanist Czech literature had rather more potential in terms of debate on values, but the values were too subtle to have a wider impact. Change came only with the work of F. Palacký, and his value-oriented concept of national history that stressed ancient Slav democracy, the Hussite Reformation and the tradition of the Bohemian Brethren. This was the first persuasive perspective in which the post-White Mountain erosion of Czech statehood and Czech culture could be condemned as a disruption or even destruction of values that were not narrowly national.

A comparable value link between the Middle Ages and the Modern age was not available in the Norwegian case, since Norwegian history lacked episodes comparable with Hussitism, and the reformation had actually had an effect opposite to that of Hussitism in terms of national development. Pride in the Vikings could not fill the gap, since aggression and brute force were not considered part of the modern system of values and the Viking model was therefore of only limited use for "national education" purposes.

What remained was idealisation of the qualities of the medieval peasants – their physical prowess, skill and industry. If this element of national history was to become functional, however, the idea of the complete interruption of national history had to be abandoned, and a concept that would recognise the Danish period as a part of national history had to be adopted instead. This change was the work of historians who came to prominence in the later 19th century and based their concept of history on identification with past generations (E. Sars). The source of the values of a national history that would bridge the gap was now the peasant community, considered to be the embodiment and bearer of the ideal of equality, constitutional principles and civic liberties. This concept also happened to be in line with the political ideology of the Venstre party, which gained power in Norway in 1883 and whose theorists included Sars himself.

Czech national history also involved idealisation of the peasant core of the nation, but a picture of continuity of peasant liberties from the Middle Ages could not be constructed. From this point of view it was the Hussite revolution that was most promising as grist to the national mill, and made possible – however vaguely – construction of the continuity of a "reformation tradition". There was yet another difference in the idealisation of the medieval peasant in the two histories: the Norwegian early medieval peasant was also a Viking, i.e. a warrior, while the peace-loving character of Czech peasants could be celebrated without too much strain.

While national history was conceived as a source of national values, the definition of these values was a process rife with criticism and internal dissension. In both national movements from the end of the 19th century we encounter alternative visions, which rejected the idealisation of certain values (in the Czech case Hussitism, and in the Norwegian case Vikings), and found different values to identify and celebrate. Nevertheless, up to the end of the century, there was a certain consensus that the study of history should be mainly directed to the search for nationally relevant values. "Revisionists" simply differed in their view of the diagnosis of these values: in Czech circles there was a running and not very productive discussion on the "meaning" of Czech history, while in Norway there was an equally unfruitful discussion on who did or did not belong to national history.

### 1.3. Who Are We?

### 1.3.1. The Definition of the Territory of National History
The Norwegian and Czech national histories were basically territorially defined by historical borders – and in the Norwegian case a long coastline as well. In the historical picture, territories that had earlier been temporarily united with Norway or Bohemia but had later become parts of neighbouring states played only marginal roles, more or less as a theme for a nostalgic sigh. This applies both to the Norwegian view of the lost regions of Jemtland, Herjedalen and Båhuslän, which had become part of Sweden in the 17th century, and to the Czech view of Lusatia and the Silesian Principality.

There was a certain difference in the internal structuring of national territories. Prague had been a royal seat since the early Middle Ages, and so Czech national history gravitated to Prague as its natural centre. Norwegian history involved several different royal seats or state centres – Trondheim, Bergen, Osloa (Kristiania) and the focal points of historical change were quite variable. The construction of Czech history showed a high degree of centralisation and concentrated on Bohemia, with Moravia always playing only a marginal role.

Setting aside the occasional nostalgic tone of longing for "lost" national territories (Jemtland, Herjedalen, Kladsko), the territorial definition of Czech and Norwegian national histories did not imply any territorial claims. This position did not exclude positive depictions and sometimes idealisation of military assaults abroad, whether Viking expeditions or the Hussite "beautiful rides", but territories that were now parts of the history of other nations were never permanently integrated into national histories. A certain ambivalence can be detected in the Czech case in relation to Slovaks, who according to the Czechoslovakist concept were for some time regarded as part of the Czech nation, and in the Norwegian case in relation to Iceland, which from 1264 had been part of Norway.

The most serious challenge to the territorial definition and integrity of Czech national history came from outside, and finds no parallel in Norwegian history. Insofar as German historians identified the history of the Holy Roman Empire with the history of the German nation, it followed that the history of the Czech Lands became part of German history. This was a schema later (and at first not very consistently) reflected in the identification of the German minority in the Czech Lands with German history, a strategy that posed a challenge to the integrity of the political framework of Czech national existence. At this point we reach the question of whether all the inhabitants of a "national" historical whole were to be included in national history.

### 1.3.2. Who Belongs to National History?

The definition of Norwegian and Czech national history involved thematisation – albeit with different degrees of intensity and different results – of the question of whether the entire population of the historical whole (territory) was part of the image of national history, or only a core population. Specifically this meant the question of the place of the German inhabitants of the Czech Lands in Czech national history and the Danish-speaking official class and bourgeoisie in Norwegian national history.

In the Czech case there was relatively rapid development from the concept of land (provincial) history to Palacký's concept of the history of "the Czech nation in Bohemia and Moravia". Only with the later unambiguous assertion of language as the criterion of nationality were the German-speaking inhabitants of the border areas of Bohemia and Moravia excluded. The history of these lands was then gradually occupied, as it were, by the Czech nation, although in Palacký's original conception Czech history had been distinguished by continual "contact and clash" with the German nation.

The construction of Norwegian national history likewise had to come to terms with the existence of dual ethnicity on national territory, but here ethnic difference was defined socially, not territorially: the officials and educated elites, like the bourgeoisie, spoke Danish, while the peasants and rural population in general spoke dialects of Norwegian. In contrast to the situation in the Czech Lands, however, the Danish-speaking officials and merchants put themselves at the head of the national emancipation struggle and identified with the Norwegian nation. Given that the first syntheses of national history were written by members of this group (i.e. during the 1st half of the 19th century), doubts were hardly raised at this stage point about their membership of the Norwegian nation, however harsh the condemnations of the wrongs and oppression of the period of Danish rule.

The situation was subsequently complicated by the new generations that struggled for "authentic" Norwegianness and asked whether Norway was inhabited by one nation with two cultures, or even by two nations separated by language. It is in this context that we find expression of the view that only the Norwegian peasants were the genuine bearers of Norwegian national history and heirs to the traditions of the medieval kingdom. The view was primarily taken up by radical supporters of the introduction of a new Norwegian national language (landsmaal), but did not win general agreement and was increasingly left on the margins of historical consciousness. The opinion that prevailed was that of E. Sars and his school, who saw Norwegian history as the history of a single nation (people), which had been moulded for a certain period by a dual cultural tradition, i.e. the domestic Norwegian and the Danish, which had come from outside but had undergone Norwegian adaptation. As has been suggested, this construction of history made it possible to integrate the period following the loss of Norwegian statehood into the picture of national history – not only as a time of "darkness", but as a time that brought some positive changes as well as cultural decline.

Differences in Norwegian and Czech conclusions on who belonged and who did not belong in national history were also reflected in different social definitions of national history of the early modern period. The Norwegian conception was divided, but with greater or lesser enthusiasm its proponents ultimately incorporated the Danish-speaking and so "foreign" governing class into national history of the 16th to 18th centuries. In the Czech case, as has been mentioned, the "foreign" (German) nobility remained outside the framework of Czech national history.

### 1.3.3. Where Do We Belong?

Norwegian and Czech historiographies were entirely at one with the other European national historiographies in defining the nation in relation to its surroundings, or more precisely by trying to demonstrate its distinctive and separate existence while setting its past in the more universal context of the progress of mankind. Both searched for the "place" of national history in the history of the continent, and essentially Czech and Norwegian history were both firmly placed in the context of "Western", Latin and Catholic civilisation with the proviso that they had for a certain period been wrenched away from the universalism of this civilisation. In the Czech case, this had been a matter of "internal" development in the Hussite Revolution, while in the Norwegian case, on the contrary, reformationary separation from the world of Catholicism had been imposed from without, by decision of the Danish king. Hence Hussitism could become a positive element in Czech national history, while attitudes to the reformation in Norwegian history were ambivalent: on the one hand reformation had been forced on Norway, but on the other it had become so deep-rooted that it could scarcely be banished from national life.

One might say that the reformation turned the Norwegian historical angle of vision towards North Germany and Britain, while the victory of the Counter-Reformation turned the Czech Lands towards the South German and Italian context, but it would be too simple to explain these orientations purely in terms of religious affinities. The orientation of trade was evidently more important. Thus the North Sea linked Norway with England, Scotland and the North-West coast of the empire, and this situation was reflected in the strong presence of these regions in the picture of national history. The commercial and political ties with the North that had begun to develop in the Czech Lands at the end of the 16th century were cut off in the post-White Mountain period, and so the more distant Hungarian Lands loomed larger in the international context of Czech national history than the closer German North. It should of course be remembered that "closeness" was relative: distances did not look the same from Prague and Moravia. We can find the same difference in the contours of the Norwegian historical context as seen from Østland near Oslofjord and from the West Coast.

In the Norwegian and Czech constructions of history neighbours always constituted a dangerous force regardless of the how close or distant they seemed, and it was as enemies that they were incorporated into the context of national history. The difference lies in the fact that for Norway, enemy (or threatening) neighbours were primarily defined as states (Sweden, Denmark), and only occasionally as ethnic groups as well, while the enemies of Czechs were defined above all in ethnic terms (Germans and occasionally Magyars), and only in some cases as states as well. The enemy could also be defined dynastically, and it is significant that while in 19th-century Czech history the image of the Habsburgs acquired ever more negative features, the image of the Oldenburg dynasty, which had played a similar role in Norwegian history, tended to shed its originally strongly negative features. Another difference derives from the fact that while up to the 15th century Norway had been roughly equivalent to her neighbours as a potential enemy and rival, and was so depicted, in the Czech concept of national history the German enemy was always presented as clearly the stronger. Although in more than one historical episode the "Germans" had actually been represented by one of the weaker German neighbouring states (Saxony, Bavaria, Austria), this made no difference to the use of these episodes to generate the paradigm of national threat from a more powerful enemy.

Neighbours did not, of course, have to be perpetual enemies. Certain elements of the Scandinavianism that tried to minimise conflict with the Northern neighbour states not only in the present but also in the picture of the past crept into the Norwegian construction of history. In the Czech Lands one might find a parallel in the idea of a common Austrian homeland and the peaceful, mutually beneficial co-existence of different nations in the framework of the Habsburg Monarchy. Theoretically, Pan-Slavism might also be counted a supranational aspect with positive connotations in the construction of Czech history, but it was expressed relatively rarely, for example to emphasise the relationship of the Czech Lands to Slavic Poland.

We can trace some similarity in the fact that both constructs of national history were initially born as negative reactions to impulses from outside, i.e. to the picture of these nations created by the historiography of neighbours. In the Norwegian case construction of national history begins as polemic against the Danish view of Norway as an integral part of Denmark, while in the Czech case it starts from the early 19th century as defensive polemic against the German historiography that incorporated the Czech Lands into German history.

## 2. Second Comparison: The History of the Greek and Turkish Nations

### 2.1. Historical Development

It is clear at first glance that in contrast to the histories of Czechs and Norwegians, the histories of the Greeks and Turks differ from each other dramatically. While in the case of the Greeks, the ancient period was the time of the greatest glory and prosperity, the earliest Turkish history is known only to Turkish specialists. In the Middle Ages, there were few similarities between the Byzantine Empire and the Seljuk Turks, who were gradually settling Anatolia, and in the 14th century, when the power of Byzantium was already on the wane, the best-known of Turkish states, the Ottoman Empire, was just beginning to expand.

Furthermore, unlike the histories of Czechs and Norwegians, Turkish and Greek history is intertwined in important ways. The Byzantine rulers encountered and clashed with the Seljuks, and later it was the conquest of Constantinople by the Ottoman forces under Mehmed II that ended the existence of the Byzantine state in 1453. From this moment, the history of the Greeks was the history of a part of the Ottoman Empire.

The Ottoman state reached the high point of its advance and geographical expansion in the 16th century, when it covered a huge area from North Africa to South-East and Central Europe. Although in the following period expansion came to a halt and the Ottoman state was faced by a series of problems, including that of how to administer so vast an area, Ottoman sovereignty over a large part of South-East Europe, the Balkans, lasted up to the 19th century and in some cases the beginning of the 20th century.

The Greeks enjoyed a quite exceptional position among the subject peoples of the Ottoman Empire. The Greek patriarch was the head of the Orthodox Church and all Orthodox inhabitants of the empire, whatever their ethnicity, came under his jurisdiction. Greek priests enjoyed privileged status among Ottoman Christians and Greek church schools represented one of the few opportunities for Orthodox Christians of different ethnic origins to get an education. Greek merchants gradually acquired an important position in Ottoman trade. Greeks were employed as interpreters by the Ottoman government and its administration. One particularly important element was formed by the "Phanariots", rich and influential Greeks from one of Istanbul's districts; it was from Phanariot ranks that the ruler of the Danubian principalities of Moldavia and Wallachia was appointed. In their way, the Greeks were the most privileged, but also the most advanced ethnic group in the Ottoman Empire.

The Greek national movement thus developed relatively early. It linked cultural revival with attempts at political emancipation, partly under the influence of Greeks living in the Diaspora beyond the frontiers of the Ottoman Empire. Following the Greek rebellion and intervention by the great powers, the Kingdom of Greece was founded in 1830, headed by a king of Bavarian origin, but the new Greek state included only part of the territory historically or presently inhabited by Greeks, and was under the influence of three protectors – England, France and Germany. There was a resurgence of the Greek national movement at the end of the 19th century.

It is imprecise to see the Turks as the "ruling nation" of the Ottoman Empire. The Ottoman state was markedly cosmopolitan, and under the impact of the European powers but also the national liberation movements of subject nations (first and foremost the Greeks), the Turks were themselves searching for national identity from the last third of the 19th century. All this was connected to the process of modernisation, which in the 19th century included extensive efforts at reform affecting most areas of the Ottoman state and the life of its inhabitants. A short constitutional experiment in 1876 was eventually followed in 1908 by the Young Turk Revolution, which limited the absolute power of the sultan by a constitution and parliament.

Ottoman territory continued to shrink as a result of the Balkan Wars in 1912–13 and the Ottoman Empire finally collapsed after the 1st World War, when it had allied with Germany. The founding of a new Turkish Republic in 1923 in place of the multi-national Islamic Ottoman Empire followed armed conflict with Greece, whose armies, supported by the Allies, had occupied part of Ottoman territory.

### 2.2. What Do We Draw on from the Past?

### 2.2.1. The Historiographical Tradition

The development of national consciousness fundamentally changed Turkish and Greek views of their respective national pasts. It is arguable, indeed, that these changes were even more fundamental than in the case of Norwegian or Czech constructs of history. One very distinctive aspect of the Turkish situation, however, was the difference in the historiographical tradition that preceded the rise of nationalism. Official Ottoman historiography, the historiography of a powerful empire rich in literary culture, was extensive and relatively advanced. As with the history of other empires it was naturally concerned with the state and its rulers. In the official conception, the beginning of history was linked to the birth of Islam, the arrival of the Seljuks in Anatolia and the origins of the Ottoman dynasty. The latter was sometimes designated a Turkish dynasty, but this was not important for the interpretation of Ottoman history.

In the case of the Greeks, the main type of historical writing in the Ottoman period up to the 18th century was chronicles. Their subject was church history, i.e. the history of Orthodox Christendom, and their goal was to present examples of moral improvement for Christians, and not just for Greeks. This was a type of history on which it was difficult for modern national historiography to build. Up to the 19th century, history was not understood as the history of the Greek nation, but the 18th century had already seen the first changes, and a turning away from traditional chronicles. A new interest in international political history and a trend to secularisation emerged. Historical development was no longer considered to be given by God and no longer limited to church history. The Enlightenment had a major influence, strengthening interest in Antiquity and hence a sense of the distinctive character of Greeks.

The Ottoman Turks and the Greeks had one starting-point in common: a lack of knowledge of their earliest history. A certain knowledge of the ancient past lived on among the few Greek men of learning, above all from the ranks of the church, and survived in less systematic form among less educated Greeks, but in general, especially in the initial period of Ottoman rule, the Greeks did not regard themselves as the heirs of the cultural tradition of Ancient Greece. In the same way the Ottoman Turks, including Ottoman historians, had gradually "forgotten" that Turkish tribes had existed even before the acceptance of Islam and the establishment of the Ottoman Empire.

Another important similarity was the fact that in both cases it was an external factor, and even the same factor – the work of European historians and other scholars – that contributed to the "discovery" of these "roots", and the beginnings of national histories.

### 2.2.2. Sources of Information

European science and scholarship, specifically historiography, archaeology and linguistics, had a huge influence on the construction of Turkish and Greek national histories. First, they brought new, often basic information about the Greek and especially the Turkish past, and so replaced or supplemented the "domestic" sources. Second, and above all, this information led to fundamental changes in the concepts of national history.

The study of old Chinese and Arab Islamic sources and archaeological research in what is today Mongolia brought new information about the history of the Turkish tribes before their arrival in Anatolia and conversion to Islam. Scholarship demonstrated that the Turks had already produced written records and state formations even at this early date. In 1869, a leading Ottoman-Turkish intellectual wrote an article celebrating the values of Turkish civilisation from earliest times, which he actually based on the historical introduction to a Turkish Grammar by A.L. Davids. Necib Asım's Turkish History of 1899, which was a markedly free translation of the "Introduction à l'histoire de l'Asie" by the French historian and librarian Léon Cahun of 1896, played an important part in the process of raising national consciousness. European works thus led to change in the Turks' own view of their past, and to the discovery and celebration of the Pre-Islamic Turks. Under the influence of the opinions of European Enlightenment thinkers, the Greek historians likewise started to celebrate the period of Ancient Greece. In the same way it was the work of a European, the German Fallmerayer, that later contributed to the incorporation of the Byzantine Empire into the Greek concept of national history.

Thus in the first phase, Western works had more influence on the construction of national histories than the Turkish or Greek historiographical traditions themselves. Although attitudes to the West European states in the Ottoman Empire and later in the Kingdom of Greece were ambivalent and often negative, conceptions of national history did not originally emerge in opposition to, but in harmony with (some) European works. This was of course only one line of development. Later, the effort to defend the nation and its past from accusations or contempt from Europeans became an important impulse in historical writing. In Greece, this tendency grew after the establishment of the independent state and the decline of West European Philhellenism as Western Europeans expressed disappointment with contemporary Greece as compared to the glory of Antiquity. In the Ottoman Empire the defensive impulse appeared after the mid-19th century, when learned people gained a more detailed knowledge of the prejudices of European authors and historians, and it gathered headway thereafter. In the later period, national history was constructed in opposition to the West and Western historiography.

### 2.2.3. Continuity and Discontinuity

In the first phase of both Turkish and Greek national awareness, historical writing linked the newly imagined communities to the earliest periods of their history. Greeks of the turn of the 18th and 19th century were presented as the heirs of Ancient Greece and Ottoman Turks of the late 19th century as the descendants of the Turkish nomads in Central Asia. The view of Turkish history, however, changed only very slowly. While the Ottoman Empire survived, the tendency to construct the past as the history of the Ottoman Empire remained relatively important, and even predominant. The idea that the Ottoman Empire followed on from the earlier history of Pre-Islamic Turkish tribes was gradually introduced into this official version, and only later did the Ottoman Empire come to be regarded as a part of Turkish history.

The question of the continuity of national history has probably been the key issue in modern Greek national historiography. The discovery of the past came in two phases. In the first it was a matter of the discovery, celebration and idealisation of Antiquity, and in the second the re-evaluation of Byzantium. The discovery of Antiquity was already underway at the end of the 18th century under the influence of the Enlightenment. Greek men of learning, such as Adamantios Korais, started to stress that present-day Greeks were the direct descendants of famous ancestors, the Ancient Greeks. Liberation from Ottoman rule would therefore mean the revival of Ancient Greece in all its power. It should be noted that many Philhellenist Western European authors (such as Herder), whose interest in Ancient Greece influenced the Greeks themselves, wrote in similar terms.

The following periods of national history, Byzantium and especially the period of Ottoman-Turkish rule in the Greek case (and the Ottoman period itself in the eyes of Turkish nationalists), were regarded as secondary and decadent, and as eras from which it was necessary to distance oneself. The Enlightenment thinkers in Europe, and under their influence learned Greeks as well, condemned Byzantium as the embodiment of despotism and corruption. Even after the founding of the Greek state the history of mankind was taught in an Enlightenment spirit. The beginning of Greek history was associated with the glory of Ancient Greece. The second milestone was 1821, the birth of the Greek state. The interval, i.e. not only the period of Ottoman rule, but also Byzantium, represented a dark period, the decline of the Greeks.

Change in this view of Greek history was generated by the needs and realities of the present. Modern Greek society had a much more immediate and obvious connection with Byzantine (mainly Orthodox) elements than with ancient elements, and identified itself primarily on the basis of religion, i.e. with Orthodox Christendom. Political motives also played their part – the Bavarian king could hardly find the necessary legitimisation of his power and monarchy in Antiquity. Moreover, after the foundation of the Greek state the church, under pressure from the new regime, was moving away from the Patriarchate of Constantinople, and so new sources of unity were being sought in the interests of both church and state. It has also been argued that the views of Jacob Philipp Fallmerayer, who at the beginning of the 1830s claimed that the influx of Slav and Albanian elements meant that modern Greeks had no connection with the Ancient Greeks, were a major or even a crucial factor.

In his five-volume history of the Greek nation, Konstantinos Paparrigopoulos, the author of the new conception incorporating Byzantium into Greek history, proclaimed the unbroken continuity of Greek history from the Ancient World to the present. He saw Greek history as divided into three great epochs and two periods of bondage. The first glorious epoch was the period of Ancient Greece up to 146 BC. This was followed by the Roman occupation, the first era of foreign rule. The second great epoch was Byzantium to the Fall of Constantinople in 1453, followed by the dark period of Ottoman rule and then by partial emancipation in 1821. The prospective culmination of Greek history was to be the fulfilment of the great idea (Megale idea) – the union of all Greek elements and the territory of Classical Greece and Byzantium in one state.

In Ottoman-Turkish historiography, change came only after the mid-19th century. Under the influence of European works Turkish men of learning began to discover the history of the Pre-Islamic Turkish tribes before their arrival in Anatolia and the kinship of the Turks with the Mongols and the Turkic ethnic groups in Central Asia. In other words, they started to develop an interest in the history of the Turks rather than the history of the Ottoman Empire. The first change in the conception of history was thus the incorporation of the pre-Ottoman period of Turkish tribes. As has been suggested, so long as the Ottoman Empire survived, the traditional approach to history that saw the Ottoman period as its core and crown and emphasised political and military events tended to predominate, although historians began to use new sources (including European sources), and to interpret history rather than simply narrate in chronicle style. Gradually, and above all under the influence of the work of Ziya Gökalp in the 1910s, a second change occurred: Ottoman history was presented as a period of "darkness" and decline, especially in comparison with the preceding period of Turkish history. The third change was a new interest in "forebears" which included a tendency to incorporate into national history such ancient civilisations as had once been found on what had become (even marginally) "Turkish" territory – i.e. the Sumerians and the Hittites (and for lack of proof to the contrary even the Etruscans). The tendency to repress the Ottoman period and distance oneself from it culminated in the historiography of the inter-war Kemalist Turkish Republic, in which the Ottoman Empire was accorded so little attention in official conceptions of history that the half a millennium of empire might never have existed.

For Greeks, not surprisingly, it was the Ottoman Empire and the Turks, and later sometimes "oriental" influences on the character of the Greeks, that were to blame for the Greek decline. It is noteworthy that Ottoman-Turkish intellectuals in their turn blamed decline mainly on Greek-Byzantine influences, alongside Persian and Arab influences.

### 2.2.4. Values

Among the basic values projected from the present onto the past the most striking was that of "civilisation". The Greeks regarded themselves as the cradle of European civilisation and this argument had strong contemporary overtones, especially when Western European authors cast doubts on the Greek present after the founding of the independent state. According to Paparrigopoulos the Ancient Greeks had discovered the parliamentary form of government and modern Greeks had managed to avoid the disunity that had afflicted the ancient world by accepting a monarchic form of government from the Byzantine system.

Among the Turks, claims about civilisation as a historic national value were more polemic: as in other areas, Turkish intellectuals tried to show that from their earliest beginnings Turks had been one of the most advanced nations – old Turkish civilisation had more than equalled world civilisations of the time (unlike later Ottoman civilisation) and had even foreshadowed some of the values of the modern West European civilisation of the 19<sup>th</sup> century. Democracy, linked to the nomadic way of life, the equality of women and shamanism were put forward as the most important of such values. The place of Islam was debatable, and only sometimes, and with reservations, was it interpreted as part of the national past. It was also often seen as an obstacle to progress and a cause of decline. The perspective on Islam changed with time, and also varied between authors in the same period, and it remains a living question in Turkish history. There was also a tendency to celebrate the Turkish common people, although this was expressed less in historiography than elsewhere.

Language, which had a close relation to history, was an important value. One result of the discovery of the Greek ancient past before 1821 was a growing polemic on which language should be used for the revival of Greece. There were three currents of thought. According to the first, which predominated in the new Greek state, Greeks could revive the greatness of their ancestors only by reviving their original language. According to the second, the new Greek should use vernacular demotic Greek as its basis. This current of thought was associated with a Romantic interest in the past, including the Byzantine period and its popular culture. Adamantios Korais stood somewhere in the middle, defending the contemporary spoken language, but recommending that it be purged of foreign (especially Turkish) words and constructions.

Turkish discussion on the character of the language in the Ottoman Empire ran along very similar lines. Purists (sometimes employing nationalist arguments) wanted to purge Turkish of Arabic and Persian words and grammatical constructions. Their opponents declared that in that case nothing much would be left of Turkish and unity with Islam would be lost, and preferred to stress the Ottoman (Islamic) rather than the Turkish character of the language. Here too there were supporters of compromise, who wanted the language to be simplified but to retain essential Arab-Persian elements. In the Turkish Republic the turn away from the Arab-Islamic-Eastern tradition was symbolised by the replacement of Arabic by Latin script.

It is worth mentioning that in neither case were these language proposals distinctively connected with a single social group. Although intellectuals believed that the ordinary Turkish people spoke the "purer" Turkish, people on both sides of the debate came from the same (educated, elite) classes. There was likewise no social division between supporters of the three linguistic "camps" in Greece.

### 2.3. Who Are We?

### 2.3.1. The Territorial Dimension

The territorial aspect took very different form in the construction of Greek and Turkish national histories as compared to the Czech and Norwegian cases. Above all, the territorial definition of national society was not a solid or indisputable given. Nor did

Greek or Turkish historians show any concern with this vagueness as a theme of debate. It is significant that the Turkish and Greek territorial claims overlapped, in the present (and hence in history too). It was an issue for the Greeks that their new state was far from containing all Greeks. The consequences of the "Megale idea", the great idea of the revival of the former Byzantium including Constantinople-Istanbul, were reflected in views of history, but the frontiers of an ideal Greek state were not firmly defined, and the views of historians differed. Contemporary considerations sometimes had an effect here, above all the existence of the Greek state, and also the ethnic aspect, i.e. where Greeks presently lived on the territory of the Ottoman Empire, and not simply where the Byzantine borders had once been located.

For Turks the territorial aspect played a rather different role. As national consciousness emerged, so too did interest in the past of the region settled mainly by Turks, i.e. Anatolia. This territory was associated with the Turkish common people as the purest representative of "surviving" Turkishness. The national movements of non-Turkish peoples, the Armenians, Greeks and later the Kurds, also played their part in arousing Turkish interest in Anatolia, and the Turkish character of the region in the past and present was strongly emphasised to counter their demands. The moving of the capital of the Turkish Republic from Ottoman Istanbul to Ankara in the heart of Anatolia was a radical expression of the rejection of the Ottoman Empire in the new conception of national history.

### 2.3.2. Who Belongs to National History?

In the later 19th century, when the new conception of Turkish history was beginning to make headway but the ideology of Ottomanism (with its defence of the Ottoman Empire and assertion of the equality of all its inhabitants as citizens who would have the good of their homeland at heart) prevailed at the political level, all the inhabitants of the Ottoman Empire had a place in national history. Not even the incorporation of the pre-Islamic history of the Turks meant the limitation of the historic community purely to ethnic Turks, since this was not in the interest of the maintenance of the empire. In Pan-Turkist thought the Turks were linked to the Turkic peoples of Central Asia, but there continued to be a certain tension between the existing Ottoman Empire and the Turkish element as the foundation of identity and bearer of national history. The emphasis on the past of Anatolia as Turkish territory, including its ancient civilisations, was another factor contributing to ambiguity. Overall we can perhaps identify one common thread in concepts of history from the Ottoman Empire to the Turkish Republic. It is that the people who live on the territory of a given state at a given moment are part of the national history: first, the inhabitants of the contemporary Ottoman Empire (minus the newly emancipated Greeks and Slavs) and later, the inhabitants of the Turkish Republic.

Nor was the Greek view of who belonged to national history entirely clear. On the one hand it was not disputed that even people who had remained outside the frontiers of the new Greek state were part of Greek history. On the other hand, in contrast to the Great Idea (Megale idea) of the renewal of the glory of Byzantium including Istanbul/Constantinople and other Greek/Byzantine territories of the Ottoman Empire, some intellectuals emphasised the contemporary geopolitical factor, the existence of the Greek state.

### 2.3.3. Where Do We Belong?
In both cases the place of the national community – past and present – in relation to Europe was a major question, specifically in relation to "European Civilisation" and to the dichotomy of West and East.

The Greeks were regarded by West Europeans as cultural forefathers and Greece as the cradle of European society, and this was how the Greeks saw themselves, but when many Europeans took a superior attitude to contemporary Greece, Greek intellectuals responded with an ambivalent view of Western Europe and its civilisation. Nonetheless, Greek historians continued to distance themselves from the Ottoman, Oriental past. The Ottoman Empire and the Turks were conceived as the main enemy in the present and in history. Historiography presented Greeks as a bridge between East and West. At the same time, the Greeks were identified with Orthodoxy, not simply as a part of the Orthodox world, but as the embodiment and leaders of that world.

Although for many Ottoman-Turkish intellectuals the link with the East and above all with Islam was the most important element, it was orientation towards the West that predominated in mainstream national discourse. Turkish authors considered the Arabs less educated and successful, and claimed that it was the Turks who had preserved the unity of Islam after the Arab decline and had defended the Arabs themselves. While pre-Islamic history created closer links with the Turkic tribes of Central Asia and hence the warrior Mongols, Tartars and Huns, interest in ancient civilisations clearly connected the Turks with Europe.

The attempt to demonstrate that Turks belong to Western, democratic European civilisation played a significant part in the Ottoman Empire and later in the Turkish Republic (athough paradoxically the West European powers were the main enemy of the Turks in history). This aspiration was behind the celebration of ancient civilisations on the territory of Anatolia, and insistence on the democratic spirit of the old, pre-Islamic Turks and on democracy as a part of national character.

## 3. Conclusion

While the choice of four distant subjects for comparison may seem rather ambitious, the two brief comparative studies have shown that application of a comparative approach can illuminate many aspects of national history and place them in wider context. It now remains to be seen whether we can derive any fruitful general-isations from comparison of the four constructions of national history. What stands out most clearly is the perhaps rather banal fact that history was always one of the basic constitutive elements in the formation of national identity and one of the main political arguments formulated in the name of the nation. It is no accident that in all four countries historians (or other scholars concerned with history) made major contributions to the formulation of the national programme and national policy.

All the national historiographies that we have considered had to address and resolve the problem of discontinuity in their national histories. The most elaborate and thorough treatment of the problem is to be found in the case of Norwegian history, where the "gap", originally regarded as a tragedy, was bridged in the later 19th century by orientation to the continuity of social and economic relations. The same kind of process can be found in more dilute form in Czech history. All four national historiographies thematised the question of the reasons for discontinuity. Initially, the prevailing approach was an unambiguous (and simple) identification of a "culprit" (in the Norwegian case, the Danish kings, in the Czech case, the Habsburgs and in the Greek case, the Ottoman Turks while in the Turkish case, there was no single "culprit"). Gradually, however, the search for a "culprit" was combined with critical self-examination, which also identified causes of decline in the internal history of the nation.

Only in the Czech case did the construction of national history rest on the continuity of a historiographical tradition that supplied not only a territorial definition of national history but the very concept or "definition" of the nation itself. Norwegian history used sagas and medieval chronicles as a substitute for this continuity. Its territorial definition was made easier by geographical conditions. In the Greek and Turkish cases, the absence of a nationally exploitable historiography that could be updated was compensated for by the "depth" of the historical perspective, reaching back to Ancient Greece and the pre-Ottoman period, respectively. While this compensation may have had an important psychological function, it was an insufficient basis for the clear and realistic historical definition of national territory that would have ruled out territorial overlaps and the resulting territorial claims and counter-claims.

In all the cases considered, "ethnicisation" was part of the construction of national history. Sooner or later members of the national community in former centuries came to be defined on an ethnic basis. This tendency corresponded to the general trend prevailing in most national movements but raised a series of difficulties over answers to the question of who belonged to national history. In Norway, there was a search for "genuine" ethnicity and integrating criteria of "Norwegianness", while in the Greek case the trend led to longing for the integration of the Greek Diaspora. In the Czech case, the German minority was excluded from national history, while in the Turkish case, on the contrary, there were efforts at the artificial incorporation of non-Turkish ethnic groups into the newly established construct of the political nation.

Historians of all four nations posed the question of the place of their history in a wider context. All had to come to terms with views from outside, which in the Greek and Turkish cases were initially to a greater or lesser extent capable of integration into the concepts of national history. In the Norwegian and especially the Czech case, views from the outside were incompatible with the construction of national history. It is not surprising that historians always sought the most flattering contexts for their histories, and tried to show that their nation had moved in the "best society". The historical stories on which they drew were not and usually could not have been entirely invented, but the choice of motifs that could be "brought up to date", the selection of predecessors in the national struggle, and the definition of what had to be excluded from national history were nonetheless fundamentally influenced by the contemporary needs of the national movement. The changes and modifications to the image of national histories that occurred in the course of the formation of nations themselves testify to the close connection between the historiography and current events.

It is notable that in the construction of these four national histories there always seems to be a search for an "updateable" national function or even a national mission as the intermediary for the transmission of values between cultures, i.e. the assumption of the role of a "bridge" between what was regarded as the more advanced "Western" and less advanced "Eastern" civilisation. Linked to this theme was the conception of national histories as sources of values for the contemporary national struggle. Naturally the dimension of the present played a major role in the construction of national histories. Attitude to the question of continuity and discontinuity was itself a highly topical issue, and was based on present political needs and opinions on what was beneficial for the nation and what was (or had been) harmful.

At the risk of a certain simplification we can say that the degree of integration of times of "darkness" into national histories depended on the position of the main "culprits", or representatives of past "darkness" in relation to the national movement concerned. In the first phase of the Norwegian national movement the period of Danish rule had been rejected as one of complete decline, and its subsequent incorporation into the construct of national history reflected not only the new emphasis on ethnic continuity but also the fact that by the later 19th century, Denmark was no longer regarded as a threat or even an enemy to the Norwegian national struggle.

In the formation of the Turkish picture of national history, the development of opinion was in the opposite direction – from the inclusion of the Ottoman period as part of national history to its condemnation as an epoch of cosmopolitanism and universal decadence. Even then, however, the attitudes motivated by the increasing Turkish national awareness involved distancing from the Ottoman era rather than its complete banishment from national history. In this case too, one important factor was political development, since after the establishment of the Turkish Republic, the cosmopolitan and Islamic Ottoman Empire of the past was not in practice the enemy of modern Turkish identity.

In contrast, the time of "darkness" was still dark in the eyes of Czech and Greek historians at the end of the 19th century. For the Czech national movement Vienna and the Habsburg government remained the enemy. No doubts were raised about the "national", i.e. ethnic continuity of the Czech common people and conversely, the German-speaking nobility and elites were being excluded from national history, with reference to the way in which they were distancing themselves from the current Czech national community.

In the construction of Greek history, political and social changes were reflected in the gradual incorporation of the Byzantine Empire into a national historical picture that had originally focused only on Classical Greece. The era of the Ottoman Empire that followed Byzantium was still regarded as a period of bondage, and this was definitely connected to the fact that the Ottoman Empire (and later Turkey) remained an enemy that controlled territories to which the Greeks laid claim and where a sizeable Greek minority still lived.

The answer to the question of who belonged to national history was also influenced by the form of the present-day national "enemy". In Palacký's conception, history became the history of the ethnic Czechs, while the German-speaking inhabitants of the Czech Lands who did not accept Czech national identity were shifted into the role of rival not only in the present but also in the past. The entirely reverse development in Norway, where "foreign", i.e. Danish-speaking elites gradually became acceptable in the picture of national Norwegian history, can be explained by the fact that it was precisely these elites who headed the rising Norwegian national movement.

A similar problem did not arise in the construction of Greek and Turkish national history. In the Greek case, the ethnic definition of the nation was unambiguous, but doubts about the ethnic continuity of the Greek population from ancient times played an important role. The "Megale idea", however, was not based on ethnicity, but on historical-geographical criteria. In the Turkish case, ethnicity played a role primarily in the new focus on the pre-Islamic period of nomadic Turkish tribes. This concept of national history was, however, at odds with the distinctively civic definition of the nation that included all inhabitants of the Ottoman Empire and later Turkey within the nation.

Present-day motivations were no less striking in the case of the values exalted in national history. Despite all their differences, in all four cases we can find the idealisation of principles of equality or democracy in the life of ancient forebears. Here we clearly have a projection of the contemporary values of civil society. Given that medieval society was very far from exhibiting a democratic order, there was no alternative but to connect the ideals of democracy and equality with the early pre-feudal periods of national history.

### SELECTED BIBLIOGRAPHY

**Czechs**
PLASCHKA, Richard, *Von Palacký bis Pekař*. Graz/Köln 1955.
ZACEK, Joseph F., *Palacky: The Historian as Scholar and Nationalist*. The Hague/Paris 1970.
RAK, Jiří, *Bývali Čechové… České historické mýty a stereotypy*. Praha 1994.
ŠTAIF, Jiří, *Historici, dějiny, společnost. Historiografie v českých zemích od Palackého a jeho předchůdců po Gollovu školu, 1790–1900*. Praha 1997.

**Norwegians**
DAHL, Ottar, *Norsk historieforsning i 19. og 20. arhundre*. Oslo 1976.
FALK, Bernhard P., *Geschichtsschreibung und nationale Ideologie. Der norwegische Historiker Johan Ernst Sars*. Heidelberg 1991.
FULSAS, Narve, *Historie og nasjon. Ernst Sars og striden om norske kultur*. Oslo 1999.
SØRENSEN, Øystein, 'The Development of a Norwegian National Identity during the Nineteenth Century', *Nordic Paths to National Identity*, Øystein Sørensen (ed.), Oslo 1994, 165–183.
SØRENSEN, Øystein (ed.), *Jakten pa det norske*. Oslo 1998.

**Greeks**

CLOGG, Richard, 'The Greeks and their Past', *Historians as Nation-Builders. Central and South-East Europe*, Dennis Deletant – Harry Hanak (eds.), London 1988, 15–31.

GAZI, Fotini-Effi – LAMBROS, Spyridon (1851–1919), *'Scientific' History in national perspective in nineteenth-century Greece*. PhD dissertation, European University Institute, Florence 1996.

GOURGOURIS, Stathis, *Dream Nation. Enlightenment, Colonization and the Institution of Modern Greece*. Stanford 1996.

PAPOULIA, Basilike, 'Die Osmanenzeit in der griechischen Geschichtsforschung seit der Unabhängigkeit', *Die Staaten Südosteuropas und die Osmanen*, Hans Georg Majer (ed.), München 1989.

TZERMIAS, Pavlos, *Neugriechische Geschichte. Eine Einführung*. Tübingen 1986.

VRYONIS, Speros, 'Recent Scholarship on Continuity and Discontinuity of Culture: Classical Greeks, Byzantines, Modern Greeks', *The 'Past' in Medieval and Modern Greek Culture*, Vryonis, Speros, Jr. (ed.), 237–256.

**Turks**

COPEAUX, Etienne, *Espaces et temps de la nation turque. Analyse d'une historiographie nationaliste 1931–1993*. Paris 1997.

ZIYA, Gökalp, *The Principles of Turkism*. Leiden 1968.

KURAN, Ercüment, 'Ottoman Historiography of the Tanzimat Period', *Historians of the Middle East*, Lewis, Bernard – Holt, P.M. (eds.), London/New York/Toronto 1962, 422–429.

LEWIS, Bernard, 'History-writing and National Revival' Turkey, *Middle Eastern Affairs*, IV, 1953, 218–227.

VRYONIS, Speros, Jr., *The Turkish State and History. Clio Meets the Grey Wolf*. New Rochelle 1993.

# XV

# The Czech Discourse on Europe, 1848–1948

To analyse the meaning of Europe in the Czech national context, it is vital to distinguish two levels: first, the general placement of 'Us' into a broader, macroregional and continental context, and secondly, the discourse on Europe, which is explicitly oriented to the term itself. For this reason, this contribution is divided into two parts, the first giving an overview of Czech history, the second based on sources.

## A Czech Overview

Similar to all European national movements, the Czech national movement offered a new, modern identity and had to define this identity in order to place the Czech nation into the broader regional and continental context. This search was complicated by the fact that the definition of the Czech place in Europe was characterized by severe ambivalence borne from history and geography. This involves a number of factors.

First, since the Middle Ages, the Czech lands were included in the Holy Roman Empire, but they were never fully integrated into this Empire and kept their status of state. As a result of this, German historians, who identified their national history with the history of the Holy Roman Empire, regarded Czech history as a part of German history, while Czech historians, for their part, constructed their own national history independent of Germans.

Second, from a linguistic point of view, the Czechs were a Slavic nation and had their own literary language from the late Middle Ages, but they were entwined in the German linguistic environment and culture. Third, Czech lands, and especially Bohemia, constitute a historical and closed geographical territory with an extraordinary stable political border and administrative structure, but this territory has been inhabited not just by the Czech-speaking majority, but also by a German-speaking minority which in the mid-nineteenth century opted for German national identity.

Fourth, the Czechs inhabited a territory that could be classified neither as the 'West' nor as the 'East' of Europe. Fifth, almost all the population of Bohemia were Roman Catholics, but in the fifteenth and sixteenth centuries there was a Protestant majority which was forced to convert to Catholicism after 1620. Under these conditions, it is not surprising that we can distinguish five competing identities in Bohemia at the threshold of the inauguration of the Czech national movement:

- an Austrian dynastic state identity
- an identity with the historical land of the kingdom of Bohemia
- a Slavic identity
- a linguistically-defined Czech (originally ethnic) identity
- a linguistically-defined German (originally ethnic) identity.

The decisive turn came with the 1848 Revolution, when only two of these identities survived – the Czech and German ones – and were no longer defined as ethnic but as political identities. Since then, one can observe in Bohemia a competition and political struggle between the German element, represented by a wealthy bourgeoisie and a section of the old elites, and the Czech element. In opposition to the apparent cultural and material superiority of Germans, Czech intellectuals and politicians tried as early as the 1860s to find spiritual inspiration and cultural support in non-German parts of Europe, first in Russia and France, and then later also in the Anglo-Saxon world. Further, before the end of the nineteenth century, the literature of other 'small nations' was systematically translated and reviewed, including that of Scandinavian and Polish writers. This naturally predestined the European orientation of Czech culture – or better, that of leading Czech intellectuals and artists. They did not accept the alternative of becoming merely 'translated Germans' but rather demonstrated their ability to create an original national culture.

Some kind of cultural syncretism emerged, where the Slavic component was also strongly represented. Nevertheless, the position between East and West often drew the reflection: are we Eastern or Western people? We are partially Western and partially Eastern but we inherited from both parts their feebleness, wrote the poet J.S. Machar at the threshold of the twentieth century. It was not easy to solve the problem by introducing the construct of Central Europe because this term was, at least until the First World War, filled by the German nationalist concept of 'Mitteleuropa'.

*The Czech Discourse on Europe, 1848–1948*

At the end of the nineteenth century, Czech society achieved a full social structure and was differentiated into several political streams corresponding to the general trend of European political development. Czech politicians, like the politicians of all Europe's fully-formed nations, regarded their nation as a 'personality' and demanded full equality with other nations irrespective of their size, including also the German nation. This demand was unacceptable to the German 'Herrenvolk' mentality, which resulted in an increasing national tension. In spite of this high self-consciousness, Czech politics did not formulate any demand for political independence until 1914.

This changed with the First World War: increasing numbers of intellectuals and politicians joined the group around T.G. Masaryk who decided to emigrate and to support the entente powers in order to fight for national independence. The Czech syncretism of Western and Eastern cultural orientation seemed to be confirmed by political developments. Nevertheless, Masaryk won the acknowledgement of independence after the October revolution, only through the decision of the Western powers and under condition of the waging of an open war between the Czech legions and the Bolshevik troops in Siberia. This fact was decisive for the political and cultural orientation of the Czechoslovak state after 1918 in favour of the Western powers and, above all, in favour of France. To the large majority of Czechs the meaning of Europe was limited to the West.

It is in this sense that one must interpret the strong accentuation of the need for the improvement of Czech culture in order to correspond to 'European criteria'. Nevertheless, some relics of Slavism remained after the October revolution: cultural contacts with the Soviet Union were rather strong and even if political sympathy with the new regime were originally limited to the extreme left, the defence treaty with both France and the Soviet Union from 1935 was accepted by the majority of the population.

The 1938 Munich Conference and Agreement severely challenged the Czech sense of Western identity: people felt betrayed by the Western powers. This caused a new revival of Slavism manifested in sympathy for the Soviet Union among the majority of the population and by no means only among leftists. These sympathies seemed to be confirmed by the results of the Second World War.

New reflections concerning the Czech place in Europe emerged. The slogan, originally formulated by President Beneš, was very influential: under present conditions, we are not living between the West and the East, but between Germany and Russia (Soviet Union). This concept was accompanied by the myth about the Czech mission in post-war Europe:

to become a bridge which could mediate an exchange of both cultural and political values between West and East.

Events turned this in a very different way. Europe was divided by the cold war and Czechoslovakia was included in the Soviet sphere and classified, above all in the West, as a part of the East. This was not accepted by the Czech population: the concept of Central or Middle Europe was used, even though in a very unreflective sense. Even the official state ideology never dared to qualify Czechs as part of Eastern Europe. The Eastern orientation was substituted by Slavism (itself becoming increasingly artificial) and by the construct 'community of socialist countries'.

During the 1980s, some dissenting intellectuals formulated a new version of the myth of Central Europe. It was based on reflection on one aspect of the 'tragedy' of the region: the West's non-acceptance of the Czechs, who were not a part of the East, but maintained Western traditions under Soviet rule, which was itself the historical mission of Central Europe. In the early 1990s, to be European meant also to be above all Central European (as a part of Western culture).

After 1990, this ideological concept lost its political anti-communist connotation, but it survived transformed in two fashions. For the main part, it contributed some feelings of value to the general consciousness of the self-evident allegiance to Central Europe, but for the other part, it degenerated into a nostalgic conception of Central Europe, which was interpreted as a lost Habsburg heritage and is still presented as such in the revue *Střední Evropa* (Central Europe) by a group of conservative intellectuals. Some of this group use the concept of Central Europe not as a complementary element of the European identity as represented by the EU, but on the contrary, according to their opinion, the traditional, 'true' European values, represented by the Central European heritage, are violated by EU technocracy and centralism. It is difficult to say just how strongly these ideas influenced Czech public opinion.

## The 'Narrow' Meaning of Europe

The second part of this contribution aims to analyse the meaning of Europe in the narrow sense by concentrating on the term 'Europe', itself. Only those texts are included wherein 'Europe' is explicitly verbalized and defined, above all in relation to the emerging modern Czech national identity. What will not be included is the general 'European horizon', the interest of Czech writers and politicians in other countries, and in the European context of their writings, translations and other activities.

The Czech Discourse on Europe, 1848–1948

A specific limitation concerns the fact that the word 'Europe' was very frequently used as *terminus technicus* of geography or even politics, without being conceptualized as a classificatory scheme. Reflections on Europe as a quality, as a dimension of national identity were rather rare in Czech discourse, compared for instance to similar reflections on the relationship with Germans, or on the Slavic identity. This under-representation did not change until the 1990s when, on the contrary, the concept of Europe became a very fashionable component of cultural and political rhetoric.

The presented results are not based on an exhaustive study of all manner of sources, but rather on a selection of texts, which include the most important politicians and intellectuals between the mid-nineteenth and mid-twentieth centuries. For this reason, no quantification could be used and the analysis aims to find out basic trends, types and periods. It is presumed that these results will be corrected or modified through systematic research, which will analyse newspapers and journals, etc. This is not only presumable, but also desirable. With few exceptions (cf. Hahnová 1997a) no such research exists in the Czech republic.

## What is Europe?

The general overview of the development of the meaning of Europe is based on data from three national Encyclopaedias, each of which being of representative importance to Czech national culture. The oldest one was published from the early 1860s, the second around the year 1900 and the third one at the end of 1920s. Naturally, we find in these texts an extensive geographical, biological, etc. description of Europe, but besides this are also some significant features of what is regarded as the proper meaning, the 'quality' of Europe. This meaning was different in the various Encyclopaedias and these differences are rather symptomatic.

The oldest Encyclopaedia stressed that 'Europe was exceeding all other continents through its power and the level of education' and was somehow 'predestined' by its geographical position to become the centre of trade and civilization of all the world. This modernizing understanding of Europe was accompanied by the opinion that Europe was developing towards a civil society, equality of citizens and peasant liberation – all these progressive changes were regarded as resulting from the French revolution ('Evropa', in: *Riegrův slovník naučný, II*, 1862: 528). This article expressed the opinion of the editor, František L. Rieger, who soon became the leading personality among the Czech liberals.

*Miroslav Hroch*

The Otto-Encyclopaedia shared the opinion that Europe exceeded all other continents and that it was moving toward civic freedoms, but it put the origins of the idea of freedom in the Middle Ages, when Europe was fighting against the 'barbarians' from the East – Huns, Mongolians and Turks. Besides this, we find a further specification: Europe as 'some sort of federation of nations' whose further improvement depended on the opportunity given to each of these nations to contribute to European development. In this process of improvement and growth, an important role would fall upon 'young nations' and their ability to be more efficient than 'older' ones, who could sometimes be in decline. ('Evropa' in: *Ottův slovník naučný, VIII*, 1997 [1894]: 854–5). This Encyclopaedia expressed the concepts of the new generation of the Czech positivist scholars.

The Masaryk Encyclopaedia again included the meaning of Europe as being the most prosperous among all the continents (with a short reference to North America), and as being a continent of many nations and nation states. The central characteristic was nevertheless regarded as European cultural specificity based on Christian tradition and on highly developed historicism. In this respect it mentioned the discussion on whether Russia belonged to Europe – or was outside of it ('Evropa', in *Masarykův slovník naučný, II*, 1926). This Encyclopaedia claimed to represent the official (political) concepts of the newly formed Czechoslovakia, but it did not necessarily express the opinions of scholars.

The development of the meaning of Europe roughly corresponds to the development of the priorities in Czech national discourse: from the successful struggle for civil rights through the successful struggle for national emancipation to the efforts at Europeanization of cultural life in the newly founded nation state. Naturally, this is only a hypothetical generalization and it will be the aim of following reflections to assess if the shift of emphases observed in the three Encyclopaedias really corresponded to the general trend of Czech discourse on Europe.

Besides the analysis of the change in time, it is preferable to break up the analysis according to the three basic meanings of 'Europeanness':

- Europe as a normative context and moral engagement
- Europe as a value to be protected
- being proud of belonging to Europe.

Nevertheless, we cannot neglect the fact that there were also alternatives to European identity, which are presented below.

*The Czech Discourse on Europe, 1848–1948*

*Europe as a Normative Context and Moral Engagement*

The conservative Czech historian, W.W. Tomek, included in his memoirs an ironically written episode from the 1848 Revolution in Prague. In an almost empty street, a young man started to built a barricade. Some anxious women tried to persuade him to stop doing it, but he answered with a high voice: 'Let me to do it, all Europe is watching us' (Tomek 1904: 286–7). Tomek did not know that these words could be heard rather often in Vienna and other cities at that time. Nevertheless, he preserved important evidence that among the Czech population also, some people spontaneously regarded Europe – the revolutionary Europe, not the feudal one – as a normative model. This included both political identification with Europe and the concept of European identity as a moral imperative of their behaviour.

There is no spontaneity without previous communication. The founder of the modern Czech political programme, journalist Karel Havlíček-Borovský, in his articles in 1848–49 presented Europe as a protagonist of progress on the way 'from absolutism towards liberty'. (Havlíček-Borovský 1956: 409). Further, both Czechs and other Slavic nations had to join this progressive path. František Palacký, the then most prominent historian and unofficial leader of the Czech national movement, expressed a similar view in the manifesto of the Slavic Congress, which opened in Prague in June 1848. According to this proclamation, Slavic nations sought to participate in the 'new history of Europe' because they were definitely not enemies of freedom (Palacký 1977: 183–4).

Dreaming about establishing a Czech democratic republic, the radical democrat Emanuel Arnold related his dream to Europe: this republic would adopt 'European ideas' and spread its light through Europe (Arnold 1848: 162). Some years before 1848, a small group of Czech democrats had already considered the necessity to 'concentrate themselves around the European family as their centre of action', following the example of the Poles (Záček 1948: 202).

With some exaggeration, we can say that Europe entered Bohemia for the first time through the revolutionary process and the struggle for constitutional rights. Therefore, it is understandable that very soon some patriots tried to take credit for the fact that in earlier times, Czechs were pioneers of the European way towards freedom: the Czech nation was the first one in Europe which started (in the Hussite movement) the struggle for freedom against absolutism. It was a struggle not only for their own freedom, but also for the liberation of 'all nations' (Sojka 1953: 6).

Europe was a normative context for the Czechs not only as the model of civic virtues, but also as the focal point of education. According to F.L. Rieger, who later became the national leader after Palacký, all European nations were moving toward higher education and civilization – some nations started earlier, while others like the Slavs would have to follow them as soon as possible: 'The time for Slavic enlightenment is coming'. In the past, Czechs had occupied an important position among educated nations, and this would have to be the case again (Rieger 1923: 89, 94).

In the 1840s, some intellectuals expected relevant advantages for the speed of Czech cultural improvement due to Bohemia's position in the middle of Europe, 'at the crossroad of almost all cultures of our continent'. This advantage of geographical position is related to values: the position in the middle of Europe, in its 'heart', could be interpreted as a position in the centre of European virtues (Nebeský 1953: 35).

This was nevertheless not a Czech exception: several decades earlier similar ideas were developed by early German patriots for their own nation (Jahn 1817, 11). The Czech specificity could consist – so Palacký asserted – of transmitting and unifying different cultural elements, such as Germanic, Roman and Slavic ones. The myth of the middle as a positive value survived until the twentieth century and inspired the later ideology of 'Central Europe' developed by Czech dissidents in the 1980s. In this concept, belonging to Central Europe is – as a specific form of being European – a matter of national pride (see below).

To understand this opinion, we have to notice that besides being aware of the struggle for freedom as a normative context of Europe, Czech politicians felt inspired also by another trend which they voluntarily accepted as a 'European norm': the process of nation-formation. Czech national leaders could declare their movement as a natural component of the generally accepted 'principle of nationality'. 'A strong feeling of national revival is moving all Europe', wrote Nebeský in the 1860s (Nebeský 1953 [1845]: 15). As a nation, Czechs became compatible with all other Europeans. 'Europe knows us and appreciates our honest efforts in the name of the true humanity', declared Rieger in 1873, and three years later he stressed that Czechs knew that they had played an important role for Europe and that they still signified something for it (Rieger 1923: 185, 199).

The idea of belonging to the general European national movement was further developed by T.G. Masaryk in the 1890s. He regarded the Czech national movement as a natural part of that movement which in Europe started with the French revolution. In this perspective, national movement and the struggle for freedom formed one unit: 'Since the end of the

*The Czech Discourse on Europe, 1848–1948*

eighteenth century, a progressive and liberal minded movement emerged both in Bohemia and in all Europe' (Masaryk 1990 [1894]: 17). Symptomatically, in this book Masaryk regarded Czech nation-building as strongly influenced by the moral and cultural traditions of the Reformation which had given a new sense to European society and its history. It was not by chance that Masaryk developed this concept at the same time as the Otto-Encyclopaedia regarded nation-formation as one of the European specificities.

This operation included a symptomatic syllogism: if we understand the normative European values as both civic and national ones, then all our political activities (including the national ones) that follow this path can be regarded as being in favour of Europe. To accept European values obliged or legitimated the Czechs to continue and to strengthen their national movement.

This syllogism was implicitly integrated by the Czech national movement at least at the beginning of the twentieth century, if not earlier. It was then explicitly used as a political argument in the Czech anti-Habsburg struggle during the First World War. Masaryk presented this struggle as being in the name of old European values. 'The real federation of nations will only appear, if all nations will be free and join each other. This is the trend of European development.' Supporting this goal were the entente powers fighting the war. Only if Europe accepted the democratic ideas of the entente powers would the federation of nations become easier (Masaryk 1994 [1918]: 102–3).

Under conditions of war, Masaryk formulated his concept of the post-war European values in his pamphlet *New Europe* (1994 [1918]) which was addressed above all to European politicians. The central position was democracy: europeanization meant democratization. Nevertheless, the basic and inevitable condition for this democratization was moral re-education of nations according to the principles of rationality, humanity and Christian spirituality. Symptomatically Masaryk ended his pamphlet with a rather pathetic sentence: 'Jesus, not Caesar – this is the slogan of the democratic Europe' (Masaryk 1994 [1918]: 192).

Even though the existence of the Czech nation after the achievement of independence was still not self-evident, the Czech understanding of European specificity moved from the picture of the continent of nations toward the concept of a Europe whose nations were joined by a common cultural atmosphere and heritage. Principles of rationality and spirituality seemed to be more important, because they were less self-evident than principles of national self-determination or those of liberalism. To be European within this concept meant to share a common culture.

This concept of Europe was explicitly analysed by František Krejčí, a philosophy professor in Prague. His book was a singular attempt to analyse systematically the relationship between the Czech and European identities (Krejčí 1931). Krejčí defined Europe as a continent with the highest quality of arts and with the most extensive spread of arts and other cultural artefacts among the population.

This Europe gradually became a cultural community, a community of spirit, which was formed from ancient times through the Christian Middle Ages to the Early Modern time, where the borders of cultural community corresponded to the geographical unit 'Europe' – i.e., they included also Russia. Hence, deduced Krejčí, the criterion of being European: it was the level of participation of a given community (nation) in the consumption of European cultural production, above all literature and music, measured through the quantity of translations, concerts, reviews. In this sense, the point of departure of Czech Europeanness was represented by two important Czech poets in the last third of the nineteenth century. One of them, Jaroslav Vrchlický, systematically translated the most important works of various European literatures into the Czech language; the other, Julius Zeyer, used in his poems and novels motifs from the history of almost all European cultures from Ireland to Russia (Krejčí 1931: 197).

It was, however, not only consumption of European culture but also the active contribution to the improvement of this culture that, according to Krejčí, marked the level of being European. In the case of the Czech nation, he regarded their achievements in the field of music as the most important contribution to European culture. Nevertheless, he argued, Czech Europeanness reached its height in the work of Masaryk, who was able to demonstrate the transition from cultural to political Europeanness. Krejčí, who regarded the cultural unity of Europe as the main precondition for political unity, regarded Masaryk as a pioneer of this trend (Krejčí 1931: 203).

Some years later, F.X. Šalda, who became one of the most influential intellectuals of his time, gave a less optimistic evaluation of the relation between Czechs and Europe. To him, Europe was defined by a common culture, above all by the cultural heritage of Western universalist Christianity. He regarded this culture as a normative context also for Czech cultural development. It was the moral imperative for Czech national culture to contribute to the European one. Hence his critical call for applying the highest artistic criteria in the national context: to become really European, Czech culture had to relinquish its 'petty-bourgeois' mentality and its 'fainthearted taste' in favour of heroism and originality of progressive ideas. Nationalism was – as an outdated heritage from the past – not compatible with this concept of European culture (Šalda 1934–1935: 226).

## Europe as a Value, to be Protected

The argument in favour of European defence against external danger is a topic traditional to almost all reflections on Europe. It is also present in the Czech discourse, nevertheless not without some paradoxical features. In April 1848, the German Vorparlament, preparing for German unification, invited Palacký, as the representative of Czechs, to participate in the elections for the Parliament in Frankfurt. Palacký refused this invitation in a famous letter where he not only stressed the difference between the German and Czech nations, but also warned against destroying the Habsburg monarchy by realizing the Great-Germany concept of unification. He described the Habsburg monarchy as the 'most Eastern' European great power, saying it had 'by the call of nature and of history, the mission to be a protector and guard of Europe against all kinds of Asian elements'. These elements, under given conditions, were represented by both the Ottoman and the Russian Empires. Russia was dangerous not because it was Slavic but because it was an absolutist system suppressing all liberties. He continued: 'If the state of Austria would not exist, we would have in the interest of Europe' to try to construct it (Palacký 1977: 161). Implicitly, this warning included a denunciation of the Great-Germany concept as one that indirectly endangered Europe, because it opened the door to Eastern invasion.

It would be an erroneous simplification to say that Palacký's warning was confirmed in 1849, when Russian troops invaded Hungary and suppressed the national revolution there: this intervention was invited from Vienna just to protect Austrian absolutism. Another 'European' observation of Palacký's falls into an ironical context: shortly before the Russian intervention, Palacký declared the internal stability of Austria to be of importance for all Europe (Palacký 1977: 222).

The Czech vision of the European enemy switched very radically twenty years later, when Czech politicians, deeply disappointed by Austro-Hungarian dualism which totally neglected Czech claims, made a demonstrative journey to Russia in 1867. It was Rieger, above all, who included the topic of European defence in his speeches. He stressed the positive role of the Russians who had saved Europe from Mongols and Turks and made a parallel between the two protectors of Europe, i.e. Russians standing against the danger from the East, and Czechs doing likewise for 'the civilization of all Europe' in their struggle against the Germans. Naturally, this concept was more or less a rhetorical exercise (Rieger 1923: 81).

Nevertheless, we cannot say that it left no stains. The positive appreciation of the role of Russians as protectors of Europe against the danger from the East can be found in the Otto-Encyclopaedia. Russians, it notes, took over from the Roman Empire the role of defending Europe against barbarians, the Ural-Altaic tribes and Mongolians. On the other side, the encyclopaedia stressed expansion as the historical 'mission' of Europe, with the mission fulfilled above all by two powers: Great Britain in the West and Russia in the East (*Ottův slovník naučný VIII* 1997 [1894]: 905).

The efforts to stress Czech participation in the defence of Europe also included some historical arguments. Perhaps the most popular of these was the peace project elaborated by the Czech king, George of Podiebrad, who in 1464 (ten years after the fall of Constantinople) sent a delegation to the French king, proposing a coalition of Christian rulers against the common enemy – the invading Ottomans. Naturally, this project enjoyed no success and was soon forgotten, but under conditions of the nineteenth-century discourse of Europe, this political initiative could be interpreted as an expression of a long-standing Czech devotion to the defence of European interests and values. Significantly, this interpretation was restored to life by the reformist communist ideologists in the 1960s.

At the threshold of the First World War, Masaryk accepted the entente powers' axiom that it was a war protecting European democracy. He modified this in his book 'New Europe' to the concrete sense that it was a struggle against anti-democratic Pan-Germanism and against the degenerated dynastic principle of Habsburg rule. He claimed that if the liberation of citizens and nations belonged to the aims of this war, then it could not be fulfilled without the liberation of Czechs and the constitution of their nation state. (Masaryk 1994: 160). In other words, if Europe was defined by the plurality of fully-fledged democratic nations, then the construction of Czechoslovakia would help to protect 'European principles' of democracy against alien, anti-democratic (and hence anti-European) Pan-Germanism.

The success of the Bolshevik revolution in Russia opened a new level of European defence-discourse. In Western Europe of that time, the idea of defending democracy and capitalism coincided strongly with the idea of defending European values. This was also partially the case in Czechoslovakia. Nevertheless, it seems to me that the 'main-stream' of Czechoslovak politics and culture did not exclude Russia from the European context.

*The Czech Discourse on Europe, 1848–1948*

Relevant authors, such as Beneš and Peroutka, often stressed that Russia remained a part of the European continent, peculiar above all through its backwardness in comparison with other parts of Europe and because it had never experienced capitalism and civil society (Krejčí 1931:170–1). On the other hand, Krejčí, who strongly defended the Europeanness of pre-Revolutionary Russia, put this adherence into question. The reason for him was that Soviet Russia refused to participate in European culture – and cultural community was to Krejčí the basic criterion of being European. (Bugge in Hahnová 1997a, 104).

## Belonging to Europe as a Matter of National Pride

It would be one-sided to conclude that the Czech national movement tried to strengthen its self-consciousness only by emphasizing its European merits. For the decisive part of Czech intellectuals, journalists and politicians, the European horizon of Czech national existence was a commonplace, which did not need to be argued using European 'merits'. Describing his experiences in Russia, Havlíček compared – as early as the 1840s – life in Russian towns with life 'in other European cities', such as London, Paris or Vienna. At the very same time, he described his hierarchy of identities: 'I am Czech, in addition also Slav, European, human being' (Havlíček 1924: 67, 200). Symptomatically, a half-century later, Masaryk explicitly appreciated and shared this statement (Masaryk 1990 [1894]: 344–5).

During the 1848 Czech Revolution, Europe was mentioned not only as a classificatory scheme, as mentioned above, but also as an expression of a proud self-consciousness: Czechs were participating in a European revolution through their own will and decision. In a speech to his comrades, the student leader J.V. Frič said in June 1848: 'Europe is waiting for you – you have to become the starting point of the European revolution!' (Frič 1889: 121). According to the opinion of a young lecturer in modern history, Anton Heinrich Springer, it was the mission of Slavs (implicitly of Czechs) to create a social state (Pfaff 1997: 189, 191–2). Also during the following decades, Europe was a self-evident part of Czech politics and cultural consciousness. In this sense, Czech politicians argued with Vienna, Czech culture tried to find a way out from provincialism. At the turn of the century, the young Šalda included Czech literature within the European context. With the same self-evidence, the European context included, according to him, both Western Europe and Russia: he had no difficulty in analysing the work of Duhamel and Čechov in one and the same review. The *Manifesto* of the 'Czech Moderne' from 1894, in which Šalda also participated, self-consciously criticized the 'European bourgeoisie' for having forgotten the achievements of revolutions and for neglecting the people. The *Manifesto* explicitly refused nationalist limitations and professed its allegiance to European Modernism (Šalda 1950: 361–2).

Thirty years later, in his essay on 'Czechs and Europe', Šalda regarded the position in the middle of Europe as an extraordinary favourable precondition for a 'European engagement' of Czech culture: 'I believe in the mission in the middle of Europe' (Šalda 1934–5: 228). In this connection, Šalda was only one of many authors who included their discourse on Europe in the discourse on Central Europe. The Czech consciousness of belonging to Central Europe could be interpreted as a distinct national value.

This somewhat spontaneous understanding of becoming European through being Central European reached a new level in the 1980s. Milan Kundera and other authors afforded good ideological grounds for it: their concept of Central Europe was totally compatible with modern Europeanness. Three out of four elementary central-European features were also fully related to Europe as a whole: first, the shared elitarian culture second, the shared system of values; and third, the diversity of cultures which enriched each other. Only the fourth characteristic was, according to Kundera, a specifically central-European one: the repeated experience of having been defeated and held captive. In connection to this fourth peculiarity some authors stressed that under conditions of oppression, intellectuals such as scientists, writers and scholars were able to keep their influence: also this phenomenon was regarded as exclusively European. Nevertheless, almost all this discussion proceeded outside of the Czech territory and never became a part of the internal Czech national discourse: it was and continued to be an international discourse among cosmopolitan intellectuals, such as Kundera, Konrad, Milosz and Havel. As a consequence of it, the concept of Central Europe in the Czech discourse of Europe played a less relevant role than was the case in Western Europe (Kundera 1984; Havel 1994; Lord 1999).

*Alternative European and Anti-European Visions*

The Czech discourse on Europe also included another – negative version – represented above all by the myth of Czech historical exceptionality and by the Slavic myth. In the first case the 'collective memory', the historical consciousness, played a decisive role, but in the second case only a supplementary one. The Hussite myth followed from the fact that during the Hussite revolution 1419–34 Czech adherents of the reformer Jan Hus successfully defeated several crusades from Germany and other European countries. This fact could be instrumentalized in the course of the national movement as a tool of anti-German and anti-Catholic agitation. Nevertheless, it could scarcely be used as a tool of European identity. On the contrary: the national pride of the 'anti-European' resistance could be fed.

'You never trembled by fear face to face to Europe', proclaimed the poet Rudolf Mayer of his fatherland in the 1860s. 'All Europe was in fear of the Czech material power', which was fighting for its truth, wrote at the same time the biographer of Czech patriots, Sojka (Macura 1997: 10). The novel *Against Everybody* (*All*), written by A. Jirásek, glorified the Hussite wars against feudal Europe and became something of a bestseller. On the place of the first glorious Hussite victory, on the hill Vítkov (nowadays in a suburb of Prague) a commemorial tablet was placed in 1910 with an inscription saying: 'At that time, there existed two parties: Europe and we. And Europe was bloodless and pale' (Macura 1997:10). Using these examples, V. Macura constructed a 'dichotomy' of pro- and anti-European feelings in Czech public opinion. This construction seems, nevertheless, not to be very convincing. In this relation, the value of Czechs was based on their (positively connotated) difference from the (feudal) European context. At the same time, these texts admit their fascination with the rich, well-equipped Europe. The victories of the poor Czechs gained greater importance, because they were achieved against such a strong enemy.

While the Hussite struggle against 'all' was situated in the fifteenth century and could be interpreted as a path-breaking attempt to open the way toward freedom (i.e., one compatible with the general trend to European modernization), another anti-European criticism was a genuine nineteenth-century phenomenon. This attitude toward Europe emanated from the conviction that Czech identity was above all compatible with Slavic, not European, identity. Even though this was originally a rather marginal phenomenon, it has to be represented by one example in this context. The poet Svatopluk Čech, very popular in his time, published a long poem in 1878 telling a story about a proud vessel called 'Europe'. As a result of a revolt, outlaws from its steerage took over rule of the ship, but then quarrelled with each other and were unable to find a consensus. Eventually, the ship with a red flag on the mast (an allegory of the Commune of Paris) capsized and sank. Six years later, Čech published another allegory – a poem 'Slavia', presenting a ship sailing for a happy future, as a 'morning star of new worlds', even though the crew was poor and rejected by the rich. The poverty, nevertheless, was accompanied by spiritual virtues that are higher than traditional (i.e. Western) virtues (Čech 1884, 1886). This alternative vision was naturally inspired by Russian Slavophilism, but had its specific anti-German background. The Slavic alternative was used in the context of a defence against the concept of Germanic and Roman Europe that was propagated by German nationalists in order to exclude Slavs from Europe. This concept seemed to offer to the Czechs two alternatives: either to remain European becoming Germans, or to remain Slavic Czechs and exclude themselves from Europe.

Russian discourse played the central role in this discussion about the size of Europe. It was in this context that Masaryk decided to write an ambitious interdisciplinary monograph on 'Russia and Europe' (Masaryk 1995–96 [1913]). Masaryk did not exclude Russia from Europe but regarded it as a specific part of it: 'Europe is not essentially foreign to Russia, but Russia still did not master it totally'. Russia represents in his view 'the childhood of Europe': Russia is what Europe was (ibid.: 15). For this reason, the relationship between Russia and Europe is a matter of comparison of two parts of Europe standing on different levels of development. Russia was behind Europe, behind the European Enlightenment and constitutionalism, but its educated elites do not regard this time-lag (belatedness) as relevant, since they were convinced they were spiritually superior to Europe. Russia was, according to Masaryk, decadent and theocratic. On the other side, Europe was weakened through its internal struggles for democracy and social justice, while Russia, should it cure its sickness, could become the most powerful state in Europe (ibid.: 370).

A new variant of anti-European alternatives emerged in inter-war Czechoslovakia. Some radical left intellectuals saw an alternative in the new social system of the young Soviet Union. Former anarchist and later communist Stanislav Kostka Neumann, a poet, wrote: 'Europe, you are not more, what you were' – you are not any more the spiritual Europe but Europe of murdering weapons (Hahnová 1997a: 29). The new world, the new culture was born in the East.

This anti-Europeanism received political support after 1948, but even from 1945 young Czech writers attacked Europe as 'rotten', as a satellite of American imperialism, as a traitor of its own ideals, as a system that tolerated fascism in Spain and Portugal, etc. Later on, Europe changed in the eyes of some communist poets into 'casemates', or 'pyramids of nuclear shelters', inhabited by 'fossils of men and wrecks of women'.

*The Czech Discourse on Europe, 1848–1948*

The late Zdenek Nejedlý (1950: 69) gave a theoretical background: the true Europe moved to the territory of the USSR. Even though the rhetoric and the vocabulary changed, the basic concept remained: the 'socialist countries' were a part of Europe, they accepted its best traditions and offered to all Europe a progressive alternative. There were two important features which both parts of Europe had in common: common history and shared cultural tradition.

## Conclusions

The concept of Europe never played a dominating, decisive role in Czech national discourse and not even in Czech political vocabulary. It never became a mobilizing slogan of politics, despite the fact that from the end of the nineteenth century the mostly spontaneously accepted European horizon strongly influenced the concept of Czech culture. The discourse on Europe cannot be neglected, above all due to the introduction of different connotations and interpretations into Czech national consciousness. These connotations survived, sometimes non-verbalized and 'unconsciously', until the present time.

The conceptualization of Europe in Czech discourse had three successive levels which were mutually compatible. These three levels roughly corresponded to the development of the Czech national movement and Czech society. Initially, it was above all a continent, which introduced liberal and democratic changes in its revolutionary way toward civil society. Later on, at the second level, Europe was understood also as a community of free nations and as a protector of unfree nations. In the third level, which grew to dominance during the inter-war period, the concept of Europe was based on the community of high culture.

The Czech understanding of Europe until the Second World War was complicated by its position in the middle – between East and West Europe. This position was sometimes interpreted also as a position between Germans and Slavs (or Russians) and contributed to a dichotomy in the understanding of Europe. This East-West dichotomy played a different role according to the changing political circumstances in the Habsburg monarchy and in Central Europe.

Under conditions of German domination, the Slavic component was rather strongly represented, and after the defeat of Germany, under conditions of Russian-Soviet domination, the Western component became dominant and the Slavic component was almost totally forgotten. Despite all of these contextual changes, the concept of Europe was verbalized as a positive value. We do not have enough data, however, to allow us to generalize our observations. It seems still not to be a given fact that the integration of Europe influenced not only journalists but also the broad Czech public as a mobilizing, constitutive factor for civic engagement.

## References

Arnold, E. (1848), *Děje husitů* [History of the Hussites], Prague, reprinted in: '*Čeští revoluční demokraté*', Prague.

Frič, J.V. (1889), *Pameti IV.*, Prague.

Hahnová, E. (ed.) (1997a), *Evropa očima Čechů* [Europe through Czech eyes], Prague.

—— (1997b), 'Češi a imaginární hranice mezi západem a východem Evropy' [The Czechs and the imaginary border between the West and East of Europe] in E. Hahnová (ed.), *Evropa očima Čechů* [Europe through Czech eyes], Prague.

Havel, V. (1994), *Toward a Civil Society: Selected speeches and writings 1990–1994*, Prague.

Havlíček-Borovský, K. (1924), Vybrané spisy [Selected Works] II, Prague.

—— (1956), *Politik a novinář* [The politician and journalist], Prague.

Jahn, F.L. (1817), *Das deutsche Volkstum*, Leipzig.

Krejčí, F.V. (1931), 'Češství a Evropanství'. 'Úvahy o naší kulturní orientaci' [The title is difficult to translate: 'Czech national feeling and European identity'], Prague.

Kundera, M. (1984), 'The tragedy of Central Europe', in *New York Review of Books*.

Lord, C. (ed.) (1999), *Central Europe: Core or Periphery?*, Copenhagen.

Macura, V. (1997), 'Semiotika Evropy', in: Hahnová (ed.), *Evropa očima Čechů*, Prague.

Masaryk, T.G. (1990 [1894]), *Česká otázka: Naše nynější krize* [The Czech question: Our contemporary crisis], Prague.

—— (1994 [1918]) *Nová Evropa* [New Europe], Prague.

—— (1995–96 [1913]), *Rusko a Evropa* I-III, Prague.

*Masarykův slovník naučný, II* (1926), Prague.

Nebeský, V.B. (1953 [1845]), 'O potřebě oslavit dějiny národa [On the need of the glorification of Czech history], in Ibid., *O literature* [On literature], Prague.

Nejedlý, Z. (1950), 'O Evrope', in *Var 3*, Prague.

*Ottův slovník naučný, VIII* (1997 [1894]), Prague.

*The Czech Discourse on Europe, 1848–1948*

Palacký, F. (1977), *Úvahy a projevy* [Reflections and speeches], Prague.

Pfaff, I (1997), 'Češi mezi západem a východem Evropy v 19.století [The Czechs between the West and the East of Europe], in E. Hahnová (ed.), Evropa očima Čechů, Prague.

Rieger, F.L. (1923), *Řeči dra Františka Ladislava Riegra* [F.L. Rieger's speeches], I, 1868–78, Prague.

*Riegrův slovník naučný* (1862), *II*, Prague.

Šalda, F.X. (1934–1935), Češství a Evropa [The Czechness and Europe], in: *Šaldův Zápisník*, Prague.

___ (1950), *Kritické projevy* [Critical writings] 2, Prague.

Sojka, J.E. (1953 [1862]), Naši mužové [Our men], Prague.

Svatopluk Č. (1884), týž, 'Slavie', Prague.

―― (1886), *Evropa*, Prague.

Tomek, W.W. (1904), *Paměti z mého života* [Memory of my life], Prague.

Žáček, V. (1948), *Češi a Poláci v revoluci 1848, I* [Czechs and Poles in the Revolution of 1848], Prague.

# XVI

## DIE ROLLE DES ZENTRALEUROPÄISCHEN HANDELS IM AUSGLEICH DER HANDELSBILANZ ZWISCHEN OST- UND WESTEUROPA 1550—1650

### I.

Zu den schwierigsten Aufgaben der Wirtschaftsgeschichte gehört die Erforschung der Handelsbilanz. Es ist kein Zufall, daß viele Handbücher vor dieser Aufgabe zurückschrecken[1]. Dabei stoßen wir hier auf einen Fragenkomplex, der nicht nur das Ausmaß jeder Handelsbeziehung festlegt, sondern auch ihre soziale und wirtschaftliche Bedeutung beleuchtet. — Wenn wir den mitteleuropäischen Handel in seinen gesamteuropäischen Zusammenhängen sehen wollen — und dies ist für die frühe Neuzeit bereits unerläßlich —, dann bieten uns die Verbindungen zwischen ihm und dem Ost-West-Handel, repräsentiert durch seine wichtigste, die baltische Richtung, einen willkommenen Ausgangspunkt. Diese Beziehung verdichtet sich besonders aufschlußreich in dem Problem der Handelsbilanz. Im Hinblick auf den gegenwärtigen Stand der Forschung ist es mir nicht möglich, endgültige Lösungen vorzulegen, vielmehr muß ein Zwischenbericht genügen, eine Konfrontierung mit unseren bisherigen Kenntnissen, der Versuch einer allgemeinen, übergreifenden Fragestellung für die künftige, heute so sehr spezialisierte Forschung.

Der große Strukturwandel, der während des 16. Jahrhunderts die Ostsee unter den Handelsverbindungen zwischen Ost- und Westeuropa an die erste Stelle schob, hat auch die binnenländischen Handelswege nicht unberührt gelassen. In diesem Zusammenhang hat sich die steigende Bedeutung der Flußwege als Bindeglieder zu den Seehäfen eines regen Interesses der Forscher erfreut. Daneben

---

[1] Vgl. die dem internationalen Handel gewidmeten Kapitel in The Cambridge Economic History of Europe IV., Cambridge 1967. Dagegen bei W. Kula, Problemy i metody historii gospodarczej (Probleme und Methoden der Wirtschaftsgeschichte), Warszawa 1963, S. 206 ff.

2

bestand natürlich auch weiterhin der Warentransport in westöstlicher und ostwestlicher Richtung auf dem Landwege fort, d. h. die Routen durch Zentraleuropa, die jedoch weniger Beachtung fanden. Wieweit berührten sich beide Handelssysteme und wieweit beeinflußten sie sich gegenseitig? Die Frage nach ihrer Wechselwirkung ist von allgemeiner Bedeutung und vor allem mit jener der Handelsbilanz eng verknüpft.

Die Gesamtbilanz des Ostseehandels wird allgemein als aktiv für den Osten bezeichnet; dies war schon den Zeitgenossen und ist ebenso der modernen Geschichtsforschung bekannt[2]. So hat A. E. Christensen den Versuch unternommen, die Handelsbilanz an der Ostsee quantitativ zu erfassen. Er hat den Warenumsatz im Öresund berechnet: 70 % des Wertes fallen auf den westwärts gehenden, 30 % des Wertes dem ostwärts gehenden Warenstrom zu. Später zweifelte er jedoch selbst an der Zuverlässigkeit dieser Zahlen und begnügte sich mit einer allgemeinen Grundcharakteristik[3], die mit den Schätzungen der niederländischen, englischen oder polnischen Handelsbilanz, die wir kennen, übereinstimmt[4]. Ähnliche Resultate zeigen die Schätzungen der russischen Handelsbilanz mit dem Westen[5]. Auch die genaueren Angaben, die wir für einzelne

---

[2]) Zu den zeitgenössischen Vorstellungen vgl. A. ATTMAN, Den ryska marknaden i 1500-talets baltiska politik (Der russische Markt in der baltischen Politik des 16. Jahrhunderts), Uppsala 1944, S. 74 ff.; S. I. ARCHANGELSKIJ, Anglo-gollandskaja torgovlja s Moskvoj v XVII. v. (Der englisch-holländische Handel mit Moskva im 17. Jahrhundert), Istoričeskij sbornik 5., Moskva—Leningrad 1936, S. 7.

[3]) A. E. CHRISTENSEN, Sundzollregister und Ostseehandel. Resultate und Probleme, Conventus primus historicorum Balticorum Rigae 1937, Riga 1938, S. 398 f.; DERSELBE, Dutch Trade on the Baltic about 1600. Studies in the Sound Register and Dutch Shipping Records, Copenhagen, The Hague 1941, S. 428.

[4]) A. E. CHRISTENSEN, Dutch Trade a.a.O., S. 231 u. 390 ff.; C. H. WILSON, Treasure and the Trade Balancies, The Economic History Review, Ser. II. 2., 1949, S. 152 ff.; R. W. K. HINTON, The Eastland Trade and the Common Weal in the 17th Century, London 1959, S. 22 ff. u. 48 f.; A. ATTMAN, Den ryska marknaden a.a.O., S. 112; R. RYBARSKI, Handel i polityka handlowa Polski w XVI stuleciu (Der Handel und die Handelspolitik Polens im 16. Jahrhundert) I., Poznań 1928, S. 247 ff.; E. LIPIŃSKI, Studia nad historią polskiej myśli ekonomicznej (Studien zur Geschichte der polnischen nationalökonomischen Theorie), Warszawa 1956, S. 212; S. HOSZOWSKI, The Polish Baltic Trade in the 15—18th Centuries. Poland at the XIth Internat. Congress of Hist. Sciences, Warszawa 1960, S. 124.

[5]) M. MAŁOWIST, Poland, Russia and Western Trade in the 15th and 16th Centuries, Past and Present 1958, S. 34; für die spätere Zeit belegt bei L. LEHRFREUND, Die Entwicklung der deutsch-russischen Handelsbeziehungen, Leipzig 1921,

Ostseehäfen besitzen, zeigen dieselbe für den Osten aktive Handelsbilanz. Das Übergewicht des Exports aus dem Osten schwankt dem-
nach zwischen 25 % und 40 % des Gesamtwertes[6]. Daneben können
wir uns auf eine Reihe von monographischen Studien berufen, die
den einzelnen Handelszentren gewidmet sind[7]. Aber auch hier ist
das letzte Wort noch nicht gesprochen.

Einige Forscher haben jedoch Einwände gegen die Behauptung,
die Bilanz des Ost-West-Handels sei für den Osten eindeutig aktiv,
vorgebracht. Sie waren es, die auf den erwähnten Zusammenhang
zwischen dem Ostseehandel und dem Warentransport auf dem
Landwege aufmerksam gemacht haben[8]. Dieser Zusammenhang,
trifft er zu, würde nicht nur Warenmenge, Nachfrage und
Angebot der Güterarten, sondern auch das Gesamtbild der Handelsbilanz mitbestimmen. Dabei spielt natürlich nicht nur der direkte Fernhandel zwischen Ost- und Westeuropa, sondern auch der
Warenaustausch innerhalb Mittel- und Ostmitteleuropas eine Rolle.
Es ist bezeichnend für die Umwege unserer historischen Erkenntnis,

---

S. 29 ff.; A. S. MELNIKOVA, Sistěmatizacija monet Michaila Fedroviča (Die Münz-
systematisierung unter Michail Fedrovič), Archeografičeskij ježegodnik 1958, S. 68,
79 u. 83); G. MICKWITZ, Die Hansakaufleute in Wiborg 1558—1559, Historiallinen arkisto 45., S. 101 f.; zum Geld- und Edelmetallimport nach Rußland vgl.
V. A. KORDT, Očerk snošenij Moskovskogo gosudarstva s Respublikoju Sojedině̌n-
nych Niderlandov po 1631 g. (Abriß der Beziehungen zwischen dem Moskauer
Staate und der Republik der Vereinigten Niederlande bis zum Jahre 1631). Sbornik
Imperatorskogo Istoričeskogo Obščestva 116., St. Petersburg 1902, S. LXXI f. u.
CCLXXXII.

[6]) A. ATTMAN, Den ryska marknaden a.a.O., S. 105.

[7]) Für die Handelsbilanz in Riga vgl. neben A. ATTMAN, Den ryska marknaden a.a.O., S. 104 u. 107 auch C. JENSCH, Der Handel Rigas im 17. Jahrhundert, Mitteilungen aus der livländischen Geschichte 14., Riga 1930, S. 87 f.; E.
DUNSDORFS, Der Außenhandel Rigas im 17. Jahrhundert, Conventus primus histo-
ricorum Balticorum, Rigae 1937, Riga 1938, S. 464. Für die preußischen Häfen
H. RACHEL, Die Handels-, Zoll- und Akzisepolitik Brandenburg-Preußens bis
1713, Acta Borussica, Berlin 1911, S. 369. Für Viborg vgl. G. MICKWITZ, Die
Hansakaufleute a.a.O., S. 110 ff. und A. ATTMAN, Den ryska marknaden a.a.O.,
S. 103. Für Gdańsk (Danzig) vgl. die Studie von M. Bogucka in dem vorliegenden
Bande.

[8]) A. E. CHRISTENSEN, Sundzollregister a.a.O., S. 329 f.; DERSELBE, Der han-
delsgeschichtliche Wert der Sundzollregister, Hansische Geschichtsblätter 1934, S.
28 ff.; E. F. HECKSCHER, Öresundsräkenskaperna och deras behandling (Sundzollregister und ihre Behandlung), Historik tidskrift 1942, S. 174 f.; P. JEANNIN,
L'économie française au milieu du 16e siècle et le marché russe, Annales ESC IX.,
1954, S. 23 ff.

4

daß die ersten Vermutungen von der Bedeutung Zentraleuropas
für den Ausgleich der Handelsbilanz im Ost-West-Handel nicht von
mitteleuropäischen, sondern von schwedischen Historikern geäußert
wurden. Es ist zu bedauern, daß diese Hinweise, die bereits vor
mehr als 20 Jahren gegeben worden sind, von den mitteleuropäischen Forschern ungenutzt, ja oft sogar unbemerkt blieben.

A. Attman hat 1944 überzeugend nachgewiesen, daß der Gesamtwert der aus den baltischen Häfen ausgeführten Waren ungefähr das Doppelte des Gesamtwerts der Einfuhr ausmachte[9]). Er
ließ aber ein anderes Problem offen, das für den mitteleuropäischen
Handel von zentraler Bedeutung ist. Als er die Handelsbilanz für
Narva am Anfang des 17. Jahrhunderts berechnete, mußte er feststellen, daß die aus dem Westen gebrachten Geldsummen und Edelmetalle kaum zur Deckung der Hälfte der für den Westen passiven
Bilanz ausreichen konnten[10]. Wie wurde der Rest des Exportwertes
bezahlt? Attman begnügte sich mit der wenig begründeten Vermutung, daß die Differenz durch Geldimport in andere Ostseehäfen
ausgeglichen wurde. Diese These hat jedoch berechtigte Kritik her-
vorgerufen. Ein anderer schwedischer Historiker, S. A. Nilsson, hat
der Teilerkenntnis Attmans allgemeinere Bedeutung zugemessen
und darauf aufbauend eine feinere Rekonstruktion des Ost-West-
Handels und der daraus resultierenden Handelsbilanz zu geben
versucht. Er kam zu der Ansicht, daß der fragliche Bilanzüberschuß
des osteuropäischen Handels nur teilweise durch Münzgeld und
münzbare Edelmetalle aus Westeuropa ausgeglichen wurde. Den
Rest hätten Wechsel gedeckt, die im Westen eingelöst worden seien.

---

[9]) S. A. Nilsson, Den ryska marknaden i 1500-talets baltiska politik, Scandia
XVI., 1944, S. 181 äußert sich kritisch dazu, daß Attman seine Resultate aus dem
Ostbaltikum auf Rußland überträgt und daß er die Handelsbilanz auf Grund der
Preise im Durchfuhrhafen anstatt der Preise am Marktort berechnet. Der Bilanz-
unterschied war jedoch so hoch, daß ihn eine eventuelle Umrechnung auf Grund
der Preise in Westrußland (wenn wir solche in ausreichenden Reihen hätten) vielleicht mildern, kaum aber annulieren konnte; in dieser Hinsicht können wir den
methodischen Vorgehen Attmans (Ryska marknaden a.a.O., S. 113) Recht geben.
Dagegen betrachten wir die mangelhafte Kenntnis der mitteleuropäischen Fachliteratur als einen wesentlichen Mangel in der Arbeit Attmans, ebenso wie in der
Kritik Nilssons.
[10]) Der Unterschied zwischen dem Import- und Exportwerte machte in Narva
583 000 dlr. aus; davon waren 244 000 dlr. durch Zufuhr von Edelmetallen (über
200 000) und des Geldes gedeckt, während die andere Hälfte des Unterschiedes
ungedeckt blieb; A. Attman, Den ryska marknaden, a.a.O., S. 84 ff.

Für diese Wechsel hätte man dann nach Osten keineswegs Geld exportiert, sondern vor allem in Leipzig Waren gekauft, die durch Zentraleuropa auf dem Landwege transportiert worden seien. Die Vermittlung hätte zum größten Teil bereits in den Händen osteuropäischer Kaufleute gelegen[11]. Diese Auffassung Nilssons, die sich in erster Linie auf einen Rückschluß von den mit Sicherheit ermittelten Zuständen des 18. Jahrhunderts stützt, hat in Schweden Zustimmung gefunden[12]. Den Wirtschaftshistorikern der mitteleuropäischen Länder blieb sie aber, von einigen Ausnahmen abgesehen[13], so gut wie unbekannt. Sprachliche Gründe haben dabei wohl eine gewisse Rolle gespielt; es scheint, daß die Devise „Slavica non leguntur" auch für die „Nordica" („Scandinavica") ihre Gültigkeit hat[14].

## II.

Das Problem der Handelsbilanz, wie es sich aus den Forschungen der beiden schwedischen Historiker ergibt, stellt uns vor zwei wichtige Fragen, die bisher aber kaum gestellt worden sind und weitere Forschungen fordern:

1. Inwieweit wirkte der zentraleuropäische Handel als Vermittler für den osteuropäischen Fernhandel?
2. Welche Bedeutung hatte die binnenländische Parallelroute, wie hoch ist der Wert ihres Handelsumsatzes im Vergleich zu Struktur und Umfang des Ostseehandels?

---

[11]) S. A. NILSSON, Den ryska marknaden, a.a.O., S. 183 ff.

[12]) Das autoritäre Urteil S. BOLINS sah hier eine der besten Leistungen S. A. NILSSONS; S. BOLIN, Sju svenska historiker, Scandia XXII., 1950, S. 230 f.

[13]) Hier sei in erster Linie die Arbeit von E. HARDER genannt; Seehandel zwischen Lübeck und Rußland im 17.—18. Jahrhundert, nach Zollbüchern der Nowgorodfahrer, Zeitschrift des Vereins für Lübeckische Geschichte und Altertumskunde 41., 1961, S. 43 ff. u. 42. 1962, S. 5 ff.

[14]) In diesem Zusammenhang haben die kritischen Bemerkungen von H. WECZERKA in seinen Besprechungen der Arbeit von F. LÜTGE, Strukturwandlungen im ostdeutschen und osteuropäischen Fernhandel des 14. bis 16. Jahrhunderts, Bayerische Akad. d. Wiss., Phil.-hist. Kl., Sitzungsberichte 1964, H.l., eine allgemeinere Bedeutung; vgl. Hansische Geschichtsblätter 83., 1965, S. 161 f. und Zeitschrift für Ostforschung 16., 1967, S. 135 ff.

6

Natürlich mußten auch die inneren Handelsbeziehungen im zentraleuropäischen Raum durch diesen Zusammenhang berührt werden — vorausgesetzt, daß wir die Hypothese Nilssons akzeptieren, handelt es sich doch um eine Hypothese, die erst überprüft werden muß. Ich möchte sie mit einigen Gegebenheiten des zentraleuropäischen Handels konfrontieren, die wiederum von S. A. Nilsson nicht beachtet wurden, bzw. nicht beachtet werden konnten. Wie auch immer das Resultat einer solchen Konfrontierung ausfallen mag, eines steht fest: wir gewinnen einen neuen Blickwinkel und neue Ansatzpunkte, die auf so manche uns nur scheinbar gut bekannte Tatsachen ein neues Licht werfen. In gewissen Phasen der Forschung können neue Fragestellungen ebenso wichtig sein wie neue Detailergebnisse. Man stimmt im allgemeinen in der Auffassung überein, daß die westeuropäischen Kaufleute im Osthandel Wechsel benutzt haben[15]. Die niederländischen Wechsel sollen — nach A. E. Christensen — in Antwerpen, später dann in Amsterdam eingelöst worden sein, die englischen — nach R. W. K. Hinton — oft in Amsterdam, aber auch in Frankreich[16]. In der Beurteilung der Bedeutung dieser Wechsel für den Handel sind die Ansichten allerdings geteilt. Hier sei vor allem die schon genannte Diskussion zitiert, an der sich mitteleuropäische Historiker nicht beteiligten. Auf der anderen Seite blieb sie ihrerseits fast ohne Kenntnis der zentraleuropäischen Fachliteratur, und zwar nicht nur der slawischen. Ch. Wilson polemisierte 1949 gegen die ältere Ansicht E. F. Heckschers, daß Wechsel zum Ausgleich der Handelsbilanz in Ost- und Ostmitteleuropa verwandt wurden. Seiner Meinung nach ist die Differenz in der Bilanz doch in vollem Umfang durch Geld und Edelmetalle gedeckt worden, da dieser Handel bilateral und nicht

---

[15] E. F. HECKSCHER, Öresundsräkenskaperna, a.a.O., S. 174 f.; DERSELBE, Sveriges ekonomiska historia från Gustav Vasa I., 1., Stockholm 1936, S. 64 f. Die großen Hansestädte haben sogar besondere Wechselordnungen erlassen; M. NEUMANN, Geschichte des Wechsels im Hansagebiet bis zum 17. Jahrhundert, Erlangen 1863, S. 181. C. H. WILSON beschränkt die Wirkung des Wechsels nur auf den Bilateralhandel; vgl. Treasure and Trade Balances, a.a.O., S. 156 ff.

[16] Vgl. A. E. CHRISTENSEN, Dutch Trade, a.a.O., S. 390 f. Ebenda auch ein konkretes Beispiel der Handelsbeziehungen der Firma van Adrichem zu Gdańsk (Danzig); S. 231 ff. Ein anderes Beispiel der Benutzung von Wechsel (der Kaufmann Dalz aus Antwerpen 1573—75) bei A. ATTMAN, Den ryska marknaden, a.a.O., S. 73. Über Wechsel im englischen Handel vgl. R. W. K. HINTON, The Eastland Trade and the Common Weal in the 17th Century, London 1959, S. 114 f.

multilateral gewesen sei — was Voraussetzung für die Verwendung von Wechseln wäre[17]. Heckscher polemisierte lebhaft gegen Wilson[18], wie später auch J. Sperling, der die Gepflogenheiten des 17. Jahrhunderts von denen der späteren Zeit unterschieden wissen will. Von hier aus versucht er, die Frage zu beantworten, ob Wechsel benutzt wurden und inwieweit der Handel bilateral oder multilateral abgewickelt wurde[19]. Er sieht den Gebrauch von Wechseln schon für das 16. Jahrhundert als zweifelsfrei erwiesen, ein Übergewicht des „multilateral trade" jedoch erst seit der Mitte des 17. Jahrhunderts für gegeben[20]. Damit kommt ein weiteres Problem, die Frage nach dem multilateralen Handel, in unser Blickfeld.

Wenden wir uns für einen Augenblick wieder Narva zu. Die dort zum Ausgleich der Bilanz in Frage kommenden Wechsel mußten westeuropäischer, bzw. mitteleuropäischer Herkunft sein. Verfolgen wir nämlich den Anteil der Kaufmannsgruppen an der Bilanzdifferenz, bzw. die Handelsbilanz einzelner Handelsgruppen, so stellen wir fest, daß die Bilanzdifferenz der Handelsunternehmen der Kaufleute von Tallin (Reval) und von Narva zugunsten des Ostens nur etwas über 33 000 dlr ausmachte, die der westeuropäischen jedoch 206 000 dlr, d. h. 31 % ihrer Umsätze[21]. Im Rußlandhandel hat man die in Westeuropa einlösbaren Wechsel ohne Zweifel benutzt[22]. Ferner waren in Lviv (Lemberg) englische, Leipziger und

---

[17]) Vgl. den oben genannten Aufsatz C. H. WILSONS, Treasure and Trade Balances, S. 152 ff.

[18]) E. F. HECKSCHER, Multilateralism, Baltic Trade and the Mercantilists, The Ecconomic History Review 2. Ser., III., S. 219 ff. Die Antwort C. H. WILSONS, Treasure and Trade Balances; Further Evidence, ebenda, IV., S. 231 ff.

[19]) J. SPERLING, The International Payments Mechanism in the Seventeenth and Eighteenth Centuries, ebenda XIV., S. 446 ff.

[20]) Ebenda, S. 456 u. 459.

[21]) A. ATTMAN, Den ryska marknaden, a.a.O., S. 89. Prozentual ausgedrückt sollten die westeuropäischen Kaufleute nachträglich (eventuell durch Wechsel) noch 31 % ihres Exports bezahlen; die Talliner dagegen nur 3 % ihres Exportwertes!

[22]) V. A. KORDT, Očerk, a.a.O., S. CCLXV. Ein konkretes Beispiel: 1631 besuchte den niederländischen Gesandten in Moskva ein Offizier im zaristischen Dienst, der fragte, ob man damit rechnen könne, daß der erhaltene Wechsel auf 60 000 Rubel in den Niederlanden ausgezahlt werde — vgl. Otčet Alberta Burcha i Jogana Feldtrilla o posolstvé jich v Rossiju v 1630—31 godach (Bericht der Gesandten Albert Burgh und Joh. Feldtdrill von ihrer Gesandtschaft nach Rußland in den Jahren 1630—1631), Sbornik Imperatorskogo Istoričeskogo Otščestva 116., St. Petersburg 1902, S. 133. Die Episode selbst könnte jedoch auch als Beweis dienen, daß diese Art des Zahlungsverkehrs nicht üblich war. Oder war es die Höhe der Geldsumme, die Anlaß zur Anfrage gegeben hat?

Danziger Wechsel seit dem Ende des 16. Jahrhunderts geläufig[23]. Das geldarme Litauen kannte zumindest den Schuldbrief und den gezogenen Wechsel (Tratte)[24]. Es wurden also ohne Zweifel Wechsel für den Ausgleich der Handelsbilanz benutzt. Solche Beweisführung löst aber das Problem der Handelsbilanz an sich nicht, da dabei offen bleibt, wie die auf diese Weise gewonnenen Summen verwandt wurden. Keinesfalls konnte der Wechsel thesauriert werden — und das ist der wesentliche Unterschied zu Bargeld und Edelmetallen. Man mußte die Wechsel irgendwo eingelöst und dafür Geld oder Waren, bzw. beides nach Osten gebracht haben. Es spricht alles dafür, daß dies auf dem Landwege geschah.

## III.

Bevor wir uns die Frage stellen, welche Waren so getauscht wurden und welche Wege sie wählten, müssen wir die Rolle von Leipzig klären. Hat sich Leipzig an dem Ausgleich der Handelsbilanz beteiligt? Wieweit stimmt die Hypothese, wenn wir Leipzig in unsere Betrachtung mit einbeziehen[25]? Wir haben aus dem 16. Jahrhundert einige Belege für Wechselsendungen von Gdańsk (Danzig) nach Leipzig[26]. Auch jüdische Kaufleute aus Lviv (Lemberg) ließen sich die für ihre Waren ausgestellten Wechsel in Leipzig auszahlen[27]. In einem Fall begegnen wir einer Transaktion, die dem Modell Nilssons völlig entspricht, und zwar im Handelsverkehr zwischen Leipzig

---

[23]) M. BALABAN, Żydzi lwowscy na przełomie XVI go i XVII go wieku, (Die Lemberger Juden an der Wende des 16. und 17. Jahrhunderts), Monografie z Historyi Żydów w Polsce III., Lwów 1906, S. 573.

[24]) A. WAWRZYŃCZYK, Studia z dziejów handlu Polski z Wielkim Księstwem Litewskim i Rosją w XVI wieku (Studien zur Geschichte des polnischen Handels mit dem Großfürstentum Litauen im 16. Jahrhundert), Warszawa s. d., S. 112 f.; über die Geldzustände in Litauen vgl. ebenda S. 103 ff. Auf einige konkrete Beispiele kommen wir in einem anderen Zusammenhang noch zurück.

[25]) Die neueren (aber auch die älteren, die S. A. NILSSON nicht kannte) Forschungsergebnisse ermöglichen es uns, die Hypothese neu nachzuprüfen; für den Leipziger Handel benutzte nämlich S. A. NILSSON nur die Arbeiten von GH. NETTA und E. HASSE.

[26]) M. NEUMANN, Geschichte des Wechsels, a.a.O., S. 87, 158, 203 f.; ebenda auch Belege für die Verbindung zwischen Gdańsk (Danzig) und Wrocław (Breslau).

[27]) M. BALABAN, Żydzi lwowscy, a.a.O., S. 371 f. Die Benutzung der Leipziger Wechsel im Lemberger Handel war allgemein üblich; ebenda S. 373.

und Litauen aus dem Jahre 1540[28]. Überdies finden wir Leipziger Kaufleute 1589 in den Dorpater Zollregistern als die stärkste Gruppe vertreten[29]. Die Anwesenheit osteuropäischer Kaufleute in Leipzig während der zweiten Hälfte des 16. Jahrhunderts ist allerdings nur durch wenige direkte Hinweise belegt. Leipzig wird allgemein als der Markt bezeichnet, wo sich die Nürnberger mit den polnischen und ukrainischen Kaufleuten trafen[30]. Nachweisbar sind polnische Kaufleute für die erste Hälfte des 17. Jahrhunderts[31], litauische gelegentlich am Ende des 16., mit Sicherheit aber erst gegen Ende des 17. Jahrhunderts[32]. Jüdische Kaufleute aus Polen und Rußland sind erst seit Anfang des 18. Jahrhunderts in größerer

---

[28]) Der reiche Jude aus Tykocin (Städtchen zwischen Augustów und Brijansk) Ilja Mojsejewitsch Doktorowitsch kaufte damals in Leipzig Kleinodien im Werte von 1900 Gulden. Dafür hat er sich verpflichtet, dem Agenten eines Nürnberger Kaufmanns 400 Zentner Leinen nach Vilnius zu liefern. Als Pfand hat er in Leipzig seine Pelzware hinterlassen; vgl. A. WAWRZYŃCZYK, Studia z dziejów handlu, a.a.O., S. 101. Da die Lieferung von Leinen nur auf dem Wasserwege denkbar ist, mußte diese Transaktion zugleich für die baltische Handelsbilanz zu Buche schlagen. Auch wenn diese Episode gut in das Modell NILSSONS paßt, heißt das noch nicht, daß solche Vorgänge die einzig möglichen des Bilanzausgleichs werden konnten.

[29]) Leider sind die Zollangaben nur für das Jahr 1589—90 bekannt. Die Leipziger verzollten damals die meisten von allen in der Dorpater Kammer durchgeführten Ochsenhäute und Tuche, fast den ganzen importierten Pfeffer (jedoch eine geringe Qualität), die Hälfte des Hanfes, ein Fünftel des Leinens; R. RYBARSKI, Handel i polityka handlowa, a.a.O., II., S. 260 ff.

[30]) Neben der Arbeit von S. A. NILSSON vgl. E. KROKER, Handelsgeschichte der Stadt Leipzig, Beiträge zur Stadtgeschichte VII., Leipzig 1925, S. 47 f. u. 78 f.; H. KRETZSCHMER, Sachsen und der deutsche Osten, Deutschland und der Osten Bd. 21., Leipzig 1943, S. 129 f.

[31]) M. FREUDENTHAL, Leipziger Messgäste. Die jüdischen Besucher der Leipziger Messen in den Jahren 1675—1764, Frankfurt/M. 1928, S. 174 f.; M. WOLAŃSKI, Związki handlowe Śląska z Rzecząpospolitą w XVII wieku ze szczególnym uwzględnieniem Wrocławia, Prace Wrocławskiego Towarzystwa naukowego, Ser. A. Nr. 77., (Die Handelsverbindungen Schlesiens mit Polen im 17. Jahrhundert mit besonderer Berücksichtigung von Breslau), Wrocław 1961, S. 133 f.

[32]) Bei A. WAWRZYŃCZYK, (Studia z dziejów handlu Polski, a.a.O., S. 16), finden wir Leipzig unter jenen mitteleuropäischen Städten genannt, in welche die Litauer (bes. aus Vilnius) gereist sind. In den von der Verfasserin angeführten Quellennachweisen ist jedoch Leipzig nicht vertreten (ebenda, S. 100). Auch für die Behauptung, daß der aufkommende litauisch-russische Handel die Blüte des Leipziger Marktes mitbedingte, gibt es bei A. WAWRZYŃCZYK weder Hinweise noch Beweise (ebenda, S. 72). Die einzigen positiven Angaben wieder bei M. FREUDENTHAL, Leipziger Messgäste, a.a.O., S. 216. Dagegen scheint die Anwesenheit der litauischen Kaufleute in Poznań im 16. Jahrhundert unbestreitbar (A. WAWRZYŃCZYK, a.a.O., S. 52.

10

Zahl vertreten[33]. Noch im Jahre 1685 stellten die osteuropäischen jüdischen Kaufleute nur 8 % aller jüdischen Kaufleute, die nach Leipzig kamen[34]. Die hohen Zahlen der osteuropäischen Kaufleute in Leipzig stammen also erst aus dem 18. Jahrhundert[35]. Wenn wir diese Zahlenreihe nach rückwärts extrapolieren, erhalten wir für das 17. Jahrhundert sehr geringe Zahlen. Die schnelle Steigerung während des 18. Jahrhunderts ist nicht nur auf die allgemeine Entfaltung des europäischen Handels zurückzuführen, sondern auch auf die preußische Handelspolitik nach der Eroberung Schlesiens[36]. Übrigens wurden damals die Wechsel in den Händen osteuropäischer Kaufleute weniger in Amsterdam als vielmehr in Hamburg und London präsentiert[37]. Damit ist die Möglichkeit, von den Verhältnissen des 18. auf die des 17. Jahrhunderts zu schließen, ernsthaft in Frage gestellt. Die Anwesenheit großer Kaufmannsgruppen aus Osteuropa bedeutet jedoch nicht, daß diese lediglich Einkäufer waren. Sie brachten im 17. Jahrhundert die osteuropäischen Waren (wie z. B. Felle, Pelze und Wachs), die bis dahin über Poznań (Posen) oder Frankfurt/Oder geliefert worden waren, direkt nach Leipzig[38]. Der Aufenthalt osteuropäischer Kaufleute in dieser Stadt diente somit auch zu jenem Zeitpunkt nicht nur Einkäufen. Es sei auch hervorgehoben, daß die schon für die zweite Hälfte des 16. Jahrhunderts in Leipzig nachgewiesenen jüdischen Kaufleute aus

---

[33]) FREUDENTHAL, Leipziger Messgäste a.a.O., S. 141.

[34]) Ebenda, S. 16 f. u. 21 f.

[35]) Im Jahre 1747 waren es über 80 (aus Rußland und Polen), im Jahre 1780 schon über 400 (darunter jedoch auch die jüdischen) im Jahre 1800 über 1200; E. HASSE, Geschichte der Leipziger Messe, Preisschriften der Jablonowskischen Gesellschaft zu Leipzig XXV., Leipzig 1885, S. 305 ff. Auch in Wrocław hat übrigens die Anzahl der russischen Kaufleute im 18. Jahrhundert wesentlich zugenommen; vgl. S. KÜHN, Die wirtschaftliche Verbundenheit des Sudetenraumes von 1640 bis in die 2. Hälfte des 18. Jahrhunderts, Schlesisches Jahrbuch für deutsche Kulturarbeit im gesamtschlesischen Raume IX., 1937, S. 85 ff.

[36]) G. FISCHER, Aus zwei Jahrhunderten Leipziger Handelsgeschichte 1470—1650. Die kaufmännische Einwanderung und ihre Auswirkungen, Leipzig 1929, S. 348; E. HASSE, Geschichte, a.a.O., S. 153 f. Schon während des 17. Jahrhunderts haben jedoch die Breslauer Kaufleute ihre Selbständigkeit im Handel mit Rußland allmählich verloren; M. WOLAŃSKI, Związki handlowe, a.a.O., S. 97 und 132.

[37]) E. HASSE, Geschichte, a.a.O., S. 285 und 300.

[38]) Ebenda, S. 154 und 327; A. WAWRZYŃCZYK, Studia z dziejów, a.a.O., S. 44, 46 f., 51 f.; R. RYBARSKI, Handel i polityka handlowa, a.a.O., I., S. 89 f. u. 170.

Osteuropa stets als Verkäufer (Vieh, Felle), nicht aber als Einkäufer bezeichnet werden[39]. Um das Jahr 1600 überwog noch der Export aus Osteuropa nach Leipzig über Poznań, Wrocław (Breslau) und Lübeck[40]. Auch in dem Export aus Leipzig nach Osteuropa waren die Hauptvermittler deutsche und allenfalls noch großpolnische Kaufleute[41]. Somit fehlen die notwendigen Beweise für die von Nilsson umrissene Rolle Leipzigs im Ausgleich der Handelsbilanz zwischen Ost und West im 16. und 17. Jahrhundert.

Wenn wir die Anwesenheit zahlreicher Kaufmannsgruppen aus Osteuropa in Leipzig vor 1650 als unbeweisbar ablehnen, wird auch die Vermutung fraglich, daß der zur Diskussion gestellte Bilanzausgleich nur innerhalb des bilateralen Handels getätigt wurde. Zumindest müßten die Bilanzdifferenzen des baltischen durch den zentraleuropäischen Osthandel vorwiegend multilateral ausgeglichen worden sein. Wahrscheinlich aber ist der gesamte Ost-West-Handel multilateral abgewickelt worden. Aber dürfen wir überhaupt von einem wichtigen Warentransport auf dem Landwege nach Osten sprechen? Welche Warenmengen konnten auf dem Landwege in solcher Quantität und unter solchen Bedingungen nach dem Osten gebracht werden, daß auf diese Weise die unausgeglichene Handelsbilanz, zumindest teilweise, hätte beeinflußt werden können? Es mußte sich um wertvolle und leicht transportierbare Waren handeln[42], damit sich der weite Transport lohnte, dessen Kosten häufig unberücksichtigt bleiben. Zugleich ist nach Warensorten zu forschen, die nach Osteuropa in der fraglichen Zeit — sei es auf neuen Transportwegen, sei es in bisher ungekannter Quantität — geliefert worden sind. Es sei angemerkt, daß bei der folgenden Analyse von der allgemein verbreiteten Annahme ausgegangen wird, daß der Ost-

---

[39]) In den Leipziger Ratsprotokollen; E. Kroker, Handelsgeschichte, a.a.O., S. 87 f. Die Lübecker und Breslauer Kaufleute haben osteuropäische Waren regelmäßig nach Leipzig geliefert; vgl. ebenda, S. 47.

[40]) G. Fischer, Aus zwei Jahrhunderten Leipziger Handelsgeschichte, a.a.O., S. 348.

[41]) Ebenda, S. 94 u. 167.

[42]) Die Kaufleute aus Vilnius unterschieden in einem Protest gegen die Zollerhöhung 1621 ganz eindeutig die „teueren Sachen", welche auf dem Landwege gehandelt werden, von den billigen, für die sich der Wasserweg empfiehlt; vgl. A. Prochaska, Protest kupców wileńskich z 1621 r., Kwartalnik historyczny VII., 1893 (Der Protest der Kaufleute von Wilna 1621), S. 442 f.

12

West-Handel auf dem Landwege in seinem Gesamtwert mit dem des Seehandels vergleichbar ist. Diese Annahme wäre im einzelnen nachzuprüfen.

## IV.

Auf diesem Hintergrund sind für unsere Problematik in erster Linie die Kolonialwaren, insbesondere die Gewürze, wichtig. Gewürze waren Handelsartikel, die auch bei einem Transport auf dem Landwege befriedigende Erlöse versprachen, nicht nur wegen ihres hohen Wertes bei niedrigem Gewicht, sondern auch deshalb, weil ein eventueller Verkauf unterwegs möglich war[43].

Der alte Kolonialhandel durchquerte Europa in ost-westlicher, bzw. süd-nördlicher Richtung. Auch nach dem Fall von Konstantinopel sind Gewürze und andere Kolonialwaren noch zu einem großen Teil von Osten her (Trapezunt—Kaffa—Lviv/Lemberg) eingeführt worden, außerdem von Süden über Venedig nach Zentraleuropa und weiter über Lübeck in das Ostseegebiet[44]. Erst im 16. Jahrhundert wurde Lisboa das Eingangstor für den europäischen Gewürzimport[45]. Von da an gingen Pfeffer und andere Gewürze auf dem Seewege nach Hamburg, Gdańsk (Danzig) und in andere Häfen Nordosteuropas[46]. Diese Entwicklung wirkte sich auch auf

---

[43]) Für Polen Belege bei R. RYBARSKI, Handel i polityka handlowa, a.a.O., I., S. 149.

[44]) Von grundsätzlicher Bedeutung ist hier das Werk von M. MAŁOWIST, Kaffa, kolonia genueńska na Krymie i problem wschodni w latach 1453—1476, Warszawa 1947 (Kaffa, die Kolonie Genuas und das östliche Problem 1453—1475). Geschichte und Urkunden der Rigafahrer in Lübeck im 16. und 17. Jahrhundert. Bearb. von F. SIEWERT, Hansische Geschichtsquellen N. F. Bd. I., Berlin 1897, S. 191. Vgl. auch W. A. WAGNER, Handel dawnego Jaroslawia do polowiny XVII wieku, Lwów 1929 (Der Handel des alten Jaroslav bis zur Mitte des 17. Jahrhunderts), S. 136.

[45]) Die Folgen für den Ostseehandel: Geschichte und Urkunden, a.a.O., S. 5; für Kraków S. KUTRZEBA, Handel Krakowa w wiekach średnich na tle stosunków handlowych Polski (Der Krakauer Handel im Mittelalter im Rahmen des polnischen Handels), Rozprawy Akademii Umiejętności, hist.-fil. ser. II., t. XIX., Kraków 1903, S. 114 f.

[46]) H. KELLENBENZ, Der Pfeffermarkt und die Hansestädte, Hansische Geschichtsblätter 74., 1956, S. 19 ff.; DERSELBE, Autour de 1600: Les Frères Fugger et le marché international du poivre, Annales ESC XI., 1956, S. 9 und 22. Dort weitere Literatur.

die zentraleuropäischen Gewürzhandelswege aus. Die Ergebnisse der bisherigen Forschung bieten uns ein widerspruchsvolles Bild der Lage. Die Richtungen, in denen Gewürze durch Zentraleuropa gingen, überschnitten sich einige Jahrzehnte lang, da die Vermittlerrolle des venezianischen Imports bis in die dreißiger Jahre des 17. Jahrhunderts hinein fortbestand und es andererseits den Nürnbergern gelang, Verbindung zu den neuen Handelswegen herzustellen[47].

Aufschlußreich ist die Stellung von Poznań (Posen) im Gewürzhandel, da diese Stadt einerseits Verbindungen nach Gdańsk (Danzig) und Litauen unterhielt, zum anderen bis zur Mitte des 16. Jahrhunderts besonders eng mit Oberdeutschland verknüpft war[48]. So erhielt Poznań (Posen) einmal Gewürze aus Hamburg über Wrocław (Breslau) geliefert, zum anderen durch die Leipziger und Frankfurter und drittens durch die Kaufleute aus Gdańsk (Danzig) mit Weiterlieferung nach Wrocław[49]. Zu bemerken ist, daß der Umfang des Pfefferhandels in der zweiten Hälfte des 16. Jahrhunderts wuchs. Auch die Stellung von Kraków (Krakau) im Gewürzhandel ist nicht eindeutig. Bis Mitte des 16. Jahrhunderts scheint die Zufuhr aus dem Süden zu überwiegen, sie geht später zurück, während sich der geringe Import über Wrocław (Breslau) auch in diesen späteren Jahrzehnten gehalten hat. Neu hinzu kamen gegen Ende des 16. Jahrhunderts Lieferungen aus Toruń (Thorn) und Gdańsk (Danzig)[50].

Für die hier zu überprüfenden Formen des Ost-West-Handels ist eine Nachricht vom Jahre 1590 besonders wichtig, die vom Pfeffer-

---

[47]) H. KELLENBENZ, Autour de 1600, a.a.O., S. 14; DERSELBE, Der Pfeffermarkt und die Hansestädte, a.a.O., S. 48 f.

[48]) Da in diesen Sammelband ein Beitrag des polnischen Historikers M. GRYCZ eingereiht wurde, verzichteten wir auf eine nähere Behandlung seiner Arbeiten. Weiter vgl. R. RYBARSKI, Handel i polityka handlowa, II., S. 86 u. 108; L. KOCZY, Handel Poznania do połowy wieku XVI., (Der Posener Handel bis zur Mitte des 16. Jahrhunderts), Poznań 1930, S. 300 ff. Unter den Vermittlern ist eine klare Verschiebung zugunsten der polnischen, bzw. litauischen Kaufleute zu erkennen.

[49]) R. RYBARSKI, Handel i polityka handlowa, a.a.O., I., S. 150 ff.; L. KOCZY, Handel Poznania, a.a.O., S. 302. Bei H. WOLAŃSKI ist jedoch diese Richtung für Wrocław nicht aufzufinden (Związki handlowe Śląska, a.a.O.).

[50]) R. RYBARSKI, Handel i polityka handlowa, a.a.O., II., S. 86, 108, 202; H. WOLAŃSKI, Związki handlowe śląska, a.a.O., S. 224 f.

import in Tartu (Dorpat) berichtet, der durch Leipziger auf dem Landwege erfolgte[51]. Für Gdańsk (Danzig) ist zu fragen, ob die Belege über einen großen Pfeffer- und Gewürzhandel, die um das Jahr 1590 zu datieren sind, nicht nur von einer kurzfristigen Konjunktur Zeugnis geben[52]. Allerdings geht aus den Sundzollregistern eindeutig hervor, daß der Umfang der Kolonialwarenlieferungen während der ersten Hälfte des 17. Jahrhunderts zunimmt[53].

Wir können noch eine andere Möglichkeit zur eingehenderen Betrachtung der Gewürzhandelsrichtungen nutzen und zwar den Vergleich der Preise in verschiedenen Städten zur selben Zeit, wie er dank den polnischen Preisstatistiken möglich geworden ist[54]. Es ist von der Tatsache auszugehen, daß eine Ware durch den Weitertransport in der Regel teurer wird. Je weiter also eine Ware transportiert wurde, desto teurer wurde sie verkauft. Diese vergleichende

---

[51]) R. RYBARSKI, Handel i polityka handlowa, a.a.O., II., S. 236. Dabei wird unter den auf dem Seewege aus Lübeck gegen Osten weitergeführten Warengattungen Kolonialware nur verhältnismäßig selten genannt; vgl. E. HARDER, Seehandel zwischen Lübeck und Rußland, a.a.O., S. 96.

[52]) Wir wissen nämlich, daß sich die in Danzig residierenden Kaufleute wegen Absatzschwierigkeiten beklagt haben; A. E. CHRISTENSEN, Dutch Trade, a.a.O., S. 386. Die größeren Mengen der Kolonialwaren, die auf dem Seewege gegen Ende des 16. Jahrhunderts zuströmten, mußten die Preise im Detailhandel herabdrükken und dadurch besonders den bisherigen Handel auf dem Landwege schädigen. Das kann man an den Pfefferpreisen in Gdańsk (Danzig) sehr gut verfolgen; vgl. J. PELC, Ceny w Gdańsku w XVI i XVII wieku (Die Preise in Danzig im 16. und 17. Jahrhundert), Badania z dziejów społecznych i gospodarczych, Nr. 21., Lwów 1937.

[53]) Auch wenn die Gewichts- und Wertrelationen schwer festzustellen sind, spiegelt sich der Aufstieg in folgenden Zahlen:

|      |        |        |           |           |        |
|------|--------|--------|-----------|-----------|--------|
| 1604 | wurden | 124    | Fässer und | 200 Pfund | verzollt, |
| 1609 |        | 164,5  | „         | 7 106     | „      |
| 1619 |        | 2034   | „         | 86 401    | „      |
| 1624 |        | 1412,5 | „         | 38 702    | „      |
| 1629 |        | 54     | „         | 409 000   | „      |
| 1639 |        | 3      | „         | 1 216 428 | „      |
| 1644 |        | —      | „         | 2 402 857 | „      |
| 1649 |        | 30     | „         | 1 366 633 | „      |

Tabeller over Skibsfart og Varetransport gennem Öresund 1497—1660, ed. N. E. BANG, I., København, Leipzig 1906; vgl. auch die Berechnung bei A. E. CHRISTENSEN, Dutch Trade, a.a.O., S. 465 f.

[54]) Polen wird hier nicht nur wegen seiner Schlüsselstellung in dem Ost-West-Handel als Beispiel gewählt, sondern auch deshalb, weil in anderen Gebieten Mitteleuropas die Preisstatistiken im erwünschten Umfang und für die gesuchten Warensorten nicht vorliegen.

Analyse, die, wie gesagt, leider nur für Pfeffer und teilweise für Safran möglich ist, bietet uns einige interessante Einblicke[55]. Die Safranpreise waren während der sechziger Jahre des 16. Jahrhunderts in Warszawa (Warschau) niedriger als in Kraków (Krakau), in den folgenden zwei Jahrzehnten hat sich die Lage umgekehrt. Seit den neunziger Jahren und bis in die Mitte des 17. Jahrhunderts hinein waren die Preise dann in Warszawa (Warschau) niedriger. In Lublin sind die Preise ungefähr die gleichen wie die in Kraków (Krakau)[56]. Die Pfefferpreise waren bis 1591 in der Regel in Gdańsk (Danzig) höher als in Kraków, während die Preise in Warszawa ungefähr zwischen diesen beiden Werten lagen. Nur in einzelnen Jahren war die Relation umgekehrt, so zum Beispiel 1575, als die Preise in Warszawa die höchsten waren. Seit dem Jahre 1591 waren die Preise in Gdańsk immer wesentlich niedriger als in Kraków, mit Ausnahme der Jahre, die wegen einer tiefergehenden Handelskrise bekannt geworden sind[57]. Die Pfefferpreise in Lublin scheinen dagegen nicht wesentlich anders als in anderen Städten des polnischen Binnenlandes gewesen zu sein. Diese Entwicklung wird nachstehend graphisch verdeutlicht.

---

[55]) Die Preise für Gdańsk (Danzig) berechnet nach J. PELC, Ceny, a.a.O., die Preise in Kraków bis 1600; DERSELBE, Ceny w Krakowie w l. 1369—1600, Badania z dziejów spolecznych i gospodarczych 14., Lwów 1935; die Preise daselbst nach 1600 bei E. TOMASZEWSKI, Ceny w Krakowie w l. 1601—1795, Badania..., 15., Lwów 1934; Die Preise in Warszawa W. ADAMCZYK, Ceny w Warszawie w XVI i XVII w., Badania..., 24., Lwów 1938; Die Preise in Lublin; DERSELBE, Ceny w Lublinie od XVI do końca XVIII wieku, Badania..., 17., Lwów 1935.

[56]) Bei Safran, wo die Lage im Grunde ähnlich, im Detailverlauf jedoch vielfältiger gewesen ist, muß man bei dem unterschiedlichen Verlauf der Preiskurve in Betracht ziehen, daß sich seit der 2. Hälfte des 16. Jahrhunderts die Zufuhr von Safran aus Mähren und Ungarn nach Polen verstärkte; A. V. FLOROVSKIJ, Českoruské obchodní styky v minulosti X.—XVIII. století, Praha 1954 (Die tschechisch-russischen Handelsbeziehungen in der Vergangenheit X.—XVIII. Jahrhundert), S. 155 ff. Aus diesem Grunde verzichten wir auf eine Konfrontierung der Preiskurven von Safran mit denen von Pfeffer.

[57]) Dieses Verhältnis kommt im Jahre 1618 (für die folgenden zwei Jahre fehlen die Angaben) und im Jahre 1630 vor. Zu den Krisenjahren vgl. A. SZELĄGOWSKI, Pieniądz i przewrót cen w XVI i XVII wieku w Polsce (Das Geld und die Preisrevolution in Polen des 16.—17. Jahrhunderts), Lwów 1902, S. 181. Von englischer Seite vgl. R. W. K. HINTON, The Eastland Trade, a.a.O., S. 13 ff.; J. D. GOULD, The Trade Depression of the Early 1620's, The Economic History Review Ser. 2., VII. S. 82 ff.; R. ROMANO, Tra XVI e XVII secolo. Una crisi economica, Rivista Storica Italiana LXXIV, 1962, S. 521 ff. Zum Krisenjahr 1630 vgl. M. HROCH, Obchod a politika za třicetileté války (Handel und Politik während des Dreißigjährigen Krieges), Sborník historický XIII., 1964, S. 215 ff.

16

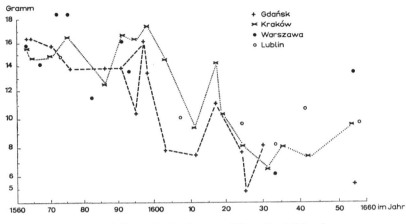

Die Pfefferpreise in Gramm Silber für 1 Pfund

Man erkennt eine klare Linie, die jedoch noch mit Quellen anderer Art konfrontiert werden müßte: Bis in die achtziger Jahre des 16. Jahrhunderts hinein scheint der Gewürzhandel ohne stabile und direkte Verbindung der Route über die Ostsee und der Route über die Binnenländer verlaufen zu sein, wie der von einander unabhängige Verlauf der Preiskurven zeigt. Danach erhöhten sich die Pfefferpreise radikal von Gdańsk (Danzig) aus, je weiter der Pfeffer nach Süden und Osten vordrang. In den Krisenjahren des Ostseehandels, das heißt in einigen Jahren des Dreißigjährigen Krieges, scheint sich der Landweg ostwärts wieder verselbständigt zu haben. Jedenfalls konnten Gewürze für den Bilanzausgleich auf dem Landwege in viel stärkerem Maße vor Ende des 16. Jahrhunderts in Frage kommen als danach.

Einige Historiker halten an der Annahme fest, daß der Gewürzimport nach Rußland weiter auf den altgewohnten Handelswegen vom Osten und Südosten her erfolgte. Für diese Behauptung finden sich jedoch in der von uns betrachteten Zeitspanne kaum Belege[58].

---

[58] Ein charakteristisches Beispiel finden wir bei M. V. FECHNER, Torgovlja russkogo gosudarstva so stranami Vostoka v XVI věkě, (Der Handel des russischen Staates mit den Ländern des Ostens im 16. Jahrhundert), Moskva 1952, wo eindeutig von dem Gewürzimport aus Asien die Rede ist. Wenn wir aber die Quellennachweise für die Pfefferpreise in dieser Arbeit verfolgen, dann stellen wir fest, daß fast alle aus Nordrußland stammen — also näher zu den Import-

Im Gegenteil: es gibt Projekte, einen Transithandelsweg über Rußland auszubauen, der unter anderem auch Gewürze nach Persien vermitteln sollte[59]. Die Zufuhr von Gewürzen nach Rußland aus dem Westen scheint gegen Ende des 16. Jahrhunderts überwogen zu haben. Direkte Belege sind häufig für die Ostseehäfen und später auch für den nördlichen Seeweg über Archangelsk vorhanden[60]. Auf dem Weitertransport ins Binnenland wurde ein Teil der Gewürze bereits unterwegs auf den nordrussischen Lokalmärkten verkauft[61]. Der russische Handel rechnete am Anfang des 17. Jahrhunderts fest

wegen aus Westeuropa liegen; vgl. ebenda, S. 100 f. Wenn es doch zum Gewürzimport aus dem Osten kam, handelte es sich um ganz spezifische Warensorten und um kleine Quantitäten; A. SZELĄGOWSKI, Z dziejów wspólzawodnictwa Anglii i Niemiec Rosji i Polski (Aus der Geschichte des Wettbewerbes zwischen England und Deutschland, Rußland und Polen), Lwów 1910, S. 43 f. B. T. KURC, Snošenije Kilburgera o russkoj torgovlje v carstvovanije Alekseja Michajloviča (Bericht Kilburgers über den russischen Handel während der Regierung von Alexej Michailowitsch), Sbornik studenčeskogo istorikoetnograf. kružka pri Universitětě sv. Vladimira. vyp. VI., Kijev 1915, str. 302.
[59]) Auf Grund der Beschreibung des russischen Handels von P. LOOFELT vgl. bei A. ATTMAN, Den ryska marknaden, a.a.O., S. 115; A. V. FLOROVSKIJ, Českoruské obchodní styky, a.a.O., S. 235 f. Zum Holsteinischen Projekt des Persienhandels vgl. E. M. KIECKSEE, Die Handelspolitik der Gottorfer Herzöge im 17. Jahrhundert, Diss. Kiel 1952, S. 54 ff. u. 79 ff. zu den kurländischen Projekten, vgl. O. H. MATTIESSEN, Die Kolonial- und Überseepolitik der kurländischen Herzöge im 17. und 18. Jahrhundert, Stuttgart 1940. Zusammenfassend zu dieser Problematik JE. S. ZEVAKIN, Persidskij vopros v russko-jevropejskich otnošenijach XVII. v., (Die persisch-russische Frage in den Beziehungen zwischen Rußland und Europa), Istoričeskije zapiski S., 1940, S. 133 ff.
[60]) Nach dem Bericht Kilburgers beschreibt den Handel H. KOSTOMAROV, Očerk torgovli Moskovskogo gosudarstva v XVI. i XVII. stoletijach (Abriß des Handels des Moskauer Staates im 16.—17. Jahrhundert), Sobranije sočiněnij kn. t. 20., St. Petersburg 1905, S. 381. Vgl. auch V. A. KORDT, Očerk snošenij, a.a.O., S. CCLXXXII. Im Zusammenhang damit sind auch die — jedoch selten vorkommenden — Belege für den Gewürzhandel in den nordrussischen Zollbüchern als Beweis für den Import aus Westeuropa zu betrachten; leider fehlen aber in den Zollbüchern genauere Angaben über die Herkunft der Ware; vgl. Tamožennyje knigi Moskovskogo gosudarstva XVII věka, t. I. Severnyj rečnyj puť: Ustug Velikij, Solvyčegodsk, Totma v 1633—1636 gg. (Die Zollbücher des Moskauer Staates aus dem 17. Jahrhundert, Bd. I. Der nördliche Flußweg), Moskva—Leningrad, 1950, S. 528, 532 u. a.
[61]) V. A. KORDT, Očerk snošenij, a.a.O., S. CCLXXXII; A. C. MERZON, JU. A. TICHONOV, Rynok Usťjuga Velikogo v period skladyvanija vserossijskogo rynka (XVII. věk) (Der Markt von Usťjug Velikij zur Zeit der Formierung des Gesamtrussischen Marktes im 17. Jahrhundert), Moskva 1960, S. 289. Dazu auch die oben erwähnten Belege aus den Tamožennyje knigi Moskovskogo gosudarstva (vgl. Anm. 60).

mit dem Gewürzimport über Westeuropa[62], wobei wir den Anteil der Binnenland-Route im allgemeinen hoch einschätzen dürfen. Freilich: seit dem Ende des 16. Jahrhunderts stieg auch hier die Bedeutung des Ostseeweges.

Auch andere Warensorten verdienen neben den Gewürzen im Hinblick auf den West-Ost-Handel unsere Aufmerksamkeit. Es steht eindeutig fest, daß ein Teil der für Osteuropa bestimmten westlichen Tuchproduktion auch in der frühen Neuzeit weiter auf dem Landwege durch Zentraleuropa transportiert wurde. Dieser Transportweg des Tuches wird neben dem über die Ostsee als der zweite wichtige Handelsweg allgemein anerkannt[63]. Er war ebenso für die polnischen wie für die litauischen und westrussischen Gebiete von großer Bedeutung[64]. Selbst bei den billigeren Tuchsorten lohnte sich der weite Transport auf dem Landwege[65], der die Flüsse überschritt[66]. Dabei soll außer Poznań auch Leipzig eine gewisse Rolle gespielt haben[67]. Neben den westeuropäischen Tuchen sind aus Mitteleuropa auch Stoffe ostwärts geliefert worden, wie vor allem Tuche mittlerer Qualität (aus Großpolen und den böhmischen Län-

---

[62] Die „Torgovaja Kniga" von Moskva aus dem Ende des 16. — Anfang des 17. Jahrhunderts verfolgt die Preisentwicklung (bzw. das Preisniveau) der Gewürze nicht im Osten, sondern im Westen, in Holland. I. P. SACHAROV, Torgovaja kniga. Zapiski otdělenija russkoj i slavjanskou archeologii Imp. Russ. Archeolog. Obščestva I., St. Petersburg 1851; § 45, 54, 73, 114, 116 ff.

[63] R. RYBARSKI, Handel i polityka handlowa, a.a.O., I., 162; II. S. 170 ff.; A. E. CHRISTENSEN, Sundzollregister und Ostseehandel, a.a.O., S. 399; A. MĄCZAK, Rola kontaktów z zagranicą w dziejach sukiennictwa polskiego XVI. i pierwszej połowy XVII. wieku, Przegląd historyczny XL III., 1952, S. 243 ff.; DERSELBE, Sukiennictwo wielkopolskie XIV—XVII wieku (Die Tuchproduktion in Großpolen im 14.—17. Jahrhundert), Warszawa 1955, S. 209, 229, 232 f.

[64] R. RYBARSKI, Handel i polityka handlowa, a.a.O., I. S. 171 f., 176 u. 178; H. ŁOWMIAŃSKI, Handel Mohylewa w XVI wieku (Der Mogilewsker Handel im 16. Jahrhundert), studia historyczne ku czci St. Kutrzeby II., Kraków 1938, S. 25 ff.; W. RUSIŃSKI, Rozwój gospodarczy ziem polskich w zarysie (Umriß der Wirtschaftsentwicklung der polnischen Länder), Warszawa 1963, S. 103 f. Nur zur Ergänzung des Gesamtbildes sei an dieser Stelle der Tuchimport Ungarns aus dem Westen erwähnt.

[65] Belegt überzeugend bei A. MĄCZAK, Sukiennictwo wielkopolskie, a.a.O., S. 205.

[66] R. RYBARSKI, Handel i polityka handlowa, a.a.O., I., S. 162.

[67] Der Stadtrat von Leipzig warnte vor den allzu harten Maßnahmen gegen die fremden Kaufleute mit der Begründung, daß der Handelsweg ostwärts an Leipzig vorbei geführt werden könnte; E. KROKER, Handelsgeschichte der Stadt Leipzig, a.a.O., S. 125 ff.; vgl. auch E. HASSE, Geschichte der Leipziger Messe, a.a.O., S. 457 f.

dern) und Leinen (aus Schlesien, Sachsen, Lausitz und Nordböhmen)[68]. Ein Quantitätenvergleich zwischen dem Ostseeweg und der Landroute durch Zentraleuropa ist jedoch kaum durchführbar[69]. Wir begnügen uns mit der Feststellung, daß es sich um Werte handelte, die nicht weit entfernt voneinander waren.

Schließlich noch eine knappe Übersicht über die kleineren Warengruppen. Unter ihnen wird der größte Wert den Luxuswaren (Kleinodien, Goldschmiedearbeiten, wertvoll bearbeiteten Stoffen) zugeschrieben[70]. Weiter hatten Papier[71], Eisenwaren (Messer, Sensen und

[68]) A. WAWRZYŃCZYK, Studia z dziejów handlu Polski, a.a.O., S. 58; A. MĄCZAK, Sukiennictwo wielkopolskie, a.a.O., S. 207 f. und Taf. 6; R. RYBARSKI, Handel i polityka handlowa, a.a.O., I., S. 170 und II., S. 89 ff.; M. BALABAN, Żydzi lwowscy, a.a.O., S. 394.

[69]) Die Tatsache, daß die zentraleuropäischen, insbesondere die polnischen Zollkammern den Warenverkehr in einem viel kleinerem Umfang notiert haben als die Sundzollregister, hilft in unserer Fragestellung nicht weiter, da sich darin in erster Linie eine verschiedenartig gehandhabte Zollregistrierung widerspiegelt, nicht aber mit Sicherheit ein unterschiedlicher Warenumsatz. Dies bleibt noch eine offene Frage für die künftige quellenkritische Forschung; R. RYBARSKI, Handel i polityka handlowa, a.a.O., I., S. 162 f.

[70]) Schon Ivan IV. beauftragte oft die ausländischen aber auch die russischen Kaufleute zum Einkauf von Juwelen in Antwerpen bzw. Amsterdam; nicht anders war es auch in der 1. Hälfte des 17. Jahrhunderts; vgl. V. A. KORDT, Očerk snošenij, a.a.O., S. XVII und XXIV f., für das 17. Jahrhundert S. CCLXXII. Womit sollten diese bezahlt werden? — Die Hälfte der Goldschmiedwaren, die in der Dorpater Zollkammer 1589—90 notiert sind, war von den Leipziger Kaufleuten eingeführt worden; vgl. R. RYBARSKI, Handel i polityka handlowa, a.a.O., II., S. 266. Diese Angabe wird von Leipziger Seite durch die Auskunft über das Handelsunternehmen der Firma H. Cramer v. Clausbruch bestätigt, die nach Moskva (aber auch in die polnischen Städte) Juwelen und Edelsteine exportierte, um von dort auf dem Seewege Pelzwaren, Teer u. a. auszuführen; vgl. H. KROKER, Handelsgeschichte der Stadt Leipzig, a.a.O., S. 94. Für das 16. Jahrhundert vgl. auch H. WOLAŃSKI, Związki handlowa, a.a.O., S. 201 f. (über Wrocław nach Osteuropa). Zum Import der Luxuswaren auf dem Landwege nach Rußland, vgl. S. V. BACHRUŠIN, Očerki po istorii remesla, torgovli i gorodov russkogo centralizovannogo gosudarstva XVI.—načala XVII. věka (Studien zur Geschichte des Gewerbe und des Handels in den Städten des zentralisierten russischen Staates im 16. bis zum Anfang des 17. Jahrhunderts), Naučnyje trudy I., Moskva 1952, S. 179 f. Für das 17. Jahrhundert vgl. die Relation von P. LOOFELT, A. ATTMAN, Den ryska marknaden, a.a.O., S. 112. Dazu ein typisches Beispiel aus der späteren Zeit: der Zar hat 1627 (und wieder 1628) den Niederländer Karl Molin nach Westeuropa geschickt, um dort für den Hof eine größere Quantität von Juwelen und Luxuswaren einzukaufen; ein Teil der eingekauften Ware ging über Archangelsk, ein anderer auf dem Landwege; vgl. V. A. KORDT, Očerk snošenij, a.a.O., S. CCLXXVII.

[71]) Papier aus Polen wird erwähnt bei A. G. MAŃKOV, Ceny i jich dviženije v russkom gosudarstvě VI věka, Moskva—Leningrad 1951 (Die Preise und ihre

andere)[72] sowie Glaswaren[73] Bedeutung. Alle drei Warengruppen stammten zum überwiegenden Teil aus Mitteleuropa[74]. Sie sind nebst der Leinwand im 16. und 17. Jahrhundert jene neuen Warensorten auf dem Landwege in west-östlicher Richtung, die eine Rolle für den hier erforschten Bilanzausgleich gespielt haben könnten, besonders, nachdem wir die Bedeutung der Gewürze für diesen Ausgleich seit etwa 1590 in Frage stellen mußten. Für eine ganz spezielle Art des osteuropäischen Imports — Söldnerwerbung und Waffenlieferungen — ist die Bezahlung durch Wechsel ausdrücklich belegt. Zwei typische Beispiele: in den Jahren 1630 und 1631 wurden einige Niederländer, die im zaristischen Dienste wirkten, nach Holland, England, bzw. Schweden geschickt, um dort für die russische Armee zu werben und Waffen zu bestellen. Die damit verbundenen Kosten sollten sie mit jenen Wechseln decken, mit denen die niederländischen Kaufleute in Rußland die russischen Ge-

---

Entwicklung im russischen Staate des 16. Jahrhunderts), S. 241. Papierimport nach Litauen — vgl. A. WAWRZYŃCZYK, Studia z dziejów handlu Polski, a.a.O., S. 60. Aus (bzw. über) Leipzig gingen größere Papiermengen nach Lviv (Lemberg) — WŁ. ŁOZIŃSKI, Patrycyat i mieszczaństwo Lwowskie w XVI i XVII wieku (Das Patriziat und das Bürgertum in Lemberg des 16.—17. Jahrhunderts), Lwów 1892, S. 346. Für den Papierexport aus Böhmen finden wir Belege erst gegen Mitte des 17. Jahrhunderts bei A. V. FLOROVSKIJ, Česko-ruské obchodní styky, a.a.O., S. 167 f.

[72]) S. V. BACHRUŠIN, Očerki po istorii remesla, a.a.O., S. 179 f.; N. I. KOSTOMAROV, Očerki torgovli moskovskogo gosudarstva, a.a.O., S. 355; A. V. FLOROVSKIJ, Česko-ruské obchodní styky, a.a.O., S. 148 ff.; R. RYBARSKI, Handel i polityka handlowa, a.a.O., II., S. 70, 93 f. u. 114.; M. BALABAN, Żydzi lwowscy a.a.O., S. 394.

[73]) Zum Glasimport in Rußland N. I. KOSTOMAROV, Očerki torgovli moskovskogo gosudarstva, a.a.O., S. 376; B. T. KURC, Sočiněnije Kilburgera o russkoj torgovlě v carstvovanije Alekseja Michajloviča (Der Bericht Kilburgers über den russischen Handel zur Zeit der Regierung von Alexej Michajlowitsch), Kijev 1915, Sbornik studenčeskogo istoriko-etnografičeskogo kružka pri Universitětě sv. Vladimira, vyp. VI., S. 119, 125 f., 138 f., 323 f. Zum böhmischen Glasexport nach Osteuropa A. V. FLOROVSKIJ, Česko-ruské obchodní styky, a.a.O., S. 158 f. Import in Polen auf dem Landwege vgl. R. RYBARSKI, Handel i polityka handlowa, a.a.O., I. S. 187 f.

[74]) Wir dürfen jedoch nicht ohne weiteres voraussetzen, daß alle auf dem russischen Markte erscheinenden Waren mitteleuropäischer Herkunft nur auf dem Landwege gekommen sind; so finden wir z. B. im Jahre 1621 in Archangelsk unter den auf dem Seewege importierten Warengattungen auch ungarische Messer, mährisches Tuch, deutsche Leinwand u. ä. vgl. V. A. KORDT, Očerki snošenij, a.a.O., S. CCLXXXII f.

treidelieferungen bezahlt hatten[75]. Ferner sollten schwedische Offiziere zum Teil mit den in Hamburg und Amsterdam zu präsentie-
renden Wechseln bezahlt werden, und zwar gerade seit Anfang der
dreißiger Jahre des 17. Jahrhunderts, als das Ostbaltikum schwe-
disch wurde[76].

Wir haben uns bisher auf die ostwärts gelieferten Güter beschränkt, um die Wahrscheinlichkeit eines Bilanzausgleiches im Ostseehandel durch den Warentransport auf dem Landwege zwischen
Osteuropa einerseits und West- und Mitteleuropa andererseits zu
überprüfen. Importierte der Osten auf diesem Landwege aber wirklich höhere Werte als er nach dem Westen exportierte? Es ist gegen-
wärtig völlig ausgeschlossen, eine zuverlässige Gesamtbilanz des
Handels auf dem Landwege aufzumachen. Indes verfügen wir über
einige signifikante Teilangaben.

---

[75]) Otčet Alberta Burcha i Jogana Feltdrilla, a.a.O., S. 70 u. 133; es handelte
sich um den Oberst Dahm und um Alexander Leslie; der erstere bekam Wechsel
im Werte von 60 000 Rubel. In dem niederländischen Bericht wird dieses Ereignis
als ein selbstverständlicher Vorgang betrachtet; wir haben daher keinen Anlaß,
es als etwas Außerordentliches zu bezeichnen. Da der Getreidehandel zu den
zaristischen Monopolen gehörte, konnten die Wechsel für die verkauften Ge-
treidelieferungen direkt dem Zaren zur Verfügung stehen. Zu den Waffenlieferungen aus England für Rußland in den Jahren 1630—32 vgl. die Korrespondenz
zwischen dem Zaren Michail Fedorowitsch und dem König Karl I.; R. Schoener,
Der Briefwechsel zwischen dem Zaren Michail und den englischen Königen Jakob
I. und Karl I. als Quelle zur Geschichte der englisch-russischen Beziehungen 1613—
1645, Diss. Erlangen, 1957, S. 25, 30, 32 u. 35.
[76]) Die schwedischen „Faktoren" in Hamburg (A. Svensson) und in Amsterdam (K. v. Falkenberg) sollten die Wechsel aus dem Gewinn für das verkaufte
russische (Subsidien Rußlands an Schweden!) und livländische Getreide in den
beiden Städten einlösen und damit den Sold für die schwedischen Offiziere gewinnen; vgl. die Korrespondenz zwischen Gustav Adolf und Axel Oxenstjerna
aus dem Jahre 1630, Rikskansleren Axel Oxenstjernas Skrifter och Brefvexling, I.
Afd. 5., S. 505 f., 622 u. 627 ff. Zu der russischen Subsidienpolitik gegenüber
Schweden vgl. B. F. Poršněv, Russkije subsidiji Šveciji vo vremja Tridcatletněj
vojny (Die russischen Subsidien an Schweden während des Dreißigjährigen Krieges),
Izvěstija AN SSSR II., N. 5., 1945, S. 319 ff. Zu der damaligen Ausnahmesitua-
tion im Finanzwesen Schwedens vgl. E. Wendt, Det svenska licentväsendet i
Preussen, Uppsala 1933, S. 187; M. Hroch, K otázce působení třicetileté války
na základní vývojové tendence baltského obchodu v 17. století (Zum Einfluß
des Dreißigjährigen Krieges auf die Entwicklungstendenzen des baltischen Handels im 17. Jahrhundert), Sborník historický 13., 1965, S. 133 ff.

## V.

Die Handelsbilanz zwischen Schlesien und den polnischen Gebieten hat sich am Anfang des 17. Jahrhunderts aus einer wahrscheinlich ausgeglichenen in eine eindeutig aktive für Schlesien verwandelt. Der Wert der ostwärts geführten Waren war höher als der vom Osten kommenden[77]. Die Handelsbilanz auf dem Landwege war somit für den Osten nicht nur in Leipzig, sondern auch in Wrocław (Breslau) passiv. Die erhaltenen Bruchstücke der Zollregister von Brest vom Ende des 16. Jahrhunderts zeigen desgleichen einen überwiegenden Import aus dem Westen[78]. Für Lviv (Lemberg) ist dagegen eine für den Osten aktive Handelsbilanz zu verzeichnen; hier wurden also Geld und Edelmetalle weiter nach Osten exportiert[79]. Für Poznań (Posen) wird eine ausgeglichene Handelsbilanz grosso modo angenommen[80]. Wenn wir den für Polen bestimmten Teil des Handels von dem weiter in den Osten reichenden trennen, ergibt sich ein differenzierteres Bild. Im polnischen Teil des Handels überwog im 16. Jahrhundert der Import aus dem Westen und Süden den Export in gleicher Richtung. Ebenso scheint der Anteil der aus dem Osten stammenden Ware am Gesamtumsatz höher zu sein als der für Osteuropa bestimmten. Diese Differenz wird auch durch Belege über die Geldausfuhr aus Polen nach Litauen bestätigt[81]. Die aktive Handelsbilanz (und eine eventuelle durch das Geld nicht gedeckte Differenz) Polens an der Ostsee scheint also teilweise durch die passive Bilanz in dem zentraleuropäischen bzw. südosteuropäischen Zweig des polnischen Handels ausgeglichen worden zu sein. Zuletzt sei uns gestattet, eine Parallele

---

[77] H. Wolański, Związki handlowe Śląska, a.a.O., S. 291 f.

[78] A. Wawrzyńczyk, Studia z dziejów handlu Polski, a.a.O., S. 109.

[79] Wł. Łoziński, Patrycjat i mieszczaństwo, a.a.O., S. 42 ff.; zum polnischen Geld- und Edelmetallexport vgl. Z. Switalski, Clo z pieniędzy wywożonych za granicę Polski (Der Zoll aus der Geldausfuhr aus Polen), Przegląd historyczny 1960, S. 27 ff. Andererseits sei dazu bemerkt, daß der seit dem Mittelalter bekannte Import böhmischer Münze in Rußland im 16. Jahrhundert aufhörte — nach A. V. Florovskij, Česko-ruské obchodní styky v minulosti, a.a.O., S. 177 n. Dürfen wir diese Tatsache als einen weiteren Beweis für die Verschiebungen in der Handelsbilanz zwischen Mittel- und Osteuropa betrachten?

[80] A. Wawrzyńczyk, Studia z dziejów handlu Polski, a.a.O., S. 73 f.

[81] Die Warensorten, welche gegen Osten transportiert worden sind, konnte man unterwegs verkaufen; dagegen handelte es sich im Falle des Exportes russischer bzw. litauischer Waren westwärts meistens um solche, die auch aus den Durchfuhrgebieten (Polen, Litauen) exportiert wurden. Man kann also kaum einen Verkauf unterwegs annehmen; vgl. auch Wawrzyńczyk, a.a.O., S. 73.

zu den statistisch eindeutig gesicherten Verhältnissen der späteren Zeit zu ziehen. Ein Teil des Außenhandelsüberschusses der russischen Seehandelswege wurde laut den statistischen Angaben der Jahre 1794/95 durch die passive Handelsbilanz auf dem Landwege gegen Westen ausgeglichen[82].

Die apostrophierten Teilbilanzen schließen also den Ausgleich der baltischen Handelsbilanz durch den binnenländischen Zustrom westlicher und — wie wir oben gezeigt haben — besonders mitteleuropäischer Waren nicht aus. Doch auch hier gibt es Ausnahmen. Der Handel von und über Lviv (Lemberg) war traditionell aktiv für den Osten und der polnisch-litauische Handel (nicht aber der litauische Handel über Polen mit Zentraleuropa) weist dank des Anteils der in die Ostseehäfen zielenden Handelswaren wahrscheinlich auch eine für den östlichen Partner aktive Handelsbilanz auf.

Wir dürfen — neben der nicht eben neuen Feststellung, daß aus und durch Mitteleuropa trotz des sich vergrößernden Ostseehandels steigende Warenmengen ostwärts gegangen sind — auf Grund des bisherigen Standes der Forschung festhalten, daß ein Teil dieser Lieferungen durch Wechsel bezahlt wurde. Von den aus dem Westen kommenden Warensorten bestand nur bei den Kolonialwaren ein Handel mit derartigen Quantitäten und Wahl der Transportwege, daß man ihn in Zusammenhang mit dem uns interessierenden Problem des Ausgleiches der Handelsbilanz bringen darf. Parallel verlief jedoch der wachsende Warenexport aus den deutschen und böhmischen Ländern durch Schlesien nach Ostmittel- und Osteuropa, dessen mögliche Bedeutung für den Ausgleich der Handels- bzw. Zahlungsbilanz in der bisherigen Forschung unbeachtet ist.

Es bleibt die Frage zu stellen, wieweit die Struktur und der Umfang des baltischen und binnenländischen Handels sich gegenseitig beeinflussen bzw. ergänzen konnten[83]. Die Frage bleibt zu beantworten, wie die eine Handelsroute reagierte, wenn die andere auf diese oder jene Art gestört bzw. begünstigt wurde. Bereits aus der zwei-

---

[82] E. HARDER, Seehandel zwischen Lübeck und Rußland, a.a.O., S. 35; dadurch wurde etwa 5 % des Handelsumsatzes gedeckt. Die Verfasserin erhöht mit Recht den Prozentsatz für die älteren Handelsbeziehungen, weil sie den Anteil des Landweges an dem Handel ostwärts im 17. Jahrhundert für höher hält als in dem folgenden Jahrhundert.

[83] Aufschlußreich ist ein Vergleich des Umfangs der durch den Öresund gehenden Warenmengen mit jenen, die man auf dem Landwege transportierte. Wenn

24

ten Hälfte des 16. Jahrhunderts ist aus der russischen Geschichte bekannt, daß der Zar den binnenländischen Transithandel immer dort und zu der Zeit unterstützte, wo die Handelsverbindung zu den Ostseehäfen gestört oder abgeschnitten war[84]. Eine große Zahl anregender Parallelen bietet der Forschung die Zeit des Dreißigjährigen Krieges. Als die ersten Jahre des Krieges die Handelswege in Zentraleuropa unsicher machten, stieg die Durchfuhr westwärts im Sund ganz erheblich[85]. Zu der gleichen Zeit sprach man in Polen von dem Verfall des Ost-West-Handels auf dem Landwege[86]. Ob damit auch die aus gleicher Zeit nachweisbaren Verschiebungen des Mogilevsker Handels zugunsten der Ostseehäfen und die Vernachlässigung des Handels über Poznań (Posen) zusammenhängt[87]? In der Zeit um 1630, als die kaiserliche und dann die schwedische Handelspolitik den Ostseehandel zeitweilig erschwerten[88], stieg die Durchfuhr auf dem Landwege durch Wrocław (Breslau)[89]. Einer-

der durchschnittliche Wert des jährlichen Exports aus Polen gegen Ende des 16. Jahrhunderts zwischen 3 und 6 Millionen Gulden und während der ersten Hälfte des 17. Jahrhunderts der Ostsee-Import nach Polen auf durchschnittlich 10 Millionen jährlich geschätzt wird, machte der jährliche Import nach Kraków (Krakau) aus Schlesien während derselben Zeit 2,5 Millionen aus. Vgl. R. RYBARSKI, Handel i Polityka handlowa, a.a.O., I., S. 247 f.; A. SZELĄGOWSKI, Pieniądz i przewrót cen w XVI i XVII wieku w Polsce (Geld und die Preisrevolution im 16. und 17. Jahrhundert in Polen), Lwów 1902, S. 126 f.; H. WOLAŃSKI, Związki Śląska, a.a.O., S. 289 ff. Wir dürfen also die beiden Handelswege als vergleichbar und ihre eventuellen Zusammenhänge als wesentlich betrachten. Ihr Zusammenhang wird auch von C. H. WILSON vorausgesetzt, daß nämlich ein Finanzausgleich zwischen Ost und West schneller auf dem Landwege zu verwirklichen war, so daß die Bezahlung schneller geschehen konnte als die Lieferung der Ware auf dem Seewege; vgl. English foreign trade, a.a.O., S. 162.
[84]) A. WAWRZYŃCZYK, Studia z dziejów handlu Polski, a.a.O., S. 17 f.
[85]) Vgl. M. HROCH, Obchod mezi východní a západní Evropou v období počátků kapitalsmu (Der Handel zwischen Ost- und Westeuropa im Zeitalter des Frühkapitalismus), Československý časopis historický XI., 1963, S. 480 ff. (besonders die Tafeln im Anhang); DERSELBE, Obchod a politika za třicetileté války (Handel und Politik im Dreißigjährigen Kriege), Sborník historický 12., 1964, S. 222 ff.
[86]) A. PROCHASKA, Protest kopców wileńskich, a.a.O., S. 436 ff.
[87]) A. WAWRCZYŃCZYK, Studia z dziejów handlu Polski, a.a.O., S. 74 f.
[88]) M. HROCH, Obchod a politika za třicetileté války 234 ff.
[89]) M. WOLAŃSKI, Związki handlowe Śląska, a.a.O., S. 267. Eine Parallelerscheinung finden wir in Hamburg, wo sich während der zwanziger Jahre die Erträge aus dem Zoll fast verdoppelt haben; vom Jahresdurchschnitt 1611—20 von etwa 485 000 rtl. auf 817 000 während der Jahre 1621—25 und 842 000 in den Jahren 1626—30; berechnet nach F. VOIGT, Der Haushalt der Stadt Hamburg 1601 bis 1650, Hamburg 1916, S. 7 ff.

Die Rolle des zentraleuropäischen Handels 25

seits sind es Felle aus dem Osten, andererseits westeuropäische Tücher, deren Durchfuhr hier gerade 1629 ihren Höhepunkt erreichte und in der Quantität mit der gesamten Durchfuhr durch den Sund verglichen werden kann[90]. Der schwedische Krieg in Deutschland, die Krise des Leipziger Handels, wie ganz allgemein des Handels der deutschen Städte waren dann wieder von einer steigenden Durchfuhr im Sund begleitet[91]. Die hier angeführte Parallele, die man natürlich noch weit ausführlicher darlegen könnte, ist zu auffallend, um in das Reich des Zufälligen verwiesen zu werden.

## VI.

Fassen wir zusammen. Als unhaltbar hat sich die Vermutung erwiesen, daß es vor dem Jahre 1700 die osteuropäischen Kaufleute selbst waren, die die Wechsel, mit denen die baltische Handelsbilanz teilweise ausgeglichen wurde, nach Mitteleuropa gebracht haben. Ebenso unhaltbar ist die Annahme, daß diese Transaktionen überwiegend in Leipzig stattfanden und daß für die Wechsel dort oder anderswo nur westeuropäische Ware gekauft wurde. Dagegen konnten wir Zusammenhänge zwischen dem Ostseehandel und dem Ost-

---

[90]) M. WOLAŃSKI, Związki handlowe Śląska, a.a.O., S. 289. In Wrocław (Breslau) waren 1629 27 000 St. verzollt, während der Jahresdurchschnitt 13 000 betrug; durch Öresund wurden 1629 26 000 St. gebracht, Jahresdurchschnitt der Jahre 1620—1640: etwa 69 000 St.; berechnet nach den Angaben von R. W. K. HINTON, Eastland Trade, a.a.O., S. 227 f. Dieser Entwicklung entsprechen auch die Schwankungen des englischen Tuchexports nach Mitteleuropa (d. h. außer der Durchfuhr durch Öresund); am Anfang der zwanziger Jahre ist der Umfang stark gesunken, gegen Ende der zwanziger Jahre wieder gestiegen; noch markanter ist der Aufstieg des Exports in die Niederlande im Jahre 1628:

| Export im Jahre | 1606 | 1620 | 1622 | 1628 | 1632 |
|---|---|---|---|---|---|
| ins Reich: | 65 166 | 22 336 | 23 668 | 30 865 | 23 053 |
| in die Niederlande: | 36 170 | 35 716 | 26 518 | 65 597 | 36 425 |

— nach B. E. SUPPLE, Commercial Crisis and Change in England 1600—1642. A. Study in the Instability of a Mercantile Economy, Cambridge 1959, S. 262.

[91]) P. JEANNIN, Les comptes du Sund comme source pour la construction d'indices généraux de l'activité économique en Europe, XVIe—XVIIIe siècles, Revue historique 231., 1964, bes. S. 316 ff.; M. HROCH, Obchod mezi východní a západní, Evropou, a.a.O., S. 489 ff.; zur Konsolidierung des Handels an der Ostsee vgl. K. R. MELANDER, Die Beziehungen Lübecks zu Schweden und Verhandlungen dieser beiden Staaten wegen des russischen Handels 1643—1653, Historiallinen Arkisto XVIII., 1903, S. 9; zur Krise in Leipzig E. HASSE, Geschichte der Leipziger Messe, a.a.O., S. 113.

West-Transport auf dem Landwege nachweisen, wenn auch nicht
für alle Handelswege und nicht für alle Warengattungen. Schon
jetzt können wir sagen, daß sich der Weg über Lviv (Lemberg) von
allen anderen in vieler Hinsicht unterschied. Ferner ist die Ansicht
gerechtfertigt, daß die Bilanzdifferenz an der Ostsee zum Teil
durch Import auf dem Landwege nach Osteuropa ausgeglichen
war. Zu unterstreichen wäre hier, daß dieser Ausgleich nicht unbe-
dingt durch westeuropäische, sondern auch durch mitteleuropäische
Waren (und vielleicht sogar überwiegend durch diese) geschah. Der
Import konnte durch die Wechsel aus dem Ostseehandel gedeckt
werden, also auch im Rahmen eines Multilateralhandels.

Als eine offene Frage ist die Handelsbilanz auf den einzelnen
Handelswegen Zentraleuropas wie auch in den einzelnen Handelszentren in den Vordergrund getreten. Ihre Klärung erfordert noch
eine Reihe von Detailuntersuchungen. Auf dem hier eingeschlage-
nen Wege könnten aber auch weitere Probleme des europäischen
Handels neu beleuchtet werden. So zum Beispiel die Absatzkrise
des englischen Tuches um 1620, die oft mit der (gleichzeitigen) Krise
in Polen in Zusammenhang gebracht wird. Hier könnte der Hinweis auf die Möglichkeit, bzw. Unmöglichkeit der Deckung des
Festlandimports durch Wechsel manches klären[92]. Es ist ferner zu
fragen, welche Bedeutung die hier umrissenen Bilanzprobleme für
die Rentabilität des Handels besitzen, denn eine passive Bilanz bedeutet nicht eine passive Rentabilität, kümmerliche Handelsge-
winne des einzelnen Kaufmanns.

Aus der Analyse eines der hier vorgetragenen Aspekte der ost-
und ostmitteleuropäischen Handelsbilanz ergibt sich, daß auch dort,
wo der Handel auf kürzeren Strecken verlief, wie z. B. zwischen
Schlesien und Polen oder Breslau und den polnischen Städten (d. h.
wo die Entfernung zwischen dem Ort der Produktion und des
Konsums den zentraleuropäischen Rahmen nicht überschritt) ge-
samteuropäische Zusammenhänge beachtet werden müssen.

---

[92]) J. D. GOULD, The Trade Depression, a.a.O., S. 81 ff.; R. W. K. HINTON,
The Mercantile System in the Time of Thomas Mun, Econ. Hist. Review 2. Ser.,
VII., 1955, S. 277 ff.; B. E. SUPPLE, Currency and Commerce in the Early Seventeenth Century, Econ. Hist. Review 2. Ser., X., 1957, S. 239 ff.; DERSELBE, Commercial Crisis, a.a.O., 85 f. u. 89 ff.; A. SZELĄGOWSKI, Pieniądz i przewrót cen,
a.a.O., S. 192 ff.

Der Versuch, den zentraleuropäischen Handel in die europäischen
Handelsbeziehungen einzureihen, zeigte zugleich, daß wir — wenn
wir innerhalb des zentraleuropäischen Raumes differenzieren wollen — uns vor einer Verabsolutierung und Überschätzung der
Trennung in einen östlichen und westlichen Teil dieses Raumes
hüten sollten. Der Unterschied zwischen Süd und Nord scheint in
der behandelten Zeit — wenn auch auf Grund anderer Kriterien —
sehr wesentlich zu sein. Für die verfolgten Beziehungen zu Osteuropa war das nördliche Gebiet Zentraleuropas von erstrangiger
Bedeutung. Der südliche, das heißt der ungarisch-österreichische
Zweig des Handels, blieb im Zusammenhang mit unserer Fragestellung unberücksichtigt. Vielleicht darf hier die Parallele mit dem
Handelswege über Lviv (Lemberg) gezogen werden. Wenn uns die
hier verfolgten Handelsbeziehungen zu Osteuropa vor allem in die
nördlicheren zentraleuropäischen Städte führten — wie z. B. Leipzig, Wrocław (Breslau) oder Poznań (Posen) —, dann würde uns
die Berücksichtigung des südlichen Handelsweges und seiner Beziehung zu Ostmitteleuropa weiter nach Frankfurt/M. oder Nürnberg
führen, wo vielleicht die Schaltstelle der Verbindung beider Haupt-
zweige des Ost-West-Handels durch Mitteleuropa zu suchen wäre.
Auch wenn künftige Forschungen die hier aufgezeigten Zusammenhänge nicht im vollen Umfang bestätigen sollten, wird das Ziel,
das wir verfolgt haben, doch erreicht sein: durch das vorgestellte
Modell regionale Mikroanalysen mit neuen Fragen zu versehen.

# XVII

## DIE REZEPTION DER FRANZÖSISCHEN REVOLUTION ALS INDIKATOR DES FORTSCHRITTS?

Die Bedeutung der Französischen Revolution für die Geschichte Europas steht außer Frage. Wenn wir in diesem Beitrag von ihrer Rezeption sprechen, dann denken wir jedoch nicht an die langfristigen Prozesse, sondern an die unmittelbare Wirkung der Revolution während der Jahre 1789 bis 1799.[1] In der reichen Fachliteratur zu diesem Thema wird diese Wirkung zwar sehr unterschiedlich dargestellt, was aber nicht heißen soll, daß eine einfache Typologie unmöglich wäre. Es sind drei Ebenen der Auswirkung und Rezeption typologisch zu unterscheiden, auch wenn sie sich in der Realität überschnitten:

1. Die Ebene der reflektierten Kenntnisse dessen, was im revolutionären Frankreich getan und gedacht wurde; natürlich waren diese Kenntnisse nicht gleichermaßen ausführlich und nicht gleich zutreffend, und die Reflexion konnte sowohl zustimmend als auch ablehnend sein.

2. Die Ebene der Bemühungen, die Ideen und Erfahrungen der Französischen Revolution an der eigenen Realität zu messen und sie weiter zu durchdenken. Dies konnte in der Form politischer Entwürfe, philosophischer Analysen oder wirtschaftlicher Reformpläne geschehen. Diese Ebene der Rezeption war darauf ausgerichtet, einen bürgerlichen Wandel im eigenen Lande theoretisch vorzubereiten, wobei Überlegungen einer gewaltlosen Nachahmung der revolutionären Vorbilder keine Ausnahme bildeten. Man kann hier also von einer theoretisch angewandten Rezeption sprechen.

3. Die Ebene des revolutionären Handelns nach französischem Vorbild: Vorbereitungen revolutionärer Taten und Versuche, durch einen Umsturz das alte Regime abzuschaffen. Die Gewalt spielte hier eine wichtige Rolle; es kam jedoch auch zu gewaltlosen Versuchen, die nicht ohne Erfolg blieben.

Unter der Rezeption wird hier also ein breites Spektrum verstanden, das nicht nur die theoretische Reflexion und die Träume der Sympathisanten, sondern auch zielbewußtes revolutionäres Handeln umfaßt.

Es bedarf wohl keiner besonderen Begründung zu konstatieren, daß der erste Typus — die reflektierten Kenntnisse — in allen europäischen Ländern am häufigsten zu finden war. Natürlich konnten sich die Kenntnisse in jenen Ländern reibungsloser und auch unverzerrt verbreiten, wo die Zensur abgeschafft war

---

[1]  Unter den zahlreichen Neuerscheinungen, die der Rezeption der Großen Französischen Revolution gewidmet sind, fehlen leider komparative Analysen aus europäischer Sicht. Infolgedessen sind wir weiterhin auf die „klassischen" Arbeiten angewiesen, in denen jedoch der komparative Ansatz nur schwach vertreten ist wie bei *Sorel*, Albert: L'Europe et la Révolution française. 8 Bde. Paris 1886. — *Godechot*, Jacques: La Grande Nation. L'expansion révolutionnaire de la France dans le Monde 1789-1799. 2 Bde. Paris 1956. — Im vorliegenden Beitrag werden Resultate eines bescheidenen vergleichenden Versuchs des Verfassers zusammengefaßt. Vgl. *Hroch*, Miroslav / *Kubišová*, Vlasta: Velká revoluce a Evropa [Die Große Revolution und Europa]. Praha 1990.

186

(England und Dänemark), so daß die Informationen einen breiten Kreis der Gebildeten und vielleicht auch Mittelschichten erreichten. Auch der Gedankenaustausch zum Thema Revolution wurde dadurch erleichtert. Die Informationen wurden unterschiedlich ausgewertet. In diese Ebene der Rezeption gehören auch die Kritiker der französischen Ereignisse wie zum Beispiel Edmund Burke.

Die Ebene der angewandten Rezeption hat sich nicht allgemein durchgesetzt. Außerdem standen in verschiedenen Ländern andere Probleme im Vordergrund. So wurde in den englischen Korrespondierenden Gesellschaften vor allem das demokratische Prinzip der Großen Revolution und ihre Kirchenpolitik rezipiert. Unter den deutschen Anhängern der Revolution, die jedoch nicht besonders zahlreich waren, betonte man vor allem die Bürgerfreiheit, das Ideal der konstitutionellen Monarchie und die Bauernbefreiung. In Norditalien waren es der konstitutionelle Republikanismus, die bürgerlichen Freiheiten und die nationale Einheit. In Polen war die Rezeption überwiegend auf den Konstitutionalismus beschränkt, die Ideen der Demokratie wurden weniger, die der Bauernbefreiung fast gar nicht rezipiert. In Irland standen die religiöse Freiheit und die nationale Unabhängigkeit im Vordergrund. — Außerdem war überall das Problem der Gewalt im Gespräch. — Die Meinungen waren natürlich gespalten, aber es zeichnete sich ein deutlicher Unterschied zwischen den Ländern ab, in denen die Gewaltanwendung eher inspirierend wirkte (Italien, Irland, Polen), und Ländern, in denen sie eher abschreckte (deutsche Länder, Dänemark, Niederlande).

Damit kommen wir zur dritten Ebene der Rezeption — zu den Versuchen, den revolutionären Umsturz im eigenen Land durchzuführen. Dies gelang im engeren Sinne des Wortes nur in ganz wenigen europäischen Gebieten: in Italien, Belgien und im Rheinland. Hier fanden die revolutionären Veränderungen unter direkter Schirmherrschaft der französischen Armeen statt. Indirekt wurden sie auch in anderen Ländern durch militärische Drohungen ermöglicht: so in der Schweiz und in den Niederlanden, wo der Wandel sogar ohne Gewaltanwendung möglich war.

Außerhalb des Einflußbereiches der französischen Armeen sind uns Versuche direkter Nachahmung nur in zwei Randfällen bekannt. Dies war zum einen in England der Fall, wo jedoch die Frage der Wahlreform alles überschattete, so daß sich die direkte Nachahmung der Revolution meistens in äußeren Formen des Sitzungs- und Rederituals zeigte. Es war zum anderen in Wien und einigen wenigen anderen Städten der Fall, wo isolierte Enthusiasten verzweifelt an Aufstandsplänen bastelten.

Ganz auffallend sind die Unterschiede der positiven Rezeption, wenn wir nach Zahlen fragen. Zu den Idealen der Revolution bekannten sich immer nur Minderheiten einer Bevölkerung. Die absoluten Zahlen ermöglichen jedoch eine überzeugende Differenzierung der quantitativen Seite der Rezeption. Wir beschränken uns hier auf einige besonders wichtige Zahlenangaben.

Während sich im deutschen Rheingebiet an den Wahlen im Jahre 1793 nur einige Tausende beteiligten, waren es bei ähnlichen Gelegenheiten vier Jahre später in der vergleichbar großen Cisalpinischen Republik Zehntausende von Wählern. Während in Deutschland die republikanischen Jakobiner verzweifelte Einzelgänger waren, sprachen sich in den sogenannten Primarversammlungen in der Cisalpinischen Republik 70 000 für die Republik aus. In der kleinen Ligurischen Republik stimmten etwa 100 000 für die republikanische Verfassung.[2] Auch an den Abstimmungen und Wahlen in den Niederlanden, genauer gesagt in der Batavischen Republik, beteiligten sich Zehntausende von Bürgern.[3] An den großen Protestversammlungen der Londoner Corresponding Society nahmen nach nüchternen Angaben Tausende, nach enthusiastischen Angaben sogar Zehntausende teil.[4] Verglichen damit beschränkte sich die Anzahl der Revolutionäre in Rom und insbesondere in Neapel auf Hunderte, ebenso übrigens in der frankophonen Schweiz und in Polen.[5] In den deutschen, schweizerischen, österreichischen und spanischen Städten zählte man nur einige Dutzend Revolutionäre. Wie sollen diese deutlichen Unterschiede in der Intensität der Rezeption verstanden werden?

Wir dürfen davon ausgehen, daß die Rezeption der Französischen Revolution keine automatische Notwendigkeit war, und um so weniger kann sie als eine allgemeine „Gesetzmäßigkeit" bezeichnet werden. Das „Volk", daß sich automatisch für die Revolution begeistert oder durch sie inspiriert wird, gehört sicher in das mythologische Arsenal vergangener Zeiten. Es wäre jedoch ein Irrtum, wenn wir das Problem in die Sphäre des rein Zufälligen und Unberechenbaren verweisen würden. Die unterschiedliche Intensität und Qualität der Rezeption ist rational interpretierbar.

Was waren die entscheidenden Umstände und Faktoren, durch die das Vordringen der revolutionären Ideen beschleunigt bzw. verhindert wurde?

An erster Stelle soll der Faktor Kommunikation untersucht werden. Man mußte selbstverständlich von der Revolution etwas wissen, um reagieren zu können. Die Verbreitung der Informationen stieß jedoch auf mehrere Hindernisse. Vor allem war es die staatliche Kontrolle. Allgemein bekannt sind die Beschränkungen der Information durch die Behörden, durch einseitige Manipulation oder einfach durch Nachrichtensperren.

Es hing von der Einstellung der jeweiligen Regierungen ab, wie streng die Vorschriften formuliert wurden, aber die eigentliche Effektivität dieser Beschränkungen war auch durch die Leistungsfähigkeit und die Wirkungsmöglichkeiten des Polizeiapparates bedingt. Es war, um ein extremes Beispiel zu nennen, im Reich unmöglich, alle Grenzen der zahlreichen Fürstentümer zu kontrollieren. Die Reichsgrenze war ebenso porös wie das politische Leben des Reiches. Ähnlich war es in Polen. Anders war die Lage an den Grenzen der Habsburgermonarchie, Spaniens oder Rußlands.[6] Auch diejenigen Regierungen bzw. Höfe, die am

---

2  *Candeloro*, Giorgio: Storia dell'Italia moderna. Bd. 1: Le origini del Risorgimento. 3. Aufl. Milano 1961, Kap. III, 2-3.

3  *Lademacher*, Horst: Geschichte der Niederlande. Darmstadt 1983.

4  *Royle*, Edward / *Walwyn*, James: English Radicals and Reformers 1760-1848. Brighton 1982, 48 ff. — Vgl. ausführlicher *Goodwin*, Albert: The Friends of Liberty: the English Democratic Movement in the Age of the French Revolution. London 1979.

5  *Candeloro*: Storia, 251 ff. — Handbuch der Schweizer Geschichte. Bd. 2. Zürich 1977, 87 ff. — Anders gesehen bei *Bonjour*, Edgar: Geschichte der Schweizerischen Neutralität. Bd. 1. 2. Aufl. Basel 1965, Kap. 5. — Für Polen immer noch grundlegend *Leśnodorski*, Bogusław: Polscy jakobini. Karta z dziejów insurekcji 1794 r. [Polnische Jakobiner. Bild aus der Geschichte des Aufstandes von 1794]. Warszawa 1960, 164 ff. zu Wilna (Vilnius) und 395 ff. zu Warschau (Warszawa).

6  *Hroch*, Miroslav: Manipulierte Information und die gegenrevolutionäre Propaganda des alten Regimes. Saarbrücken 1989, 53 ff.

188

Anfang der Revolution zurückhaltend waren und die Kommunikation tolerierten, schwenkten mit der Zeit, besonders nach 1793, auf die Seite der erbitterten Abgrenzung um.

Es bestand jedoch auch eine andere Art von Kommunikationshindernissen, die relativ unabhängig vom staatlichen Apparat wirkten. Vor allem die Bildungsbarriere gehörte in diese Kategorie: Die Alphabetisierung der Volksschichten hatte — wenn überhaupt — erst begonnen, aber auch die Bildung der schon einigermaßen lesekundigen Mittelschicht war in den meisten Ländern immer noch an der Erziehung eines frommen, gehorsamen Untertanen orientiert. Die sprachlichen Kenntnisse bzw. Unkenntnisse vergrößerten den Abstand zu den authentischen Informationen und dadurch auch zur Revolution. Eine elementare Barriere war durch die geographische Lage bedingt: Die abseits liegenden und entfernteren Regionen waren zu einem niedrigeren Informationsstand verurteilt.

Wenn wir alle diese Kommunikationsfaktoren einbeziehen, können wir zwei Extremsituationen konstruieren: Einerseits die der optimalen Informationsmöglichkeiten, die es für die Mittelschichten in Belgien, in der frankophonen Schweiz und in England gab; andererseits der Zustand einer absoluten Informationslosigkeit in weiten Teilen von Spanien, Rußland, des Balkans, aber auch in vielen Gebieten Deutschlands und der Habsburgermonarchie.

Die günstigsten Bedingungen für die Verbreitung der revolutionären Ideen waren dort gegeben, wo die französischen Revolutionsarmeen siegreich durchgedrungen waren. Hier hat man die Informationen über die revolutionären Ereignisse und Ziele nicht unterdrückt, sondern im Gegenteil gefördert und propagiert. Trotzdem zeigt uns die empirische Forschung, daß diese Gleichung nicht stimmt. Mit Hilfe der französischen Armeen konnten zwar die einheimischen Anhänger der Revolution das alte Regime abschaffen, aber die Mentalität der Volks- und Mittelschichten wandelte sich nur langsam — in Italien schneller als in Deutschland oder der Schweiz. Auch dort, wo zuerst eine starke profranzösische Stimmung vorhanden war — wie eben in Italien —, wandten sich nach den ersten Erfahrungen mit der französischen Ausbeutung und Überheblichkeit immer mehr Bürger von den revolutionären Idealen ab.[7] Der unmittelbare Kontakt mit den französischen Revolutionsarmeen führte also nicht automatisch zur positiven Rezeption der revolutionären Programme in der Bevölkerung des betreffenden Landes.

Die Rezeption wurde nicht nur durch den einfachen Informationsstrom, sondern auch durch die gegenrevolutionäre Propaganda modifiziert. Diese Propaganda war — verglichen mit der revolutionären Propaganda —insofern in einer günstigeren Lage, als sie mit staatlicher und kirchlicher Unterstützung rechnen konnte. Sie gewann damit noch einen wichtigen Vorteil. Die revolutionäre Propaganda mußte große Entfernung (mit Ausnahme der französisch besetzten Gebiete) überbrücken, das heißt sie mußte vor allem mit dem geschriebenen Wort arbeiten. Ihre Wirkung war daher auf die Vermittlung eines lesekundigen, gebildeten Publikums angewiesen. Die gegenrevolutionäre Propaganda konnte dagegen das ganze traditionelle Kommunikationssystem des alten Regimes ausnutzen, vor allem also die mündlich vermittelte Kommunikation. Kirche und Schule spielten dabei eine zentrale Rolle. Durch Predigt und den religiös geprägten Unterricht

---

7  *Candeloro:* Storia, 265 ff.

gelangte das negative Bild der Revolution als glaubwürdige Information in die breiten Volksschichten.[8] Es ist in diesem Zusammenhang charakteristisch, daß die revolutionäre Propaganda vor allem dort in breitere Bevölkerungsschichten eindringen konnte, wo die Umstände es den Revolutionären erlaubten, mündliche Propaganda zu betreiben, d. h. legal zu wirken. Dadurch können wir die Erfolge der Rezeption in England, in Lüttich und in Warschau erklären. Damit soll jedoch nicht gesagt werden, daß die Möglichkeit der direkten Agitation schon eine Garantie für den Erfolg darstellte.

An dieser Stelle sollten wir vielleicht eine erste Bilanz ziehen. Notwendige Bedingungen für die positive Rezeption der Französischen Revolution waren: ein starker und unverzerrter Informationsfluß, ein tolerantes Regierungssystem und ein bestimmtes Bildungsniveau der Mittelschichten sowie positive Erfahrungen mit den französischen Armeen. Ungünstig für die Rezeption wirkten Informationssperren bzw. verzerrte Informationen, die politische Verfolgung aller Gegner, ein niedriges Bildungsniveau und negative Erfahrungen mit der französischen Besatzung. Wenn wir diese Elemente als ausreichend für ein Erklärungsmodell der Rezeption betrachteten, dann könnten wir an dieser Stelle abbrechen und konstatieren: Je größer die Toleranz der Regierung und je höher die Bildung, desto aktiver die Rezeption und Nachahmung der Ideen und Maßnahmen der Großen Revolution. Ein solches Modell erweist sich jedoch als allzu einfach und vor allem als realitätsfremd.

In Ländern mit ungefähr gleich starker Verbreitung der günstigen Faktoren, wie zum Beispiel England und Dänemark oder die Niederlande und das deutsche Rheingebiet, war die Rezeption prinzipiell unterschiedlich. Die oben erwähnten Faktoren sind daher als Bedingungen, nicht als Ursachen zu verstehen. Ein gewisser Umfang an Informationen und eine elementare Kommunikation bildete eine grundlegende Bedingung für eventuelle Rezeptionen. Analog können wir auch die Rolle der Bildung einstufen. Die Rolle der politischen Unterdrückung war jedoch nicht eindeutig. Sie hatte unterschiedliche Folgen, beispielsweise in den habsburgischen Ländern und in Italien. Auch die geographische Entfernung darf nicht verabsolutiert werden: Man braucht nur auf die Unterschiede in der Rezeption in den deutschen Ländern und in dem viel weiter entfernten Polen hinzuweisen.

Bevor wir nach weiteren Elementen fragen, soll noch konstatiert werden, daß sich die Unterschiede zwischen verschiedenen Ländern nicht nur in der Quantität der positiven Rezeption zeigten, sondern auch in der Abstufung des Radikalismus. Den starken Jakobinismus und Republikanismus unter den italienischen Anhängern der Revolution kann man kaum mit dem Hinweis auf höhere Bildung und stärkere Kommunikation erklären. Das gleiche gilt für den irischen Radikalismus. Wenig Möglichkeiten bietet uns dieses Modell auch bei der Frage, warum die meisten deutschen und dänischen frühen Anhänger der Revolution ihre Einstellung nach dem Sieg der Republik 1792 änderten, während die Rezeption des Jakobinismus in Polen, und nicht nur in Italien, relativ stark war.

---

8 Eine ähnliche Rolle spielte in England die Abschreckungskampagne gegen die Sympathisanten der Revolution, vgl. *Royle / Walwyn: English Radicals*, 60 ff.

Das Modell soll also wesentlich modifiziert werden. In der bisherigen Fachliteratur hat man sich über dieses Problem meistens wenig Gedanken gemacht. Man begnügte sich angesichts der ungleichen Rezeption mit einem Hinweis auf die ungleichmäßige gesamtgesellschaftliche Entwicklung der einzelnen europäischen Länder. Die rückständigeren Länder konnten einfach die Revolution nicht begreifen, während die höher entwickelten mitgemacht haben. Diese Erklärung reicht aus, wenn wir nur die ganz groben Gegenpole sehen: England und Belgien auf der einen, den Balkan oder Rußland auf der anderen Seite. Sie versagt jedoch völlig, wenn wir die unterschiedliche Rezeption in Deutschland, Italien, Polen, Irland oder Skandinavien betrachten.

Die aktive Rezeption im rückständigen Polen steht im Gegensatz zur schwachen Aufnahme in den sicherlich höher entwickelten deutschen Staaten oder in Dänemark. In Italien finden wir Revolutionäre ebenso im reichen Mailand wie im unterentwickelten Piemont, viel seltener aber in der reichen Toskana. Im fortschrittlicheren Belgien oder in den Niederlanden sollte nach dieser Vorstellung die Aufnahme der Revolution aktiver erfolgt sein als im weniger entwickelten Sachsen oder in Schlesien. In der Realität war es jedoch genau umgekehrt. Wir könnten noch weitere Beispiele aufzählen, aber schon jetzt scheint klar zu sein, daß die Rezeption nicht auf eine hochentwickelte Gesellschaft beschränkt blieb.

Ergänzend soll noch eine paradoxe Rückkoppelung dieser Korrelation zwischen Rückständigkeit und Rezeption erwähnt werden. Die Intensität der Revolutionsrezeption wurde in der zeitgenössischen Geschichtsschreibung manchmal zu einem Kriterium der „progressiven" Entwicklung hochgetrieben. Deswegen unternahmen manche Historiker krampfhafte Versuche, die Rezeption in ihrem eigenen Land so stark wie möglich darzustellen. Den letzten Anstoß zu solch wettkampfähnlichen Bemühungen gab die 200-Jahr-Feier der Französischen Revolution. Dies konnte zu einer markanten Inversion führen, wie wir sie in der Forschung zur Rezeption in Rußland finden. Die ältere französische Forschung hat mit Selbstverständlichkeit konstatiert, daß die Revolution in Rußland keine Wirkung haben konnte, weil Rußland ein rückständiges Land war. Als dann in den fünfziger Jahren der sowjetische Historiker Michail M. Štrange ziemlich reiche und überzeugende Angaben über die reflektierende Rezeption der Revolution in Rußland fand, hat er darin einen Beweis gesehen, daß die bürgerliche Einschätzung Rußlands als die eines rückständigen Staates falsch war.[9]

Den Zusammenhang zwischen der Rezeption und der Ungleichmäßigkeit der Entwicklung sollten wir jedoch nicht restlos ablehnen. Es war sicherlich kein entscheidender Zusammenhang, aber unter den Elementen der multikausalen Erklärung unseres Problems sollte er nicht fehlen. Dabei wird man auch konkretisieren müssen, in welchem Bereich wir diese Ungleichmäßigkeit beobachten. Eine Rückständigkeit des politischen Systems war nämlich in jener Zeit mit wirtschaftlichem Wachstum voll vereinbar — und auch umgekehrt. So können wir z. B. beobachten, daß die gebildeten Schichten, die schon eine gewisse Erfahrung mit dem politischen Leben der ständischen Gesellschaft besaßen — wie es in Polen der Fall war —, stärker zur positiven Rezeption der Französischen Revolution neigten als gebildete Schichten, die unter absolutistischer Herrschaft keine

---

9  *Štrange*, Michail Michailovič: Russkoje obščestvo i Francuzskaja revoljucija 1789-1799 [Die russische Gesellschaft und die Französische Revolution 1789-1799]. Moskva 1956.

politische Erfahrung gewinnen konnten, so im Fall Deutschlands. Auch hier bewegen wir uns jedoch mehr in dem Bereich der historischen Möglichkeiten, also der Bedingungen der Rezeption.

Wenn wir bei der kausalen Analyse weiterkommen wollen, müssen wir stärker den inneren Zustand der einzelnen Länder berücksichtigen. Es handelt sich vor allem um eine Gegenüberstellung der Ideale und Programme der Revolution einerseits und der inneren Konflikte des jeweiligen „rezipierenden" Landes andererseits. Es soll also komparativ geprüft werden, wo die revolutionären Ideale und Programme mit den aktuellen politischen und sozialen Problemen und Spannungen einzelner Länder bei einigen der sie bewohnenden sozialen Gruppen oder Klassen „resonierten". Dort, wo es der Fall war, daß ein Teil der Bevölkerung den Eindruck hatte, daß die Ziele und Forderungen der Franzosen den eigenen Interessen und Zielen entsprachen, erreichte die Revolution eine breitere Rezeption. Diese „Resonanz" wird hier im weitesten Sinne verstanden. Es konnte sich bei den inneren Problemen und Spannungen ebenso um grundlegende Antagonismen wie um marginale Interessengegensätze handeln, um politische oder soziale Konflikte etc. Dort, wo solche analogischen, „resonanzfähigen" Konflikte fehlten bzw. wo sie noch nicht politisch artikuliert wurden, war auch die Rezeption schwächer. Diese hypothetische Konstruktion soll im folgenden beispielhaft dargestellt werden.

Das französische Modell der Abschaffung des Feudalismus und der Bauernbefreiung konnte unter den sächsischen oder norditalienischen Bauern mobilisierend wirken,[10] nicht aber unter den schon befreiten Bauern in England oder Belgien. Das demokratische Programm resonierte mit der Wahlreformbewegung in England und fand deswegen dort viele Anhänger unter den Intellektuellen und den Mittelschichten. Das gleiche Programm klang jedoch für einen deutschen oder dänischen Bürger befremdlich und unattraktiv. In England gehörte die Reformbewegung von unten schon seit den siebziger Jahren zur politischen Tradition, nicht aber auf dem Kontinent. So bemühten sich die deutschen Jakobiner vergeblich, wenigstens den Konstitutionalismus zur Waffe gegen den feudalen Absolutismus zu machen. Ein Teil ihrer potentiellen Anhänger war nämlich mit dem Absolutismus verbunden und von ihm existentiell abhängig, ein anderer erwartete Fortschritt und Gerechtigkeit von einer weiteren Durchführung der Reformen, deren bewährter Träger ausgerechnet der aufgeklärte Absolutismus war. In den meisten deutschen Staaten fehlte also ein Konflikt, der durch die Parolen und Prinzipien der Französischen Revolution allgemein verständlich artikuliert werden konnte.

Auch dort, wo die Abhängigkeit von den Fürstenhöfen durch die französischen Armeen gebrochen wurde, hat die Mehrzahl der Bürger die konstitutionellen Programme nur zögernd oder überhaupt nicht akzeptiert. Die Tradition des Konstitutionalismus mußte erst allmählich aufgebaut werden. Außerdem spielte die abschreckende Wirkung der französischen Besatzung eine gewisse, aber wohl nicht entscheidende Rolle.

---

10  *Candeloro:* Storia, 174 ff. — *Stulz,* Percy / *Opitz,* Alfred: Volksbewegungen in Kursachsen zur Zeit der Französischen Revolution. Berlin 1956, 48 ff. und 58 ff. — Zu Schlesien: Historia Polski [Geschichte Polens]. Bd. II/2. Warszawa 1958, 49 ff.

Unter diesem Gesichtspunkt ist auch die unterschiedliche, ja entgegengesetzte Entwicklung in Deutschland und England nach 1792 interpretierbar. Die deutschen Sympathisanten lehnten die Republik und das demokratische Programm meistens noch vor dem Sieg der jakobinischen Diktatur ab.[11] Die englischen Corresponding Societies und ihre schottischen Verbündeten sahen weder in der Republik noch in der jakobinischen Verfassung einen Grund für eine Revision ihrer Einstellung zur Revolution. Der Konvent war ja aufgrund des allgemeinen Wahlrechts, das sie selbst so intensiv und ungeduldig anstrebten, entstanden.[12]

Nicht nur im Vergleich zwischen Deutschland und England, auch im Vergleich zwischen Deutschland und Italien bietet uns die Hypothese der „Resonanz" als eines entscheidenden Gliedes der Kausalanalyse den Weg zur Erklärung. Im Unterschied zu Deutschland waren die positiven Erfahrungen der italienischen Intellektuellen und auch der politisch denkenden Bürger mit Reformen im Geist des aufgeklärten Absolutismus praktisch auf die Toskana beschränkt. In den meisten anderen Staaten Nord- und Mittelitaliens verschärfte sich der Konflikt zwischen Herrschern und Anhängern der Reformen. Natürlich fanden letztere die Bestätigung ihrer Ideen in den Nachrichten aus dem revolutionären Frankreich. Zudem muß man noch in Betracht ziehen, daß die Herrscher zu ausländischen Dynastien gehörten, so daß der Kampf um politische und soziale Reformen auch einen immer deutlicheren nationalen Unterton bekam. Auch die kulturellen Bestrebungen trugen, in viel höherem Maß als in den deutschen Ländern, eine nationale Komponente in sich. Nur so kann man verstehen, daß die italienischen „Patrioten" republikanisch dachten und bereit waren, mit den Jakobinern zusammenzuarbeiten, und später dann die französischen Armeen als Befreier begrüßten.

Damit kommen wir zu einem weiteren wichtigen Bereich der Resonanz: der nationalen Idee. Nicht nur nach Italien, sondern auch nach Belgien, Polen und Irland kamen die Informationen aus dem revolutionären Frankreich ausgerechnet in einer Zeit, als in diesen Ländern der Kampf gegen die Fremdherrschaft aktuell wurde. Die Fremdherrschaft war in jedem dieser Länder durch völlig unterschiedliche soziale und politische Formationen repräsentiert: Für Irland war es das parlamentarisch regierte England, für Belgien der josephinische aufgeklärte Absolutismus, für Polen das zaristische Rußland. Der gemeinsame Nenner war jedoch in allen Fällen die Eigenständigkeit, die in verschiedenen Losungen artikuliert wurde. Nicht nur in Norditalien, sondern auch in anderen Ländern war es wichtig, daß die Resonanz nicht auf das Nationale beschränkt war. Der nationale Konflikt war immer noch mit wenigstens einem anderen verbunden. In Irland war es der Kampf um religiöse Toleranz, in Polen das konstitutionelle Streben, in Belgien der Kampf um bürgerliche Rechte.[13] Keine dieser durch Frankreich inspirierten nationalen Bewegungen war in den neunziger Jahren erfolgreich, aber die Ursachen ihres Scheiterns können nicht auf das Ausbleiben der

---

11 Vgl. z. B. *Stephan*, Inge: Literarischer Jakobinismus in Deutschland. Stuttgart 1973, 55 f.

12 *Royle / Walwyn:* English Radicals, 59 f. und 66 f. — *Goodwin:* The Friends of Liberty, 283 ff.

13 *Elliott*, Marianne: Partners in Revolution. The United Irishmen and France. London-New York 1982. — *Pirenne*, Henri: Histoire de la Belgique des origines a nos jours. Bd. IV. La révolution Brabançonne et la révolution Liégeoise. Bruxelles 1952, Ndr. 1974. — Für weitere Länder Europas vgl.: Nationalism in the Age of the French Revolution. Hrsg. von Otto *Dann* und John *Dinviddy*. London 1988.

französischen Hilfe reduziert werden, wie es in Irland und Polen der Fall war. Die revolutionären Armeen, die nach Belgien und Italien kamen, haben dort zwar das alte Regime vernichtet und die Bürgerrechte durchgesetzt, aber zugleich den Unabhängigkeitsbestrebungen ein Ende gesetzt — in Belgien sehr früh, in Italien erst in der Napoleonischen Zeit.

Wie sollen diese Beobachtungen ausgewertet werden? Die Rezeption der Französischen Revolution war in jedem europäischen Land von drei Umständen bestimmt:

1. von den allgemeinen Bedingungen, vor allem von den Kommunikationsmöglichkeiten, dem Bildungsstandard der für den Fortschritt relevanten Schichten und dem Ausmaß der staatlichen Toleranz;

2. von der Anwesenheit der französischen Armeen;

3. von der Intensität jener Gegensätze, die in dem jeweiligen Land mit den Konflikten der Revolution resonierten und die durch die Ideen der Revolution artikulierbar waren.

Von diesen drei Faktoren war nur der erste mit dem Grade der Modernisierung, also mit dem „Fortschritt", verbunden. Die Anwesenheit der französischen Armeen spielte eine ambivalente Rolle: Sie durchbrach einerseits die Informationsbarrieren und schuf dadurch Bedingungen für die Rezeption, andererseits aber wirkte sie allzuoft eher abschreckend. Der entscheidende Durchbruch zur Rezeption der revolutionären Ideen war jedoch erst durch ihre „Resonanz" mit den Konflikten des jeweiligen Landes erreichbar.

Die Revolution wurde also in jenen Ländern intensiver akzeptiert, rezipiert, nachgeahmt, wo schon in der vorrevolutionären Zeit Spannungen und Interessengegensätze herrschten — vor allem im Bereich der Bemühungen um die Überwindung des alten Feudalregimes —, die durch die Informationen aus Frankreich politisierbar und aktualisierbar geworden waren: Man konnte die Argumente und zum Teil auch die Maßnahmen der Französischen Revolution übernehmen oder sich wenigstens auf sie berufen.

Der inhaltliche und politische Charakter dieser Gegensätze war unterschiedlich. Die Tatsache, daß es sich um Konflikte mit unterschiedlichem Inhalt handelte, ist für unsere Problemstellung von zweitrangiger Bedeutung. Auch die Programme und Ideale der Französischen Revolution waren mehrschichtig und differenziert.

In einem kurzen Aufsatz kann man sich nicht die Aufgabe stellen, das komplizierte Problem der Rezeption in allen seinen Aspekten zu lösen. Wir konnten nur auf die Möglichkeiten der systematisch angewandten komparativen Methode bei der Untersuchung dieses Phänomens hinweisen. Die einzelnen Kriterien der Komparation können in Zukunft differenzierter angewandt werden, ebenso wie die territoriale Gliederung.[14] Außerdem verfolgte hier die Komparation programmatisch nur das Ziel, die Rolle der Rezeption als der eines Indikators des Fort-

---

14  Dieser Beitrag arbeitet meistens mit allgemein bekannten Tatsachen. Aus diesem Grunde verzichtet der Autor auf ausführliche Literaturhinweise, insbesondere zur deutschen Geschichte und beschränkt sich auf die dem deutschen Fachpublikum weniger geläufigen Angaben.

schritts zu beleuchten und zu entmythologisieren. Ebenso wichtig und auch komparativ analysierbar wäre die hier mit Absicht außer acht gelassene Frage, welche dauerhaften Folgen die Rezeption oder auch die Nichtannahme der Französischen Revolution für die einzelnen Länder hatte.

Um den komparativen Vorgang und seine Resultate übersichtlicher zu machen, ergänze ich diesen Beitrag durch eine stark schematisierte Tabelle, in der die Rolle der einzelnen Elemente verdeutlicht wird.[15]

---

15 Die Tabelle auf der folgenden Seite bringt einen Entwurf, der in grober Vereinfachung als provozierende Inspiration zukünftiger Forschung nützlich sein könnte.

## DIE INTENSITÄT DER REZEPTION DER FRANZÖSISCHEN REVOLUTION NACH LÄNDERN

| EINFLUSSFAKTOREN | hoch.............. | | | | | mittel............ | | | | | gering..... | | |
|---|---|---|---|---|---|---|---|---|---|---|---|---|---|
| | Belgien | Nord-Italien | Polen | Eng-land | Irland | Nieder-lande | Restl. Italien | Rhein. Dtld. | Däne-mark | Restl. Dtld. | Öster-reich | Spa-nien | Ruß-land |
| **BEDINGUNGEN** | | | | | | | | | | | | | |
| Informationen | + | + | + | + | + | + | - | + | + | + | - | - | - |
| Politische Bildung | + | + | + | + | + | + | + | + | + | - | - | - | - |
| Regierungspolitik | - | + | + | + | - | - | - | - | + | - | - | - | - |
| **KONFLIKTE** | | | | | | | | | | | | | |
| Ständische Opposition | + | + | + | - | - | - | + | - | - | - | + | + | - |
| Bauern contra Gutsherren | + | + | - | + | + | - | - | + | + | + | + | + | - |
| Konstitutionalismus | + | + | + | + | + | + | - | - | - | - | - | - | - |
| Gegen Fremdherrschaft | + | + | - | - | + | - | - | - | - | - | - | - | - |
| Anwesenheit der französischen Revolutionsarmeen | + | + | - | - | - | + | + | + | - | + | - | - | - |

Erläuterungen: unter „Informationen" wird die Intensität der objektiven Informationen aus Frankreich verstanden:
+ = relativ gut; - = relativ schlecht
unter „Politischer Bildung" wird vor allem die Bildung der Eliten verstanden
„Regierungspolitik" schließt vor allem die Haltung gegenüber politischen Gegnern (Toleranz) ein:
+ = eher tolerant; - = eher verfolgend
„Konstitutionalismus" umfaßt auch die Bemühungen um die Durchsetzung der Bürgerrechte im jeweiligen Land
+ = stärkere Bewegung vorhanden; - = Bewegung unbedeutend

# XVIII

## ZUR TYPOLOGIE DER EUROPÄISCHEN REVOLUTIONEN.
## EINIGE ÜBERLEGUNGEN ZUR NICHT BESTEHENDEN DISKUSSION

Es gibt wenige Fälle, an denen wir die Interdependenz der Gegenwartser-fahrung mit dem Wandel des Geschichtsbildes besser exemplifizieren könnten, wie im Falle der modernen Revolutionsgeschichte. Die als ein Positivum erlebte oder angestrebte Revolution, verbunden mit den optimistischen Zukunftser-wartungen, wurde auch in eine positive Einschätzung der früheren Revolu-tionen projiziert. Dabei wird nicht nur an profilierte Revolutionäre, wie etwa Karl Marx oder Jean Jaurèz, gedacht, sondern auch an die durchaus bürgerli-chen Historiker, wie etwa Michelet und Aulard[1], oder sogar an Anton Heinrich Springer, den Dozenten der Prager Universität, der 1850 eine Geschichte des „Revolutionszeitalters" publizierte[2]. Selbst der Terminus „Revolution" wird in diesen Fällen als positiver Wert empfunden.

Die Ablehnung der gegenwärtigen Revolution war andererseits mit einer kritischen Einstellung auch gegenüber den Revolutionen der Vergangenheit verbunden. Meistens gesellt sich eine negative Wertung des Begriffs dazu. Na-türlich können die beiden Konnotationen der Revolution gleichzeitig er-scheinen, wobei jedoch eine von ihnen meistens als dominierend vorkam. Unter den gegenwärtigen Zuständen gilt wohl — vor allem in den postkommunisti-schen Ländern — die negative Einschätzung der Revolutionen aller Zeiten als dominierend.

Diese politische und oft auch emotionelle Belastung des Begriffs erschwert jede Forschung, die bemüht ist, unabhängig von den Schwankungen des politi-schen Alltags zu bleiben. Eine solche von der Politik unabhängige Forschung kann zwischen zwei Auswegen wählen. Sie kann den Begriff „Revolution" als eine unbefriedigende Verallgemeinerung aus ihrem wissenschaftlichen Instru-mentarium einfach weglassen und das Wort immer nur im konkreten Kontext und im Vokabular der Zeitgenossen (natürlich auch der jeweiligen zeitbe-

---

[1] *J. Michelet:* Histoire de France. Révolution. Paris 1847—1853; *A. Aulard:* Histoire politique de la Révolution française. Origine et dévelopement de la démocratie et de la République, 1789—1804. Paris 1901.
[2] *A. H. Springer:* Geschichte des Revolutionszeitalters (1789—1848). Prag 1849.

dingten Interpretation) benutzen. Oder diese Forschung kann diesen Begriff von jeder moralisierenden Wertung völlig abstrahieren und versuchen, den Terminus „Revolution" als einen wertfreien, aber doch generalisierenden Terminus technicus zu benutzen. Beide Auswege sind nicht traditionell, dazu der erste noch kaum realisierbar. Daher scheint mir die zweite Variante doch vielversprechend bzw. einer Überprüfung wert.

Als Bedingung einer erfolgreichen Verwendung dieses Vorgangs gilt jedoch vor allem, eine typologische, differenzierende Analyse der Revolutionen zu unternehmen.

Die Typologie der Revolutionen ist keinesfalls einfach. Jede typologische Analyse muß deswegen gewisse methodische Regeln respektieren. Es sind analoge Regeln, die auch für die komparative Methode gelten, weil die Typologie eigentlich eines der möglichen Resultate der Komparation darstellt. Diese Methode verlangt zuerst von uns, drei Fragen an die Objekte der Typologie zu stellen und diese zu beantworten:

1. Das Objekt der Typologie soll definiert werden: Welche historische Realität soll verglichen und typologisch eingestuft werden?

2. Das Kriterium der Typologie muß formuliert werden, denn es gibt keine allgemeine „Typologie an sich", sondern immer nur in bezug darauf, wie die einzelnen Fälle zum Kriterium des Vergleichs bzw. der Typologie stehen.

3. Erst dann kann man nach dem eventuellen Vergleich unterschiedlicher Typen und Situationen fragen (diese Frage wird jedoch in diesem Beitrag nicht gestellt).

Der erste Vorgang — die Definition — aktualisiert den schon erwähnten Zusammenhang mit der ethischen und emotionellen Belastung des Terminus. Die Revolution wird hier also wertfrei — als eine besondere Art der Veränderung der politischen bzw. sozialen Zustände — verstanden werden, wobei es als irrelevant gelten soll, ob diese Veränderung als positiv oder negativ, als „fortschrittlich" oder „reaktionär" eingestuft wird.

Ohne hier die umfangreiche Diskussion darzustellen, möchte ich mich auf die Auffassung beschränken, die in der Revolution einen prinzipiellen, tiefgreifenden, qualitativen Wandel der ganzen politischen oder auch sozialen Systeme und Strukturen brachte bzw. versuchte[3]. Insofern ist die Revolution von der Reform unterschiedlich und auch von den Aufständen, die partielle Ziele verfolgten (wie z. B. die Gesellenunruhen bzw. Bauernaufstände). Je nachdem, wie tief dieser prinzipielle Wandel reichte, je nachdem, welche Bereiche er betraf, unterscheide ich zwei Ebenen des gesellschaftlichen Wandels:

---

[3] Diese Auffassung von der Revolution finden wir schon beim amerikanischen Soziologen *Ch. A. Ellwood:* A psychological theory of revolution. In: The American Journal of Sociology 11. 1905. S. 49 f.

22

1. Die *politische Revolution* als kurzfristige Erscheinung, als einen tiefgreifenden Wandel des politischen Systems, dem dann eventuell auch soziale Änderungen folgten bzw. folgen konnten. 2. Die *soziale Revolution*, die mit einem Wandel des gesamten sozialen und wirtschaftlichen Systems verknüpft war bzw. diesen Wandel eventuell hervorrief[4].

Während die politische Revolution als kurzfristig gilt, d. h. Monate und Jahre dauern konnte, wird die zeitliche Dimension der sozialen Revolution in Jahrzehnten bemessen: Es handelt sich also nicht um eine Revolution im vollen Sinne des Wortes, sondern nur um eine Metapher sui generis; es war ein langfristiger Prozeß des Systemwandels, an dem sich sowohl die politische Revolution, wie auch Reformen verschiedener Art gegenseitig ergänzten, wobei die Kombination von beiden, wie wir noch sehen werden, in verschiedenen Revolutionen unterschiedlich war und als typologisches Kriterium benutzt werden kann. Eigentlich handelt es sich um ein Synonym des Begriffs „Modernisierung" bzw. gesamtgesellschaftliche Transformation.

In diesem Beitrag wird vor allem von der Typologie der politischen Revolutionen die Rede sein, und erst ergänzend wird auch eine Typologie der Modernisierung bzw. der sozialen Revolution vorgestellt.

Die Typologie der politischen Revolutionen kann unter verschiedenen Aspekten bzw. durch Anwendung unterschiedlicher Kriterien der Typologie durchgeführt werden. Vorläufig kann man noch keine alles umfassende, komplexe Typologie zusammenstellen. Wir müssen vorerst mit mehreren unterschiedlichen Typologien der Revolutionen arbeiten, wobei ein und dieselbe Revolution durch die Anwendung unterschiedlicher typologischer Kriterien in unterschiedliche Nachbarschaften mit anderen Revolutionen geraten kann. Mit anderen Worten: jede Revolution kann durch mehrere typologische Zuordnungen charakterisiert werden und ihre Besonderheit wird in der spezifischen Kombination dieser Kriterien ausgedrückt. Es kann sich allerdings um keinen uferlosen „Pluralismus" der Kriterien handeln: Es gibt relevante und weniger relevante Kriterien der Typologie. Die Relevanz dieser Kriterien wird an der Aussagekraft unterschiedlicher typologischer Vorgänge für die Charakteristik der Revolution, für ihre Interpretation gemessen. In diesem Beitrag werde ich sechs solcher Kriterien von unterschiedlicher Relevanz untersuchen.

---

[4] Eine solche Unterscheidung machten mehrere marxistische Autoren der siebziger Jahre, wie z. B. *M. A. Seleznëv:* Social'naja revoljucija (Soziale Revolution). Moskva 1971; *M. Kossok und W. Markow:* Zur Methodologie der vergleichenden Revolutionsgeschichte der Neuzeit. In: *M. Kossok (Hg.):* Studien zur vergleichenden Revolutionsgeschichte 1500—1917. Berlin 1974. S. 1 ff.

ERSTES KRITERIUM: DIE GESELLSCHAFTLICHE SITUATION

An erster Stelle unter den typologischen Kriterien steht das der erreichten Stufe der gesellschaftlichen Entwicklung. Es berücksichtigt die Tatsache, daß Revolutionen unter sehr verschiedenen gesellschaftlichen, politischen und kulturellen Umständen stattfanden. Es handelt sich also um ein
„historizistisches" Kriterium, nur teilweise mit dem chronologischen Ablauf
identisch; denn infolge der ungleichmäßigen Entwicklung konnte es zu Phasenverschiebungen kommen. Als zentrale Frage steht hier, auf welche gesellschaftliche Zustände die Revolution reagierte, gegen welche Beziehungen sie
sich erhob.

Unter diesem Gesichtspunkt können vier Typen der Revolutionen charakterisiert werden:

1. Revolutionen, die sich noch tief unter den Bedingungen der alten, spätfeudalen Gesellschaft und des aufkommenden Absolutismus abspielten und
diese Zustände zu sprengen versuchten, ohne dabei zu unmittelbaren tiefgreifenden Veränderungen der herrschenden sozialen Ordnung zu führen. Als
„typisch" gelten hier die niederländische Revolution des 16. Jahrhunderts und
die englische Revolution von 1640/60. Als Übergangserscheinungen gehören
hierher einerseits die hussitische Revolution und der deutsche Bauernkrieg, andererseits die „Glorreiche Revolution" von 1688/89, die schon Elemente des
zweiten Typus in sich trug.

2. Die „klassischen" antifeudalen bürgerlichen Revolutionen, solche, die den
Weg zur bürgerlichen Gesellschaft öffneten, indem sie sowohl die Bürgerrechte
und den Konstitutionalismus wie auch die Befreiung von feudalen Privilegien
und Eigentumsreglementierungen erreichten bzw. erreichen konnten und
wollten. Als „typisch" stehen hier die Große französische Revolution von 1789,
wie auch ihre Nachahmung in Belgien und Italien, die Revolutionen von 1848
in West-, Mittel- und Südeuropa, die spanischen Revolutionen.

3. Die Revolutionen der ersten Hälfte des 20. Jahrhunderts, die sich gegen
die bürgerliche Gesellschaft und das liberal-demokratische politische System
wandten — also Revolutionen, die als antibürgerlich bezeichnet werden
könnten. Innerhalb dieser antibürgerlichen Gemeinsamkeit muß man jedoch
hier zwei deutlich abgegrenzte Subtypen differenzieren:

— die faschistischen Revolutionen in Italien, Deutschland und Spanien,

— die sozialistischen Revolutionen in Rußland, Ungarn und im Ostmitteleuropa der Nachkriegszeit, wo nicht nur ein neues politisches System, sondern auch eine neue soziale Ordnung eingeführt wurde.

Die beiden Subtypen sind insofern unterschiedlich, als man sie eventuell als
zwei selbständige Typen voneinander trennen könnte.

24

4. Die antiautoritären Revolutionen der Gegenwart, die sich sowohl gegen faschistische wie auch gegen kommunistische Diktaturen wandten und die „Erneuerung" des bürgerlichen, politischen und sozialen Systems beabsichtigten. Diese eindeutige Forderung der Rückkehr zu einem schon früher existierenden System mag gewisse Skepsis gegenüber dem Gebrauch des Terminus Revolution für diese Kategorie der Veränderungen erwecken. Warum spricht man nicht von einer Restauration? Diese Skepsis ist solange berechtigt, bis sich die Folgen, die Resultate dieser Ereignisse voll erkennen und analysieren lassen. Erst mit einem gewissen zeitlichen Abstand wird man beurteilen können, inwieweit es sich um eine einfache „Rückkehr" und inwieweit um ein neues System handelte.

Obwohl manche Fragen in der Anwendung des „historizistischen" Kriteriums noch offen bleiben, steht eines fest: eine komparative Analyse kann vor allem innerhalb der einzelnen Typen erfolgreich durchgeführt werden. Dabei können die weiteren Kriterien der Revolutionstypologie, die wir hier charakterisieren werden, zugleich und ergänzend als Kriterien des Vergleichs innerhalb der einzelnen Typen produktiv benutzt werden.

## ZWEITES KRITERIUM: DIE SUBJEKTIVEN ZIELE DER REVOLUTIONÄRE

Als ein weiteres Kriterium der Revolutionstypologie sollen die subjektiven Ziele der Revolutionäre genannt werden — ihre Vision der Zukunft. Wollten sie ein totales Neuland schaffen, etwas, was hier nie existierte, oder wollten sie etwas erneuern, was sie für gerecht, wertvoll, heilig hielten? Je nachdem, wie die Antwort lautete, können wir zwei grundlegende Revolutionstypen unterscheiden: die innovativen und die restitutiven Revolutionen. Diese Unterscheidung kann allerdings nicht verabsolutiert werden. Es gab keine rein und absolut innovative und keine rein und absolut restitutive Revolution. In jeder Revolution waren beide Aspekte vorhanden, aber doch mit unterschiedlicher Relevanz. Die innovativen Ziele scheinen zwar bei den meisten der ersten drei im Abschnitt über das Kriterium der gesellschaftlichen Entwicklung charakterisierten Typen vorherrschend, aber manchmal mit starken restitutiven Zügen kombiniert. So wollten die aufständischen Niederländer ihre alte ständische Autonomie erneuern, die englischen Puritaner kombinierten die Forderungen nach den alten Rechten des Parlaments mit der Illusion der Abschaffung des „normannischen Jochs" usw. Die Relativität der restitutiven Zielsetzung des vierten Typus der Revolutionen wurde schon oben erwähnt.

In diesem Zusammenhang soll noch eine alte Wahrheit wiederholt werden, daß nämlich die objektiven Resultate der Revolutionen den subjektiven Absichten und Zielen der Revolutionäre nie entsprachen. Keine der innovativen Revolutionen, auch wenn sie erfolgreich waren, wie z. B. die Oktoberrevolution, war total innovativ. Sie trugen immer Elemente der alten Zustände in sich. Analogisch werden wir kaum eine total restitutive Revolution finden. Übrigens, selbst die Logik der Definitionen mahnt hier zur Vorsicht: Eine in ihren Resultaten rein restitutive Systemänderung könnte nicht als Revolution bezeichnet werden: hier muß man wohl schon von einer Restauration bzw. Konterrevolution sprechen. Beispiele gibt es hier viele : Neapel 1799, Rheinland 1814, Polen 1864, Paris 1871, Ungarn 1919 usw. Alle diese Beispiele haben jedoch einen gemeinsamen Nenner: die Veränderung wurde nicht durch die Kräfte „von unten", sondern „von oben" verwirklicht. Sollte dieses „von unten" als ein ergänzendes Element in die Definition des Begriffs Revolution eingeführt werden?


### Drittes Kriterium: Der revolutionäre Erfolg


Wenn wir von den Resultaten sprechen, denken wir schon an ein anderes Kriterium der Typologie: an das Kriterium des Erfolgs. Im Volksmund werden erfolgreiche, siegreiche und geschlagene, mißlungene Revolutionen unterschieden. Wo liegt jedoch die Grenze zwischen Erfolg und Niederlage? Eine Differenzierung ist hier notwendig. Vor allem unterscheiden wir zwischen Sieg und Niederlage im machtpolitischen Sinne sowie bei den objektiven Folgen und Resultaten der Revolution. Wir wissen schon, daß ein erfolgreicher machtpolitischer Wandel, der zu keinen Systemveränderungen führte, keinesfalls als Revolution, sondern bloß als Umsturz, Machtwechsel, Putsch bezeichnet werden kann.

Alle diese Tatsachen berücksichtigend, können wir jedoch vier Typen unterscheiden:

1. Die Revolution machte den erfolgreichen ersten Schritt, siegte für eine kurze Zeit, wurde jedoch bald geschlagen, ohne etwas Dauerhaftes bewirken zu können. Es sei hier Polen 1830/31, Deutschland im November 1918, Ungarn 1956, Wien im Oktober 1848, Paris 1871 genannt.

2. Die Revolution hatte nach ihrem ersten Erfolg genügend Kraft und Zeit, tiefgreifende Veränderungen durchzusetzen bzw. anzuregen, die trotz der baldigen Niederlage der Revolution doch als Teilerfolge überlebten. Als Beispiele sollen hier vor allem das Jahr 1848 in Mitteleuropa und Frankreich, Spanien 1873 u. a. genannt werden.

3. Revolutionen, die einen langfristigen Erfolg erreichten und ihre Ziele verwirklichen konnten, zuletzt jedoch geschlagen wurden, wobei ihre dauerhaften Resultate analog entsprechend dem zweiten Typus charakterisierbar sind. Dies war in England 1640/60 und in Frankreich 1789/99 der Fall, außerdem gehören hierher die meisten der antibürgerlichen Revolutionen.

4. Revolutionen, die kontinuierlich in ein neues, dauerhaftes System mün-
deten. Es waren nicht sehr viele: die niederländische Revolution (obwohl beschränkt auf den Norden), die Glorreiche Revolution in England, die belgische
von 1830, die jungtürkische, unter den außereuropäischen die amerikanische.
Es bleibt zu fragen, wo die Grenze der „dauerhaften" Erfolge liegt: kann man
in diese Kategorie auch die Oktoberrevolution einreihen, oder handelt es sich
eher um einen Übergangsfall?

### Viertes Kriterium: Der soziale Wandel als Ziel der Revolution

Mit den Fragen des Erfolgs hängt ein weiteres Kriterium der Typologie zusammen: die Frage nach der Vertretung des sozialen Wandels unter den Zielen
und Resultaten der Revolution. Wie tief wirkten die durch die politischen Erfolge der Revolution hervorgerufenen Machtverschiebungen auf die Veränderungen im sozialen Bereich? Im Falle der Niederlage: Inwiefern waren Veränderungen beabsichtigt? Hier ist wohl keine Gruppierung in Typen möglich, und
wir müssen uns mit einer Polarität begnügen. Die meisten Revolutionen lagen
nämlich zwischen zwei extremen Zielsetzungen. Einerseits ist es die Oktoberrevolution, die den Kampf um politische Macht und den politischen System-
wandel dem Programm des totalen sozialen und wirtschaftlichen Umbaus voll
untergeordnet hat, andererseits sind es einige wenige „rein" politische Revolutionen, die im sozialen Bereich weder etwas Wesentliches verändern wollten,
noch verändert haben: England 1688/89, Belgien 1830, vielleicht Spanien
1936/38.

### Fünftes Kriterium: Die kausalen Zusammenhänge

Sehr interessant, aber vorläufig kaum durchführbar, wäre die Anwendung
des Kriteriums der kausalen Zusammenhänge. Wo lagen die Voraussetzungen,
Ursachen und unmittelbaren Anregungen? An dieser Stelle können wir einen
interessanten Fragebogen zusammenstellen, der als Ausgangspunkt einer späteren komparativen Untersuchung dienen sollte. Wie stark war die innere
Spaltung der herrschenden Klasse in der Zeit vor der Revolution? Wer gab
die entscheidenden Signale: waren es die Mitglieder der alten Elite, des
„Establishments" oder die „Outsider"? Wie stark war der Anteil des Druckes
„von unten", d. h. der Volksschichten? Wie war der Anteil der Dorf- bzw. der
Stadtbevölkerung? Die Komponente der sozialen Interessengegensätze fehlte
in der Revolution wohl nie, aber ihre Stoßrichtung und die innere Struktur der

Forderungen waren sehr unterschiedlich. Für eine Typologie fehlen hier jedoch ausreichende Untersuchungen[5].

Es besteht hier noch eine weitere Schwierigkeit, die methodologischer Art ist. Die Typologie, die die kausalen Zusammenhänge als Kriterium hat, greift in einen anderen Bereich der Komparation über: in jenen Bereich nämlich, wo sich die Komparation an explikativen Zielen orientiert. Das Ziel ist in diesem Fall nicht eine Typologie, sondern ein allgemeines explikatives Modell der Revolution, um das Allgemeine vom Spezifischen in den einzelnen Revolutionen unterscheiden zu können[6].

SECHSTES KRITERIUM: DER EINFLUSS DER NATIONALEN ZIELE

Als letztes Kriterium der Typologie sei jenes genannt, das insbesondere für unseren mitteleuropäischen Raum von eigenartiger Bedeutung ist. Es ist die Rolle, der Anteil der nationalen Ziele in der politischen Revolution. Wie stark waren unter den Ursachen der Revolution die nationalen Spannungen vertreten? Und vor allem: Wie stark waren die nationalen Forderungen unter den revolutionären Zielen vertreten? Es bleibt zu fragen, ob die gewaltigen Versuche, nationale Unabhängigkeit zu erreichen, soweit sie nicht mit einer Veränderung des politischen Systems verbunden waren, noch als Revolutionen behandelt werden dürfen. Dies betrifft z. B. den serbischen Aufstand 1804 bzw. die Formierung der Nachfolgestaaten 1918/19.

Abgesehen von dieser Schwierigkeit, ist die Typologie nach dem nationalen Kriterium ziemlich einfach:

1. Revolutionen, die keine nationalen Ziele — als Forderungen nach nationaler Gleichberechtigung und Emanzipation von nationaler Unterdrückung — hatten. Das war der Fall in England 1640 ebenso wie in Frankreich 1789, in Spanien, dann auch in Rußland 1917 und bei einigen antiautoritären Revolutionen der Gegenwart wie bei Tschechen und Polen.

2. Revolutionen, in denen die nationalen Forderungen ein organischer Teil der politischen Zielsetzungen waren. So war es vor allem 1848 in der Habsbur-

---

[5] Einige Soziologen und Politikwissenschaftler haben ähnliche Fragebogen zusammengestellt, ohne jedoch die eigentliche Anlayse der empirischen Daten durchzuführen. Vgl. *L. Gottschalk:* Causes of Revolution. In: The American Journal of Sociology 50. 1944. S. 1 ff.; *R. D. Hopper:* The Revolutionary Process. A Frame for the Study of Revolutionary Movements. In: Social Forces 28. 1949/50. S. 270 ff.; *P. A. R. Calvert:* A Study of Revolution. Oxford 1970.; *V. Rittberger:* Über solzialwissenschaftliche Theorie der Revolution. Kritik und Versuch eines Neuansatzes. In: Politische Vierteljahrschrift 12. 1971. S. 492 ff.

[6] Hierher gehört die Arbeit *B. Moore jr.:* Social Origins of Dictatorship and Democracy. Lord and Peasant in the Making of the Modern World. Boston 1966.

germonarchie, aber eigentlich auch in der deutschen Revolution 1848. Hierzu gehören die antiautoritären Revolutionen der in die Sowjetunion gewaltsam eingegliederten Nationen, wie jene der Esten, Ukrainer oder Letten.
3. Die nationalen Ziele waren für das Programm der Revolution und für das Konzept des bürgerlichen Wandels bestimmend, wie z. B. bei den Iren, Polen oder Griechen. In einem gewissen Sinne waren die nationalen Ziele auch in den antibürgerlichen Revolutionen faschistischer Prägung vorhanden.

Obwohl wir uns in dieser Typologie auf politische Revolutionen konzentrierten, sollte nicht vergessen werden, daß diese Revolutionen nur dann entsprechend verstanden werden können, wenn sie in den breiteren Kontext der gesellschaftlichen Veränderung gebracht werden. Es heißt, daß wir die politische Revolution in ihrem Verhältnis zur Reform und zur sozialen Revolution — d. h. zum gesamtgesellschaftlichen Wandel — untersuchen sollten. Dies gilt auch für die typologische Charakteristik. Aus diesem Grund wird der abschließende Teil dieser Überlegungen diesem Zusammenhang gewidmet.

Dies kann wieder in Gestalt der Typologie geschehen. Wie schon oben gesagt wurde, verstehe ich unter der „sozialen Revolution" den tiefgreifenden gesamtgesellschaftlichen Wandel, durch den die alte feudal reglementierte Gesellschaft in die moderne industrielle, kapitalistisch unternehmende verwandelt wurde[7]. Eine so verstandene soziale Revolution verwirklichte sich während eines längeren Zeitabschnitts als eine Reihenfolge der politischen Revolutionen und der Reformen, von denen einige durch den Druck des Volkes zustande kamen, einige wiederum durch die Entscheidung der Herrschenden „von oben" eingeführt wurden. In allen Ländern waren weder der chronologische Ablauf noch die relative Reihenfolge der Revolutionen und Reformen gleich. Trotzdem können wir auch hier gewisse Analogien feststellen, die uns eine Typologie der sozialen Revolution ermöglichen. Diese Typologie hilft uns eigentlich, die unterschiedlichen Wege zur modernen Gesellschaft zu differenzieren.

Durch die Kombination des Stellenwerts und der Reihenfolge der politischen Revolutionen und der Reformen können fünf Typen der sozialen Revolution differenziert werden. Als politische Revolution werden hier nur die ersten zwei Typen der unter dem ersten Kriterium der gesellschaftlichen Entwicklung genannten Revolutionen, d. h. die frühen und die bürgerlichen Revolutionen, verstanden[8].

---

[7] Als eine Komponente der Modernisierung wurde die Revolution schon bei *W. W. Rostow* betrachtet: The Stages of Economic Growth. A Non Communist Manifesto. Cambridge 1960.
[8] Diese Typologie wurde in meiner älteren Arbeit ausführlicher behandelt: *M. Hroch:* Buržoazní revoluce v Evropě (Die bürgerlichen Revolutionen in Europa). Praha 1981.

1. Im Prozeß des bürgerlichen Wandels, der Modernisierung, dominierten die politischen Revolutionen, zu denen die — durch die Revolutionen hervorgerufenen oder auch vorbeugenden — Reformen in begleitender und modifizierender Beziehung standen. So verlief dieser Prozeß in Frankreich, Spanien und Italien. Nebenbei: Ist es ein Zufall, daß es sich in allen drei Fällen um romanische Nationen handelte?

2. Am Anfang des Wandels stand eine politische Revolution, aber die strukturellen Veränderungen ereigneten sich meist durch Reformen, die jedoch durch die politische Revolution ermöglicht oder stimuliert wurden. Als „klassisch" kann hier die englische Entwicklung bezeichnet werden, es gesellt sich dazu auch die niederländische Entwicklung, wo jedoch noch eine Revolution beschleunigend einwirkte.

3. Eine analoge Reihenfolge, aber unter ganz anderen gesellschaftlichen Umständen, registrieren wir auf dem Balkan. Am Anfang steht eine national befreiende Revolution, die weitere Entwicklung war überwiegend durch die Reformen geprägt.

4. Am Anfang des Wandels standen die Reformen und erst später wurde der gesellschaftliche Wandel durch eine, meistens mißlungene oder nur zum Teil erfolgreiche bürgerliche politische Revolution erreicht. So verlief die Entwicklung in Deutschland, Rußland, Norwegen und in den meisten Ländern der Habsburgermonarchie.

5. Der Wandel verwirklichte sich nur durch Reformen, mit eventuell einigen gewaltigen Ausschreitungen. Diese friedliche Entwicklung war vor allem für die skandinavischen Länder Dänemark, Finnland und Schweden charakteristisch.

Die Vielfalt der typologischen Zuordungen, die hier demonstriert wurde, bietet zwar viele interessante Informationen, darf jedoch nicht überschätzt werden. Durch typologische Zuordnungen bekommen wir zwar ein präziseres Bild, kommen aber keinen Schritt weiter in der kausalen Analyse der Revolutionen, ihrer Ursachen und Folgen. Die Vielfalt der typologischen Kriterien wurde hier hervorgehoben und „durchdekliniert". Dadurch wurde jedoch nur der erste, wenn auch unvermeidliche Schritt in der Konstruktion der systematischen Typologie der politischen Revolutionen gemacht. Der weitere Schritt sollte die Form eines Katalogs bekommen, in dem jede der Revolutionen durch mehrere typologische Zuordnungen charakterisiert wird[9]. Erst durch diesen Vorgang wird man die einzelnen Revolutionen im Kontext der europäischen Geschichte besser lokalisieren.

---

[9] Eine solche Kombination der Kriterien hat Ch. Johnson unternommen, ohne jedoch dabei sehr überzeugend zu sein. *Ch. Johnson:* Revolution and the Social System. Stanford 1964. S. 28 ff.

30

Eine Schwierigkeit wurde bisher aus unseren Überlegungen ausgeklammert. Sie ergibt sich aus der Tatsache, daß viele, ja sogar die meisten Revolutionen innerlich strukturiert, differenziert waren und daß sich dazu noch ihr Charakter und ihre Zielsetzungen — sofern sie einen längeren Erfolg verzeichneten — entwickelten und modifizierten. Dies erschwert die zuverlässige und eindeutige Anwendung insbesondere der typologischen Kriterien unter dem zweiten, vierten und fünften Kriterium. In einigen Fällen müßte deswegen ein und dieselbe Revolution — z. B. die französische von 1789 — in unserem typologischen Katalog mehrfach, d. h. in ihren unterschiedlichen Phasen, aufscheinen.

Abschließend soll betont werden, daß die Typologie solange nur eine Vorbereitung — und ein interessantes Gedankenspiel — bleibt, bis sie Unterlage und Ausgangspunkt für eine umfassendere komparative Revolutionsforschung wird. Denn ohne typologische Zuordnung kann kein Prozeß, auch nicht die Revolution selbst, komparativ untersucht werden.

# CRITERIA AND INDICATORS OF UNEVEN DEVELOPMENT:

## SOME REFLECTIONS
## ON THE OUTCOMES OF THE WORKSHOP

The whole discussion was signposted by the premise that we would be able to explain uneven development and backwardness, if we understood and analysed their indicators and criteria. We asked the following questions at the beginning:

1. Which criteria, beside the basic economic ones, can we use for investigation of our issue?
2. Is it possible to apply modern criteria to the pre-modern age, in other words, did uneven development in the Middle Ages occur according to different parameters?
3. How will the application of more precise indicators and criteria help in the more exact division of European history into regions which would replace the vulgarising counter-position "West-East"?
4. What was the relation between dependence and uneven development: can dependence as a category at all serve as an indicator of unevenness, or is it merely one of the causes of unevenness?

It became immediately obvious that, first, the discussion had to clarify the basic concept of "development" and address the question of how the phenomenon of unevenness could be related to development. If "development" means "progressive advancement from a lower to a higher level" in the general linguistic consciousness, then we have to start with determining the criteria for measuring higher and lower level of development. Further, we have to establish whether this notion of development was immanent to each set of changes in social history, as it was presumed by 18th century scholars. P. Anderson noted (and further develops this idea

* This workshop was held in Prague in December 1994 to discuss the criteria and indicators used to measure backwardness and uneven development in individual societies.

in his contribution to this volume) that uneven development had not been a problem for Adam Smith and Scottish scholars of the Enlightenment, because the Smithian model was based on unproblematic diffusion of growth. Also early works of Karl Marx on India suggested that he had accepted this model. Unevenness of development became an issue particularly in the Marxist intellectual tradition in Russia in the late 19th and early 20th century: how could Russia be fully developed politically, if it was underdeveloped economically?

In any event, the concept of uneven development, as suggested by modern historians, implies the idea of existence of some ideal type of historical development, to which we relate faster, more dynamic, slower, or zero development, or measure it by this standard. Quite spontaneously, we accept the idea that the changes occurring in various countries at various times were more or less analogous in the respective spheres of social life, whether they happened in production or politics. Development may not necessarily be understood as a fundamental change with overall societal effects, but may also mean changes in partial spheres of everyday life, culture, and politics. This may be the reason why R. Brenner's idea of stagnation as normality and development as a specificity of history did not meet with positive response among the participants. They considered it a construct which did not correspond to historical reality.

History, however, provides evidence for "decline", the opposite of development, which respects the point of change of history. J. Topolski works with the concept of decline in his contribution. Nevertheless, referring to "a change" is not sufficient in interpretations of history. The concept does not have enough substance.

Some discussants maintain that fear of differences, variety of development, lifestyles, and living standards operates in the background of analyses of unevenness as something that should be overcome. The fear seems to originate in the application of the modern ideal of equality among people to the sphere of everyday life: if people are to be equal, they ought to live in similar conditions. This does not mean that we will obtain the criteria of unevenness of development in various regions by defining differences between them.

An important part of every analysis, of course, is defining similarities and differences by a comparative approach. The criteria of unevenness can also serve as criteria or categories of comparison. We did not go into the discussion on the comparative method, but we agreed that the investigation of unevenness was carried out at two levels:

1. at the level of situations (structures), while emphasising diffe- rences between situations in various regions and whether we focus on structures which exist synchronically (at the same time), or in the same or analogous historical situations;
2. at the level of processes, when we are not dealing with the unevenness of development, which was achieved at a particular point, but primarily with uneven speed of historical changes.

We did not discuss the term "criterion" in the workshop and it is quite possible that the usage of the term was not identical in all discussants. It appeared most frequently as a synonym of "para- meter", therefore, we needed the word "indicator" – a less de- clarative term – to point out the existence of a weaker, less evidenced, or less investigated signal, by which the reality suggested certain unevenness.

The territorial aspect is the basic and inseparable attribute of unevenness, which meant that the issue of usefulness of the Wallerstein's concept of "core-periphery" in the study of unevenness of development stood in the forefront of the discussion. Belonging to either the core or the periphery is certainly in itself an indicator of unevenness, but this fact is too simple to have any significance for our analysis for the following three reasons:

Firstly, the division to the core and the periphery is too appro- ximate and, for determining unevenness, also too banal. It is true that the introduction of the term "semi-periphery" attenuates the schematic nature of the dichotomy a little, but it also brings about another problem, and that is the issue of the borders of the semi- periphery in relation to the core and periphery.

The second problem is the unevenness of development within each category mentioned above, that is, in the core, semi-periphery, and periphery. The concepts of internal core and internal periphery, pointed out by H.-H. Nolte in his criticism of I. Wallerstein, could provide useful modification.

Finally, the problem is whether and how the relation between the core, semi-periphery, and periphery can help explain unevenness

**13**

in the past. P. Anderson noted that there were at least three basic answers to this question. One of them was Wallerstein's suggestion of the negative feedback, meaning that the dependence of the periphery on the core had been disadvantageous for the periphery and increasing. The second answer was the contrary, that is, the positive feedback, which was the idea that economic dependence had been advantageous for the periphery. The third answer suggested that the relation between the two had been neutral, and therefore, irrelevant for the process of unevenness. Nevertheless, in reality, we found that all three options could be combined, or rather, that one could be replaced by another in the long-term development.

With regard to the above, the discussants had to face the question whether they were willing to accept the idea that Europe had always been divided into "core" and "peripheral" regions and possibly into other macro-regions. It was not only a question of criteria, but above all of the time aspect of unevenness: is it possible to extrapolate the modern relation between the core and the periphery to the Middle Ages? Although everybody agreed that an uneven starting line, determined by the presence or absence of Roman traditions (Roman "limes" as the initial criterion) was at the beginning of uneven development, two opinions were expressed concerning the issue of the extrapolation from modern to pre-modern society.

The first one suggests that the relationship between the core and the periphery can be considered in the same terms in the Middle Ages as in the early modern period, because we find the differences in pace as well as the dependence of the periphery on the core (H.-H. Nolte considers this thesis in his contribution to this collection of essays). The second opinion (M. Hroch, K. Kubiš) maintains that, although the relationships of dependence and differing speed of development existed in the Middle Ages, these relationships occurred in smaller territories and not on the scale of the whole continent. Rather, there were several parallel cores and peripheries, which did not have the same durability and firmness, which they began to achieve in the early modern period. I need to mention that the issue of the legacy of the Eastern Byzantine Empire was not addressed.

The Prague participants brought up a significant empirical argument against the idea of European relations of dependence in the Middle Ages, when they suggested that we were able to trace increasing correlation of European markets only in the early modern period: the correlation was signaled by the correlation of price series even in very distant trade centres. In other words: commotions and booms occurring in one market had been reflected in the oscillation of prices also in the markets without any intense direct trade links with the "epicentre" of the change. The objection against the importance of prices as an indicator of links between regions and, by that effect, of the level of their development was the small share of trade on the overall volume of production at that time.

The position of the main element of the population – the peasantry – could be another indicator of stable regionalisation, which, however, was in place from the end of the medieval period. In this respect, P. Anderson explained his division of Europe into Eastern and Western according to the establishment of serfdom of peasants: with regard to the fact that serfdom had been an important factor in hindering economic growth, countries with a prevalence of serfs could be considered as countries which were lagging behind in development. The possibility to use serfdom as a criterion of unevenness was opposed by some other participants, who asserted that serfdom had not been introduced to Balkan under the Ottoman rule and yet it was considered as a stagnating region and a part of the European "East". In relation to the division into East and West, the cultural borders between the Roman Catholic and the Orthodox churches seem to be more significant. However, whether, why, and in what aspects we can consider orthodoxy as a factor hindering development, still has to be verified.

Economic development is the most common and the most comprehensible criterion of unevenness. It is determined by gross national product, per capita income, production level in a certain "key" industry, and also by the volume of international trade. The advantage of this criterion is that it is quantifiable and, therefore, "reliable". Also, it is generally acceptable for various schools of thought: a Marxist or a conservative historian usually agree on the materialist thesis that the standard of living, depending, of course, on the level of production is a criterion of advancement in a particular country. None of the participants of the workshop questioned the importance of the criterion, but at the same time, they agreed that it could not be the only and, possibly, the decisive criterion.

Before we proceed with investigating other criteria, we must mention that the level of economic development as an indicator of

**15**

unevenness has at least three serious weaknesses: 1. It is possible to determine the exact level of development only in the "statistical" historical period, while in the "pre-statistical" period, we have to rely on indirect indicators, that is, in fact, on other criteria than income or the level of production; 2. economic development, the level of production, etc. are not determined by any unchangeable laws, but they have their own causes and preconditions, which must also be included in the indicators of unevenness; 3. it is necessary to choose the correct parameter of the level of economic development, because a bad choice can bring fatal mistakes: one example for all can be the volume of steel production, a much-used indicator of unevenness, for which there may have been a reason in the period of industrialisation, but using it later helped to foster the myth of "highly developed" countries of real socialism, and of the possibility to gain supremacy over capitalism by increasing this production.

The discussants also repeatedly pointed out that urbanisation was a significant criterion of the level of development alongside with economic development. This included the density of urban population, but more importantly, the changes of the city social structure and the function of the city in society (L. Klusáková). The criteria of the agrarian character of towns differed from region to region. We can easily determine the density of towns, but a comparative study of their social structures and their functions still remains to be done in future. We can pronounce a hypothesis now that the countries of European "West" and "East" showed great unevenness precisely in the last two aspects. The market function of towns, which can be measured by a number of indirect indicators, can serve as an indicator of uneven development especially in the pre-industrial period. In this respect, the category of proto-industrialisation, asserted by De Vries under the term of "industrious revolution", has certain validity. The category expresses a significantly broader spectre of indicators than merely the volume and organisation of production.

The frequency of markets and the volume of market transactions was undoubtedly dynamised by the relation to the rural areas. It was extremely important whether farmers attended the markets regularly, or whether the merchants mediated their connection with the market directly in the village. The former indicates a possibility of faster development, while the latter a barter economy and therefore slow development – this argument presupposes that the countryside preserved its agrarian character and that part of the craft production was not transferred from towns to villages. The degree of development of the domestic market, in which the town functions as an elementary "core", determined the level of development of the particular country and its degree of dependence. V. Dvořáková formulated a thesis that the problem of dependence started with an entrance of a country (state) to the world system without having developed its domestic market.

If we apply the role of the internal and external market relations on European regions from this perspective, we get a picture which by no means confirms the general idea of the semi-periphery and periphery. Several regions belonging to the area of semi-periphery had the intensity of market relations in the pre-industrial period comparable with some of the regions belonging to the core. J. Topolski and J. Kumpera reflected that this applied particularly to some areas of Central Europe.

Competitiveness of towns regarding their own market relations within the domestic market, and also regarding the introduction of innovations and spreading the mentality of change is another important function which can serve as a criterion of unevenness (M. Hiettala; she pursues the thought further in her paper).

The economic criteria which form the basis for the concept of the core – periphery dichotomy confirm the higher level of development in the countries belonging to the core. At the same time, however, they show that such differentiation, although made more flexible by the introduction of the concept of the semi-periphery, is too simplistic and needs to be modified by the identification of regions within the periphery and the semi-periphery, which functioned as cores for vast internal peripheries. This group includes, for example, Catalonia in the Iberian Peninsula, or industrialised parts of Saxony and the Czech Lands, the Milan Region, etc. L. Klusáková investigates the issue of indicators of unevenness, which are valid only for a particular region. It would certainly be possible to develop a programme for comparisons of different speeds of development of these internal cores and to project them to the proto-industrial period.

Production does not increase by its own activity, the differences in the speed and the structure of economic development are neither contingent, nor do they happen through any automatic development of the labour force. That is why already the discussion over the factors of medieval unevenness paid a lot of attention to the issues of spreading innovations in production processes. The discussants agreed that innovations could be accepted and spread only if there were conditions for the increase of the demand for them, that is, if they met the needs of some part of society. The demand could be represented, for example, by the interests of states or rulers in a specific product, for example, in gunpowder and guns. H.-H. Nolte maintains that, in this respect, the competitive European structure differed significantly from a monolithic structure, as was the case, for example, in China. Here the opinions on whether military superiority can or cannot be a criterion of development varied.

P. Anderson objected that, in that case, the successful military operations of Nomads could be regarded as evidence of their high level of development. A counter-argument can be that guns played a key role in the expansion of the countries of the European core overseas, and that they also took part in the formation of the world system.

The Orientalists (Faroqui, Strnad) noted that the example with gun powder could not be generalised for other commodities. In other spheres, the demand for and the need of goods, often connected with the changes of fashion and lifestyle, took similar forms in Asia and Europe. More developed Asian states were fragmented societies as was the case in Europe, but they were not so competitive, which was a consequence of a different political and social system.

It is difficult to compare the stimuli of faster or slower acceptance of innovations and, therefore, to overrate their role of indicators of unevenness. This is true primarily for the changing and diversifying needs, whose impact and importance historians usually deduce from their consequences. The role of needs can be characterised in the role of an indicator of unevenness at least in one aspect, and that is, as J. Strnad noted, the position needs and consumption had in the value system of particular society. He used the example of India to illustrate that society, whose elites did not emphasise consumption and the growth of the living standard, stimulated the development of production far less that European societies, in which the needs changed quickly, diversified, and increased particularly from the late Middle Ages. Could this be a criterion and also one of the causes of unevenness of the development of Indian and (West)European societies?

The general social climate, the "intellectual atmosphere stimulating innovation" (R. Brenner) played a key role. Although everybody agreed with this statement, the utility of the atmosphere as an indicator of unevenness is problematic, because it can hardly be subjected to comparative analysis. Furthermore, V. Dvořáková and L. Klusáková pointed out that the "innovative spirit" was not of a purely spiritual nature, but it required certain objective conditions with respect to the level and organisation of production, to education, and to differences in civilisation and affluence of society. Although there was a considerable difference of opinion as to the uses of wealth, the decision whether money should be used as a treasure or as capital did not depend only on a wish of an individual: we have to consider the mechanisms deciding about the dominance of one or the other function, which differed in time and place.

The relation between the increasing and diversifying needs on the one hand, and the possibilities to meet them on the other belonged to the objective factors determining the social climate (J. Topolski). If the national product did not grow as fast as the needs or expectations of their fulfilment, social tensions grew and could even effect the willingness to accept innovations, and the production activity in general.

Thus not only different understanding of needs, but also different understanding of profit can be considered an indicator of unevenness. The profit-mentality was a new element, which developed with the "spirit of capitalism", and which then stimulated enterprising and, consequently, the speed of growth. This mentality was absent in the aristocracy of many countries, not only in Poland as J. Topolski noted, but, also in Spain and, to a great extent, in France and Germany. In some cases, the profit-mentality of the bourgeoisie was influenced by aristocratic value systems: the discussants, however, differed in their opinions on this influence in the cases of England and Germany. Nevertheless, they generally agreed that the profit-mentality could be an important indicator or at least a tool for an interpretation of unevenness. The problem still remains, how to determine differences in the intensity of this mentality, which seems to be possible to diagnose only by means of indirect indicators.

The opinion of H.-H. Nolte that over-population with ensuing emigration could be an indicator of unevenness incited a controversy. First of all, it was necessary to limit the validity of this thesis, evidenced by the example of migration for work from Lower Saxony, to the internal periphery. Then it became apparent that it was necessary to distinguish between the significant increase of population and over-population resulting in emigration. The reason was that in many regions the growing population had found livelihood thanks to the development of local domestic production (proto-industrialisation in some parts of Saxony, Silesia, in north Bohemia, etc.). This phenomenon should then be considered as an indicator of the creation of an internal core, rather than an indicator of backwardness, which migration for work certainly was. The question which still remains open is, whether we can consider all the regions which were the destinations of migrations as belonging to the core or an internal core. People went to seek work in the Netherlands, but less in England. In fact, people often left England and went to seek work elsewhere, especially overseas. The whole agrarian colonialisation in the Middle Ages as well as in the 18th and the 19th centuries, after all, was directed mostly from regions considered as more developed to less developed areas. This means that neither demographic growth nor migration could serve as clear criteria of faster or slower development.

M. Hroch pointed out already in the discussion on the economic criteria that the regionalisation of Europe by educational criteria would – especially regarding the 18th and the 19th centuries – differ significantly from the regionalisation according to the production activity. Central Europe (German, Austrian, and Bohemian territories), followed by Sweden and other Scandinavian countries would be the most developed region from the viewpoint of literacy. On the one hand, providing literacy was a pre-condition of social growth, and also of spreading innovation, we cannot underrate or marginalise the importance of the criterion. On the other hand, the introduction of compulsory years of school attendance and systematic education of the masses was possible only at a certain level of economic development and affluence of population, that is, it was more likely to appear in the countries belonging to the semi-periphery, than to the periphery.

A number of examples gives evidence that literacy and education of the masses became the state interest in the countries, whose governments realised the correlation between education and economic prosperity, and made deliberate efforts to support education and educational institutions. At the same time, however, we must not forget that compulsory school education was a means of educating the subjects to loyalty to the sovereign and aristocratic masters. The participants agreed on the generalised opinion that the support of literacy and education of the masses were typical for the efforts of the states from the semi-periphery to catch up with or at least to get closer to the level of the countries of the core. That was the case of Prussia, the Habsburg monarchy, Hessen, Sweden, etc. P. Anderson stressed the case of Sweden, where the successful concept of mass education quite clearly contributed to the acceleration of industrialisation.

The Czech participants quoted the case of the Habsburg monarchy for the illustration of the dependence of successful efforts to increase literacy on economic and social conditions. While the more developed western part (Austrian and Bohemian Lands) introduced general school education very quickly, the state educational policy was put to practice much later in the less developed Hungarian territory. Similar differences can be traced also in the various parts of the Prussian state. In this sense, literacy can thus serve indirectly as a criteria of unevenness.

In this respect, a separate issue is the extent to what education supports adaptability, which V. Dvořáková considered an important criterion especially for the 20th century development. She pointed the difference between individual adaptability and the adaptability of the social system. In the former socialist countries the system showed very low adaptability.

Literacy and mass education are not the only signs of the educational level of population. The scientific capacity must also be considered. The map of Europe would again look different from this perspective. H.-H. Nolte suggested the number of individuals with academic education, or the capacity and the number of academic associations, institutions, etc. as a simple indicator. Faroqui objected that, in the most developed countries, as, for example, in England, academic development had been spontaneous, and that care of education, especially technological and scientific, had not been institutionalised on the basis of interests of the state or aristocratic rulers for a long time. The other participants accepted her opinion that state support of science and research had been an expression of the effort to catch up with the more developed countries. At this point, we have to consider that we can trace such efforts not only in the countries of the semi-periphery, but also in countries like Russia.

J. Musil asked whether and to what extent we could use literature and artistic production in general as a criterion of unevenness, and obtained very disparate responses. Main arguments included the difficulty in determining the quality of literary production on the one hand, and problematic evaluation according to quantitative indicators, as for example, the number of books published or the size of theatre-going population, on the other. Here J. Strnad reflected that such approach would imply that all civilisations had had a similar system of values and cultural forms. This was certainly not the case. In any event, the participants of the workshop considered it as a given that the quality of literary production had not been in linear correlation with the speed and the level of economic development. The hypothesis that art production could be stimulated by the tension between the realisation of economic (and social) backwardness and the educational level of the population was also discussed.

On the contrary, the hypothesis of L. Klusáková that the degree of participation and, more generally, the degree of development of the political system from absolutism to parliamentarism could be a criterion of unevenness received little attention. The role of the political system became the subject of a lively discussion in connection with the problem of unevenness in contemporary history. Faroqui noted that political systems in many countries (Turkey, a large part of Latin America) created atmosphere which forced educated individuals to exile. Consequently, the backwardness of these countries deepens also in the area of education. H. Agnew objected that the degree of democratisation was not necessarily the primary factor in this problem, but the ability of the governments to adapt to new conditions (as for example, in Singapore). This again emphasised the importance of adaptability as a criterion of unevenness. V. Dvořáková explores the possibility of applying the development from authoritarian regime to democracy to contemporary history.

An engaging and long discussion developed in response to the question of applicability of the approaches discussed above to the post-1917 development, when a dichotomy of economic systems was created: a socialist system based on centrally planned economy, and a capitalist system based on market relations. Does it follow that a dual system of indicators of unevenness is necessary, depending on which system we want to consider?

The argument of supporters of the view that the world remained one system even after 1917 was that the Soviet Union was linked to the capitalist world through trade and the political tension culminating in the polarity of the two super-powers after 1945. P. Anderson objected that foreign trade represented only a minute component of Soviet economy. According to him, the fact that the Soviet Union was involved in the struggle of the super-powers did not suggest that both powers together formed an economic system.

A specific, but, unjustly, only briefly-discussed question was the subjective perception of unevenness by the contemporares themselves. It was left at the mention of several examples suggesting that, in this respect, we should distinguish, whether unevenness was observed as "higher stage" or as backwardness, and then investigate whether each of these perspectives was seen from "the outside" (outside observers, diplomats, travellers) or from "the inside". Contemporaries observed the situation in their own society, but also in comparison with other societies, and reflected the general trends: growth or decline. Although, it is quite possible that, in many cases, the meanings of the terms like, for example, backwardness, high degree of development, development, or stagnation were symbolic, which does not preclude their politicisation. The participants agreed that the issue of perception of one's own backwardness or in foreign countries should be subjected to a comparative study, and would deserve a separate conference.

At the general level, it seems that perception in the countries of the periphery and the semi-periphery, rather than anywhere else, stimulated activisation or motivation of actions. However, it was not always the case: people began to realise unevenness of development or their possible backwardness only after they achieved a certain level of education and information about broader geographic relations and, above all, people with certain social status. Then, it took a while before they stopped taking that situation for granted and started looking at it as at a state which should be overcome or minimalised. Here J. Musil noted that different types of backwardness mobilised people in different ways: some were merely acknowledged with indifference, while others were incitements for activisation.

An interesting fact is that an act of wilfulness was sometimes behind the demand for overcoming backwardness, as was the case particularly in the absolutist era. The need to overcome backwardness served as a reason, or rather an excuse, for establishing autocratic regimes or dictatorships also in our times. An interesting project would be to conduct a broader comparative analysis on the subject, and to explore the potential correlation between the social position of the observer and the motivation effect of the perception of backwardness. Other responses, like for example, the opinion that backwardness is a result of oppression by another country or of bad luck, are likely to appear, too.

The fundamental result of the workshop was the confirmation of the original hypothesis that there was no single criterion of unevenness, but a plurality of criteria. J. Musil defined four categories of the criteria: social in terms of wealth, economic in terms of dynamics of production, cultural, and political. We could, undoubtedly, divide each of them into sub-criteria or sub-indicators. Especially, we could find differences in the degree of the creation of favourable atmosphere for introduction of innovations at the economic level, in the degree of literacy at the cultural level, and in the degree of participation at the political level. At the same time, we have to consider the question of compatibility, i. e., of the possibility to combine the criteria and indicators derived from the four categories and which should, theoretically, be applicable parallelly to society living in the same region.

A more difficult problem is defining the correlation between all the above levels, and also between all the indicators. Were they related hierarchically or did their importance change with time and place? It is certain that they were related, but they were not in permanent harmony: high level of economic development was not necessarily followed by high educational level, or the degree of democratisation did not always correspond with the degree of social stratification.

Considering the plurality of criteria, we could explore their possible combinations which would best characterise the specificity of development of countries, nations, or states concerned. This approach may work especially in comparisons within the periphery or the semi-periphery, rather than at the general level of the co-reperiphery relation. What would be the result of a comparison of, for example, contemporary Ireland and the Baltic countries, or Sweden and the Austrian countries from this perspective? Even more interesting may be the application of the "criteria hierarchy" on the analysis of internal peripheries. In this case, we would be comparing regions within a territory showing concord in some criteria (e. g., political system, literacy), while distinct regionalisation in others. The time allocated to the workshop did not allow more detailed exploration of these issues and will have to be subject to further research.

We did not formulate any final conclusions, but some results of the engaging discussion are so distinct that I can take the liberty to sum them up into several points. Above all, the importance of supplementing any considerations of causes and consequences of unevenness and backwardness with questions about the selection of appropriate criteria and indicators for determining unevenness or backwardness was confirmed. We can define exactly what the subject of our considerations is and what we analyse only by taking this approach.

In spite of the fact that, as we mentioned above, the criteria of unevenness were considered in a very broad sense and included also indicators, our discussion showed that:

1. In the case of contemporary history, unevenness cannot be reduced to differences in economic growth between "the West" and "the East" with other levels of unevenness following from that;
2. Unevenness in the production sphere did not determine unevenness in all other spheres (The assertion that it was thus determined sounds as if it was a legacy of a vulgarised materialist application of the theory of "structure and superstructure".)

It is necessary to observe in which sphere of social life unevenness appeared, which spheres we compare, and which period we consider. There is no phenomenon of uneven development "an sich", which would be constant in European or world history. Only then, when we are aware of the differentiations we have to make, we can proceed with the analysis of causal relations, that is, to investigate the causes and consequences of unevenness. The same applies to research on subjective perception of unevenness and "backwardness".

By way of conclusion, it is only appropriate to ask, together with M. Hiettala, whether the whole discussion of unevenness is useful. What methodological inspiration it can bring to the historian who, after all, leans toward empiricism rather than theory? Is the effort to explain unevenness not motivated simply by unconscious fear of non-sameness which is an accompanying phenomenon of inequality of the regions of the world?

At this point, we can list several examples of uses of the approach we chose for investigation of the phenomenon of uneven development for a professional analysis:

1. It is, above all, a warning against too simple explanations of historical phenomena, events, and processes from the point of view of "backwardness" or "high level of development", however paradoxically it may sound. It is enough to mention, how many historical studies open or end with (usually) unfounded references to higher or lower level of development of a given region.
2. If we approach the phenomenon of unevenness with its complexity in mind, as we showed above, it will be much easier for us to define the specifics or general characteristics of development of the region in question: combinations of the criteria of unevenness offer so far little used possibilities.
3. If we explore history in all its variance, and attempt a causal analysis of this variance, the knowledge of the criteria of unevenness will help us in specifying and searching for driving and hindering forces of historical development.
4. Relational topics, which belong to the most frequent components of historical research, are justly considered a potential tool for a comparative analysis. They can contribute to our knowledge of uneven levels of development in the researched countries, but we have to consider also the reversed order of relations: political, economical, and cultural relations between regions, states, or nations can be properly analysed only if we know the characteristics of these regions from the perspective of uneven development and its criteria.
5. Studies of human behaviour and its motivation have paid so far little attention to the motivating (or demotivating) role of realisation of backwardness of one's own or other region. The perception of unevenness (no matter whether true or imagined) helped to stimulate enterprising spirit and spread innovations on the one hand, but also to incite political and military conflicts on the other, in many cases in the past. Therefore, it has to be included in among the factors which co-determined causal relations of historical development.

(Translated by Libora Indruchová)

# INDEX

Africa: XII 9; XIV 25
Agnew, Hugh: XIX 22
Alexander II: VII 98
American Revolution: IX 108
Amsterdam: XVI 6
Anatolia: XIV 31ff.
Anderson, Benedikt: VII 92; IX 111; XII 9
Anderson, Perry: XIX 11, 14f., 23
Antverpen: XVI 6
Archangelsk: XVI 17
Armenians: III 75; VIII 205
Attman, Artur: XVI 4
Asia: XIX 18
Austria: IV 73; VII 98; VIII 191, 203;
    XIII 104; XV 253; XIX 24
Austro-Hungary: VIII 195
Austro-Marxists: VII 102

Balibar, Étienne: VII 102
Balkans: VI 266; VIII 205; IX 107; XI 269;
    XVII 188ff.; XVIII 29; XIX 15
Baltics: V 72; VIII 191, 198, 200; XIX 24
Barcelona: VI 271f.
Basques: IV 77; VIII 203; X 37
Bauer, Otto: VII 102; XII 3
Belgium: IV 78; XVII 186ff., 192;
    XVIII 23, 26
Bellay, Jean du: V 75
Belles-lettres: XIII 100f.
Beneš, Eduard: XV 245
Bergen: XIV 21
Bernheim, Ernest: III 74
Bismarck, Otto v.: VII 95
Bohemia: I passim; II 95 ff.; IV 79; V 70,
    72, 91; X 39; XV 243, 250f.;
    XIII 103; XIV 17ff.; XIX 20
Bolzano, Bernard: II 103f.
Bosnia: VIII 194, 204; X 42
Brandenburg: XIII 106
Bratislava: VI 271
Brenner, Robert: XIX 12, 19
Britain see Great Britain
Brittany, Brittons: V 75; VII 98; VIII 192
Budapest: VI 272

Bulgaria, Bulgarians: IV 73; V 97;
    VIII 194; X 41; XI 270; XIII 97
Byelorussians: IV 77; VII 98; VIII 191;
    X 37, 41
Byzantine Empire: XIV 25, 28ff.; XIX 14

Castilia: X 37
Catalonia, Catalans: III 80; IV 72, 77f.;
    V 71, 79, 83; VI 259ff.; VII 96;
    X 37; XIX 17
Catholic Church, Catholicism: II 97;
    VI 265; XIII 103f.; XIV 23 XV 244;
    XIX 15
Caucasus: X 42
Cech, Svatopluk: XV 257
Central Europe: II 100; III 75 79; IV 77;
    VIII 202; X 35; XI 265f.; 271;
    XV passim; XVI 12, 19ff.;
    XIX 17, 20
China: XIX 18
Christensen, Axel E.: XVI 2, 6
Communism: X 44; XI 268, 276
Constantinople: XIV 29
Cossaks: VI 273
Counter-Reformation II 98; XIII 102ff.;
    XIV 23
Croatians, Croats: IV 72f.; V 81, 84; VI 259;
    VIII 193, 204; X 37, 39ff.; XI 266
Czech lands, Czechs: I passim; II passim
    IV 72, 77f.; V 71, 77, 81; VI 259f.,
    263ff.; VIII 195f.; X 37, 39ff.;
    XI 266; XIII 101ff.; XIV 15ff., 34f.;
    XVI 23; XVIII 27; XIX 17
Czechoslovakia: VII 99; VIII 196f., 203f.;
    X 41

Dalmatia: X 39
Dann, Otto: XII 5
Denmark, Danes: IV 71; VI 260, 263ff.;
    VIII 191, 193, 197, 203; X 37;
    XI 269; XIV 17, 24; XVII 186, 189;
    XVIII 29
Deutsch, Karl W.: XII 2
Dostoievski, Fiodor M.: XI 267

Dublin: VI 271f.
Dutch *see* Netherlands
Dvorakova, Vladimira: XIX 17, 19, 21

Eastern Europe: III 75, 79; X 35, 37, 43;
    XI *passim*; XV 246; XVI *passim*;
    XIX 15
Engels, Friedrich: IX 101f., 113ff.
England, Englishmen: III 77; IV 71, 81;
    V 70, 73; VII 101; X 37; XI 269;
    XIII 97; XIV 23ff.; XVI 20;
    XVII 186, 189; XVIII 25ff.; XIX 20
Estonia, Estonians: IV 72f., 77; V 77, 79,
    91; VI 261ff.; X 37, 39f.; XI 267,
    272
Europe: IV 77; VII 91ff. X 37; XI 272,
    275f.; XII 10; XV 242ff.
European Union: XI 276

Fallmerayer, Jacob Philipp: XIV 28
Faroqhi, Suraya: XIX 18, 22
Fichte, Johann Gottlieb: II 105; V 85
Finland, Finns: III 77; IV 72, 77; V 77, 81;
    VI 260, 265; VII 103; VIII 200, 203,
    206; X 37; XIII 97; XVIII 29
Fishman, Joshua: V 74, 88; VIII 193
Flanders: V 70, 75
Flemings: III 80; V 81, 84; VII 101;
    VIII 203; IX 106; X 37
France: II 100; III 81; IV 71; V 70, 73ff.;
    VII 94, 101; VIII 200, 202f.; X 37;
    XI 268, 275; XIII 98; XIV 25;
    XV 244; XVI 6; XVII *passim*;
    XVIII *passim*; XIX 19
Frankfurt/M: XV 253; XVI 27
Frankfurt/Oder: XVI 10
Franz I: (Emperor): II 101
French Revolution: II 95, 100; VII 94f., 99;
    IX 105ff.; XVII *passim*; XVIII 23
Frisians: VIII 192, 194

Galicia: VIII 192, 205
Gdansk: XVI 8
Gellner, Ernest: II 95; VII 92, 99ff.; IX 111;
    XI 267; XII 5f.
Germany, Germans: II 95f.; III 77, 80f.;
    IV 73; V 80, 94; VI 265; VII 99;
    VIII 191ff., 202f., 206; X 39;
    XI 266f., 270f., 275; XIII 97, 101ff.;
    XIV 19ff.; XV 243, 245, 253, 257ff.;
    XVII 186ff.; XVIII 23, 29;
    XIX 19f.
Glorious Revolution: XVIII 23, 26
Great Britain: IV 78; X 37; XI 268, 275;
    XIV 23

Greece, Greeks: II 96; IV 72, 77, 81;
    VII 97f.; VIII 191, 201, 203; X 37;
    XI 271; XIV 15, 25ff.; XVIII 28
Greenfeld, Liah: XII 7

Habsburg monarchy: II 96, 100; V 73, 82;
    VII 98; IX 113f.; X 37; XI 269;
    XIII 103; XIV 19, 24, 33; XVII 187;
    XVIII 27ff.; XIX 21
Hamburg: XVI 10ff.
Haskalah: III 75, 78
Hayes, Carlton J.: IX 105; XII 4
Herder, Johann Gottfried: II 105; V 85;
    VII 94; XII 4; XIV 28
Herjedalen: XIV 21
Herzl, Theodor: III 75
Hessen: XIX 21
Hietala Marjatta: XIX 25
"historical nations": X 39
Hobsbawm, Eric: XI 267; XII 9
Hohenzollern: XIII 106f.
Holland: XVI 20
Holy Roman Empire: XIV 21
Hroch, Miroslav: XIX 20
Hungary: V 70, 80, 83; VII 97, 99, 102f.;
    VIII 191, 196ff.; X 39, 41;
    XI 271, 275; XIII 98; XIV 23;
    XVIII 23, 25
Huns: XIV 32
Hus, Jan: XIII 104
Hussites: II 102; XV 249, 257;
    IX 106; XIII 102ff.; XIV 17, 20

Iceland: XIV 21
Illyrism: IV 79; V 84; VII 99
Ireland, Irish: III 77; IV 78, 81; VI 259,
    261ff.; VII 97, 99, 103; IX 107;
    X 37; XVII 186, 190; XVIII 28
Italy, Italians: VIII 191, 193, 200f., 203;
    XI 271, 275; XIII 97; XVII 186ff.;
    XVIII 23, 29

Jaurez, Jean: XVIII 20
Jemtland: XIV 21
Jews: III 73, 77ff.; VI 261; VIII 191, 205
Joseph II: II 98
Jungmann, Josef: II 104ff.

Kalmar Union: IX 106; XIV 17
Kautsky, Karl: IX 114
Kedourie, Elie: XII 1
Kiev: VI 271f.
Klusáková, Luda: XIX 16f.
Kohn, Hans: VII 94; IX 105; XI 267;
    XII 1, 5

Korais, Adamantios: XIV 28
Krakow: XVI 15
Kumpera, Jan: XIX 17
Kundera, Milan: XV 256

"Landespatriotismus" land-patriotism:
    II 104ff.; III 77; VII 96
Latin America: XIX 22
Latvia, Latvians: III 80; IV 72f., 79;
    V 77, 79; X 37, 39; XI 272; XIII 97;
    XVIII 28
Leipzig: XVI 5, 8ff., 25
Lemberg, Eugen: IX 111; XII passim
Leopold II.: II 101
Liège: XVII 189
List, Friedrich: IX 101ff., 112f.
Lithuania, Lithuanians: III 80; IV 72, 79;
    V 77, 80, 91; VI 261f.; VIII 196f.;
    X 39ff.; XI 272; XIII 97; XVI 13, 22
London: VI 272; IX 104; XVI 10
Lublin: XVI 15
Lusatia: VIII 192, 205
Lviv: XVI 7f., 23, 26ff.

Macedonians: VI 261ff.; X 41; XI 267
Magyars: III 77; IV 72f., 78; V 68, 77f., 94;
    VIII 200; X 39; XIV 24
Maria Theresia II: 98, 101
Marx, Karl: IX 101ff., 111f.; XVIII 20;
    XIX 12
Masaryk, Thomas Garrigue: XI 267;
    XV 245, 248, 250f.;
Masurs: VIII 198
Matice: I passim
Megale idea: XIV 29, 35
Middle Ages: IV 75; V 70, 89; VII 94;
    X 36; XI 267f.; XIII 98, 102ff.;
    XV 243; XIX 14, 18, 20
Minority: IV 73; VIII passim; XI 272;
    XIV 22
Mitteleuropa: XV 244
Moldova: XI 272
Mongolians: XIV 27; XV 248, 252
Moravia: I 35; II 97, 99; IV 79; VI 266;
    VIII 195; X 39; XIII 103; XIV 22
Musil, Jiri: XIX 22ff.
Muslims: VIII 194; XI 270

Napoleonic Wars: II 101; VII 98
Narva: XVI 7
Neapel: XVIII 25
Netherlands: IV 71; VII 94; IX 106;
    X 37; XI 268; XIII 97; XVI 20;
    XVII 186f., 190; XVIII 23; XIX 20
Nilsson, Sven A.: XVI 4ff., 11

Nolte, Hans-Heinrich: XIX 13, 18f., 21
Nomads: XIX 18
Non-dominant ethnic group: IV 71; X 39
Norway, Norwegians: II 96; IV 72, 77f.;
    V 71, 83; VII 97, 103; X 37;
    XIV 15ff., 33f.; XVIII 29
Nurnberg: XVI 27

October Revolution: XV 245; XVIII 24ff.
Oslo: XIV 21
Ostsee: XVI 2 16
Ottoman Empire, Ottomans: III 80; IV 73,
    81; V 73; VII 98; VIII 191; IX 113;
    X 37; XI 269; XIV24ff.; XV 254

Palacky, Frantisek: XIII 103; XIV 20, 35;
    XV 249ff.
Palestine: III 75, 79
Pan-Slavism: IX 114; XIV 24
Paparrigopoulos, Konstantinos: XIV 28f.
Paris: XVIII 25
Patriotism: II 103; XI 267
Phanariots: XIV 25
Piemont: XVII 190
Poland, Poles: III 75; IV 72; V 70;
    VI 259f., 263ff.; VII 97, 103;
    VIII 191, 196, 203f.; X 41; XI 267,
    270; XIII 97; XIV 24; XVI 9 22ff.;
    XVII 187, 192f.; XVIII 25, 28
Pomaks: VIII 194
Portugal, Portuguese: X 37; XIII 97
Poznan: VI 259, 265f.; XVI 10f., 22ff.
Prague: I 96, 101; VI 271f.; VIII 195;
    XIV 21
Protestants: II 96f.
Prussia: V 72; VIII 198; XIII 107f.;
    XIX 21

Reformation: II 98; V 106; XIII 104; XIV 20
Revolution, 1848: XIII 104; XV 244, 249;
    XVII passim; XVIII 23
Rokkan, Stein: XII 10
Roma: VIII 191
Romania, Romanians: III 77; VIII 191, 193,
    197; IX 114; X 40; XIII 98
Romanticism: VII 94
Rome: XVII 187
Rousseau, Jean-Jacques: V 85
Russia, Russians: II 100; III 80; IV 71, 73;
    V 73, 80, 83, 94; VI 259ff.; VII 98;
    VIII 196, 200, 205; X 37, 40;
    XI 267, 269f.; XV 244, 252ff.;
    XVI 9, 20; XVII 187f., 190f.;
    XVIII 23, 29; XIX 12, 21
Ruthenians: VIII 194

Sami: VIII 192;
Sars, Johan Ernst: XIV 22
Saxony: XIX 17, 20
Scandinavia: XVII 190; XIX 20
Schelling, Friedrich Wilhelm: V 85
Schleswig: VI 260ff.; VIII 193, 197, 203
Scotland, Scottish: V 84; VII 96; XIV 23
Selim III: VII 98
Seljuks: XIV 25f.
Serbia, Serbs: IV 72f., 81; V 84; VII 97f.;
    VIII 191, 197, 201ff.; X 40f.;
    XI 267, 270
Silesia: XVI 22f., 26; XVII 190; XIX 20
Singapore: XIX 22
Slavic Congress, Slavism: XV 247, 249
Slavonia: X 39
Slavophiles: XI 269
Slavs: XV 258
Slovakia, Slovaks: IV 72f.; V 77, 80;
    VI 265, 268; VII 96, 99; VIII 193,
    196ff.; X 39, 41; XI 270; XIII 98;
    XIV 21
Slovenia, Slovenes: IV 72f., 77; V 77, 84;
    VIII 193, 203; X 37, 41
Smith, Adam: XIX 12
Smith, Anthony D.: II 96; IV 75; VII 92;
    VIII 192; XII 10
Sorbians: V 72; VIII 192, 198, 205
Sorokin, Pitrim: XII 7
Soviet Union: IX 101; X 39; XI 272;
    XVIII 28; XIX 23
Spain, Spanish: II 100; IV 71; VI 260, 265;
    X 37; XI 269; XVII 187f.; XVIII 23,
    25ff.; XIX 19
Springer, Anton Heinrich: XV 255; XVIII 20
St Olaf: XIV 18
St Wenceslas: XIV 18
Stalin, Joseph: XII 2
Strnad, Jaroslav: XIX 18
Sweden, Swedes: III 77; IV 71; V 80;
    VII 94, 102; VIII 203, 206; X 37;
    XIV 17, 19, 24; XVI 20; XVIII 29;
    XIX 20f., 24
Switzerland, Swiss: V 84; XVII 187

Szporluk, Roman: IX 101ff., 111f.

Tallinn: VI 271ff.; XVI 7
Tartars: VIII 205; XIV 32
Tartu: XVI 14
Tilly, Charles: XII 10
Tocqueville, Alexis de: VII 95
Topolski, Jerzy: XIX 17, 19
Toruń: XVI 13
Transylvania: III 77; IV 73; VIII 191, 193
"Trivialliteratur": XIII 101f.
Trondheim: XIV 21
Turkish Republic: XIV 26ff.
Turkey, Turks: VIII 205; XI 270; XIV 24ff.;
    XIX 22
Tyrol: VIII 203

Ukraine, Ukrainians: III 80; IV 72; V 77f.,
    80, 83; VI 259ff.; VII 98; VIII 191,
    198, 203; IX 114; X 41; XVIII 28
Ulster: VIII 203
Upper Silesia: V 72

Vienna: XIV 34; XVIII 25
Vikings: XIV 19ff.
Vlachs: VIII 205
Volga: VIII 194
"Volksdeutsche": X 40

Wales, Welsh: III 80; V 70, 79; VII 98, 102;
    X 37
Wallerstein, Emmanuel: IV 76; XIX 13
Warszawa: XVI 14; XVII 189
Weber, Max: XII 4
Wehler, Hans-Ulrich: XII 6
Western Europe: III 79; X 43; XI 265f.,
    271, 275; XIX 15f.
Wroclaw: XVI 11ff., 22ff.

Young Turk Revolution: XIV 25
Yugoslav Army: X 41
Yugoslavia: VIII 203f.; X 42f.

Zionism: III passim; VIII 205